D0993861

Blackstone's
Magistrates' Court Handbook 2012

Andrew Keogh

OXFORD
UNIVERSITY PRESS

OXFORD
UNIVERSITY PRESS

Great Clarendon Street, Oxford OX2 6DP

Oxford University Press is a department of the University of Oxford.
It furthers the University's objective of excellence in research, scholarship,
and education by publishing worldwide in

Oxford New York

Auckland Cape Town Dar es Salaam Hong Kong Karachi
Kuala Lumpur Madrid Melbourne Mexico City Nairobi
New Delhi Shanghai Taipei Toronto

With offices in

Argentina Austria Brazil Chile Czech Republic France Greece Guatemala
Hungary Italy Japan Poland Portugal Singapore
South Korea Switzerland Thailand Turkey Ukraine Vietnam

Oxford is a registered trade mark of Oxford University Press
in the UK and in certain other countries

Published in the United States
by Oxford University Press Inc., New York

British Library Cataloguing in Publication Data
Data available

Typeset by Cenveo, Bangalore, India
Printed in Great Britain
on acid-free paper by
L.E.G.O. S.p.A.—Lavis TN

ISBN 978–0–19–969282–8

10 9 8 7 6 5 4 3 2 1

Preface to the 2012 Edition

This book aims to provide the busy magistrates' court advocate with an accurate, portable, and concise guide to the main procedures, offences, and sentences encountered on a daily basis. Inevitably, given a key objective is to produce a title for use in court on a daily basis, the balance between having a complete guide and a portable one remains on a knife-edge. I once again hope that the correct balance has been struck.

Reviewers of the last edition took the considerable trouble to feedback on its shortcomings and I hope that these have been adequately addressed in this new edition. Readers will find a number of new sections, including extradition—an important and complex area of work experienced by London duty solicitors in particular. Ideas for further development are always welcome.

Appendix 2, Court Appointed Legal Representatives, is reproduced by kind permission of the Bar Council and the Criminal Bar Association.

This book is dedicated to Roiseen, Barnaby, and Edgar.

The law is cited as it stood on 11 April 2011.

Andrew Keogh
Manchester

Contents

Part A Procedure and Evidence

Contents

Part B Youth Court

Part C Offences

Part D Sentencing

Contents

Icons List

The following icons are used throughout this book:

DO Dangerous Offender

EW Either Way

▦ Sentence

SO Summary Only

▢ Cross reference to *Blackstone's Criminal Practice 2012*

Table of Cases

Table of Cases

Table of Cases

Table of Cases

Table of Cases

Table of Cases

Table of Primary Legislation

Table of Primary Legislation

Table of Primary Legislation

Table of Primary Legislation

Table of Primary Legislation

Table of Primary Legislation

Table of Primary Legislation

Table of Secondary Legislation

Table of Conventions

Table of Practice Directions

Part A
Procedure and Evidence

A1 **Abuse of Process**

A1.1 Introduction

Abuse of process is something so unfair and wrong with the prosecution that the court should not allow a prosecutor to proceed with what is, in all other respects, a regular proceeding: *Hui-chi Ming v R* [1992] 1 AC 34.

A stay on these grounds falls into two main categories:

- where a fair trial is impossible;
- where there is a misuse of court process (where it offends the court's sense of justice and propriety to be asked to try the accused in the circumstances of the particular case).

It follows that a stay of proceedings based on an abuse of process will be rare and should only be allowed in exceptional circumstances (see *Attorney-General's Reference No 1 of 1990* (1992) 95 Cr App R 296), and if the court process can compensate for any unfairness or wrongs, so as to allow for a fair trial, that is the way in which it should proceed.

On an application to stay for abuse of process it is for the defendant to satisfy the court on a balance of probabilities, that no fair trial is possible. The application should be decided on material adduced by prosecution and defence, with both parties having the right (subject to usual judicial discretion) to call evidence (*R v Clerkenwell Magistrates' Court, ex p Bell* [1991] Crim LR 468).

The practice direction (see **A1.3**) in relation to abuse of process applications in the magistrates' court should be followed (with suitable adjustment) in all magistrates' court cases as a matter of good practice.

A1.2 Relevant cases

A1.2.1 *Missing evidence*

There is no general duty on the prosecution to retain CCTV evidence that might have given insight into whether a warning was given to a detainee during a breath test procedure; this would be the case whether or not the issue was raised prior to trial (*Morris v Director of Public Prosecutions* [2008] EWHC 2788 (Admin)).

In *R v Feltham Magistrates' Court and another, ex p Ebrahim* [2001] EWHC Admin 130 the court observed:

> It must be remembered that it is a commonplace in criminal trials for a defendant to rely on 'holes' in the prosecution case, for example, a failure to take fingerprints or a failure to submit evidential material to forensic examination. If, in such a case, there is sufficient credible evidence, apart from the missing

evidence, which, if believed, would justify a safe conviction, then a trial should proceed, leaving the defendant to seek to persuade the jury or magistrates not to convict because evidence which might otherwise have been available was not before the court through no fault of his. Often the absence of a video film or fingerprints or DNA material is likely to hamper the prosecution as much as the defence.

In relation to this type of case Lord Lane CJ said in *Attorney-General's Reference (No 1 of 1990)* at p 644A–B that no stay should be imposed:

. . . unless the defence shows on the balance of probabilities that owing to the delay he will suffer serious prejudice to the extent that no fair trial can be held: in other words, that the continuance of the prosecution amounts to a misuse of the process of the court.

Paragraphs 29 to 31 of the judgment set out a number of like cases and are essential reading for any advocate contemplating an abuse of process application on the basis of incomplete evidence.

A1.2.2 *Failure to supply advance information*

There is no jurisdiction to stay proceedings for failures in service of advance information, the appropriate remedy was to adjourn (*R v Leeds Youth Court, ex p P(A)* [2001] EWHC 215 (Admin)), although repeated failure to breach the rules may provide for a stay in truly exceptional circumstances (*R v Willesden Magistrates' Court, ex p Clemmings* (1988) 152 JPN 46). A threat to stay a prosecution if there were further disclosure breaches did not give rise to any legitimate expectation on the part of the defendant so as to require the court to carry through its threat on the next occasion (*R v Leeds Youth Court, ex p AP and others* [2001] EWHC 215 (Admin)).

A1.2.3 *Improper motive*

The fact that this is a mixed motive for launching a private prosecution will only justify a stay if the conduct of the prosecutor is truly oppressive, as it was obvious that many private prosecutions would be brought with mixed motives (*Dacre v City of Westminster Magistrates' Court* [2009] 1 Cr App R 6).

In *Nembhard v Director of Public Prosecutions* [2009] EWHC 194 (Admin) the court ruled that a magistrates' court was correct to refuse to stay proceedings on the ground that a request to produce traffic documents was motivated by improper considerations—namely a desire to harass the defendant. In such cases the proper course of action would be either to stay the prosecution pending determination of the issue by the High Court, or a judicial review of the decision to prosecute. This case is an important reminder that in instances where an abuse of state power is being alleged a magistrates' court has no jurisdiction to stay proceedings (*R v Horseferry Road Magistrates' Court, ex p Paul James Bennett* (1994) 1 AC 42).

A1.2.4 *Delay*

In the absence of other compelling reasons a lengthy delay, in itself, does not justify a stay of criminal proceedings (*Spiers v Ruddy* [2008] 1 AC 873, PC).

In *Ali v Crown Prosecution Service* [2007] EWCA Crim 691 proceedings brought seven years after the incident should have been stayed as important documentary evidence, relevant to assessing the victim's credibility, had been lost. The court emphasized that:

> . . . this is a rare case where prejudice following from the delay was not alleviated and probably could never have been cured during the course of the trial.

In *R (Flaherty) v City of Westminster Magistrates' Court* [2008] EWHC 2589 (Admin), the last two years of a ten-year delay in enforcing a confiscation order was attributable to the prosecution. The proceedings ought to have been stayed as confiscation proceedings must be determined within a reasonable time.

Earlier cases, such as *R v Clerk to the Medway Justices, ex p DHSS* [1986] Crim LR 686, DC, in which a prosecution was stayed where the prosecution laid the information on the last day before it was time-barred, should be treated with extreme caution in the light of considerable and more recent appellate-level scrutiny of the principles that apply. It is almost inconceivable that the *Medway* case would be similarly decided today.

A1.3 **Practice direction**

The following arrangements will take effect immediately:

> ### Consolidated Criminal Practice Direction, part IV.36
> **IV.36 Abuse of process stay applications**
> **(IV.36.1)**
> In all cases where a defendant in the Crown Court proposes to make an application to stay an indictment on the grounds of abuse of process, written notice of such application must be given to the prosecuting authority and to any co-defendant not later than 14 days before the date fixed or warned for trial ('the relevant date'). Such notice must:
> (a) give the name of the case and the indictment number;
> (b) state the fixed date or the warned date as appropriate;
> (c) specify the nature of the application;

(d) set out in numbered sub-paragraphs the grounds upon which the application is to be made;
(e) be copied to the Chief Listing Officer at the Court centre where the case is due to be heard.

(IV.36.2)

Any co-defendant who wishes to make a like application must give a like notice not later than 7 days before the relevant date, setting out any additional grounds relied upon.

(IV.36.3)

In relation to such applications, the following automatic directions shall apply:
(a) the advocate for the applicant(s) must lodge with the Court and serve on all other parties a skeleton argument in support of the application at least 5 clear working days before the relevant date. If reference is to be made to any document not in the existing trial documents, a paginated and indexed bundle of such documents is to be provided with the skeleton argument;
(b) the advocate for the prosecution must lodge with the Court and serve on all other parties a responsive skeleton argument at least 2 clear working days before the relevant date, together with a supplementary bundle if appropriate.

(IV.36.4)

All skeleton arguments must specify any propositions of law to be advanced (together with the authorities relied upon in support, with page references to passages relied upon), and where appropriate include a chronology of events and a list of dramatis personae. In all instances where reference is made to a document, the reference in the trial documents or supplementary bundle is to be given.

(IV.36.5)

The above time limits are minimum time limits. In appropriate cases the Court will order longer lead times. [. . .]

 See *Blackstone's Criminal Practice 2012* D3

A2 **Adjournments**

A2.1 **Time limits applicable to adjournments**

It should be noted that remand limits apply to remands under the Magistrates' Courts Act 1980 (eg ss 5,10, 11, 17, 130 etc). Therefore, when a person is sent for trial to the Crown Court, the eight-clear-day limit on initial remand (if in custody) does not apply as the court has not remanded the case.

Adjournment for trial	No limit (MCA 1980, s 10)
Adjournment after conviction but before sentence—for the purpose of reports/enquiries	Maximum four weeks, unless the defendant is in custody, when it is then three weeks.
Prior to conviction following remand into custody	Maximum eight clear days for first remand. On a subsequent remand the maximum period is 28 days provided that it will be possible for the next stage in the proceedings (not simply an onward remand) to be completed. A defendant can consent to onward remands in his absence and this will often be done when the proceedings cannot be materially progressed within a four-week period.
Prior to conviction—on bail	Maximum eight days unless defendant and prosecution consents (MCA 1980, s 128(6)).

A2.2 **Principles to be applied**

In recent years there has been a perception, if not the reality, of an adjournment culture. All eyes are now firmly focused on speeding cases through the system as fast as possible. This is an aim generally shared by both defence and prosecution alike, but there are still many instances where an adjournment is required. In such instances advocates can expect those applications to be closely scrutinized.

A common issue that arises is in relation to adjournments for the purposes of legal aid being granted. Much will depend on the circumstances, and in particular, how much time the defendant has had, if any, to arrange appropriate representation. The court will also be mindful of payments that can be made to firms if legal aid is refused—thereby diluting the force of any argument that work would otherwise be unfunded. That said, support can be found for an adjournment in the case of *Berry Trade Limited v Moussavi* [2002] 1 WLR 1910:

> . . . The question which the judge had to ask was a different question, whether Mr Moussavi had had an effective opportunity for applying for public funding. The weight to be accorded to giving him this opportunity must, in these circumstances, outweigh other considerations, such as the convenience to other parties and the use of court resources.

Any submission by the court that this is a civil case and therefore has no relevance to a criminal case does not withstand scrutiny.

Where a defendant was unable, through no fault of his own, to call an important witness, an adjournment should be granted to give an opportunity for that witness to be traced and steps taken to secure attendance (*Khurshied v Peterborough Magistrates' Court* [2009] EWHC 1136 (Admin)). In *Essen v Director of Public Prosecutions* [2005] EWHC 1077 (Admin), the court was concerned with a failure of the CPS, due to administrative error, to warn its witnesses for trial. The court held that in the absence of some other counterprevailing factor an adjournment ought not to be granted. The fact that a crime may go unpunished is not sufficient as:

> in that case no prosecutor, however dilatory, need attend to the requirement to be ready for trial on the set date . . . The prejudice to the defendant [of an adjournment in those circumstances] was manifest. The CPS had no ground for seeking clemency. It was the sole author of its own misfortune.

A prosecutor should always be given some time to make inquiries as to why a witness is not present (*R v Swansea Justices, ex p Director of Public Prosecutions* The Times, 30 March 1990).

If the prosecution has failed to carry out its statutory duties in relation to disclosure under the Criminal Procedure and Investigations Act 1996, an adjournment should be granted to the defence (*Swash v Director of Public Prosecutions* [2009] EWHC 803 (Admin)).

A failure to make proper inquiry into a defendant's absence, which had it been carried out would have led to the adjournment of the matter, will result in any resulting conviction following trial in absence being quashed (*R (James) v Tower Bridge Magistrates' Court*, unreported, 9 June 2009, DC).

Where a defendant provides a medical note in relation to non-attendance, a court should give reasons for finding such medical excuses spurious, it being rarely if ever appropriate to reject a medical certificate (even if not meeting the normal requirements as to information required) without first giving the defendant an opportunity to respond (*Evans v East Lancashire Magistrates' Court* [2010] EWHC 2108 (Admin)).

In *R v Bolton Magistrates' Court, ex p Merna* [1991] Crim LR 848 the court said:

> if the court suspects the [medical] grounds to be spurious or believes them to be inadequate, the court should ordinarily express its doubts and thereby give the defendant an opportunity to seek to resolve the doubts. It may call for better evidence, require further inquiries to be made or adopt any other expedient fair to both parties. The ultimate test must always be one of fairness and if a defendant claims to be ill with apparently responsible professional support for his claim, the court should not reject that claim and

proceed to hear the case in a defendant's absence without satisfying itself
that the claim may properly be rejected and that no unfairness will thereby
be done.

If a defendant raises matters for the first time in the proceedings (so-
called 'ambush defences'), the court is fully justified in adjourning
the matter in order to allow the prosecution to properly deal with
them (eg *R (Lawson) v Stratford Magistrates' Court* [2007] EWHC
2490 (Admin) where compliance with signage regulations in relation
to a prosecution for speeding were raised for the first time in cross-
examination).

In *R (Taylor) v Southampton Magistrates' Court*, unreported, 18
November 2008 it was held that during a trial for failing to comply
with a notice under section 172 of the Road Traffic Act 1988, a District Judge was right to adjourn the case in order for the prosecution to
be able to gather evidence (if such evidence existed) to prove service of
the notice. There was no question of bias even though the court acted
of its own motion. What is interesting about this case is that there
was no issue of 'ambush', the prosecution having not only been put to
proof of all issues, but the specific issue having been raised. That was
not enough for the court in this instance, in the absence of a positive
defence case that the notice had not in fact been served.

In *Crown Prosecution Service v Picton* [2006] EWHC 1108 (Admin)
the court laid down the following general approach:

(1) A decision whether to adjourn is a decision within the discretion of the
trial court. An appellate court will interfere only if very clear grounds for
doing so are shown.

(2) Magistrates should pay great attention to the need for expedition in the
prosecution of criminal proceedings; delays are scandalous; they bring the
law into disrepute; summary justice should be speedy justice; an application
for an adjournment should be rigorously scrutinized.

(3) Where an adjournment is sought by the prosecution, magistrates must
consider both the interest of the defendant in getting the matter dealt with,
and the interest of the public that criminal charges should be adjudicated
upon: the guilty convicted as well as the innocent acquitted. With a more
serious charge, the public interest that there be a trial will carry greater
weight.

(4) Where an adjournment is sought by the accused, the magistrates must
consider whether, if it is not granted, the accused will be able fully to present
his defence and, if he will not be able to do so, the degree to which his ability
to do so is compromised.

(5) In considering the competing interests of the parties, the magistrates
should examine the likely consequences of the proposed adjournment,
in particular, its likely length, and the need to decide the facts while
recollections are fresh.

(6) The reason that the adjournment is required should be examined and, if it arises through the fault of the party asking for the adjournment, that is a factor against granting the adjournment, carrying weight in accordance with the gravity of the fault. If that party was not at fault, then that may favour an adjournment. Likewise, if the party opposing the adjournment has been at fault, then that will favour an adjournment.

(7) The magistrates should take appropriate account of the history of the case, and whether there have been earlier adjournments and at whose request and why.

(8) Lastly, of course, the factors to be considered cannot be comprehensively stated but depend upon the particular circumstances of each case, and they will often overlap. The court's duty is to do justice between the parties in the circumstances as they have arisen.

In *Aravinthan Visvaratnam v Brent Magistrates' Court* [2009] EWHC 3017 (Admin) the court made these observations:

The prosecution must not think that they are always allowed at least one application to adjourn the case. If that idea were to gain currency, no trial would ever start on the first date set for trial.

So these are the competing considerations. I have no doubt that there is a high public interest in trials taking place on the date set for trial, and that trials should not be adjourned unless there is a good and compelling reason to do so. The sooner the prosecution understand this—that they cannot rely on their own serious failures properly to warn witnesses—the sooner the efficiency in the Magistrates' Court system improves. An improvement in timeliness and the achievement of a more effective and efficient system of criminal justice in the Magistrates' Court will bring about great benefits to victims and to witnesses and huge savings in time and money.

A2.3 Simple Speedy Summary Justice

In essential case management, applying the Criminal Procedure Rules it is stated:

At every hearing, (however early): Unless it has been done already, the court must take the defendant's plea [Crim PR 3.8(2)(b)]. This obligation does not depend on the extent of advance information, service of evidence, disclosure of unused material, or the grant of legal aid.

 See *Blackstone's Criminal Practice 2012* D5

A3 Admissibility and Exclusion of Evidence

A3.1 Admissibility and exclusion

Given that magistrates deal with questions of both fact and law, the voir dire procedure adopted in the Crown Court is not appropriate in summary proceedings when issues of admissibility arise. The timing of any challenge is a matter for the court and there is no right to have issues of admissibility determined as a preliminary issue (*R v Epping and Ongar Justices, ex p Manby* [1986] Crim LR 555). It has been ruled that a court has no power to delegate issues of admissibility to another bench (*R v Ormskirk Justices, ex p Davies* (1994) 158 JP 1145); however section 8A of the Magistrates' Courts Act 1980 now provides for pre-trial rulings on issues of admissibility (see **A3.2**). Previous rulings on admissibility can be reversed, but this should happen only exceptionally (see **A.9** for relevant cases).

When a party is seeking to exclude evidence under section 76 of the Police and Criminal Evidence Act 1984 a voir dire will be required as there is no discretion under section 76 (as opposed to section 78) and the prosecution carries the burden of disproving unfairness (*Vel v Owen* [1987] Crim LR 496). An application to exclude under section 76 can be heard during committal proceedings (*R v Oxford City Justices, ex p Berry* [1988] QB 507).

Police and Criminal Evidence Act 1984, s 76

(1) In any proceedings a confession made by an accused person may be given in evidence against him in so far as it is relevant to any matter in issue in the proceedings and is not excluded by the court in pursuance of this section.

(2) If, in any proceedings where the prosecution proposes to give in evidence a confession made by an accused person, it is represented to the court that the confession was or may have been obtained—
   (a) by oppression of the person who made it; or
   (b) in consequence of anything said or done which was likely, in the circumstances existing at the time, to render unreliable any confession which might be made by him in consequence thereof,

the court shall not allow the confession to be given in evidence against him except in so far as the prosecution proves to the court beyond reasonable doubt that the confession (notwithstanding that it may be true) was not obtained as aforesaid.

(3) In any proceedings where the prosecution proposes to give in evidence a confession made by an accused person, the court may of its own motion

---

require the prosecution, as a condition of allowing it to do so, to prove that the confession was not obtained as mentioned in subsection (2) above.

(4) The fact that a confession is wholly or partly excluded in pursuance of this section shall not affect the admissibility in evidence—

  (a) of any facts discovered as a result of the confession; or

  (b) where the confession is relevant as showing that the accused speaks, writes or expresses himself in a particular way, of so much of the confession as is necessary to show that he does so.

(5) Evidence that a fact to which this subsection applies was discovered as a result of a statement made by an accused person shall not be admissible unless evidence of how it was discovered is given by him or on his behalf.

(6) Subsection (5) above applies—

  (a) to any fact discovered as a result of a confession which is wholly excluded in pursuance of this section; and

  (b) to any fact discovered as a result of a confession which is partly so excluded, if the fact is discovered as a result of the excluded part of the confession.

(7) Nothing in Part VII of this Act shall prejudice the admissibility of a confession made by an accused person.

(8) In this section 'oppression' includes torture, inhuman or degrading treatment, and the use or threat of violence (whether or not amounting to torture).

(9) Where the proceedings mentioned in subsection (1) above are proceedings before a magistrates' court inquiring into an offence as examining justices this section shall have effect with the omission of—

  (a) in subsection (1) the words 'and is not excluded by the court in pursuance of this section', and

  (b) subsections (2) to (6) and (8).

When a party is inviting a court to exercise its discretion to exclude evidence under section 78 of the Police and Criminal Evidence Act 1984, the court has a choice as to whether to deal with the issue when it arises, or once all evidence has been heard. The voir dire procedure is appropriate to such applications as an accused may otherwise be denied the opportunity to remain silent in relation to the substantive matter. An objection under section 78 cannot be taken during committal proceedings. In *Halawa v Federation Against Copyright Theft* [1995] 1 Cr App R 496, the court laid down the following principles:

* Absent a good reason, the defendant is entitled to a voir dire on the issue of exclusion under section 78.
* If section 78 is being argued as an alternative to section 76 a voir dire should be held.
* It will generally be appropriate to hear all of the prosecution evidence before embarking on a voir dire in relation to the disputed parts.

- If the argument is only to the circumstances in which evidence was gathered a voir dire may not be necessary. If however the defendant contradicts the evidence it is more likely that a voir dire is appropriate.
- The defence must be in a position to assist the court in determining the extent of any challenge.

Police and Criminal Evidence Act 1984, s 78

(1) In any proceedings the court may refuse to allow evidence on which the prosecution proposes to rely to be given if it appears to the court that, having regard to all the circumstances, including the circumstances in which the evidence was obtained, the admission of the evidence would have such an adverse effect on the fairness of the proceedings that the court ought not to admit it.

(2) Nothing in this section shall prejudice any rule of law requiring a court to exclude evidence.

(3) This section shall not apply in the case of proceedings before a magistrates' court inquiring into an offences as examining justices.

A3.2 Pre-trial rulings

Sections 8A–8B of the Magistrates' Courts Act 1980 provide:

Magistrates' Courts Act 1980, ss 8A–8B

8A Power to make rulings at pre-trial hearing

(1) For the purposes of this section a hearing is a pre-trial hearing if—
   (a) it relates to an information—
      (i) which is to be tried summarily, and
      (ii) to which the accused has pleaded not guilty, and
   (b) it takes place before the start of the trial.

(2) [. . .]

(3) At a pre-trial hearing, a magistrates' court may make a ruling as to any matter mentioned in subsection (4) if—
   (a) the condition in subsection (5) is met,
   (b) the court has given the parties an opportunity to be heard, and
   (c) it appears to the court that it is in the interests of justice to make the ruling.

(4) The matters are—
   (a) any question as to the admissibility of evidence;
   (b) any other question of law relating to the case.

(5) [. . .]

(6) A ruling may be made under this section—
   (a) on an application by a party to the case, or
   (b) of the court's own motion.

(7) For the purposes of this section and section 8B, references to the prosecutor are to any person acting as prosecutor, whether an individual or body.

8B Effect of rulings at pre-trial hearing

(1) Subject to subsections (3) and (6), a ruling under section 8A has binding effect from the time it is made until the case against the accused or, if there is more than one, against each of them, is disposed of.

(2) The case against an accused is disposed of if—

    (a) he is acquitted or convicted,

    (b) the prosecutor decides not to proceed with the case against him, or

    (c) the information is dismissed.

(3) A magistrates' court may discharge or vary (or further vary) a ruling under section 8A if—

    (a) the condition in section 8A(5) is met,

    (b) the court has given the parties an opportunity to be heard, and

    (c) it appears to the court that it is in the interests of justice to do so.

(4) The court may act under subsection (3)—

    (a) on an application by a party to the case, or

    (b) of its own motion.

(5) No application may be made under subsection (4)(a) unless there has been a material change of circumstances since the ruling was made or, if a previous application has been made, since the application (or last application) was made.

(6) A ruling under section 8A is discharged in relation to an accused if—

    (a) the magistrates' court commits or sends him to the Crown Court for trial for the offence charged in the information, or

    (b) a count charging him with the offence is included in an indictment by virtue of section 40 of the Criminal Justice Act 1988.

 See *Blackstone's Criminal Practice 2012* **F1–F2**

A4 **Advance Information**

A4.1 **Summary**

See **A4.2** which details the rules pertaining to advance information. Rule 21 provides for advance information in relation to all cases that can be tried in a magistrates' court, so cures the previous anomaly that (strictly) denied the defendant advance information in relation to summary only matters.

Rule 21 needs to be read in conjunction with *The Director's Guidance on the Streamlined Process* which details the police and prosecution policy in relation to file preparation and supply of advance information.

In cases where a guilty plea is anticipated and charge is authorized by the police the prosecution will serve:

- The Police Report.
- Victim personal statement (if any) and key witnesses statements taken to support a no comment interview.
- Any visually recorded evidence (CCTV and/or photographs) which shows the involvement of the offender or illustrates an important feature of the case; eg photograph of bodily injury of the victim.
- A schedule of previous convictions and cautions (if any).
- A schedule of any offences to be taken into consideration (MG18).

In cases that are commenced following statutory charging the following will be served:

Police Report or the MG3 summary and the following additional statements or material where appropriate:

- Copies of the key MG11 witness statements and a copy of any victim personal statement if taken.
- Any visually recorded evidence (CCTV and/or photographs) which clearly shows the involvement of the offender or illustrates an important feature of the case; eg photograph of bodily injury of the victim.
- A schedule of the defendant's previous convictions and cautions.
- A schedule of any offences to be taken into consideration (MG18).

It can be seen from Rule 21 and the CPS guidance that prosecutors enjoy a wide discretion as to what is served prior to plea.

Frequent problems arise in relation to the service of video and other evidence. If the Crown is not relying on the undisclosed video evidence then no issue in relation to advance information arises. In *R v Calderdale Magistrates' Court, ex p Donahue and others* [2001] Crim LR 141 it was accepted by the prosecution, that a video was a document for the purposes of the advance information rules. In a later case the prosecution declined to make the same concession and the matter may have to be litigated again as delays in entering plea due to awaiting video evidence may be thought by some to fly in the face of the streamlined process and CJSSS and in some areas, including the author's, courts are increasingly reluctant to order service of such items: see: *R v Croydon Magistrates' Court, ex p Director of Public Prosecutions* [2001] EWHC Admin 552, and in particular the comments at paragraphs 24–26):

24. LORD JUSTICE BROOKE: I agree. I wish only to add a few words in relation to the case of R v Calderdale Magistrates' Court, ex parte Donahue and Cutler (unreported Crown Office transcript 18th October 2000). As Harrison J has observed, that case was decided on the foundation of a concession recorded by Bell J in paragraph 24 of his judgment that a document meant anything in which information of any description was recorded for the purposes of the interpretation of the Magistrates' Court (Advance Information) Rules 1985.

25. The definition of the word 'document' goes back into our legal history. In R v Hunt [1820] 3 Barn & Ald 566, 574, it was decided that a flag or banner bearing words or inscriptions should not be regarded as a document for the purpose of that part of law of evidence in which a distinction was made between documents on the one hand and material objects on the other. In Bartholomew v Stephens [1839] 3 C&P 728 a notice board prohibiting trespassing was similarly not treated as a document, as opposed to a material object. Coming forward to the last century, in R v Daye [1908] 2 KB 333, Darling J said at page 340 that he did not assent to the argument that a thing was not a document unless it be a paper writing:

'I should say it is a document, no matter on what material it be, provided it is writing or printing capable of being made evidence.'

26. In a number of modern statutes an express definition of the word 'document' is included, and it is defined as meaning 'anything in which information of any description is recorded'. This definition appears in section 43 of the Gaming Act 1968, in schedule 2 paragraph 5(1) of the Criminal Justice Act 1988, referring to part 2 of that Act, in section 13 of the Civil Evidence Act 1995, and in section 5A(4) of the Magistrates' Court Act 1980 (as amended). It does not appear in the Magistrates' Court (Advance Information) Rules 1985, and it would fall for decision in another case in which a concession is not made, as it was made in ex parte Donahue, as to whether a video or other material which (might qualify as a document within the meaning of the statutory definition to which I have referred) needs to be produced pursuant to those rules when the prosecutor has already adduced a fair summary of the facts and matters on which he is going to rely.

A4.2 Extent of disclosure

Rule 21 of the Criminal Procedure Rules provides:

Criminal Procedure Rules 2010, Part 21

21.1 When this Part applies

(1) This Part applies in a magistrates' court, where the offence is one that can be tried in a magistrates' court.
(2) The court may direct that, for a specified period, this Part will not apply—
    (a) to any case in that court; or
    (b) to any specified category of case.

21.2 Providing initial details of the prosecution case

The prosecutor must provide initial details of the prosecution case by—
(a) serving those details on the court officer; and
(b) making those details available to the defendant,
at, or before, the beginning of the day of the first hearing.

21.3 Content of initial details

Initial details of the prosecution case must include—
(a) a summary of the evidence on which that case will be based; or
(b) any statement, document or extract setting out facts or other matters on which that case will be based; or
(c) any combination of such a summary, statement, document or extract; and
(d) the defendant's previous convictions.

 See *Blackstone's Criminal Practice 2012* **D5**

A5 Amending Charge

A5.1 Amendment within the time limit

It should not be thought that prosecutors have an unfettered right to seek to amend charges that are not subject to any limitation of time (ie indictable and indictable only charges). Amendments should be granted where the application is judged to be proper and appropriate (*R v Redbridge Justices, ex p Whitehouse* [1992] 94 CAR 332).

In *Director of Public Prosecutions v Hammerton* [2009] EWHC 921 (Admin) the court applauded a refusal to amend a charge alleging an either-way offence with one triable summarily only, when the application had been made on the day that the original offence was due to be committed to the Crown Court for trial. Reflecting the substantial change in attitude required by all parties in order to make the criminal justice system more effective, the court observed:

> All the cases cited to me pre-date the Criminal Procedure Rules. The courts, including the magistrates' courts, now have the Criminal Procedure Rules to apply and in particular they have the overriding objective to consider. That is something the magistrates clearly would have had in mind. It is, therefore, not for the Crown Prosecution Service simply to assume to itself the way in which a proceeding will be conducted. For example, as the magistrates here noted, there had been ample time for the Crown Prosecution Service to assess the position before the date of actual committal. The magistrates' courts are concerned with the speedy and efficient administration of justice (also evidenced, for example, by the successful introduction of the CJSSS scheme throughout magistrates' courts in England and Wales). It is wholly unsurprising, to my mind, that the magistrates here were thoroughly dissatisfied with the last minute nature of this application.
>
> . . .
>
> where a lesser charge is to be substituted, first, it must be proper and appropriate to the facts of the case; secondly the application should be made promptly and not left until the last minute, at all events without any proper explanation; and, thirdly, an eye should also be kept on considerations of the good administration of justice and the wider picture: as the facts of this case illustrate, by reason of the situation of any co-accused.

In the author's view, the effect of *Hammerton* is already being overstated by defence advocates and a careful reading of the case will reveal a decision peculiar to its own facts and falling well short of providing any kind of precedent for future cases. It is notable that many of the features of *Hammerton* can be seen in earlier decisions such as *R (Crown Prosecution Service) v Everest* [2005] EWHC 1124 (Admin).

A5.2 Amendment outside the time limit

An amendment outside the time limit, in order to allow the prosecution to proceed with a summary only offence which would otherwise be time-barred, may be permitted provided that the new offence is based on the 'same misdoing' and that it is in the interests of justice to allow the amendment (*R v Scunthorpe Justices, ex p McPhee and Gallagher* (1998) 162 JP 635, DC). The principles considered in *Hammerton* (above) apply when considering the overall interests of justice.

The following principles emerge from *Scunthorpe Justices*:

(1) The purpose of the six-month time limit imposed by section 127 of the 1980 Act is to ensure that summary offences are charged and tried as soon as reasonably practicable after their alleged commission.

(2) Where an information has been laid within the six-month period it can be amended after the expiry of that period.

(3) An information can be amended after the expiry of the six-month period, even to allege a different offence or different offences provided that:
   (i) the different offence or offences allege the 'same misdoing' as the original offence; and
   (ii) the amendment can be made in the interests of justice.

The phrase 'same misdoing' should not be construed too narrowly. It means that the new offence should arise out of the same (or substantially the same) facts as gave rise to the original offence.

In *Shaw v Director of Public Prosecutions* [2007] EWHC 207 (Admin) the court ruled that an amendment to charge an offence which was based on similar misdoing ought not to have been permitted as the original offence carried only a financial penalty whereas the new offence carried imprisonment. The court ruled similarly in *R (Crown Prosecution Service) v Everest* [2005] EWHC 1124 (Admin), observing that the new offence carried a higher penalty, had a statutory offence and that the defendant was not legally represented.

The amendment of a charge to substitute failing to provide a specimen of breath, with one of failing to provide a specimen of urine was held to be proper in *Williams v Director of Public Prosecutions* [2009] ECHC 2354 (Admin), although the court did allow the appeal as the alteration had not been made in a timely fashion (applying *Hammerton*). Readers will note that *Williams* reverses the earlier case cited in the 2010 edition at **A5.2**.

The imposition of a higher fine (if convicted of the new charge) would not in itself be enough to justify the refusal of an otherwise sound amendment (*R v Newcastle Upon Tyne Justices, ex p Poundstretcher*, unreported, 2 March 1998).

An out of time amendment to allege a different defendant is not permissible (*Sainsbury's Supermarkets Ltd v HM Courts Service* [2006] EWHC 1749 (Admin)).

A6 **Appeals and Reopening**

A6.1 **Appeals**

An appeal against conviction and/or sentence lies as of right to the Crown Court. A notice of appeal must be served within 21 days of final disposal of the case.

It is not the normal practice to grant bail pending an appeal (and there is no statutory right to bail) unless the appeal is against conviction and the defendant was convicted after trial. In *R v Imdad Shah* (1980) 144 JP 460, the court rejected an argument that bail should be granted where the sentence was a short one and there was a risk that the sentence would be served prior to the appeal being heard. The court ruled that in such cases an early listing should be sought. In *R (G) v Inner London Crown Court* [2003] EWHC 2715 (Admin) the applicant successfully judicially reviewed a decision by a Crown Court to refuse bail in a 'short sentence' case.

Section 108 of the Magistrates' Courts Act 1980 provides:

Magistrates' Courts Act 1980, s 108

(1) A person convicted by a magistrates' court may appeal to the Crown Court—
  (a) if he pleaded guilty, against his sentence;
  (b) if he did not, against the conviction or sentence.

(1A) Section 14 of the Powers of Criminal Courts (Sentencing) Act 2000 (under which a conviction of an offence for which an order for conditional or absolute discharge is made is deemed not to be a conviction except for certain purposes) shall not prevent an appeal under this Act, whether against conviction or otherwise.

(2) A person sentenced by a magistrates' court for an offence in respect of which an order for conditional discharge has been previously made may appeal to the Crown Court against the sentence.

(3) In this section 'sentence' includes any order made on conviction by a magistrates' court, not being—
  (b) an order for the payment of costs;
  (c) an order under section 37(1) of the Animal Welfare Act 2006 (which enables a court to order the destruction of an animal); or
  (d) an order made in pursuance of any enactment under which the court has no discretion as to the making of the order or its terms
  and also includes a declaration of relevance, within the meaning of section 23 of the Football Spectators Act 1989.

(4) Subsection (3)(d) above does not prevent an appeal against a surcharge imposed under section 161A of the Criminal Justice Act 2003.

A6.2 **Reopening cases**

A6.2.1 *Jurisdiction*

Magistrates' Courts Act 1980, s 142

(1) A magistrates' court may vary or rescind a sentence or other order imposed or made by it when dealing with an offender if it appears to the court to be in the interests of justice to do so, and it is hereby declared that this power extends to replacing a sentence or order which for any reason appears to be invalid by another which the court has power to impose or make.

(1A) The power conferred on a magistrates' court by subsection (1) above shall not be exercisable in relation to any sentence or order imposed or made by it when dealing with an offender if—

(a) the Crown Court has determined an appeal against—

(i) that sentence or order;

(ii) the conviction in respect of which that sentence or order was imposed or made; or

(iii) any other sentence or order imposed or made by the magistrates' court when dealing with the offender in respect of that conviction (including a sentence or order replaced by that sentence or order); or

(b) the High Court has determined a case stated for the opinion of that court on any question arising in any proceeding leading to or resulting from the imposition or making of the sentence or order.

(2) Where a person is convicted by a magistrates' court and it subsequently appears to the court that it would be in the interests of justice that the case should be heard again by different justices, the court may so direct.

(2A) The power conferred on a magistrates' court by subsection (2) above shall not be exercisable in relation to a conviction if—

(a) the Crown Court has determined an appeal against—

(i) the conviction; or

(ii) any sentence or order imposed or made by the magistrates' court when dealing with the offender in respect of the conviction; or

(b) the High Court has determined a case stated for the opinion of that court on any question arising in any proceeding leading to or resulting from the conviction.

(3) Where a court gives a direction under subsection (2) above—

(a) the conviction and any sentence or other order imposed or made in consequence thereof shall be of no effect; and

(b) section 10(4) above shall apply as if the trial of the person in question had been adjourned.

(4) [repealed]

(5) Where a sentence or order is varied under subsection (1) above, the sentence or other order, as so varied, shall take effect from the beginning of the day on which it was originally imposed or made, unless the court otherwise directs.

A6.2.2 *Principles*

Section 142 relates to criminal proceedings and has no application to other areas of magistrates' court jurisdiction such as liability orders (*Liverpool City Council v Plemora Distribution Limited* [2002] EWHC 2467 (Admin)) and detention and forfeiture in relation to proceeds of crime. Further, the court enjoys no common law jurisdiction to reopen civil matters such as an anti-social behaviour order (*Samuda v Birmingham Justices* [2008] EWHC 205 (Admin)). Persons made subject to a hospital order under section 37(3) of the Mental Health Act 1983 fall within the definition of 'offender', and a person can use section 142 to reopen a hearing determining the issue under the Mental Health Act (*R (Bartram) v Southend Magistrates' Court* [2004] EWHC 2691 (Admin)). An order to commit an offender to prison for non-satisfaction of a confiscation order made under the Proceeds of Crime Act 2002 in the Crown Court is capable of being reopened.

The court has power to revisit the issue of a warrant following non-payment of fines. A court does not have the power to rescind a costs order made in favour of a defendant who was not convicted as the section related only to orders post conviction (*Coles v East Penwith Justices* The Times, 27 July 1998).

The nature of the remedy afforded under this Act is akin to a 'slip rule', allowing a court to rectify a clear mistake or injustice. An applicant who had entered an unequivocal plea of guilty cannot apply to reopen plea under this section (*R v Croydon Youth Court, ex p Director of Public Prosecutions* [1997] 2 Cr App R 411). Section 142 should not be used to advance new arguments, nor should it be used as an 'appeal' mechanism against an earlier decision (*Zykin v Crown Prosecution Service* [2009] EWHC 1469 (Admin)). Applications based on a change of law between conviction and application should not be entertained under normal principles of finality of judgment.

A prosecutor cannot apply to reopen proceedings that have previously been withdrawn (*R (Green and Green Scaffolding Ltd) v Staines Magistrates' Court* (2008) 172 JP 353).

A6.2.3 *Applications*

An application may be made orally or in writing; the applicant does not have to attend the hearing. All parties must be given notice of the application and be heard if they so wish. Section 142(1A) and (2A) set out the instances when a remedy under this provision is denied on account of an alternative avenue of appeal having been taken.

There is no statutory time limit on reopening but the former 28-day rule should act as a salutary guideline. Applications made much beyond this date might be properly refused on interests of justice grounds as

'Delay in matters of this sort is always harmful, memories fade, records may be lost and the essence of doing justice is that it should be done expeditiously' (*R v Ealing Magistrates' Court, ex p Sahota* The Times, 9 December 1997). It is not, however, a decisive factor. It is not enough for the magistrates simply to say that the length of time is such that it is no longer proper to open the case under section 142. More substantial reasoning than that has to be given, so that the applicant (and any court on appeal) can understand why it is no longer proper to deal with the matter.

Applications can be made by both defence and prosecution, but the exercise of such discretion in favour of a prosecutor will be rare, and can never extend to the overturning of an acquittal. A prosecutor could properly make an application to reopen where the court had erroneously failed to impose penalty points or some other appropriate order. Similarly, if the court had been unaware of factors relevant to sentence it could be invited to reopen sentence, even if that meant a risk that it would be increased. However, if it is appropriate for the powers under section 142 to be used to increase sentence, then the power must be exercised very speedily (*R (Holme) v Liverpool Magistrates' Court* [2004] EWHC 3131 (Admin); in this case the court declined to allow the prosecution to exercise the power. Advocates facing this type of application should refer to the full judgment).

A defendant who had been convicted in absence can properly attempt to reopen under this section. Culpability on the part of the offender is relevant to whether it is in the interests of justice to reopen, but it is not determinative. It will normally be in the interests of justice for a defendant to be able to defend himself, and unless the evidence indicates that his absence from trial is deliberate and voluntary, a rehearing would normally be the appropriate course (*R (Morsby) v Tower Bridge Magistrates' Court* [2007] EWHC 2766 (Admin)). Any inconvenience to the court in allowing a reopening can never outweigh the interests of justice (*R (Blick) v Doncaster Magistrates' Court* (2008) 172 JP 651).

A6.2.4 *Interests of justice*

Justices are given wide discretion in determining what are relevant factors in relation to interests of justice, but decisions must be based on sound judicial reasoning. A defendant's late arrival at court was held not to be a proper ground, in itself, to refuse a rehearing (*R v Camberwell Green Magistrates' Court, ex p Ibrahim* (1984) 148 JP 400). Factors a court ought to consider include:

- why the convicted person did not appear at the original trial (if that was the case);
- timeliness of the application;
- reason for any delay;

- importance of the decision being questioned—note that the importance to all parties, including defendant, prosecution, and other interested parties (such as victim), should be assessed;
- inconvenience and prejudice caused to opposing parties;
- whether a more appropriate appeal remedy is available. It will not be appropriate to allow a reopening where a defendant is denied a right of appeal due to an unequivocal guilty plea (*R v Croydon Youth Court, ex p Director of Public Prosecutions* [1997] 2 Cr App R 411).

In addition, the court must always consider rule 1 of the Criminal Procedure Rules and the overriding objective.

 See *Blackstone's Criminal Practice 2012* **D29**

A6.2.5 *Effect of reopening*

A conviction will be set aside, as will any sentence or ancillary orders flowing from it. The matter is treated as adjourned for trial. Justices who sat on the original hearing, or the hearing to reopen, cannot sit on the adjourned trial. The prosecution retain the right to offer no evidence and the court lacks power to insist that a prosecutor proceeds with the case (*R (Rhodes-Presley) v South Worcestershire Magistrates' Court* [2008] EWHC 2700 (Admin)).

If a sentence or order is reopened, the court may vary or rescind the original finding and substitute any other lawful sentence or order that would have been available to the court at the original hearing. The new orders take effect from the date of the old order unless the court directs otherwise. A court must be careful not to offend against any legitimate expectation given to the offender (*Jane v Broome* The Times, 2 November 1988).

A6.3 **Reopening of guilty plea**

Criminal Procedure Rules, r 37.9

Application to withdraw a guilty plea

(1) This rule applies where the defendant wants to withdraw a guilty plea.
(2) The defendant must apply to do so—
   (a) as soon as practicable after becoming aware of the reasons for doing so; and
   (b) before sentence.
(3) Unless the court otherwise directs, the application must be in writing and the defendant must serve it on—
   (a) the court officer; and
   (b) the prosecutor.

---

(4) The application must—

    (a) explain why it would be unjust not to allow the defendant to withdraw the guilty plea;

    (b) identify—

        (i) any witness that the defendant wants to call, and

        (ii) any other proposed evidence; and

    (c) say whether the defendant waives legal professional privilege, giving any relevant name and date.

The following principles emerge from the authorities:

- The fact that the defendant was not legally represented when he entered his guilty plea is not grounds alone for allowing a change of plea (*R v South Tameside Magistrates' Court, ex p Rowland* [1983] 3 All ER 689).

- A misunderstanding as to the nature of the charge being pleaded to may justify a change of plea (and may well be an equivocal plea in any event) (*P Foster Haulage Ltd v Roberts* [1978] 2 All ER 751).

- Evidence of the previous guilty plea may be adduced at any later trial, although its probative value will generally be so low that a court ought to decline to admit it (*R v Rimmer* [1972] 1 WLR 268).

In *S (An Infant) v Recorder of Manchester* [1971] AC 481 the court held:

The power to reopen plea was a discretionary one;

The power ought to be used sparingly;

The power is available up until sentence has been passed;

The question for the court is whether justice requires the change of plea to be permitted.

A7 **Bad Character**

A7.1 **Introduction**

The admissibility of bad character is regulated by sections 98–113 of the Criminal Justice Act 2003, all previous common law rules having been replaced. The Act is concerned with the admission of bad character in relation to:

- the defendant;
- any co-defendant;
- a person other than a defendant in the case.

As will be seen from the Criminal Procedure Rules below there is a strict regime for the admittance of evidence of bad character. The court has the power to exclude otherwise admissible evidence of bad character on the grounds of non-compliance, if the effect would be to prejudice a party, for example by way of ambush defence (*R v Musone* [2007] EWCA Crim 1237). Provided that there is no prejudice a court is free to admit evidence of bad character if to do so would satisfy the overriding objective of rule 1 of the Criminal Procedure Rules. Attempts to argue that evidence ought to be admitted following procedural non-compliance only in exceptional cases have been rejected (*R (Robinson) v Sutton Coldfield Magistrates' Court* [2006] EWHC 307 (Admin)). In *Robinson*, the court did however say that:

> . . . a court would ordinarily wish to know when the relevant enquiries had been initiated, and in broad terms why they have not been completed within the time allowed. Any application for an extension will be closely scrutinised by the court. A party seeking an extension cannot expect the indulgence of the court unless it clearly sets out the reasons why it is seeking that indulgence.

Rule 35 of the Criminal Procedure Rules 2010 regulates the admission of bad character evidence.

A7.2 **What is bad character?**

The Act defines bad character as the commission of an offence, or other 'reprehensible behaviour'. It is important to note the effect of section 98 (see **A7.3**) which has the effect of excluding much bad character from the statutory scheme, allowing for its admissibility subject only to the normal rules of probity and relevance.

In considering whether or not a party has committed an offence, regard can be had to:

- previous convictions;
- previous police warnings, reprimands, or cautions;

- offences for which the person has not been tried;
- offences for which the person has been acquitted (*R v Z* [2000] 2 AC 483), or found unfit to be tried (*R v Renda* [2005] EWCA Crim 2826).

Other examples include telling lies, taking illegal drugs (*R v AJC* [2006] EWCA Crim 284), being sexually promiscuous (*R v Ball* [2005] EWCA Crim 2826), and collecting photographs of people being violently attacked (*R v Saleem* [2007] EWCA Crim 1923).

The Act also covers those with a disposition towards reprehensible conduct, for example an admission that a person is sexually attracted to children (*R v S* [2007] EWCA Crim 1387, but see also *R v Fox* [2009] EWCA Crim 653 where such evidence ought not to be admitted).

It is important to note that a defendant is entitled to dispute that he is guilty of a matter that has resulted in conviction (or caution), the procedure for doing so is discussed in *R v C*, unreported, 17 December 2010).

There are some particular considerations at play when admitting police cautions as evidence of bad character. In *R v Olu and others* [2010] EWCA Crim 2975 the court held:

> We accept the submission that there is a very considerable difference not only between a caution and a conviction for the reasons given in the authorities to which we have referred, but there is also a very considerable difference between an admission contained in a caution without legal advice having been given and an admission made in a caution after legal advice or before a court by a plea. In such circumstances, the giving of legal advice or the formality of a court appearance will have made clear to the person the consequences of his admission. The processes that lead to a caution can differ widely between police area and police area; a court would be shutting its eyes to reality if it assumed that, where a person was not legally represented, the consequences of admitting an offence and accepting a caution were fully explained to a person in a manner that he understood the serious adverse consequences that would follow and what he was giving up by not exercising his right to legal advice—namely that what he was admitting would give him a criminal record, that the caution would be maintained on his PNC record for very many years and that it would be used against his interests in certain circumstances.

Penalty notices for disorder cannot, in themselves, be adduced as evidence of bad character (*R v Hamer* [2010] EWCA Crim 2053), nor can unsubstantiated allegations contained in crime reports (*R v Braithwaite* [2010] EWCA Crim 1082).

A7.3 Bad character excluded from application

Section 98 provides:

Criminal Justice Act 2003, s 98

References in this Chapter to evidence of a person's 'bad character' are to evidence of, or of a disposition towards, misconduct on his part, other than evidence which—

(a) has to do with the alleged facts of the offence with which the defendant is charged, or

(b) is evidence of misconduct in connection with the investigation or prosecution of that offence.

At a more obvious level this means that the allegation itself (obviously of misconduct) does not need to be subject to an application to admit bad character. It also covers the following:

- evidence of a previous conviction that might be a component of the offence alleged (eg a conviction for assault against a child in relation to a cruelty charge in relation to that same child *R v R* [2006] EWCA Crim 3196);
- preparatory acts, eg purchase of a murder weapon;
- background evidence (eg an act that provided motive for the offence: *R v Saleem* [2007] EWCA Crim 1923 and *R v McNeill* [2007] EWCA Crim 2927).

A7.4 Non-defendant's bad character

Section 100 provides:

Criminal Justice Act 2003, s 100

(1) In criminal proceedings evidence of the bad character of a person other than the defendant is admissible if and only if—

(a) it is important explanatory evidence,

(b) it has substantial probative value in relation to a matter which—

(i) is a matter in issue in the proceedings, and

(ii) is of substantial importance in the context of the case as a whole, or

(c) all parties to the proceedings agree to the evidence being admissible.

(2) For the purposes of subsection (1)(a) evidence is important explanatory evidence if—

(a) without it, the court or jury would find it impossible or difficult properly to understand other evidence in the case, and

(b) its value for understanding the case as a whole is substantial.

(3) In assessing the probative value of evidence for the purposes of subsection (1)(b) the court must have regard to the following factors (and to any others it considers relevant)—

(a) the nature and number of the events, or other things, to which the evidence relates;

(b) when those events or things are alleged to have happened or existed;

(c) where—

    (i)   the evidence is evidence of a person's misconduct, and

    (ii) it is suggested that the evidence has probative value by reason of similarity between that misconduct and other alleged misconduct,

  the nature and extent of the similarities and the dissimilarities between each of the alleged instances of misconduct;

(d) where—

    (i)   the evidence is evidence of a person's misconduct,

    (ii) it is suggested that that person is also responsible for the misconduct charged, and

    (iii) the identity of the person responsible for the misconduct charged is disputed,

  the extent to which the evidence shows or tends to show that the same person was responsible each time.

(4) Except where subsection (1)(c) applies, evidence of the bad character of a person other than the defendant must not be given without leave of the court.

A7.5 Defendant's bad character

Section 101 provides:

> ### Criminal Justice Act 2003, s 101
>
> (1) In criminal proceedings evidence of the defendant's bad character is admissible if, but only if—
>
>   (a) all parties to the proceedings agree to the evidence being admissible,
>
>   (b) the evidence is adduced by the defendant himself or is given in answer to a question asked by him in cross-examination and intended to elicit it,
>
>   (c) it is important explanatory evidence,
>
>   (d) it is relevant to an important matter in issue between the defendant and the prosecution,
>
>   (e) it has substantial probative value in relation to an important matter in issue between the defendant and a co-defendant,
>
>   (f) it is evidence to correct a false impression given by the defendant, or
>
>   (g) the defendant has made an attack on another person's character.
>
> (2) Sections 102 to 106 contain provision supplementing subsection (1).
>
> (3) The court must not admit evidence under subsection (1)(d) or (g) if, on an application by the defendant to exclude it, it appears to the court that the admission of the evidence would have such an adverse effect on the fairness of the proceedings that the court ought not to admit it.
>
> (4) On an application to exclude evidence under subsection (3) the court must have regard, in particular, to the length of time between the matters to which that evidence relates and the matters which form the subject of the offence charged.

A7.6 Important explanatory evidence

Section 102 provides:

Criminal Justice Act 2003, s 102

For the purposes of section 101(1)(c) evidence is important explanatory evidence if—
(a) without it, the court or jury would find it impossible or difficult properly to understand other evidence in the case, and
(b) its value for understanding the case as a whole is substantial.

A7.7 Matter in issue between defendant and prosecution

Section 103 provides:

Criminal Justice Act 2003, s 103

(1) For the purposes of section 101(1)(d) the matters in issue between the defendant and the prosecution include—
    (a) the question whether the defendant has a propensity to commit offences of the kind with which he is charged, except where his having such a propensity makes it no more likely that he is guilty of the offence;
    (b) the question whether the defendant has a propensity to be untruthful, except where it is not suggested that the defendant's case is untruthful in any respect.
(2) Where subsection (1)(a) applies, a defendant's propensity to commit offences of the kind with which he is charged may (without prejudice to any other way of doing so) be established by evidence that he has been convicted of—
    (a) an offence of the same description as the one with which he is charged, or
    (b) an offence of the same category as the one with which he is charged.
(3) Subsection (2) does not apply in the case of a particular defendant if the court is satisfied, by reason of the length of time since the conviction or for any other reason, that it would be unjust for it to apply in his case.
(4) For the purposes of subsection (2)—
    (a) two offences are of the same description as each other if the statement of the offence in a written charge or indictment would, in each case, be in the same terms;
    (b) two offences are of the same category as each other if they belong to the same category of offences prescribed for the purposes of this section by an order made by the Secretary of State.
(5) A category prescribed by an order under subsection (4)(b) must consist of offences of the same type.
(6) Only prosecution evidence is admissible under section 101(1)(d).

A7.8 Matter in issue between the defendant and a co-defendant

Section 104 provides:

Criminal Justice Act 2003, s 104

(1) Evidence which is relevant to the question whether the defendant has a propensity to be untruthful is admissible on that basis under section 101(1)(e) only if the nature or conduct of his defence is such as to undermine the co-defendant's defence.

(2) Only evidence—
   (a) which is to be (or has been) adduced by the co-defendant, or
   (b) which a witness is to be invited to give (or has given) in cross-examination by the co-defendant,
   is admissible under section 101(1)(e).

A7.9 Evidence to correct a false impression

Section 105 provides:

Criminal Justice Act 2003, s 105

(1) For the purposes of section 101(1)(f)—
   (a) the defendant gives a false impression if he is responsible for the making of an express or implied assertion which is apt to give the court or jury a false or misleading impression about the defendant;
   (b) evidence to correct such an impression is evidence which has probative value in correcting it.

(2) A defendant is treated as being responsible for the making of an assertion if—
   (a) the assertion is made by the defendant in the proceedings (whether or not in evidence given by him),
   (b) the assertion was made by the defendant—
      (i) on being questioned under caution, before charge, about the offence with which he is charged, or
      (ii) on being charged with the offence or officially informed that he might be prosecuted for it,
      and evidence of the assertion is given in the proceedings,
   (c) the assertion is made by a witness called by the defendant,
   (d) the assertion is made by any witness in cross-examination in response to a question asked by the defendant that is intended to elicit it, or is likely to do so, or
   (e) the assertion was made by any person out of court, and the defendant adduces evidence of it in the proceedings.

(3) A defendant who would otherwise be treated as responsible for the making of an assertion shall not be so treated if, or to the extent that, he withdraws it or disassociates himself from it.

(4) Where it appears to the court that a defendant, by means of his conduct (other than the giving of evidence) in the proceedings, is seeking to give the

---

court or jury an impression about himself that is false or misleading, the court may if it appears just to do so treat the defendant as being responsible for the making of an assertion which is apt to give that impression.

(5) In subsection (4) 'conduct' includes appearance or dress.

(6) Evidence is admissible under section 101(1)(f) only if it goes no further than is necessary to correct the false impression.

(7) Only prosecution evidence is admissible under section 101(1)(f).

A7.10 Attack on another person's character

Section 106 provides:

Criminal Justice Act 2003, s 106

(1) For the purposes of section 101(1)(g) a defendant makes an attack on another person's character if—

(a) he adduces evidence attacking the other person's character,

(b) he (or any legal representative appointed under section 38(4) of the Youth Justice and Criminal Evidence Act 1999 (c. 23) to cross-examine a witness in his interests) asks questions in cross-examination that are intended to elicit such evidence, or are likely to do so, or

(c) evidence is given of an imputation about the other person made by the defendant—

(i) on being questioned under caution, before charge, about the offence with which he is charged, or

(ii) on being charged with the offence or officially informed that he might be prosecuted for it.

(2) In subsection (1) 'evidence attacking the other person's character' means evidence to the effect that the other person—

(a) has committed an offence (whether a different offence from the one with which the defendant is charged or the same one), or

(b) has behaved, or is disposed to behave, in a reprehensible way;

and 'imputation about the other person' means an assertion to that effect.

(3) Only prosecution evidence is admissible under section 101(1)(g).

 See *Blackstone's Criminal Practice 2012* F12

A8 **Bail**

A8.1 **Introduction**

The starting point is that there is a presumption in favour of bail being granted in criminal proceedings (see **A8.2** for the position in relation to defendants charged with murder appearing before a magistrates' court). That presumption does not however apply in the following cases:

- in extradition proceedings or in connection with a warrant issued in the Republic of Ireland;
- following committal to the Crown Court for sentence or for breach of a Crown Court order;
- after conviction, unless the proceedings are adjourned for inquiries to be made or a report to be prepared for sentence;
- on appeal against conviction or sentence;
- following a breach of bail.

Where the defendant aged 18 or over has tested positive for heroin, cocaine, or crack cocaine and is unwilling to undergo an assessment into their drug misuse and/or any proposed follow-up treatment, different rules apply. The defendant cannot be granted bail unless the court is satisfied that there is no significant risk of an offence being committed on bail.

Schedule 1, paragraph 6A of the Bail Act 1976 provides:

Bail Act 1976, Sch 1 paras 6A, 6B, and 6C

6A Subject to paragraph 6C below, a defendant who falls within paragraph 6B below may not be granted bail unless the court is satisfied that there is no significant risk of his committing an offence while on bail (whether subject to conditions or not).

6B (1) A defendant falls within this paragraph if—

    (a) he is aged 18 or over;

    (b) a sample taken—

        (i) under section 63B of the Police and Criminal Evidence Act 1984 (testing for presence of Class A drugs) in connection with the offence; or

        (ii) under section 161 of the Criminal Justice Act 2003 (drug testing after conviction of an offence but before sentence),

    has revealed the presence in his body of a specified Class A drug;

(c) either the offence is one under section 5(2) or (3) of the Misuse of Drugs Act 1971 and relates to a specified Class A drug, or the court is satisfied that there are substantial grounds for believing—

    (i) that misuse by him of any specified Class A drug caused or contributed to the offence; or

    (ii) (even if it did not) that the offence was motivated wholly or partly by his intended misuse of such a drug; and

(d) the condition set out in sub-paragraph (2) below is satisfied or (if the court is considering on a second or subsequent occasion whether or not to grant bail) has been, and continues to be, satisfied.

(2) The condition referred to is that after the taking and analysis of the sample—

  (a) a relevant assessment has been offered to the defendant but he does not agree to undergo it; or

  (b) he has undergone a relevant assessment, and relevant follow-up has been proposed to him, but he does not agree to participate in it.

(3) In this paragraph and paragraph 6C below—

  (a) 'Class A drug' and 'misuse' have the same meaning as in the Misuse of Drugs Act 1971;

  (b) 'relevant assessment' and 'relevant follow-up' have the meaning given by section 3(6E) of this Act;

  (c) 'specified' (in relation to a Class A drug) has the same meaning as in Part 3 of the Criminal Justice and Court Services Act 2000.

6C Paragraph 6A above does not apply unless—

  (a) the court has been notified by the Secretary of State that arrangements for conducting a relevant assessment or, as the case may be, providing relevant follow-up have been made for the local justice area in which it appears to the court that the defendant would reside if granted bail; and

  (b) the notice has not been withdrawn.

Bail may only be granted in exceptional circumstances where a defendant is charged with or convicted of an offence of:

- murder, or
- attempted murder, or
- manslaughter, or
- rape, or
- attempted rape, and

the defendant has been previously convicted in the UK of any such offence or of culpable homicide. (If the previous conviction was manslaughter or culpable homicide the provision only applies if they received a sentence of imprisonment/long-term detention.) When section 144 and Schedule 17 paragraph 3 of the Coroners and Justice Act 2009 are in force, convictions in EU Member States can be taken into account.

Bail need not be granted to a person on bail at the time of committing an indictable only offence or an offence triable only on indictment (Bail Act 1976, Sch 1 para 2A).

Sections 14 and 15 of the Criminal Justice Act 2003 are partially in force and currently apply only to those charged with offences carrying life imprisonment. The 2003 Act inserted paragraphs 2A (subject to transitional provisions) and 9AA into Schedule 1 to the Bail Act 1976. The effect of the two amendments is that if at the time of allegedly committing the offence, the accused was on bail, he may not be granted bail, in the case of an adult, unless the court is satisfied that there is no significant risk of his committing an offence while on bail (whether subject to conditions or not). In the case of a person under 18 years, in deciding whether there are substantial grounds for believing that the defendant, if released on bail (whether subject to conditions or not), would commit an offence while on bail, the court shall give particular weight to the fact that the defendant was on bail in criminal proceedings on the date of the offence.

Criminal Justice Act 2003, s 14

(1) For paragraph 2A of Part 1 of Schedule 1 to the 1976 Act (defendant need not be granted bail where he was on bail on date of offence) there is substituted—

'2A (1) If the defendant falls within this paragraph he may not be granted bail unless the court is satisfied that there is no significant risk of his committing an offence while on bail (whether subject to conditions or not).

(2) The defendant falls within this paragraph if—

(a) he is aged 18 or over, and

(b) it appears to the court that he was on bail in criminal proceedings on the date of the offence.'

(2) After paragraph 9 of that Part there is inserted—

'9AA (1) This paragraph applies if—

(a) the defendant is under the age of 18, and

(b) it appears to the court that he was on bail in criminal proceedings on the date of the offence.

(2) In deciding for the purposes of paragraph 2(1) of this Part of this Schedule whether it is satisfied that there are substantial grounds for believing that the defendant, if released on bail (whether subject to conditions or not), would commit an offence while on bail, the court shall give particular weight to the fact that the defendant was on bail in criminal proceedings on the date of the offence.'

A8.2 **Right to apply for bail**

An application for bail can be made at the first hearing of the case before a magistrates' court, save in respect to a defendant facing a charge of murder (or murder and any other charge(s)), in which case the issue of bail must be resolved before a Crown Court judge within 48 hours (excluding public holidays) beginning the day after the defendant's appearance in the magistrates' court (Coroners and Justice Act 2009, s 115). If bail is refused, an application can be made at the subsequent hearing, and can be based on the same grounds as the first. A refusal of bail on the grounds of insufficient information should not be counted as a decision to refuse bail, thereby exhausting one of the two attempts (*R v Calderdale Justices, ex p Kenedy* The Times, 18 February 1992). Similarly, a remand in absence should be discounted (*R v Dover and East Kent Justices, ex p Dean* The Times, 22 August 1991).

Note, however, that if a fully argued application is not made by the defendant at the first hearing the effect is that one opportunity to argue for bail is lost, meaning that if bail is refused at the subsequent hearing, the two opportunities for bail are spent. Similarly, if an argument is made at the first hearing, but not at a second hearing, there is no right to a second application for bail at the third hearing. Advocates should always obtain certificates of full argument in order to support any further Crown Court bail application (Bail Act 1976, s 5(6A)).

Following two refusals to grant bail, further applications can be made if there has been a change in circumstances, eg:

- Change in the case alleged against the defendant (this often arises when committal papers are served with a draft indictment) (*R v Reading Crown Court, ex p Malik* [1981] QB 451 and *R v Slough Justices, ex p Duncan* [1981] QB 451).
- Increased surety (*R v Isleworth Crown Court, ex p Commissioners of Customs and Excise* The Times, 27 July 1990).
- Passage of time (*Neumeister v Austria (No 1)* (1979–80) 1 EHRR 91).

In *R (B) v Brent Youth Court* [2010] EWHC 1893 (Admin) the court held that a change of address presented for residence purposes amounted to a change of circumstances. It was not necessary that any new factor be exceptional in nature. The correct test is whether there are any new considerations which were not before the court when the accused was last remanded in custody. Similarly an argument that the prosecution case against the defendant was significantly weaker than at first presented would qualify as a change in circumstance. The court ended by saying:

> even if the Bench had been entitled to form the view that each and every argument as to fact or law was an argument which it had heard previously, it manifestly failed to go on to consider whether, notwithstanding that, it should nonetheless consider substantively a bail application, given the

provisions of Section 44 [Children and Young Persons Act 1933], having regard to the welfare of a child or young person.

A8.3 Refusing bail

A court can refuse bail on the grounds that the defendant is already a serving prisoner (para 4 remand), or that there is insufficient information on which to base a decision (para 5 remand). Refusal of bail can be based upon the defendant's own protection, or for a defendant under 17 years, his own welfare.

The seriousness of the offence in itself (and the likely penalty) cannot of itself justify a refusal of bail on the inference that the person is likely to abscond (*Lettelier v France* (1992) 14 EHRR 83), although a judge is perfectly entitled to regard that as a significant factor (*R (Thompson) v Central Criminal Court* [2005] EWHC 2345). Before bail can be refused on the grounds of interfering with witnesses or obstructing justice the prosecution must point to an identifiable risk and provide supporting evidence (*Clooth v Belgium* (1991) 14 EHRR 717).

Section 114 of the Coroners and Justice Act 2009 amends the Bail Act with the following consequences (although in practice they add very little):

- If the defendant is charged with murder, the defendant may not be granted bail unless the court is of the opinion that there is no significant risk of the defendant committing, while on bail, an offence that would, or would be likely to, cause physical or mental injury to any person other than the defendant.
- If the court is satisfied that there are substantial grounds for believing that the defendant, if released on bail (whether subject to conditions or not), would commit an offence while on bail, the risk that the defendant may do so by engaging in conduct that would, or would be likely to, cause physical or mental injury to any person other than the defendant.

Following changes enacted by the Criminal Justice and Immigration Act 2008, there are three categories of offences to consider:

- indictable imprisonable offences;
- summary only imprisonable offences (which includes offences triable summarily only due to the value of the offence, eg criminal damage); and
- summary only non-imprisonable offences.

A8.4 Indictable imprisonable offences

Bail can be refused if there are substantial grounds for believing that, if released on bail, the defendant would:

- fail to surrender;

- commit further offences; or
- interfere with witnesses or otherwise obstruct the course of justice.

A8.5 Summary only imprisonable offences

Bail can only be refused on one or more of the following grounds:

- failure to surrender (if the defendant has previously failed to surrender);
- commission of further offences (if the instant offence was committed on bail);
- fear of commission of offences likely to cause another person to suffer or fear of physical or mental injury;
- the defendant's own protection (for his own welfare if a child);
- the defendant is serving custody;
- fear of failure to surrender, commission of offences, interference with witnesses, or obstruction of justice (if the defendant has been arrested for breach of bail in respect of the instant offence); and
- lack of sufficient information.

A8.6 Summary only non-imprisonable offences

Bail can only be denied if there has been a previous failure to surrender in the proceedings and the court believes that if granted bail he would fail to surrender again, or:

- for the defendant's own protection (for his own welfare if a child);
- where the defendant is already in custody;
- following a breach of bail, or the defendant absconding, there are substantial grounds for believing that if released on bail the defendant would:
    (a) fail to surrender;
    (b) commit further offences; or
    (c) interfere with witnesses or otherwise obstruct the course of justice.

A8.7 Conditional bail

Conditional bail can be imposed if the court believes there to be a risk that:

- the defendant will fail to surrender;
- the defendant will commit an offence while on bail;
- the defendant would interfere with witnesses or obstruct justice;
- the defendant would not cooperate with the making of pre-sentence or other reports; or
- the defendant would not attend appointments with his legal adviser.

A person granted bail on a charge of murder must be required to undergo a psychiatric examination (Bail Act 1976, s 3(6A)):

Bail Act 1976, s 3(6A)

(6A) In the case of a person accused of murder the court granting bail shall,
unless it considers that satisfactory reports on his mental condition have
already been obtained, impose as conditions of bail—

(a) a requirement that the accused shall undergo examination by two
medical practitioners, for the purpose of enabling such reports to be
prepared; and

(b) a requirement that he shall for that purpose attend such an institution
or place as the court directs and comply with any other directions which
may be given to him for that purpose by either of those practitioners.

(6B) Of the medical practitioners referred to in subsection (6A) above at least
one shall be practitioner approved for the purposes of section 12 of the
Mental Health Act 1983.

A8.8 Electronic monitoring

Section 3AA deals with electronic monitoring for children and young
persons; section 3AB deals with adults; and section 3AC is applicable
to all defendants.

Bail Act 1976, ss 3AA(1)–(5), 3AB, and 3AC(1)–(2)

3AA Conditions for the imposition of electronic monitoring requirements: children and young persons

(1) A court may not impose electronic monitoring requirements on a child or
young person unless each of the following conditions is met.

(2) The first condition is that the child or young person has attained the age of
twelve years.

(3) The second condition is that—

(a) the child or young person is charged with or has been convicted of a
violent or sexual offence, or an offence punishable in the case of an
adult with imprisonment for a term of fourteen years or more; or

(b) he is charged with or has been convicted of one or more imprisonable offences which, together with any other imprisonable offences of
which he has been convicted in any proceedings—

(i) amount, or

(ii) would, if he were convicted of the offences with which he is
charged, amount,

to a recent history of repeatedly committing imprisonable offences
while remanded on bail or to local authority accommodation.

(4) The third condition is that the court is satisfied that the necessary provision
for dealing with the person concerned can be made under arrangements
for the electronic monitoring of persons released on bail that are currently
available in each local justice area which is a relevant area.

(5) The fourth condition is that a youth offending team has informed the court
that in its opinion the imposition of electronic monitoring requirements will
be suitable in the case of the child or young person.

. . .

> **3AB Conditions for the imposition of electronic monitoring requirements: other persons**
>
> (1) A court may not impose electronic monitoring requirements on a person who has attained the age of seventeen unless each of the following conditions is met.
> (2) The first condition is that the court is satisfied that without the electronic monitoring requirements the person would not be granted bail.
> (3) The second condition is that the court is satisfied that the necessary provision for dealing with the person concerned can be made under arrangements for the electronic monitoring of persons released on bail that are currently available in each local justice area which is a relevant area.
> (4) If the person is aged seventeen, the third condition is that a youth offending team has informed the court that in its opinion the imposition of electronic monitoring requirements will be suitable in his case.
>
> **3AC Electronic monitoring: general provisions**
>
> (1) Where a court imposes electronic monitoring requirements as a condition of bail, the requirements must include provision for making a person responsible for the monitoring.
> (2) A person may not be made responsible for the electronic monitoring of a person on bail unless he is of a description specified in an order made by the Secretary of State.

A8.9 Prosecution appeals against the grant of bail

The Bail (Amendment) Act 1993 allows a prosecutor to appeal the grant of bail in any case where the offence is imprisonable. The prosecution must have objected to bail, and following the grant of bail, must orally in court state their intention to appeal the decision. A written notice must be served on both the court and defendant within two hours of the oral notice having been given. A delay of five minutes in giving an oral indication to the court (and after the defendant had been taken from the courtroom) was deemed to comply with the Act in *R v Isleworth Crown Court, ex p Clarke* [1998] 1 Cr App R 257. In *R (Jeffrey) v Crown Court at Warwick* [2003] Crim LR 190, a written notice was served three minutes late due to no fault on the part of the prosecutor. A challenge to the validity of that service failed and the court suggested that section 1(7) of the Act should have read into it the following words:

> . . . unless such failure was caused by circumstances outside the control of the prosecution and not due to any fault on its part.

Service of the written notice on a jailer who hands the notice to a defendant suffices, and solicitors who accept such notices do so on the implicit understanding that they will be immediately communicated to the defendant. Note, however, that there is no obligation for a solicitor to be a party to the prosecution appeals process; one wonders why any solicitor would see such participation as being in line with his duty to the client.

A8.10 Breach of bail

Following an alleged breach of bail, the defendant must be brought before a magistrates' court within 24 hours of arrest. This means that the hearing must commence at court within those 24 hours, and any delay must result in the defendant's automatic release from custody (*R v Governor of Glen Parva Young Offender Institution, ex p G (A Minor)* [1998] 2 Cr App R 349). A court can, however, bring a defendant into the dock and then adjourn the hearing until later in the court list (*R (Hussein) v Derby Magistrates' Court* [2001] 1 WLR 254), subject to the proviso that the breach must be resolved within the 24-hour period. A magistrates' court has no power simply to commit an offender to the Crown Court in order for the breach to be decided (*R v Teeside Magistrates' Court, ex p Ellison* (2001) 165 JP 355).

Only one magistrate needs deal with an alleged bail breach and there is no requirement for formal evidence to be called by prosecution or defence. There is no defence of 'reasonable excuse' in relation to the breaking of bail conditions (*R (Vickers) v West London Magistrates' Court* [2004] Crim LR 63), although the reasons for breach would be relevant to the determination of whether or not to grant bail.

In *R v Liverpool Justices, ex p Director of Public Prosecutions* (1992) 95 Cr App R 222, the court laid down the following guidance for a court to follow when considering bail breaches:

- strict rules of evidence did not apply and hearsay was admissible;
- the court must consider the type of evidence called and take account of the fact that there had been no cross-examination;
- the prosecution and defence can call witnesses if they so wish, and the other party has the right to cross-examine;
- the defendant has a right to give oral evidence.

In practice a statement will be read to the court, it follows as a result of the above that no issue in relation to hearsay arises (*R (Thomas) v Greenwich Magistrates' Court* [2009] EWHC 1180 (Admin)).

If the breach is not proved the defendant must be released on the same conditions as existed previously. If the breach is proved that does not mean an automatic remand into custody, it is simply a factor to be considered when the court decides on whether or not it should rebail.

A8.11 Criminal procedure rules applicable to the grant of bail (rule 19)

Part 19 of the Criminal Procedure Rules 2010 applies to bail.

A8.12 Provision of bail for juveniles

See **B3**.

A8.13 Appeals in relation to bail

A8.13.1 *Appeal against conditional bail*

If a defendant is dissatisfied with the conditions of bail he may appeal to the Crown Court, provided that he has first applied to a magistrates' court to vary those conditions and has been unsuccessful. An appeal only lies in relation to the following conditions:

- residence (but not in relation to any bail hostel);
- surety or security;
- curfew;
- non-contact.

A8.13.2 *Appeal against refusal of bail*

Following full argument in the magistrates' court (and a certificate of full argument having been issued) an appeal lies as of right to the Crown Court.

There is no longer any appeal route to the High Court, save in an exceptional case by way of judicial review.

 See *Blackstone's Criminal Practice 2012* **D7**

A9 **Binding Rulings**

Section 8B of the Magistrates' Courts Act 1980 allows a magistrates' court to make binding rulings. Section 8B provides:

Magistrates' Courts Act 1980, s 8B

(1) Subject to subsections (3) and (6), a ruling under section 8A has binding effect from the time it is made until the case against the accused or, if there is more than one, against each of them, is disposed of.

(2) The case against an accused is disposed of if—
   (a) he is acquitted or convicted,
   (b) the prosecutor decides not to proceed with the case against him, or
   (c) the information is dismissed.

(3) A magistrates' court may discharge or vary (or further vary) a ruling under section 8A if—
   (a) the condition in section 8A(5) is met,
   (b) the court has given the parties an opportunity to be heard, and
   (c) it appears to the court that it is in the interests of justice to do so.

(4) The court may act under subsection (3)—
   (a) on an application by a party to the case, or
   (b) of its own motion.

(5) No application may be made under subsection (4)(a) unless there has been a material change of circumstances since the ruling was made or, if a previous application has been made, since the application (or last application) was made.

(6) A ruling under section 8A is discharged in relation to an accused if—
   (a) the magistrates' court commits or sends him to the Crown Court for trial for the offence charged in the information, or
   (b) a count charging him with the offence is included in an indictment by virtue of section 40 of the Criminal Justice Act 1988.

Because of the binding nature of these rulings, it is not open to a later bench simply to reverse the ruling because it would have reached a different conclusion.

In *Brett v Director of Public Prosecutions* [2009] EWHC 440 (Admin), the court took a far less restrictive approach than that taken in previous cases in holding a judge to have erred in feeling that he was bound by a previous ruling under section 8A of the Magistrates' Courts Act 1980. What is certainly clear from pre- and post-section 8A case law, is that a later court cannot simply annul a previous decision on the sole ground that it simply disagrees with it (*Crown Prosecution Service v Gloucester Justices and Loveridge* [2008] EWHC 1488 (Admin)). In *R (Jones) v South East Surrey Local Justice Area*, unreported, 12 March 2010, the court having previously disallowed a prosecution application to adjourn, later granted it due to the fact that the information presented on the renewed application was different, and that it was in the interests of justice that the previous ruling be reversed.

Where the court acts of its own motion to vary a previous ruling, the grounds for discharge or variation are simply the interests of justice, and where an application is made by a party, there is an additional requirement for proof of material change of circumstances (*Crown Prosecution Service v Gloucester Justices and Alan Loveridge* [2008] EWHC 1488 (Admin)).

 See *Blackstone's Criminal Practice 2012* **D21**

A10 **Case Management**

A10.1 **Overview**

The last few years have seen substantial changes in relation to case management, and all parties are expected to proactively manage cases through the system. Courts take on a supervisory responsibility to ensure that justice is achieved in a cost-effective way. The most notable impact has been in relation to so-called 'ambush defences', and a widely held view among criminal lawyers that there is no duty to declare their hand in advance. That notion has been exploded through a number of cases (see **A10.3**) and all advocates can now expect robust challenges to that type of practice. It is worth noting, however, that no court to date has sought to address the wider question of how the rules ought to coexist alongside an advocate's duty to their client—for an academic perspective on this issue see: Cape, E (2006) 'Rebalancing the Criminal Justice Process: Ethical Challenges for Criminal Defence Lawyers', 9 *Legal Ethics* 1, 56–79.

A10.2 **Application of the rules to civil proceedings**

The Criminal Procedure Rules have no application in relation to civil procedure in the magistrates' court, nor do the Civil Procedure Rules apply.

Rule 3A of the Magistrates' Court Rules 1981 (as inserted by SI 2009/3362) provides the court with case management powers identical to those enjoyed in relation to criminal cases.

A10.3 **The overriding objective and case management**

Rules 1 and 3 deal with the overriding objective and case management powers. Rules 1 and 3 are reproduced in **Appendix 4**.

A10.4 **Defence witnesses—notification of intention to call**

Section 34 of the Criminal Justice Act 2003 inserted section 6C into the Criminal Procedure and Investigations Act 1996. Section 6C imposes duties on a defendant proposing to call defence witnesses at trial. Failure to comply is most likely to result in an adjournment and wasted costs, so solicitors should ensure that they have taken all reasonable steps to ensure that a defendant is made aware of his obligations to provide such information. It is likely that the prosecution will take advantage of any information supplied and supply it to the police, resulting in witness statements being produced. A code of practice governing this is available at: <http://www.opsi.gov.uk/acts/acts 1996/related/ukpgacop_19960025_en.pdf>.

A10.4.1 *Duty to provide details and keep disclosure under review*

Within 14 days of the prosecutor complying with initial disclosure:

Criminal Procedure and Investigations Act 1996, s 6C

(1) The accused must give to the court and the prosecutor a notice indicating whether he intends to call any persons (other than himself) as witnesses at his trial and, if so—
   (a) giving the name, address and date of birth of each such proposed witness, or as many of those details as are known to the accused when the notice is given;
   (b) providing any information in the accused's possession which might be of material assistance in identifying or finding any such proposed witness in whose case any of the details mentioned in paragraph (a) are not known to the accused when the notice is given.
(2) Details do not have to be given under this section to the extent that they have already been given under section 6A(2). [Alibi witness details included in any defence statement.]
(3) The accused must give a notice under this section during the period which, by virtue of section 12, is the relevant period for this section. [Set as 14 days by virtue of SI 2010/214.]
(4) If, following the giving of a notice under this section, the accused—
   (a) decides to call a person (other than himself) who is not included in the notice as a proposed witness, or decides not to call a person who is so included, or
   (b) discovers any information which, under subsection (1), he would have had to include in the notice if he had been aware of it when giving the notice,
   he must give an appropriately amended notice to the court and the prosecutor.

A10.4.2 *Time limits*

Criminal Procedure and Investigations Act 1996 (Defence Disclosure Time Limits) Regulations 2011, regs 2 and 3

2.—(1) The relevant period for section 5 (compulsory disclosure), section 6 (voluntary disclosure) and section 6C (notification of intention to call defence witnesses) begins with the day on which the prosecutor complies or purports to comply with section 3 (initial duty of the prosecutor to disclose).

(2) In a case where Part 1 applies by virtue of section 1(1) (application of Part 1 in respect of summary proceedings), the relevant period for section 6 and section 6C expires at the end of 14 days beginning with the first day of the relevant period.

(3) In a case where Part 1 applies by virtue of section 1(2) (application of Part 1 in respect of Crown Court proceedings), the relevant period for section 5 and section 6C expires at the end of 28 days beginning with the first day of the relevant period.

(4) Where the relevant period would expire on a Saturday, Sunday, Christmas Day, Good Friday or any day that under the Banking and Financial Dealings Act 1971 is a bank holiday in England and Wales, the relevant period is treated as expiring on the next day that is not one of those days.

(5) Paragraphs (2) and (3) are subject to regulation 3.

3.—(1) The court may by order extend (or further extend) the relevant period by so many days as it specifies.

(2) The court may only make such an order—
    (a) on an application by the accused; and
    (b) if it is satisfied that it would be unreasonable to require the accused to give a defence statement under section 5 or section 6, or give notice under section 6C, as the case may be, within the relevant period.

(3) Such an application must—
    (a) be made within the relevant period;
    (b) specify the grounds on which it is made; and
    (c) state the number of days by which the accused wishes the relevant period to be extended.

(4) There is no limit on the number of applications that may be made under paragraph (2)(a).

A10.5 Case law

There has been a constant stream of case law in relation to case management and the issues essentially boil down to the courts deprecating any attempts to take a tactical advantage.

In *Writtle v Director of Public Prosecutions* [2009] EWHC 236 (Admin) the court held:

1. the present regime of case management should in general ensure that the issues in the case are identified well before a hearing. There will, of course, be cases where something occurs in the course of a trial which may properly give rise to a new issue, but this was not such a case. The days when the defence can assume that they will be able successfully to ambush the prosecution are over.

2. A challenge to the way a procedure was carried out (in this case in relation to evidential samples) was more than merely factual such that the defence were doing nothing more than putting the prosecution to proof.

The court adopted the earlier ruling in *Malcolm v Director of Public Prosecutions* [2007] EWHC 363 (Admin) in which Burnton J stated that it is the duty of the defence to make clear to the prosecution and the court at an early stage both the defence and the issues it raises:

In my judgment, [counsel's] submissions, which emphasised the obligation of the prosecution to prove its case in its entirety before closing its case, and certainly before the end of the final speech for the defence, had an anachronistic, and obsolete, ring. Criminal trials are no longer to be treated as a game, in which each move is final and any omission by the prosecution leads to its failure. It is the duty of the defence to make its defence and the issues it raises clear to the prosecution and to the court at an early stage. That duty is implicit in rule 3.3 of the Criminal Procedure Rules, which requires the parties actively to assist the exercise by the court of its case management powers, the exercise of which requires early identification of the real issues. Even in a relatively straightforward trial such as the present, in the magistrates' court (where there is not yet any requirement of a defence statement or a pre-trial review), it is the duty of the defence to make the real issues clear at the latest before the prosecution closes its case.

In *Director of Public Prosecutions v Bury Magistrates' Court* [2007] EWHC 3256 (Admin) the court deprecated the practice of the defence failing to notify the court of prosecution failures when certifying a case ready for trial, in order to take a tactical advantage. Further, that defence breach of the rules may impact on the amount of any costs to be recovered (in this case wasted costs).

In *R (Lawson) v Stratford Magistrates' Court* [2007] EWHC 2490 (Admin) it was held that a court was correct to allow a prosecution adjournment in order to address issues raised for the first time by the defence during a closing speech. The issues related to signage and device calibration.

A10.6 Essential case management: apply the Criminal Procedure Rules

Magistrates have been issued with the following guidance:

- It is important to note that all participants in criminal cases, including magistrates, District Judges, and Justices' Clerks must follow and apply the Criminal Procedure Rules. The Rules are not mere guidance. Compliance is compulsory. The word 'must' in the Rules means must.
- The expression 'court' includes magistrates, District Judges, and Justices' Clerks exercising judicial powers (Crim PR 2.2(1)).

- Exceptions to the rule requiring the plea to be taken are rare and must be strictly justified.
- For a full version of the guidance, see: <http://www.justice.gov.uk/criminal/procrules_fin/rulesmenu.htm>.

(A) *Generally*

The court must further the Overriding Objective of the Rules by actively managing each case [Crim PR3.2(1)].

The parties must actively assist the court in this without being asked [Crim PR 3.3(a)].

But at every hearing, including a trial, it is the personal responsibility of the magistrates or district judge to manage the case actively [Crim PR 3.2].

Unnecessary hearings should be avoided by dealing with as many aspects of the case as possible at the same time [Crim PR 3.2(2)(f)].

(B) *The first hearing taking the plea*

At every hearing, (however early): Unless it has been done already, the court must take the defendant's plea [Crim PR 3.8(2)(b)]. This obligation does not depend on the extent of advance information, service of evidence, disclosure of unused material, or the grant of legal aid.

If the plea really cannot be taken, or if the alleged offence is indictable only, the court must find out what the plea is likely to be [Crim PR 3.8(2)(b)].

(C) *If the plea is 'guilty'*

The court should pass sentence on the same day, if at all possible (unless committing for sentence).

If information about the defendant is needed from the Probation Service, it may be that a report prepared for earlier proceedings will be sufficient or (depending on local arrangements) a 'fast delivery' report (oral or written) may be made that day.

If a 'Newton' hearing is needed, the court, with the active assistance of the parties, must identify the disputed issue [Crim PR 3.2(2)(a); 3.3(a)] and either, if possible, determine it there and then or, if it really cannot be determined, give directions specifically relating to that disputed issue so that the next hearing is the last.

(D) *If the plea is 'not guilty'*

The key to effective case management is the early identification by the court of the relevant disputed issues [Crim PR 3.2(2)(a)].

From the start, the parties must identify those issues and tell the court what they are [Crim PR 3.3(a)]. If the parties do not tell the court, the court must require them to do so.

The relevant disputed issues must be explicitly identified and the case must be managed by the court so that the 'live' evidence at trial is confined to those issues.

The parties must complete the prescribed case progression form [Crim PR 3.11; Consolidated Practice Direction V.56.2] and the court must rigorously consider each entry on the form in order to comply with its duty actively to manage the case by making properly informed directions specific to each case.

Only those witnesses who are really needed in relation to genuinely disputed, relevant issues should be required to attend. The court must take responsibility for this (not simply leave it to the parties) in order to comply with the Overriding Objective of the Rules [Crim PR 1.1(2)(d), (e)].

The court's directions must include a timetable for the progress of the case (which can include a timetable for the trial itself) [Crim PR 3.8(2)(c)].

The time estimate for the trial should be made by considering, individually, how long each 'live' witness will take having regard to the relevant disputed issue(s).

(E) *The parties' obligations to prepare for trial include:*

Getting witnesses to court [Crim PR 3.9(2)(b)].

Making arrangements for the efficient presentation of written evidence/other material [Crim PR 3.9(2)(c)].

Promptly warning the court and other parties of any problems [Crim PR 3.9(2)(d)].

(F) *At trial*

Before the trial begins, the court must establish, with the active assistance of the parties, what disputed issues they intend to explore [Crim PR 3.10(a)].

The court may require the parties to provide:

- A timed, 'batting order' of live witnesses [Crim PR 3.10(b)(i), (ii), (ix)].
- Details of any admissions/written evidence/other material to be adduced [Crim PR 3.10(b)(vi), (vii)].
- Warning of any point of law [Crim PR 3.10(b)(viii)].
- A timetable for the whole case [Crim PR 3.10(b)(ix)].

During the trial the court must ensure that the 'live' evidence, questions, and submissions are strictly directed to the relevant disputed issues.

A10.7 **Law Society Practice Note**

All advocates should have access to the Law Society Practice Note in relation to the Criminal Procedure Rules which accurately sets out the legal position in relation to a number of recurring issues:

<http://www.lawsociety.org.uk/documents/downloads/practicenote_criminalprocedurerules.pdf>.

A10.8 **Sanctions**

Failure to abide by rules brings sanctions specified by statute (eg adverse inferences). A failure by a defendant to serve a defence statement did not amount to a contempt of court on either the part of the advocate or defendant (*R v GR* [2010] EWCA Crim 1928).

 See *Blackstone's Criminal Practice 2012* **D4**

A11 **Clerks Retiring with Justices**

The Consolidated Criminal Practice Direction provides:

Consolidated Criminal Practice Direction, part V.55

(V.55.1)

A justices' clerk is responsible for:

(a) the legal advice tendered to the justices within the area;

(b) the performance of any of the functions set out below by any member of his staff acting as legal adviser;

(c) ensuring that competent advice is available to justices when the justices' clerk is not personally present in court; and

(d) the effective delivery of case management and the reduction of unnecessary delay.

(V.55.2)

Where a person other than the justices' clerk (a 'legal adviser'), who is authorised to do so, performs any of the functions referred to in this direction he will have the same responsibilities as the justices' clerk. The legal adviser may consult the justices' clerk or other person authorised by the justices' clerk for that purpose before tendering advice to the bench. If the justices' clerk or that person gives any advice directly to the bench, he should give the parties or their advocates an opportunity of repeating any relevant submissions prior to the advice being given.

(V.55.3)

It shall be the responsibility of the legal adviser to provide the justices with any advice they require properly to perform their functions, whether or not the justices have requested that advice, on:

(a) questions of law (including European Court of Human Rights jurisprudence and those matters set out in section 2(1) of the Human Rights Act 1998);

(b) questions of mixed law and fact;

(c) matters of practice and procedure;

(d) the range of penalties available;

(e) any relevant decisions of the superior courts or other guidelines;

(f) other issues relevant to the matter before the court; and

(g) the appropriate decision-making structure to be applied in any given case.

In addition to advising the justices it shall be the legal adviser's responsibility to assist the court, where appropriate, as to the formulation of reasons and the recording of those reasons.

(V.55.4)

A justices' clerk or legal adviser must not play any part in making findings of fact, but may assist the bench by reminding them of the evidence, using any notes of the proceedings for this purpose.

(V.55.5)

A justices' clerk or legal adviser may ask questions of witnesses and the parties in order to clarify the evidence and any issues in the case. A legal adviser has a duty to ensure that every case is conducted fairly.

(V.55.6)

When advising the justices the justices' clerk or legal adviser, whether or not previously in court, should:

(a) ensure that he is aware of the relevant facts; and

(b) provide the parties with the information necessary to enable the parties to make any representations they wish as to the advice before it is given.

(V.55.7)

At any time justices are entitled to receive advice to assist them in discharging their responsibilities. If they are in any doubt as to the evidence which has been given, they should seek the aid of their legal adviser, referring to his notes as appropriate. This should ordinarily be done in open court. Where the justices request their adviser to join them in the retiring room, this request should be made in the presence of the parties in court. Any legal advice given to the justices other than in open court should be clearly stated to be provisional and the adviser should subsequently repeat the substance of the advice in open court and give the parties an opportunity to make any representations they wish on that provisional advice. The legal adviser should then state in open court whether the provisional advice is confirmed or if it is varied the nature of the variation.

(V.55.8)

The performance of a legal adviser may be appraised by a person authorised by the magistrates' courts committee to do so. For that purpose the appraiser may be present in the justices' retiring room. The content of the appraisal is confidential, but the fact that an appraisal has taken place, and the presence of the appraiser in the retiring room, should be briefly explained in open court.

(V.55.9)

The legal adviser is under a duty to assist unrepresented parties to present their case, but must do so without appearing to become an advocate for the party concerned.

(V.55.10)

The role of legal advisers in fine default proceedings or any other proceedings for the enforcement of financial orders, obligations or penalties is to assist the court. They must not act in an adversarial or partisan manner. With the agreement of the justices a legal adviser may ask questions of the defaulter to elicit information which the justices will require to make an adjudication, for example to facilitate his explanation for the default. A legal adviser may also advise the justices in the normal way as to the options open to them in dealing with the case. It would be inappropriate for the legal adviser to set out to establish wilful refusal or neglect or any other type of culpable behaviour, to offer an opinion on the facts, or to urge a particular course of action upon the justices. The duty of impartiality is the paramount consideration for the legal adviser at all times, and this takes precedence over any role he may have as a collecting officer. The appointment of other staff to 'prosecute' the case for the collecting officer is not essential to ensure compliance with the law, including the Human Rights Act 1998. Whether to make such appointments is a matter for the justices' chief executive.

 See *Blackstone's Criminal Practice 2012* D22.51

A12 Commencing Proceedings

A12.1 Consent to prosecute

Section 25 of the Prosecution of Offences Act 1985 provides:

> **Prosecution of Offences Act 1985, s 25**
>
> (1) This section applies to any enactment which prohibits the institution or carrying on of proceedings for any offence except—
>   (a) with the consent (however expressed) of a Law Officer of the Crown or the Director; or
>   (b) where the proceedings are instituted or carried on by or on behalf of a Law Officer of the Crown or the Director;
>   and so applies whether or not there are other exceptions to the prohibition (and in particular whether or not the consent is an alternative to the consent of any other authority or person).
> (2) An enactment to which this section applies—
>   (a) shall not prevent the arrest without warrant, or the issue or execution of a warrant for the arrest, of a person for any offence, or the remand in custody or on bail of a person charged with any offence; and
>   (b) shall be subject to any enactment concerning the apprehension or detention of children or young persons.
> (3) In this section 'enactment' includes any provision having effect under or by virtue of any Act; and this section applies to enactments whenever passed or made.

It is by no means clear, but highly likely, that were proceedings to have been commenced without the requisite authority, they will be a nullity (*R v Clarke and McDaid* [2008] 1 WLR 338, HL). Consent must be obtained by the time the charge is entered into the court register (*R v Lambert* [2009] 2 Cr App R 523(32)).

A crown prosecutor can give consent where the consent of the Director of Public Prosecutions is required (Prosecution of Offences Act 1985, s 1(7)).

Section 26 of the 1985 Act deals with proof of consent:

> **Prosecution of Offences Act 1985, s 26**
>
> Any document purporting to be the consent of a Law Officer of the Crown, the Director or a Crown Prosecutor for, or to—
> (a) the institution of any criminal proceedings; or
> (b) the institution of criminal proceedings in any particular form;

and to be signed by a Law Officer of the Crown, the Director or, as the case may be, a Crown Prosecutor shall be admissible as prima facie evidence without further proof.

A12.2 Time limits

A12.2.1 *Overview*

Generally speaking, summary proceedings must be started within six months of the criminality complained of.

Section 127 of the Magistrates' Courts Act 1980 provides:

Magistrates' Courts Act 1980, s 127

(1) Except as otherwise expressly provided by any enactment and subject to subsection (2) below, a magistrates' court shall not try an information or hear a complaint unless the information was laid, or the complaint made, within 6 months from the time when the offence was committed, or the matter of complaint arose.

(2) Nothing in—
  (a) subsection (1) above; or
  (b) subject to subsection (4) below, any other enactment (however framed or worded) which, as regards any offence to which it applies, would but for this section impose a time-limit on the power of a magistrates' court to try an information summarily or impose a limitation on the time for taking summary proceedings,
  shall apply in relation to any indictable offence.

(3) . . .

(4) . . .

The following principles emerge from the case law:

- The date of the offence is excluded from the time calculation (*Radcliffe v Bartholomew* [1892] 1 QB 161).
- In relation to a continuing offence it is the date of the last act that is relevant (*Director of Public Prosecutions v Baker* [2004] EWHC 2782 (Admin)).
- Month means calendar month.
- Limitation ends at midnight on the last day.
- If there is doubt as to whether an information has been laid in time it must be resolved in favour of the defendant (*Lloyd v Young* [1963] Crim LR 703).

See **A5** for the rules relating to amendment of a charge to substitute an offence that would otherwise be time-barred.

A12.2.2 *Exceptions*

A large number of offences that can only be tried summarily are, in certain circumstances, exempt from the six-month time bar.

In relation to some offences time only runs from when an offence is 'discovered' by the prosecutor, which means when there was a reasonable belief that an offence had been committed (*Tesco Stores Limited v London Borough of Harrow* (2003) 167 JP 657, DC).

 See *Blackstone's Criminal Practice 2012* **D2**

A13 Constitution and Jurisdiction

A13.1 The magistrates' court

The magistrates' court (which includes a youth court) is a creature of statute created under the Magistrates' Courts Act 1980.

Magistrates' Courts Act 1980, s 148

(1) In this Act the expression 'magistrates' court' means any justice or justices of the peace acting under any enactment or by virtue of his or their commission or under the common law.

(2) Except where the contrary is expressed, anything authorised or required by this Act to be done by, to or before the magistrates' court by, to or before which any other thing was done, or is to be done, may be done by, to or before any magistrates' court acting in the same local justice area as that court.

A13.2 Constitution and place of sitting

Magistrates' Courts Act 1980, s 121

(1) A magistrates' court shall not try an information summarily or hear a complaint except when composed of at least 2 justices unless the trial or hearing is one that by virtue of any enactment may take place before a single justice.

(2) A magistrates' court shall not hold an inquiry into the means of an offender for the purposes of section 82 above or determine under that section at a hearing at which the offender is not present whether to issue a warrant of commitment except when composed of at least 2 justices.

(4) Subject to the provisions of any enactment to the contrary, a magistrates' court must sit in open court if it is—
   (a) trying summarily an information for an indictable offence,
   (b) trying an information for a summary offence,
   (c) imposing imprisonment,
   (d) hearing a complaint, or
   (e) holding an inquiry into the means of an offender for the purposes of section 82.

(5) A magistrates' court composed of a single justice shall not impose imprisonment for a period exceeding 14 days or order a person to pay more than £1.

(6) Subject to the provisions of subsection (7) below, the justices composing the court before which any proceedings take place shall be present during the whole of the proceedings; but if during the course of the proceedings any justice absents himself, he shall cease to act further therein and, if the remaining justices are enough to satisfy the requirements of the preceding provisions of this section, the proceedings may continue before a court composed of those justices.

(7) Where the trial of an information is adjourned after the accused has been convicted and before he is sentenced or otherwise dealt with, the court which sentences or deals with him need not be composed of the same justices as that which convicted him; but, where among the justices composing the court

which sentences or deals with an offender there are any who were not sitting when he was convicted, the court which sentences or deals with the offender shall before doing so make such inquiry into the facts and circumstances of the case as will enable the justices who were not sitting when the offender was convicted to be fully acquainted with those facts and circumstances.

A13.3 Territorial jurisdiction

The court has jurisdiction over:

- offences committed in England and Wales;
- offences committed elsewhere when statute so prescribes;
- offences committed by an English citizen aboard a UK ship, or any foreign ship where he does not belong (Merchant Shipping Act 1995, s 281(a));
- offences committed by a non-UK citizen aboard any UK ship on the high seas (Merchant Shipping Act 1995, s 281(b));
- offences committed on an aircraft in flight over the UK.

 See *Blackstone's Criminal Practice 2012* **D3**

A13.4 Diplomatic immunity

Member of a diplomatic mission, their staff, and families enjoy diplomatic immunity from prosecution provided that their arrival into the UK has been notified under the Vienna Convention on Diplomatic Relations. A failure to notify presence in the UK prevents the defendant from claiming immunity (*R v Lambeth Justices, ex p Yusufu* [1985] Crim LR 510). There is no duty on the accused to raise immunity, although it would clearly be sensible to do so at the earliest stage. Any prosecution and proceedings, save where a waiver has been granted by the chief representative (or his agent) of the mission concerned, is void (*R v Madan* [1961] Crim LR 253). It remains unclear as to whether a waiver can be granted retrospectively.

A13.5 Prosecutions by local government

In some instances prosecutions commenced by local government bodies can only be brought for offences committed within their local area unless authority to prosecute has been delegated to them by the other relevant local body. If in doubt as to the authority to prosecute, consideration should be given to sections 101 and 202 of the Local Government Act 1972 and the cases of *Brighton and Hove County Council v Woolworths* [2002] EWHC 2656 (Admin) and *R (Donnachie) v Cardiff Magistrates' Court* [2009] EWHC 489 (Admin).

 See *Blackstone's Criminal Practice 2012* **A8.17** and **D2.15**

A14 **Committal, Sending, and Transfer for Trial**

A14.1 **Overview**

In the following instances the court may decline or be deprived of jurisdiction to try a matter:

- indictable only matters—sent to the Crown Court;
- either-way matters where jurisdiction is declined or the defendant has elected Crown Court trial—committed to the Crown Court. Note: it is likely that during the life of this book all offences in this category will simply be sent to the Crown Court immediately, instead of proceeding by way of committal;
- transfer cases—transferred to the Crown Court;
- voluntary bill of indictment (not covered in this book).

Method	Notes
Committal proceedings. Section 6 of the Magistrates' Courts Act 1980	Committal can be by consent if a prima facie case (s 6(2)), or via contested hearing (s 6(1)). No right to require oral evidence and no defence evidence allowed. Court has no discretion to exclude evidence under Police and Criminal Evidence Act 1984, ss 76, 78. The court may commit on any indictable offence (although if different from the one charged it may proceed if it wishes to try the matter summarily: *R v Cambridge Justices, ex p Fraser* [1985] 1 All ER 668). Court can also commit summary offences to be tried on the indictment, eg common assault (Criminal Justice Act 1988, s 40). Court can commit other summary offences if they are imprisonable or carry discretionary or obligatory disqualification from driving (Criminal Justice Act 1988, s 41). Provided the defendant is represented the case can be committed in his absence (*R v Liverpool Magistrates' Court, ex p Quantrell* [1999] Crim LR 734).

| Sending.
Section 51 of the Crime and Disorder Act 1998
Note: Section 41 of and Schedule 3 to the Criminal Justice Act 2003 greatly extend the powers to send cases to the Crown Court. At the time of writing only section 51A is in force in relation to youths who might fall to be sentenced under dangerous offender provisions. It is highly likely that the remaining amendments (sections 51 to 51E) will come into force during the life of this book, so they too have been reproduced below. | The court will send the indictable only matter, along with any related either-way matters. This may involve sending one or more co-defendants. Note: A sending is not a remand within the meaning of ss 128, 128A MCA 1980, and therefore the initial 8 day limitation on a remand in custody does not apply.
An either-way offence is related to an indictable offence if the charge for the either-way offence could be joined in the same indictment as the charge for the indictable offence.
A summary offence is related to an indictable offence if it arises out of circumstances which are the same as or connected with those giving rise to the indictable offence. The court can also send related summary offences if they are imprisonable or carry discretionary or obligatory disqualification from driving.
It does not matter that all matters are not sent on the same occasion.
In the case of a youth charged with an adult (not necessarily on the same occasion), the youth will be sent if it is in the interests of justice to try him with the adult. There is no power to send a case to the Crown Court in the absence of a defendant, even if that person is legally represented. |
| Transfer cases.
Note: See sections 51B and 51C of the Crime and Disorder Act 1998 below for provisions that will replace this power. | Applicable to fraud cases (Criminal Justice Act 1987, s 4) and child cases (Criminal Justice Act 1991, s 53). There will be no committal proceedings as the case will be transferred forthwith. |

A14.2 Relevant legislation

Section 6 of the Magistrates' Courts Act 1980 provides:

Magistrates' Courts Act 1980, s 6

(1) A magistrates' court inquiring into an offence as examining justices shall on consideration of the evidence—
  (a) commit the accused for trial if it is of opinion that there is sufficient evidence to put him on trial by jury for any indictable offence;
  (b) discharge him if it is not of that opinion and he is in custody for no other cause than the offence under inquiry;
  but the preceding provisions of this subsection have effect subject to the provisions of this and any other Act relating to the summary trial of indictable offences.
(2) If a magistrates' court inquiring into an offence as examining justices is satisfied that all the evidence tendered by or on behalf of the prosecutor falls within section 5A(3) above, it may commit the accused for trial for the offence without consideration of the contents of any statements, depositions or other

documents, and without consideration of any exhibits which are not documents, unless—

(a) the accused or one of the accused has no legal representative acting for him in the case, or

(b) a legal representative for the accused or one of the accused, as the case may be, has requested the court to consider a submission that there is insufficient evidence to put that accused on trial by jury for the offence;

and subsection (1) above shall not apply to a committal for trial under this subsection.

Section 51 of the Crime and Disorder Act 1998 provides:

Crime and Disorder Act 1998, s 51

(1) Where an adult appears or is brought before a magistrates' court ('the court') charged with an offence triable only on indictment ('the indictable-only offence'), the court shall send him forthwith to the Crown Court for trial—

(a) for that offence, and

(b) for any either-way or summary offence with which he is charged which fulfils the requisite conditions (as set out in subsection (11) below).

(2) Where an adult who has been sent for trial under subsection (1) above subsequently appears or is brought before a magistrates' court charged with an either-way or summary offence which fulfils the requisite conditions, the court may send him forthwith to the Crown Court for trial for the either-way or summary offence.

(3) Where—

(a) the court sends an adult for trial under subsection (1) above;

(b) another adult appears or is brought before the court on the same or a subsequent occasion charged jointly with him with an either-way offence; and

(c) that offence appears to the court to be related to the indictable-only offence,

the court shall where it is the same occasion, and may where it is a subsequent occasion, send the other adult forthwith to the Crown Court for trial for the either-way offence.

(4) Where a court sends an adult for trial under subsection (3) above, it shall at the same time send him to the Crown Court for trial for any either-way or summary offence with which he is charged which fulfils the requisite conditions.

(5) Where—

(a) the court sends an adult for trial under subsection (1) or (3) above; and

(b) a child or young person appears or is brought before the court on the same or a subsequent occasion charged jointly with the adult with an indictable offence for which the adult is sent for trial,

the court shall, if it considers it necessary in the interests of justice to do so, send the child or young person forthwith to the Crown Court for trial for the indictable offence.

(6) Where a court sends a child or young person for trial under subsection (5) above, it may at the same time send him to the Crown Court for trial for any either-way or summary offence with which he is charged which fulfils the requisite conditions.

(7) The court shall specify in a notice the offence or offences for which a person is sent for trial under this section and the place at which he is to be tried; and a copy of the notice shall be served on the accused and given to the Crown Court-sitting at that place.

(8) In a case where there is more than one indictable-only offence and the court includes an either-way or a summary offence in the notice under subsection (7) above, the court shall specify in that notice the indictable-only offence to which the either-way offence or, as the case may be, the summary offence appears to the court to be related.

(9) The trial of the information charging any summary offence for which a person is sent for trial under this section shall be treated as if the court had adjourned it under section 10 of the 1980 Act and had not fixed the time and place for its resumption.

(10) In selecting the place of trial for the purpose of subsection (7) above, the court shall have regard to—

(a) the convenience of the defence, the prosecution and the witnesses;

(b) the desirability of expediting the trial; and

(c) any direction given by or on behalf of the Lord Chief Justice with the concurrence of the Lord Chancellor under section 75(1) of the Supreme Court Act 1981.

(11) An offence fulfils the requisite conditions if—

(a) it appears to the court to be related to the indictable-only offence; and

(b) in the case of a summary offence, it is punishable with imprisonment or involves obligatory or discretionary disqualification from driving.

(12) For the purposes of this section—

(a) 'adult' means a person aged 18 or over, and references to an adult include references to a corporation;

(b) 'either-way offence' means an offence which, if committed by an adult, is triable either on indictment or summarily;

(c) an either-way offence is related to an indictable-only offence if the charge for the either-way offence could be joined in the same indictment as the charge for the indictable-only offence;

(d) a summary offence is related to an indictable-only offence if it arises out of circumstances which are the same as or connected with those giving rise to the indictable-only offence.

Sections 51–51E following implementation of section 41 of and schedule 3 to the Criminal Justice Act 2003 provide:

Criminal Justice Act 2003, ss 51–51E

51 Sending cases to the Crown Court: adults

(1) Where an adult appears or is brought before a magistrates' court ('the court') charged with an offence and any of the conditions mentioned in subsection (2) below is satisfied, the court shall send him forthwith to the Crown Court for trial for the offence.

(2) Those conditions are—

    (a) that the offence is an offence triable only on indictment other than one in respect of which notice has been given under section 51B or 51C below;

    (b) that the offence is an either-way offence and the court is required under section 20(9)(b), 21, 23(4)(b) or (5) or 25(2D) of the Magistrates' Courts Act 1980 to proceed in relation to the offence in accordance with subsection (1) above;

    (c) that notice is given to the court under section 51B or 51C below in respect of the offence.

(3) Where the court sends an adult for trial under subsection (1) above, it shall at the same time send him to the Crown Court for trial for any either-way or summary offence with which he is charged and which—

    (a) (if it is an either-way offence) appears to the court to be related to the offence mentioned in subsection (1) above; or

    (b) (if it is a summary offence) appears to the court to be related to the offence mentioned in subsection (1) above or to the either-way offence, and which fulfils the requisite condition (as defined in subsection (11) below).

(4) Where an adult who has been sent for trial under subsection (1) above subsequently appears or is brought before a magistrates' court charged with an either-way or summary offence which—

    (a) appears to the court to be related to the offence mentioned in subsection (1) above; and

    (b) (in the case of a summary offence) fulfils the requisite condition,

the court may send him forthwith to the Crown Court for trial for the either-way or summary offence.

(5) Where—

    (a) the court sends an adult ('A') for trial under subsection (1) or (3) above;

    (b) another adult appears or is brought before the court on the same or a subsequent occasion charged jointly with A with an either-way offence; and

    (c) that offence appears to the court to be related to an offence for which A was sent for trial under subsection (1) or (3) above,

the court shall where it is the same occasion, and may where it is a subsequent occasion, send the other adult forthwith to the Crown Court for trial for the either-way offence.

(6) Where the court sends an adult for trial under subsection (5) above, it shall at the same time send him to the Crown Court for trial for any either-way or summary offence with which he is charged and which—

    (a) (if it is an either-way offence) appears to the court to be related to the offence for which he is sent for trial; and

    (b) (if it is a summary offence) appears to the court to be related to the offence for which he is sent for trial or to the either-way offence, and which fulfils the requisite condition.

(7) Where—

    (a) the court sends an adult ('A') for trial under subsection (1), (3) or (5) above; and

    (b) a child or young person appears or is brought before the court on the same or a subsequent occasion charged jointly with A with an indictable offence for which A is sent for trial under subsection (1), (3) or (5) above, or an indictable offence which appears to the court to be related to that offence,

the court shall, if it considers it necessary in the interests of justice to do so, send the child or young person forthwith to the Crown Court for trial for the indictable offence.

(8) Where the court sends a child or young person for trial under subsection (7) above, it may at the same time send him to the Crown Court for trial for any indictable or summary offence with which he is charged and which—

    (a) (if it is an indictable offence) appears to the court to be related to the offence for which he is sent for trial; and

    (b) (if it is a summary offence) appears to the court to be related to the offence for which he is sent for trial or to the indictable offence, and which fulfils the requisite condition.

(9) Subsections (7) and (8) above are subject to sections 24A and 24B of the Magistrates' Courts Act 1980 (which provide for certain cases involving children and young persons to be tried summarily).

(10) The trial of the information charging any summary offence for which a person is sent for trial under this section shall be treated as if the court had adjourned it under section 10 of the 1980 Act and had not fixed the time and place for its resumption.

(11) A summary offence fulfils the requisite condition if it is punishable with imprisonment or involves obligatory or discretionary disqualification from driving.

(12) In the case of an adult charged with an offence—

    (a) if the offence satisfies paragraph (c) of subsection (2) above, the offence shall be dealt with under subsection (1) above and not under any other provision of this section or section 51A below;

    (b) subject to paragraph (a) above, if the offence is one in respect of which the court is required to, or would decide to, send the adult to the Crown Court under—

        (i) subsection (5) above; or

        (ii) subsection (6) of section 51A below,

the offence shall be dealt with under that subsection and not under any other provision of this section or section 51A below.

(13) The functions of a magistrates' court under this section, and its related functions under section 51D below, may be discharged by a single justice.

51A Sending cases to the Crown Court: children and young persons

(1) This section is subject to sections 24A and 24B of the Magistrates' Courts Act 1980 (which provide for certain offences involving children or young persons to be tried summarily).

(2) Where a child or young person appears or is brought before a magistrates' court ('the court') charged with an offence and any of the conditions mentioned in subsection (3) below is satisfied, the court shall send him forthwith to the Crown Court for trial for the offence.

(3) Those conditions are—

    (a) that the offence falls within subsection (12) below;

    (b) that the offence is such as is mentioned in subsection (1) of section 91 of the Powers of Criminal Courts (Sentencing) Act 2000 (other than one mentioned in paragraph (d) below in relation to which it appears to the court as mentioned there) and the court considers that if he is found guilty of the offence it ought to be possible to sentence him in pursuance of subsection (3) of that section;

    (c) that notice is given to the court under section 51B or 51C below in respect of the offence;

    (d) that the offence is a specified offence (within the meaning of section 224 of the Criminal Justice Act 2003) and it appears to the court that if he is found guilty of the offence the criteria for the imposition of a sentence under section 226(3) or 228(2) of that Act would be met.

(4) Where the court sends a child or young person for trial under subsection (2) above, it may at the same time send him to the Crown Court for trial for any indictable or summary offence with which he is charged and which—

    (a) (if it is an indictable offence) appears to the court to be related to the offence mentioned in subsection (2) above; or

    (b) (if it is a summary offence) appears to the court to be related to the offence mentioned in subsection (2) above or to the indictable offence, and which fulfils the requisite condition (as defined in subsection (9) below).

(5) Where a child or young person who has been sent for trial under subsection (2) above subsequently appears or is brought before a magistrates' court charged with an indictable or summary offence which—

    (a) appears to the court to be related to the offence mentioned in subsection (2) above; and

    (b) (in the case of a summary offence) fulfils the requisite condition,

the court may send him forthwith to the Crown Court for trial for the indictable or summary offence.

(6) Where—

    (a) the court sends a child or young person ('C') for trial under subsection (2) or (4) above; and

    (b) an adult appears or is brought before the court on the same or a subsequent occasion charged jointly with C with an either-way offence for which C is sent for trial under subsection (2) or (4) above, or an either-way offence which appears to the court to be related to that offence,

the court shall where it is the same occasion, and may where it is a subsequent occasion, send the adult forthwith to the Crown Court for trial for the either-way offence.

(7) Where the court sends an adult for trial under subsection (6) above, it shall at the same time send him to the Crown Court for trial for any either-way or summary offence with which he is charged and which—

    (a) (if it is an either-way offence) appears to the court to be related to the offence for which he was sent for trial; and

    (b) (if it is a summary offence) appears to the court to be related to the offence for which he was sent for trial or to the either-way offence, and which fulfils the requisite condition.

(8) The trial of the information charging any summary offence for which a person is sent for trial under this section shall be treated as if the court had adjourned it under section 10 of the 1980 Act and had not fixed the time and place for its resumption.

(9) A summary offence fulfils the requisite condition if it is punishable with imprisonment or involves obligatory or discretionary disqualification from driving.

(10) In the case of a child or young person charged with an offence—

    (a) if the offence satisfies any of the conditions in subsection (3) above, the offence shall be dealt with under subsection (2) above and not under any other provision of this section or section 51 above;

    (b) subject to paragraph (a) above, if the offence is one in respect of which the requirements of subsection (7) of section 51 above for sending the child or young person to the Crown Court are satisfied, the offence shall be dealt with under that subsection and not under any other provision of this section or section 51 above.

(11) The functions of a magistrates' court under this section, and its related functions under section 51D below, may be discharged by a single justice.

(12) An offence falls within this subsection if—

    (a) it is an offence of homicide;

    (b) each of the requirements of section 51A(1) of the Firearms Act 1968 would be satisfied with respect to—

        (i) the offence; and

        (ii) the person charged with it,

        if he were convicted of the offence; or

    (c) section 29(3) of Violent Crime Reduction Act 2006 (minimum sentences in certain cases of using someone to mind a weapon) would apply if he were convicted of the offence.

51B Notices in serious or complex fraud cases

(1) A notice may be given by a designated authority under this section in respect of an indictable offence if the authority is of the opinion that the evidence of the offence charged—

    (a) is sufficient for the person charged to be put on trial for the offence; and

    (b) reveals a case of fraud of such seriousness or complexity that it is appropriate that the management of the case should without delay be taken over by the Crown Court.

(2) That opinion must be certified by the designated authority in the notice.

(3) The notice must also specify the proposed place of trial, and in selecting that place the designated authority must have regard to the same matters as are specified in paragraphs (a) to (c) of section 51D(4) below.

(4) A notice under this section must be given to the magistrates' court at which the person charged appears or before which he is brought.

(5) Such a notice must be given to the magistrates' court before any summary trial begins.

(6) The effect of such a notice is that the functions of the magistrates' court cease in relation to the case, except—

(a) for the purposes of section 51D below;

(b) as provided by paragraph 2 of Schedule 3 to the Access to Justice Act 1999; and

(c) as provided by section 52 below.

(7) The functions of a designated authority under this section may be exercised by an officer of the authority acting on behalf of the authority.

(8) A decision to give a notice under this section shall not be subject to appeal or liable to be questioned in any court (whether a magistrates' court or not).

(9) In this section 'designated authority' means—

(a) the Director of Public Prosecutions;

(b) the Director of the Serious Fraud Office;

(c) the Director of Revenue and Customs Prosecutions;

(d) [repealed]

(e) the Secretary of State.

51C Notices in certain cases involving children

(1) A notice may be given by the Director of Public Prosecutions under this section in respect of an offence falling within subsection (3) below if he is of the opinion—

(a) that the evidence of the offence would be sufficient for the person charged to be put on trial for the offence;

(b) that a child would be called as a witness at the trial; and

(c) that, for the purpose of avoiding any prejudice to the welfare of the child, the case should be taken over and proceeded with without delay by the Crown Court.

(2) That opinion must be certified by the Director of Public Prosecutions in the notice.

(3) This subsection applies to an offence—

(a) which involves an assault on, or injury or a threat of injury to, a person;

(b) under section 1 of the Children and Young Persons Act 1933 (cruelty to persons under 16);

(c) under the Sexual Offences Act 1956, the Protection of Children Act 1978 or the Sexual Offences Act 2003;

(d) of kidnapping or false imprisonment, or an offence under section 1 or 2 of the Child Abduction Act 1984;

(e) which consists of attempting or conspiring to commit, or of aiding, abetting, counselling, procuring or inciting the commission of, an offence falling within paragraph (a), (b), (c) or (d) above.

(4) Subsections (4), (5) and (6) of section 51B above apply for the purposes of this section as they apply for the purposes of that.

(5) The functions of the Director of Public Prosecutions under this section may be exercised by an officer acting on behalf of the Director.

(6) A decision to give a notice under this section shall not be subject to appeal or liable to be questioned in any court (whether a magistrates' court or not).

(7) In this section 'child' means—

    (a) a person who is under the age of 17; or

    (b) any person of whom a video recording (as defined in section 63(1) of the Youth Justice and Criminal Evidence Act 1999) was made when he was under the age of 17 with a view to its admission as his evidence in chief in the trial referred to in subsection (1) above.

51D Notice of offence and place of trial

(1) The court shall specify in a notice—

    (a) the offence or offences for which a person is sent for trial under section 51 or 51A above; and

    (b) the place at which he is to be tried (which, if a notice has been given under section 51B above, must be the place specified in that notice).

(2) A copy of the notice shall be served on the accused and given to the Crown Court sitting at that place.

(3) In a case where a person is sent for trial under section 51 or 51A above for more than one offence, the court shall specify in that notice, for each offence—

    (a) the subsection under which the person is so sent; and

    (b) if applicable, the offence to which that offence appears to the court to be related.

(4) Where the court selects the place of trial for the purposes of subsection (1) above, it shall have regard to—

    (a) the convenience of the defence, the prosecution and the witnesses;

    (b) the desirability of expediting the trial; and

    (c) any direction given by or on behalf of the Lord Chief Justice with the concurrence of the Lord Chancellor under section 75(1) of the Supreme Court Act 1981.

51E Interpretation of sections 50A to 51D

For the purposes of sections 50A to 51D above—

(a) 'adult' means a person aged 18 or over, and references to an adult include a corporation;

(b) 'either-way offence' means an offence triable either way;

(c) an either-way offence is related to an indictable offence if the charge for the either-way offence could be joined in the same indictment as the charge for the indictable offence;

(d) a summary offence is related to an indictable offence if it arises out of circumstances which are the same as or connected with those giving rise to the indictable offence.

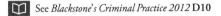 See *Blackstone's Criminal Practice 2012* **D10**

A15 **Costs (Defendants)**

A15.1 **Statutory basis for awarding defence costs**

Section 16 of the Prosecution of Offences Act 1985 provides:

> **Prosecution of Offences Act 1985, s 16**
>
> **16 Defence costs**
>
> (1) Where—
>
>   (a) an information laid before a justice of the peace for any area, charging any person with an offence, is not proceeded with;
>
>   (b) a magistrates' court inquiring into an indictable offence as examining justices determines not to commit the accused for trial;
>
>   (c) a magistrates' court dealing summarily with an offence dismisses the information;
>
> that court or, in a case falling within paragraph (a) above, a magistrates' court for that area, may make an order in favour of the accused for a payment to be made out of central funds in respect of his costs (a 'defendant's costs order').

Section 16 does not apply to proceedings in respect to breach of community penalty as the information does not charge a person with an offence. Similarly, the section has no application in relation to civil proceedings (eg in relation to anti-social behaviour orders), see below for other provisions.

Costs should generally be awarded to a defendant who can satisfy section 16. This includes:

- where the case is withdrawn so that a caution can be administered (*R (Stoddard) v Oxford Magistrates' Court* (2005) 169 JP 683);
- where there is a stay for abuse of process (*R (on the application of R E Williams & Sons (Wholesale) Ltd) v Hereford Magistrates' Court*, unreported, 2 July 2008);
- where a case is resolved by way of bind over (*Emohare v Thames Magistrates' Court* [2009] EWHC 689 (Admin)).

In *R (on the application of Spiteri) v Basildon Crown Court*, unreported, 19 March 2009, the applicant successfully appealed a refusal to make a defendant's costs order on the grounds that he was acquitted on a 'technicality'. It was held that a costs order could not be refused on the sole ground that the applicant had brought the proceedings upon himself, as more was required, such as the defendant having misled the prosecution as to the strength of the case against him. A similar point arose in *Dowler v MerseyRail* [2009] EWHC 558 (Admin), where the court ruled that when refusing costs courts should give reasons for the refusal contemporaneously with the ruling. In *R (Guney) v Central*

Criminal Court [2011] EWHC 767 (Admin), a case involving the making of a Recovery of Defence Costs Order following an acquittal, the court discusses further the issue of a defendant who brings the proceedings upon himself and misleading the prosecution as to the strength of the case against him. The same principles will apply when a court is considering refusing a defence costs order.

In *Brewer v Secretary of State for Justice* [2009] EWHC 987 (QB) the court held that a publicly funded defendant was able to recover as out-of-pocket expenses, payments made to a third party for professional services. Whether such costs would be recoverable depended upon (a) the profession of the person instructed and the services provided, (b) the reason why it was necessary and reasonable to incur the expenditure, and (c) why the work was not paid for under the representation order in force. In cases where the expenditure claimed was outside the norm, the person claiming should assist the court by providing full details of the heads of expenditure.

It is not appropriate to award costs on an appeal to the Crown Court where the appeal was allowed as an act of mercy (*R (Pluckrose) v Snaresbrook Crown Court*, unreported, 9 June 2009).

A15.2 Practice Direction: Costs in Criminal Proceedings

Part II.1 of the Practice Direction: Costs in Criminal Proceedings states:

Practice Direction on Costs in Criminal Proceedings, part II.1

II.1 In a Magistrates' Court

II.1.1

Where an information laid before a Justice of the Peace charging a person with an offence is not proceeded with, a Magistrates' Court inquiring into an indictable offence as examining Justices determines not to commit the accused for trial, or a Magistrates' Court dealing summarily with an offence dismisses the information, the court may make a defendant's costs order. An order under Section 16 of the Act may also be made in relation to breach of bind-over proceedings in a Magistrates' Court or the Crown Court (Regulation 14(4) of the General Regulations). As is the case with the Crown Court . . . such an order should normally be made unless there are positive reasons for not doing so. For example, where the defendant's own conduct has brought suspicion on himself and has misled the prosecution into thinking that the case against him was stronger than it was, the defendant can be left to pay his own costs. In the case of a partial acquittal the court may make a part order. . .

II.1.2

Whether to make such an award is a matter in the discretion of the court in the light of the circumstances of each particular case.

II.2.2

Where a person is convicted of some count(s) in the indictment and acquitted on other(s) the court may exercise its discretion to make a defendants costs order but may order that only part of the costs incurred be paid. The court should make whatever order seems just having regard to the relative importance of the two charges and the conduct of the parties generally. Where the court considers that it would be inappropriate that the defendant should recover all of the costs properly incurred, the amount must be specified in the order.

A15.3 Costs in relation to civil complaints

Section 64 of the Magistrates' Courts Act 1980 provides:

Magistrates' Courts Act 1980, s 64

(1) On the hearing of a complaint, a magistrates' court shall have power in its discretion to make such order as to costs—
   (a) on making the order for which the complaint is made, to be paid by the defendant to the complainant;
   (b) on dismissing the complaint, to be paid by the complainant to the defendant,
   as it thinks just and reasonable; but if the complaint is for an order for the periodical payment of money, or for the revocation, revival or variation of such an order, or for the enforcement of such an order, the court may, whatever adjudication it makes, order either party to pay the whole or any part of the other's costs.
(2) The amount of any sum ordered to be paid under subsection (1) above shall be specified in the order, or order of dismissal, as the case may be.

The discretion here is narrower than under section 16 above, and can only be invoked if the court either makes an order or dismisses the complaint. Accordingly, where the applicant withdraws proceedings, no costs can follow. This can be particularly unfair to respondents who have cash detained under the Proceeds of Crime Act 2002 and who can evidence early on in the proceedings the bona fides of the cash, leading to withdrawal of proceedings. It may be better, in order to secure costs, to apply for the release of the monies by way of formal order and seek the applicant's consent to that order.

Applicants may also rely upon *Baxendale-Walker v Law Society* [2007] 3 All ER 330 (and other similar cases) to avoid costs on the basis that they are public bodies acting in the wider public interest and should not be exposed to the risk of adverse costs orders. This principle has been upheld in two recent cases:

- in relation to civil proceedings commenced under Part 2 of the Proceeds of Crime Act 2002 (*Perinpanathan v City of Westminster Magistrates' Court* [2010] Civ 40). It is doubted in any case whether the court has any power at all to award costs in relation to cash seizure cases that have been successfully defended;
- in relation to proceedings under section 1 of the Crime and Disorder Act 1998 (ASBO application) (*Manchester City Council v Manchester Magistrates' Court* [2009] EWHC 1866 (Admin)).

A15.4 Costs in relation to witnesses

Costs in relation to character witnesses' attendance at court can only be recovered when the court has certified that the interests of justice required the witnesses' attendance (Costs in Criminal Cases (General) Regulations 1986 (SI 1986/1335), reg 15). Advocates should ensure that an application is made to the court either prior to or immediately after the witnesses' attendance.

See *Blackstone's Criminal Practice 2012* **D31**

A16 **Court Appointed Legal Representatives**

A16.1 **Overview**

In certain circumstances a defendant is prohibited from cross-examining witnesses. In the event that the defendant has declined or is not eligible for legal funding, the court has power to appoint a legal representative to carry out this function on behalf of the court.

Fees for this work are authorized under section 19 of the Prosecution of Offences Act 1985 and are as agreed by the court or allowed following taxation. Solicitors should not agree to fees that are less than those that would be allowed for in line with civil guideline costs rates.

The Bar Council has issued comprehensive guidance to assist counsel and it is suggested that solicitors would be well advised to follow the same (see **Appendix 2**).

 See *Blackstone's Criminal Practice 2012* **D3.75–D3.82**

A17 **Custody Time Limits**

A17.1 Overview

Category	Time limit
Either-way offences committed for trial	Maximum 70 days between first appearance and the court beginning to hear evidence in relation to committal. Maximum 56 days from first appearance to hearing evidence in a summary trial (unless case was originally destined for committal and court reverts to summary trial after 56 days have elapsed, in which case the limit is 70 days).
Summary only offences	56 days to start of summary trial.
Youths	As above, save that indictable only cases that are tried summarily in the youth court are subject to the same time limits as either-way cases (*R v Stratford Youth Court, ex p S (A Minor) [1998] 1 WLR 1758*).

A17.2 Exceptions

Defendants who abscond from prison, or who have been released on bail following expiry of a custody time limit, but are then remanded following a breach of bail, do not enjoy the protections offered by custody time limits.

If a person is granted bail and is then later remanded into custody, the earlier period on remand will count towards the custody time limit.

Custody time limits start at the end of the first day of remand and expire at midnight on the last day. A time limit expiring on one of the following days will be treated as having expired on the next preceding day which is not one of those days: Saturday, Sunday, Christmas Day, Good Friday, and bank holidays.

A17.3 Extending custody time limits

The case law on extending custody time limits is voluminous and since applications will generally be made on notice, this topic is not covered in this book (see instead *Blackstone's Criminal Practice*). In general the following considerations are relevant.

- The prosecution should give two days' notice of an intention to apply, but lack of notice is not fatal to the application and the court retains a discretion to extend the time limits (*R v Governor of Canterbury Prison, ex p Craig* [1991] 2 QB 195).
- There is no power to extend once a time limit has lapsed (*R v Sheffield Justices, ex p Turner* [1991] 2 WLR 987).

- The court must be satisfied, on a balance of probabilities that the need for the extension is due to the illness or absence of the accused, a necessary witness, a judge, or magistrate; or a postponement which is occasioned by the ordering of separate trials, or some other good and sufficient cause; and that the prosecution has acted with all due diligence and expedition.
- The following have been held to amount to good and sufficient cause: lack of court time, listing difficulties due to the nature of the case, lack of a suitably experienced judge (or lack of any judge at all). Absent exceptional circumstances, resource difficulties do not amount to a good and sufficient case.

 See *Blackstone's Criminal Practice 2012* D15.6

A18 **Disclosure**

A18.1 **Overview**

Prosecution disclosure of unused material is regulated under the Criminal Procedure and Investigations Act 1996.

Section 3 of the Act requires the prosecutor to disclose, following a not-guilty plea:

> **Criminal Procedure and Investigations Act 1996, s 3(1a)**
>
> any prosecution material which has not previously been disclosed to the accused and which might reasonably be considered capable of undermining the case for the prosecution against the accused or of assisting the case for the accused.

In the magistrates' court there is no duty to serve a defence case statement, but in the absence of one a prosecutor may not be able adequately or at all to discover which information might be disclosable.

A failure to disclose in accordance with the statutory scheme should lead to an adjournment (and possibly in an extreme case an argument in relation to abuse of process) (*Swash v Director of Public Prosecutions* [2009] EWHC 803 (Admin)). In *Swash* the court emphasized the court's case management powers and also rejected a prosecution argument that the court had no jurisdiction to adjourn—the defence remedy in relation to defects in disclosure being restricted to a section 8 application.

A18.2 **Section 8 disclosure applications**

A party aggrieved in relation to prosecution disclosure can apply to the court under section 8 of the 1996 Act, that provides:

> **Criminal Procedure and Investigations Act 1996, s 8**
>
> (1) This section applies where the accused has given a defence statement under section 5, 6 or 6B and the prosecutor has complied with section 7A(5) or purported to comply with it or has failed to comply with it.
> (2) If the accused has at any time reasonable cause to believe that there is prosecution material which is required by section 7A to be disclosed to him and has not been, he may apply to the court for an order requiring the prosecutor to disclose it to him.

(3) For the purposes of this section prosecution material is material—
  (a) which is in the prosecutor's possession and came into his possession in connection with the case for the prosecution against the accused.
  (b) which, in pursuance of a code operative under Part II, he has inspected in connection with the case for the prosecution against the accused, or
  (c) which falls within subsection (4).
(4) Material falls within this subsection if in pursuance of a code operative under Part II the prosecutor must, if he asks for the material, be given a copy of it or be allowed to inspect it in connection with the case for the prosecution against the accused.
(5) Material must not be disclosed under this section to the extent that the court, on an application by the prosecutor, concludes it is not in the public interest to disclose it and orders accordingly.
(6) Material must not be disclosed under this section to the extent that it is material the disclosure of which is prohibited by section 17 of the Regulation of Investigatory Powers Act 2000.

See *Blackstone's Criminal Practice 2012* **D9**

A19 **Evidence in Civil Cases**

A19.1 **Hearsay**

Civil behaviour orders are now commonplace in criminal cases, but very often involve issues of hearsay and the like. Hearsay evidence in civil proceedings is not regulated by the Criminal Justice Act 2003, but by Part 50 of the Criminal Procedure Rules in so far as it relates to ancillary orders in criminal proceedings.

A19.2 **Challenging the weight to be attached to hearsay evidence**

Regard should be had to section 4 of the Civil Evidence Act 1995 which provides:

Civil Evidence Act 1995, s 4

(1) In estimating the weight (if any) to be given to hearsay evidence in civil proceedings the court shall have regard to any circumstances from which any inference can reasonably be drawn as to the reliability or otherwise of the evidence.

(2) Regard may be had, in particular, to the following—

    (a) whether it would have been reasonable and practicable for the party by whom the evidence was adduced to have produced the maker of the original statement as a witness;

    (b) whether the original statement was made contemporaneously with the occurrence or existence of the matters stated;

    (c) whether the evidence involves multiple hearsay;

    (d) whether any person involved had any motive to conceal or misrepresent matters;

    (e) whether the original statement was an edited account, or was made in collaboration with another or for a particular purpose;

    (f) whether the circumstances in which the evidence is adduced as hearsay are such as to suggest an attempt to prevent proper evaluation of its weight.

A19.3 Credibility and previous inconsistent statements

Sections 5(2) and 6 of the Civil Evidence Act 1995 provide:

Civil Evidence Act 1995, ss 5(2) and 6

5 Competence and credibility

(2) Where in civil proceedings hearsay evidence is adduced and the maker of the original statement, or of any statement relied upon to prove another statement, is not called as a witness—

   (a) evidence which if he had been so called would be admissible for the purpose of attacking or supporting his credibility as a witness is admissible for that purpose in the proceedings; and

   (b) evidence tending to prove that, whether before or after he made the statement, he made any other statement inconsistent with it is admissible for the purpose of showing that he had contradicted himself.

   Provided that evidence may not be given of any matter of which, if he had been called as a witness and had denied that matter in cross-examination, evidence could not have been adduced by the cross-examining party.

6 Previous statements of witness

(1) Subject as follows, the provisions of this Act as to hearsay evidence in civil proceedings apply equally (but with any necessary modifications) in relation to a previous statement made by a person called as a witness in the proceedings.

(2) A party who has called or intends to call a person as a witness in civil proceedings may not in those proceedings adduce evidence of a previous statement made by that person, except—

   (a) with the leave of the court, or

   (b) for the purpose of rebutting a suggestion that his evidence has been fabricated.

   This shall not be construed as preventing a witness statement (that is, a written statement of oral evidence which a party to the proceedings intends to lead) from being adopted by a witness in giving evidence or treated as his evidence.

(3) Where in the case of civil proceedings section 3, 4 or 5 of the Criminal Procedure Act 1865 applies, which make provision as to—

   (a) how far a witness may be discredited by the party producing him,

   (b) the proof of contradictory statements made by a witness, and

   (c) cross-examination as to previous statements in writing,

   this Act does not authorise the adducing of evidence of a previous inconsistent or contradictory statement otherwise than in accordance with those sections.

   This is without prejudice to any provision made by rules of court under section 3 above (power to call witness for cross-examination on hearsay statement).

(4) Nothing in this Act affects any of the rules of law as to the circumstances in which, where a person called as a witness in civil proceedings is cross-examined on a document used by him to refresh his memory, that document may be made evidence in the proceedings.

(5) Nothing in this section shall be construed as preventing a statement of any description referred to above from being admissible by virtue of section 1 as evidence of the matters stated.

A20 Extradition

A20.1 Jurisdiction

The Extradition Act 2003 outlines the procedures to be adopted during the extradition process. The power to extradite rests with the Senior Magistrate and authorized District Judges, and cases are generally only heard at the City of Westminster Magistrates' Court. This chapter details the initial checks that a solicitor or barrister should make when seized of the case for the first time. Unless absolutely satisfied that extradition can properly proceed unopposed under Part 1 of the Act, recourse should be had to the detailed practitioner works.

Countries are divided into category 1 (Part 1 Extraditions) and category 2 countries (Part 2 Extraditions). Category 1 states utilize the European Arrest Warrant procedure, and extradition will generally be ordered save in the most exceptional circumstances. More robust evidential protections are in place in relation to most category 2 states. In addition, the United Kingdom also has special arrangements in place with certain states, for example the United States of America.

A20.2 The Arrest Warrant

A20.2.1 *Part 1 Extradition*

The following states have been designated under Part 1 of the 2003 Act:

Austria, Belgium, Bulgaria, Cyprus, Czech Republic, Denmark, Estonia, Finland, France, Germany, Gibraltar, Greece, Hungary, Ireland, Italy, Latvia, Lithuania, Luxembourg, Malta, the Netherlands, Poland, Portugal, Romania, Slovakia, Slovenia, Spain, and Sweden.

Following the issuing of an arrest warrant the police will execute that warrant and bring the individual before the court.

The arrest warrant should be in the standard format and detail the statutory particulars as required under section 2 of the Act.

A20.2.2 *Part 2 Extradition*

The following states have been designated under Part 2 of the 2003 Act:

Albania, Algeria, Andorra, Antigua and Barbuda, Argentina, Armenia, Australia, Azerbaijan, The Bahamas, Bangladesh, Barbados, Belize, Bolivia, Bosnia and Herzegovina, Botswana, Brazil, Brunei, Canada, Chile, Colombia, Cook Islands, Croatia, Cuba, Dominica, Ecuador, El Salvador, Fiji, The Gambia, Georgia, Ghana, Grenada, Guatemala,

Guyana, Hong Kong Special Administrative Region, Haiti, Iceland, India, Iraq, Israel, Jamaica, Kenya, Kiribati, Lesotho, Liberia, Libya, Liechtenstein, Macedonia (FYR), Malawi, Malaysia, Maldives, Mauritius, Mexico, Moldova, Monaco, Montenegro, Nauru, New Zealand, Nicaragua, Nigeria, Norway, Panama, Papua New Guinea, Paraguay, Peru, Russian Federation, Saint Christopher and Nevis, Saint Lucia, Saint Vincent and the Grenadines, San Marino, Serbia, Seychelles, Sierra Leone, Singapore, Solomon Islands, South Africa, Sri Lanka, Swaziland, Switzerland, Tanzania, Thailand, Tonga, Trinidad and Tobago, Turkey, Tuvalu, Uganda, Ukraine, the United Arab Emirates, the United States of America, Uruguay, Vanuatu, Western Samoa, Zambia, and Zimbabwe.

A request for an arrest warrant is made to the Secretary of State and will result in the wanted person being brought before the court pursuant to an arrest warrant being issued by the court (s 71).

The warrant should comply with section 70 of the Act, but it is a matter for the Secretary of the State as opposed to the court, to determine whether it does so comply.

A20.3 Funding

Extradition work is funded under the Standard Criminal Contract and an application for representation should be made in the usual way. Extradition proceedings are the only proceedings in the magistrates' court that allow for representation by Queen's Counsel. It is rare for legal aid to be refused on merits.

A20.4 The First Hearing

A20.4.1 *Timing of appearance*

In the case of a provisional arrest warrant the first appearance must be within 48 hours of arrest (weekends and holidays excepted). In all other cases the appearance must be as soon as is practicable. A failure to comply should lead to the person's discharge. Section 4(2) requires service of the warrant. The initial hearing can be adjourned to a later date.

Extradition Act 2003, ss 4–6

4   Person arrested under Part 1 warrant

  (1) This section applies if a person is arrested under a Part 1 warrant.

  (2) A copy of the warrant must be given to the person as soon as practicable after his arrest.

  (3) The person must be brought as soon as practicable before the appropriate judge.

---

    (4) If subsection (2) is not complied with and the person applies to the judge to be discharged, the judge may order his discharge.

    (5) If subsection (3) is not complied with and the person applies to the judge to be discharged, the judge must order his discharge.

    (6) A person arrested under the warrant must be treated as continuing in legal custody until he is brought before the appropriate judge under subsection (3) or he is discharged under sub-section (4) or (5).

5   Provisional arrest

    (1) A constable, a customs officer or a service policeman may arrest a person without a warrant if he has reasonable grounds for believing—

       (a) that a Part 1 warrant has been or will be issued in respect of the person by an authority of a category 1 territory, and

       (b) that the authority has the function of issuing arrest warrants in the category 1 territory.

    (2) A constable or a customs officer may arrest a person under subsection (1) in any part of the United Kingdom.

    (3) A service policeman may arrest a person under subsection (1) only if the person is subject to service law or is a civilian subject to service discipline.

    (4) If a service policeman has power to arrest a person under subsection (1) he may exercise the power anywhere.

6   Person arrested under section 5

    (1) This section applies if a person is arrested under section 5.

    (2) The person must be brought before the appropriate judge within 48 hours starting with the time when the person is arrested.

    (2A) The documents specified in subsection (4) must be produced to the judge within 48 hours starting with the time when the person is arrested but this is subject to any extension under subsection (3B).

    (2B) Subsection (3) applies if—

       (a) the person has been brought before the judge in compliance with subsection (2); but

       (b) documents have not been produced to the judge in compliance with subsection (2A).

    (3) The person must be brought before the judge when the documents are produced to the judge.

    (3A) While the person is before the judge in pursuance of subsection (2), the authority of the category 1 territory may apply to the judge for an extension of the 48 hour period mentioned in subsection (2A) by a further 48 hours.

    (3B) The judge may grant an extension if the judge decides that subsection (2A) could not reasonably be complied with within the initial 48 hour period.

    (3C) The judge must decide whether that subsection could reasonably be so complied with on a balance of probabilities.

    (3D) Notice of an application under subsection (3A) must be given in accordance with rules of court.

    (4) The documents are—

       (a) a Part 1 warrant in respect of the person;

       (b) a certificate under section 2 in respect of the warrant.

(5) A copy of the warrant must be given to the person as soon as practicable after his arrest.

(5A) Subsection (5B) applies if—

(a) the person is before the judge in pursuance of subsection (2); and

(b) the documents specified in subsection (4) have not been produced to the judge.

(5B) The judge must remand the person in custody or on bail (subject to subsection (6)).

(6) If subsection (2), (2A) or (3) is not complied with and the person applies to the judge to be discharged, the judge must order his discharge.

(7) If subsection (5) is not complied with and the person applies to the judge to be discharged, the judge may order his discharge.

(8) The person must be treated as continuing in legal custody until he is brought before the appropriate judge under subsection (2) or he is discharged under subsection (6) or (7).

(8A) In calculating a period of 48 hours for the purposes of this section no account is to be taken of—

(a) any Saturday or Sunday;

(b) Christmas Day;

(c) Good Friday; or

(d) any day falling within subsection (8B).

(8B) The following days fall within this subsection—

(a) in Scotland, any day prescribed under section 8(2) of the Criminal Procedure (Scotland) Act 1995 as a court holiday in the court of the appropriate judge;

(b) in any part of the United Kingdom, any day that is a bank holiday under the Banking and Financial Dealings Act 1971 in that part of the United Kingdom.

(9) Subsection (10) applies if—

(a) a person is arrested under section 5 on the basis of a belief that a Part 1 warrant has been or will be issued in respect of him;

(b) the person is discharged under subsection (6) or (7).

(10) The person must not be arrested again under section 5 on the basis of a belief relating to the same Part 1 warrant.

A20.4.2 *Identity*

If identity is not admitted the requesting state must be in a position to prove it on a balance of probabilities (ss 7, 78). Some examples of identification methods include: photographic or video evidence; possession of (or proximity to) papers bearing the same or essentially the same details; unusual name; fingerprints; admissions.

A20.4.3 *Consent*

A person who is legally represented (or is ineligible for legal aid, has declined it, or has had it withdrawn) may consent to extradition, but such consent cannot be revoked.

Consent should only be given when the legal adviser is satisfied that none of the statutory or other bars to extradition are at issue.

The statutory bars to extradition are:

- age (s 15);
- double jeopardy (ss 12, 80);
- earlier extradition (s 18);
- extraneous considerations (ss 13, 81);
- hostage taking (ss 16, 83);
- passage of time (ss 14, 82);
- speciality (ss 17, 95).

Other bars to extradition are:

- asylum claim (ss 39, 40, 121);
- competing claims for extradition (ss 24, 90);
- convictions in absence (ss 20, 86);
- domestic proceedings taking precedence (ss 22, 88);
- human rights considerations (s 87);
- person serving sentences (ss 23, 89);
- physical or mental health (ss 25, 91).

If consent to extradition is not given the Judge will set the appropriate timetable:

Part 1 states: 21 days from arrest, or a later date if it is in the interests of justice (Extradition Act 2003, s 8).

Part 2 states: not later than two months from first appearance, or a later date if it is in the interests of justice (Extradition Act 2003, s 75).

A20.5 Bail

Usual Bail Act considerations apply, although there is no presumption in favour of bail in conviction cases. A security or surety is generally required.

 See *Blackstone's Criminal Practice 2012* **D32**

A21 **Handcuffs Applications**

A21.1 **Introduction**

There is no statutory authority for the handcuffing of defendants at court, but common law authority exists to support its legality where there is shown to be a danger of escape or a violent breach of the peace. These are the only two factors that are relevant when considering such applications (*R v Vrastides* [1998] Crim LR 251, CA). Only in the most exceptional case should handcuffs be permitted while a defendant was giving evidence.

The court has no jurisdiction over defendants who have not arrived at court and are in transit, that being a matter for the police or prison authorities. The fact that a prisoner has arrived in handcuffs does not remove the need for the court to consider the matter afresh (*R v Cambridge Justices, ex p Peacock* (1992) 161 JP 113, DC) (save where it has already heard argument on the issue and there is no change in circumstances).

The fact that these applications are becoming commonplace does not dilute the fact that important human rights are engaged. Whether Convention rights are breached is a matter of fact and degree in each case, but advocates should have their eye on the overriding principle, namely:

> Article 3 does not bite if handcuffing has been imposed in connection with lawful detention, provided the force and public exposure does not exceed that which is reasonably considered necessary by the public authority carrying out the handcuffing. (*R (JB) v GSL Limited* [2007] EWHC 2227 (Admin).)

A21.2 **Applications**

Applications should be decided before the defendant is brought into court as the decision is that of the court and the court alone, and should always be heard *inter partes* (*R v Rollinson* (1996) 161 JP 107, CA). It is for the applicant to show that reasonable grounds exist for their use. A response that 'it was usual practice' to make an application when the prisoner had an escape marker recorded against him was not acceptable and the court should either be given detailed information on which to make a decision, or in its absence should request it (*R v Horden* [2009] EWCA Crim 288).

The CPS has issued the following guidance to prosecutors:

> The rights of the suspects need to be balanced against public safety, and legitimate reasons put forward for handcuffing in court. Any derogations from these principles must be strictly justified. Consistent with this approach,

other methods of countering any risk of escape or violence should be explored to ensure the least risk of prejudice to the suspect. This may include, for example, the presence of covertly armed police officers in court or a use of a specially protected dock. Applications for handcuffs are becoming common. It is the role of the prosecutor to make representations to the court for the handcuffing of a prisoner based on information provided by the police or court security officers. It would not be appropriate for a prosecutor to comment upon the decision to seek an order or to advise on the safety of a particular person, other than to advise on the legal parameters of the court's discretion. Therefore, a prosecutor should not advise whether a particular defendant should be handcuffed but may refuse to assist the police or security staff where an application would be outside the court's discretion. A prosecutor may also refuse to make an application where s/he is not satisfied about the nature or extent of information provided by the police or Securicor when requested to make an application.

It is not appropriate for anyone other than the prosecutor to make a direct application to the court.

To maintain consistency of approach, all requests should be channelled through the prosecutor and the application should be made, wherever possible, before the defendant is brought into court. There is nothing, however, to prevent an application being made once the court is sitting or the suspect is in the dock.

Prosecutors need to carefully examine requests to make applications for handcuffs to be worn in court, and to ensure that there are sufficient grounds for making such applications.

A court is not bound to consider the application afresh at each subsequent hearing (*R v Cambridge Justices, ex p Peacock* (1992) 156 JP 895), but if there has been a change in circumstances, such as a defendant withdrawing his initial consent following a change of representation, the court should consider the matter afresh (*R v Monk* [2004] EWCA Crim 1256).

 See *Blackstone's Criminal Practice 2012* **D1.3**

A22 **Hearsay**

A22.1 Overview

Hearsay evidence in criminal proceedings is regulated by sections 114–126 of the Criminal Justice Act 2003, and criminal procedure rules. Section 114(1)(d) is inclusionary in nature and provides for the admission of hearsay where its admission is in the interests of justice. Later sections (notably s 116) mirror older common law principles. The main legislative provisions are set out in **A22.3**.

A22.2 Criminal Procedure Rules

Part 34 of the Criminal Procedure Rules 2010 regulates the admission of hearsay evidence.

A22.3 Legislative scheme

Sections 114–120 of the Criminal Justice Act 2003 are the main statutory provisions.

Criminal Justice Act 2003, ss 114

114 Admissibility of hearsay evidence

(1) In criminal proceedings a statement not made in oral evidence in the proceedings is admissible as evidence of any matter stated if, but only if—
   (a) any provision of this Chapter or any other statutory provision makes it admissible,
   (b) any rule of law preserved by section 118 makes it admissible,
   (c) all parties to the proceedings agree to it being admissible, or
   (d) the court is satisfied that it is in the interests of justice for it to be admissible.
(2) In deciding whether a statement not made in oral evidence should be admitted under subsection (1)(d), the court must have regard to the following factors (and to any others it considers relevant)—
   (a) how much probative value the statement has (assuming it to be true) in relation to a matter in issue in the proceedings, or how valuable it is for the understanding of other evidence in the case;
   (b) what other evidence has been, or can be, given on the matter or evidence mentioned in paragraph (a);
   (c) how important the matter or evidence mentioned in paragraph (a) is in the context of the case as a whole;
   (d) the circumstances in which the statement was made;
   (e) how reliable the maker of the statement appears to be;
   (f) how reliable the evidence of the making of the statement appears to be;

(g) whether oral evidence of the matter stated can be given and, if not, why it cannot;
(h) the amount of difficulty involved in challenging the statement;
(i) the extent to which that difficulty would be likely to prejudice the party facing it.

(3) Nothing in this Chapter affects the exclusion of evidence of a statement on grounds other than the fact that it is a statement not made in oral evidence in the proceedings.

It will rarely be appropriate to use section 114 in order to circumvent section 116 (*R v Ibrahim* [2010] EWCA Crim 1176. This principle takes on a particular importance in the magistrates' court in relation to 'missing' or reluctant witnesses (for example in so-called domestic violence cases). Section 114 should not be used simply to bypass other procedures available to the prosecution, for example witness summons. In *R v Freeman* [2010] EWCA Crim 1997 the court quashed a conviction where section 114 was used in relation to a witness who had retracted their previous statement.

Regard must be had to all of the criteria in section 114(2), although not all factors need be decided in favour of admissibility.

Section 114(2)(e) requires the court to consider the reliability of the maker of the statement. Particular caution should be taken in relation to anonymous witnesses and the defence should scrutinize such applications with great care.

Criminal Justice Act 2003, ss 115–116

115 Statements and matters stated

(1) In this Chapter references to a statement or to a matter stated are to be read as follows.

(2) A statement is any representation of fact or opinion made by a person by whatever means; and it includes a representation made in a sketch, photofit or other pictorial form.

(3) A matter stated is one to which this Chapter applies if (and only if) the purpose, or one of the purposes, of the person making the statement appears to the court to have been—
  (a) to cause another person to believe the matter, or
  (b) to cause another person to act or a machine to operate on the basis that the matter is as stated.

Principal categories of admissibility

116 Cases where a witness is unavailable

(1) In criminal proceedings a statement not made in oral evidence in the proceedings is admissible as evidence of any matter stated if—
  (a) oral evidence given in the proceedings by the person who made the statement would be admissible as evidence of that matter,

---

(b) the person who made the statement (the relevant person) is identified to the court's satisfaction, and

(c) any of the five conditions mentioned in subsection (2) is satisfied.

(2) The conditions are—

(a) that the relevant person is dead;

(b) that the relevant person is unfit to be a witness because of his bodily or mental condition;

(c) that the relevant person is outside the United Kingdom and it is not reasonably practicable to secure his attendance;

(d) that the relevant person cannot be found although such steps as it is reasonably practicable to take to find him have been taken;

(e) that through fear the relevant person does not give (or does not continue to give) oral evidence in the proceedings, either at all or in connection with the subject matter of the statement, and the court gives leave for the statement to be given in evidence.

(3) For the purposes of subsection (2)(e) 'fear' is to be widely construed and (for example) includes fear of the death or injury of another person or of financial loss.

(4) Leave may be given under subsection (2)(e) only if the court considers that the statement ought to be admitted in the interests of justice, having regard—

(a) to the statement's contents,

(b) to any risk that its admission or exclusion will result in unfairness to any party to the proceedings (and in particular to how difficult it will be to challenge the statement if the relevant person does not give oral evidence),

(c) in appropriate cases, to the fact that a direction under section 19 of the Youth Justice and Criminal Evidence Act 1999 (c. 23) (special measures for the giving of evidence by fearful witnesses etc) could be made in relation to the relevant person, and

(d) to any other relevant circumstances.

(5) A condition set out in any paragraph of subsection (2) which is in fact satisfied is to be treated as not satisfied if it is shown that the circumstances described in that paragraph are caused—

(a) by the person in support of whose case it is sought to give the statement in evidence, or

(b) by a person acting on his behalf,

in order to prevent the relevant person giving oral evidence in the proceedings (whether at all or in connection with the subject matter of the statement).

In considering whether it is reasonably practicable to secure the attendance of a witness the court must consider what steps have, and have not, been taken. The reasonableness will be judged in relation to many factors including the resources available to the party (*R v Maloney* [1994] Crim LR 525).

Even where the attendance of a witness is not practicable (or some other factor in section 116 is present) the court should then go on to consider section 126 of the Act and section 78 PACE 1984 in order to decide whether the evidence ought, in fairness, to be admitted.

Criminal Justice Act 2003, ss 117–120

117 Business and other documents

(1) In criminal proceedings a statement contained in a document is admissible as evidence of any matter stated if—

    (a) oral evidence given in the proceedings would be admissible as evidence of that matter,

    (b) the requirements of subsection (2) are satisfied, and

    (c) the requirements of subsection (5) are satisfied, in a case where subsection (4) requires them to be.

(2) The requirements of this subsection are satisfied if—

    (a) the document or the part containing the statement was created or received by a person in the course of a trade, business, profession or other occupation, or as the holder of a paid or unpaid office,

    (b) the person who supplied the information contained in the statement (the relevant person) had or may reasonably be supposed to have had personal knowledge of the matters dealt with, and

    (c) each person (if any) through whom the information was supplied from the relevant person to the person mentioned in paragraph (a) received the information in the course of a trade, business, profession or other occupation, or as the holder of a paid or unpaid office.

(3) The persons mentioned in paragraphs (a) and (b) of subsection (2) may be the same person.

(4) The additional requirements of subsection (5) must be satisfied if the statement—

    (a) was prepared for the purposes of pending or contemplated criminal proceedings, or for a criminal investigation, but

    (b) was not obtained pursuant to a request under section 7 of the Crime (International Co-operation) Act 2003 (c. 32) or an order under paragraph 6 of Schedule 13 to the Criminal Justice Act 1988 (c. 33) (which relate to overseas evidence).

(5) The requirements of this subsection are satisfied if—

    (a) any of the five conditions mentioned in section 116(2) is satisfied (absence of relevant person etc), or

    (b) the relevant person cannot reasonably be expected to have any recollection of the matters dealt with in the statement (having regard to the length of time since he supplied the information and all other circumstances).

(6) A statement is not admissible under this section if the court makes a direction to that effect under subsection (7).

(7) The court may make a direction under this subsection if satisfied that the statement's reliability as evidence for the purpose for which it is tendered is doubtful in view of—

    (a) its contents,

    (b) the source of the information contained in it,

    (c) the way in which or the circumstances in which the information was supplied or received, or

    (d) the way in which or the circumstances in which the document concerned was created or received.

118 Preservation of certain common law categories of admissibility

(1) The following rules of law are preserved.

Public information etc

(1) Any rule of law under which in criminal proceedings—

    (a) published works dealing with matters of a public nature (such as histories, scientfic works, dictionaries and maps) are admissible as evidence of facts of a public nature stated in them,

    (b) public documents (such as public registers, and returns made under public authority with respect to matters of public interest) are admissible as evidence of facts stated in them,

    (c) records (such as the records of certain courts, treaties, Crown grants, pardons and commissions) are admissible as evidence of facts stated in them, or

    (d) evidence relating to a person's age or date or place of birth may be given by a person without personal knowledge of the matter.

Reputation as to character

(2) Any rule of law under which in criminal proceedings evidence of a person's reputation is admissible for the purpose of proving his good or bad character.

[Note. The rule is preserved only so far as it allows the court to treat such evidence as proving the matter concerned.]

Reputation or family tradition

(3) Any rule of law under which in criminal proceedings evidence of reputation or family tradition is admissible for the purpose of proving or disproving—

    (a) pedigree or the existence of a marriage,

    (b) the existence of any public or general right, or

    (c) the identity of any person or thing.

[Note. The rule is preserved only so far as it allows the court to treat such evidence as proving or disproving the matter concerned.]

Res gestae

(4) Any rule of law under which in criminal proceedings a statement is admissible as evidence of any matter stated if—

    (a) the statement was made by a person so emotionally overpowered by an event that the possibility of concoction or distortion can be disregarded,

    (b) the statement accompanied an act which can be properly evaluated as evidence only if considered in conjunction with the statement, or

    (c) the statement relates to a physical sensation or a mental state (such as intention or emotion).

Confessions etc

(5) Any rule of law relating to the admissibility of confessions or mixed statements in criminal proceedings.

Admissions by agents etc

(6) Any rule of law under which in criminal proceedings—

    (a) an admission made by an agent of a defendant is admissible against the defendant as evidence of any matter stated, or

(b) a statement made by a person to whom a defendant refers a person for information is admissible against the defendant as evidence of any matter stated.

Common enterprise

(7) Any rule of law under which in criminal proceedings a statement made by a party to a common enterprise is admissible against another party to the enterprise as evidence of any matter stated.

Expert evidence

(8) Any rule of law under which in criminal proceedings an expert witness may draw on the body of expertise relevant to his field.

(2) With the exception of the rules preserved by this section, the common law rules governing the admissibility of hearsay evidence in criminal proceedings are abolished.

119 Inconsistent statements

(1) If in criminal proceedings a person gives oral evidence and—
   (a) he admits making a previous inconsistent statement, or
   (b) a previous inconsistent statement made by him is proved by virtue of section 3, 4 or 5 of the Criminal Procedure Act 1865 (c. 18),
   the statement is admissible as evidence of any matter stated of which oral evidence by him would be admissible.

(2) If in criminal proceedings evidence of an inconsistent statement by any person is given under section 124(2)(c), the statement is admissible as evidence of any matter stated in it of which oral evidence by that person would be admissible.

120 Other previous statements of witnesses

(1) This section applies where a person (the witness) is called to give evidence in criminal proceedings.

(2) If a previous statement by the witness is admitted as evidence to rebut a suggestion that his oral evidence has been fabricated, that statement is admissible as evidence of any matter stated of which oral evidence by the witness would be admissible.

(3) A statement made by the witness in a document—
   (a) which is used by him to refresh his memory while giving evidence,
   (b) on which he is cross-examined, and
   (c) which as a consequence is received in evidence in the proceedings,
   is admissible as evidence of any matter stated of which oral evidence by him would be admissible.

(4) A previous statement by the witness is admissible as evidence of any matter stated of which oral evidence by him would be admissible, if—
   (a) any of the following three conditions is satisfied, and
   (b) while giving evidence the witness indicates that to the best of his belief he made the statement, and that to the best of his belief it states the truth.

(5) The first condition is that the statement identifies or describes a person, object or place.

(6) The second condition is that the statement was made by the witness when the matters stated were fresh in his memory but he does not remember

them, and cannot reasonably be expected to remember them, well enough to give oral evidence of them in the proceedings.

(7) The third condition is that—

   (a) the witness claims to be a person against whom an offence has been committed,

   (b) the offence is one to which the proceedings relate,

   (c) the statement consists of a complaint made by the witness (whether to a person in authority or not) about conduct which would, if proved, constitute the offence or part of the offence,

   (d) [repealed]

   (e) the complaint was not made as a result of a threat or a promise, and

   (f) before the statement is adduced the witness gives oral evidence in connection with its subject matter.

(8) For the purposes of subsection (7) the fact that the complaint was elicited (for example, by a leading question) is irrelevant unless a threat or a promise was involved.

 See *Blackstone's Criminal Practice 2012* **A7.74–A7.79** and **F16**

A23 **Human Rights**

Rights and Freedoms

Article 2
Right to life

1 Everyone's right to life shall be protected by law. No one shall be deprived of his life intentionally save in the execution of a sentence of a court following his conviction of a crime for which this penalty is provided by law.

2 Deprivation of life shall not be regarded as inflicted in contravention of this Article when it results from the use of force which is no more than absolutely necessary:

   (a) in defence of any person from unlawful violence;

   (b) in order to effect a lawful arrest or to prevent the escape of a person lawfully detained;

   (c) in action lawfully taken for the purpose of quelling a riot or insurrection.

Article 3
Prohibition of torture

No one shall be subjected to torture or to inhuman or degrading treatment or punishment.

Article 4
Prohibition of slavery and forced labour

1 No one shall be held in slavery or servitude.

2 No one shall be required to perform forced or compulsory labour.

3 For the purpose of this Article the term 'forced or compulsory labour' shall not include:

   (a) any work required to be done in the ordinary course of detention imposed according to the provisions of Article 5 of this Convention or during conditional release from such detention;

   (b) any service of a military character or, in case of conscientious objectors in countries where they are recognised, service exacted instead of compulsory military service;

   (c) any service exacted in case of an emergency or calamity threatening the life or well-being of the community;

   (d) any work or service which forms part of normal civic obligations.

Article 5
Right to liberty and security

1 Everyone has the right to liberty and security of person. No one shall be deprived of his liberty save in the following cases and in accordance with a procedure prescribed by law:

   (a) the lawful detention of a person after conviction by a competent court;

(b) the lawful arrest or detention of a person for non-compliance with the lawful order of a court or in order to secure the fulfilment of any obligation prescribed by law;

(c) the lawful arrest or detention of a person effected for the purpose of bringing him before the competent legal authority on reasonable suspicion of having committed an offence or when it is reasonably considered necessary to prevent his committing an offence or fleeing after having done so;

(d) the detention of a minor by lawful order for the purpose of educational supervision or his lawful detention for the purpose of bringing him before the competent legal authority;

(e) the lawful detention of persons for the prevention of the spreading of infectious diseases, of persons of unsound mind, alcoholics or drug addicts or vagrants;

(f) the lawful arrest or detention of a person to prevent his effecting an unauthorised entry into the country or of a person against whom action is being taken with a view to deportation or extradition.

2 Everyone who is arrested shall be informed promptly, in a language which he understands, of the reasons for his arrest and of any charge against him.

3 Everyone arrested or detained in accordance with the provisions of paragraph 1(c) of this Article shall be brought promptly before a judge or other officer authorised by law to exercise judicial power and shall be entitled to trial within a reasonable time or to release pending trial. Release may be conditioned by guarantees to appear for trial.

4 Everyone who is deprived of his liberty by arrest or detention shall be entitled to take proceedings by which the lawfulness of his detention shall be decided speedily by a court and his release ordered if the detention is not lawful.

5 Everyone who has been the victim of arrest or detention in contravention of the provisions of this Article shall have an enforceable right to compensation.

Article 6
Right to a fair trial

1 In the determination of his civil rights and obligations or of any criminal charge against him, everyone is entitled to a fair and public hearing within a reasonable time by an independent and impartial tribunal established by law. Judgment shall be pronounced publicly but the press and public may be excluded from all or part of the trial in the interest of morals, public order or national security in a democratic society, where the interests of juveniles or the protection of the private life of the parties so require, or to the extent strictly necessary in the opinion of the court in special circumstances where publicity would prejudice the interests of justice.

2 Everyone charged with a criminal offence shall be presumed innocent until proved guilty according to law.

3 Everyone charged with a criminal offence has the following minimum rights:

(a) to be informed promptly, in a language which he understands and in detail, of the nature and cause of the accusation against him;

(b) to have adequate time and facilities for the preparation of his defence;

(c) to defend himself in person or through legal assistance of his own choosing or, if he has not sufficient means to pay for legal assistance, to be given it free when the interests of justice so require;

(d) to examine or have examined witnesses against him and to obtain the attendance and examination of witnesses on his behalf under the same conditions as witnesses against him;

(e) to have the free assistance of an interpreter if he cannot understand or speak the language used in court.

Article 7
No punishment without law

1 No one shall be held guilty of any criminal offence on account of any act or omission which did not constitute a criminal offence under national or international law at the time when it was committed. Nor shall a heavier penalty be imposed than the one that was applicable at the time the criminal offence was committed.

2 This Article shall not prejudice the trial and punishment of any person for any act or omission which, at the time when it was committed, was criminal according to the general principles of law recognised by civilised nations.

Article 8
Right to respect for private and family life

1 Everyone has the right to respect for his private and family life, his home and his correspondence.

2 There shall be no interference by a public authority with the exercise of this right except such as is in accordance with the law and is necessary in a democratic society in the interests of national security, public safety or the economic well-being of the country, for the prevention of disorder or crime, for the protection of health or morals, or for the protection of the rights and freedoms of others.

Article 9
Freedom of thought, conscience and religion

1 Everyone has the right to freedom of thought, conscience and religion; this right includes freedom to change his religion or belief and freedom, either alone or in community with others and in public or private, to manifest his religion or belief, in worship, teaching, practice and observance.

2 Freedom to manifest one's religion or beliefs shall be subject only to such limitations as are prescribed by law and are necessary in a democratic society in the interests of public safety, for the protection of public order, health or morals, or for the protection of the rights and freedoms of others.

Article 10
Freedom of expression

1 Everyone has the right to freedom of expression. This right shall include freedom to hold opinions and to receive and impart information and ideas

without interference by public authority and regardless of frontiers. This Article shall not prevent States from requiring the licensing of broadcasting, television or cinema enterprises.

2 The exercise of these freedoms, since it carries with it duties and responsibilities, may be subject to such formalities, conditions, restrictions or penalties as are prescribed by law and are necessary in a democratic society, in the interests of national security, territorial integrity or public safety, for the prevention of disorder or crime, for the protection of health or morals, for the protection of the reputation or rights of others, for preventing the disclosure of information received in confidence, or for maintaining the authority and impartiality of the judiciary.

Article 11
Freedom of assembly and association

1 Everyone has the right to freedom of peaceful assembly and to freedom of association with others, including the right to form and to join trade unions for the protection of his interests.

2 No restrictions shall be placed on the exercise of these rights other than such as are prescribed by law and are necessary in a democratic society in the interests of national security or public safety, for the prevention of disorder or crime, for the protection of health or morals or for the protection of the rights and freedoms of others. This Article shall not prevent the imposition of lawful restrictions on the exercise of these rights by members of the armed forces, of the police or of the administration of the State.

Article 14
Prohibition of discrimination

The enjoyment of the rights and freedoms set forth in this Convention shall be secured without discrimination on any ground such as sex, race, colour, language, religion, political or other opinion, national or social origin, association with a national minority, property, birth or other status.

 See *Blackstone's Criminal Practice 2012* **A7**

A24 **Identification Evidence**

A24.1 **Turnbull direction**

In *R v Turnbull* (1976) 63 Cr App R 132, the court laid down the following guidance:

> First, whenever the case against an accused depends wholly or substantially on the correctness of one or more identifications of the accused which the defence alleges to be mistaken, the judge should warn the jury of the special need for caution before convicting the accused in reliance on the correctness of the identification or identifications. In addition he should instruct them as to the reason for the need for such a warning and should make some reference to the possibility that a mistaken witness can be a convincing one and that a number of such witnesses can all be mistaken. Provided this is done in clear terms the judge need not use any particular form of words.

> Secondly, the judge should direct the jury to examine closely the circumstances in which the identification by each witness came to be made. How long did the witness have the accused under observation? At what distance? In what light? Was the observation impeded in any way, as for example, by passing traffic or a press of people? Had the witness ever seen the accused before? How often? If only occasionally, had he any special reason for remembering the accused? How long elapsed between the original observation and the subsequent identification to the police? Was there any material discrepancy between the description of the accused given to the police by the witness when first seen by them and his actual appearance? If in any case, whether it is being dealt with summarily or on indictment, the prosecution have reason to believe that there is such a material discrepancy they should supply the accused or his legal advisers with particulars of the description the police were first given. In all cases if the accused asks to be given particulars of such descriptions, the prosecution should supply them. Finally, he should remind the jury of any specific weaknesses which had appeared in the identification evidence.

> Recognition may be more reliable than identification of a stranger; but even when the witness is purporting to recognise someone whom he knows, the jury should be reminded that mistakes in recognition of close relatives and friends are sometimes made.

> All these matters go to the quality of the identification evidence. If the quality is good and remains good at the close of the accused's case, the danger of a mistaken identification is lessened; but the poorer the quality, the greater the danger.

> In our judgment when the quality is good as for example when the identification is made after a long period of observation, or in satisfactory conditions by a relative, a neighbour, a close friend, a workmate and the like, the jury can safely be left to assess the value of the identifying evidence even though there is no other evidence to support it: provided always, however, that an adequate warning has been given about the special need for caution.

Were the Courts to adjudge otherwise, affronts to justice would frequently occur. A few examples, taken over the whole spectrum of criminal activity, will illustrate what the effects upon the maintenance of law and order would be if any law were enacted that no person could be convicted on evidence of visual identification alone.

 See *Blackstone's Criminal Practice 2012* **F18**

A25 **Legal Aid**

A25.1 Overview

Legal aid is available for criminal proceedings, subject to merits and means assessment in some cases. There is no means assessment:

- for those under 18 years;
- for those in receipt of income support, income-based job seeker's allowance (JSA), or pension credit.

Legal aid automatically extends to the Crown Court if the case is committed for sentence (note that there is no contribution payable in respect to Crown Court proceedings).

Legal aid automatically extends to any case sent, committed, or transferred to the Crown Court. Proceedings in the Crown Court are subject to a contribution dependent on means.

Appeals to the Crown Court require a fresh legal aid application to be lodged and are subject to interests of justice and means criteria. A contribution may be payable in the Crown Court dependent on means.

A25.2 Widgery criteria

When assessing whether the grant of representation is in the interests of justice regard should be had to the *Widgery* criteria, and be able to demonstrate one or more of the following:

- It is likely that I will lose my liberty.
- I have been given a sentence that is suspended or non-custodial. If I break this, the court may be able to deal with me for the original offence.
- It is likely that I will lose my livelihood.
- It is likely that I will suffer serious damage to my reputation.
- A substantial question of law may be involved.
- I may not be able to understand the court proceedings or present my own case.
- I may need witnesses to be traced or interviewed on my behalf.
- The proceedings may involve expert cross-examination of a prosecution witness.
- It is in the interests of another person that I am represented.
- Any other reasons.

Refusal on the basis of the interests of justice test can be appealed to justices and regard should be had to the following cases:

- Regard should be had to the likely penalty, not the theoretical maximum: *R v Highgate Justices, ex p Lewis* [1977] Crim LR 611.

- In *R (Punatar) v Horseferry Road Magistrates' Court* [2002] EWHC 1196 (Admin), the solicitors attended court to defend an imprisonable matter and submitted an application for representation at the end of those proceedings. At that stage the imprisonable matter had been replaced by a non-imprisonable one and legal aid was refused. The court held that the refusal was wrong in law and the court should not apply hindsight but instead look at what was in the mind of the solicitor when he made the decision to attend court.

- A 16-year-old would not have the skills to cross-examine a police officer effectively: *Scunthorpe Justices, ex p S* The Times, 5 March 1998.

- In *R (GKR Law Solicitors) v Liverpool Magistrates' Court* [2008] EWHC 2974 (Admin) the court held that it was appropriate to grant representation to a defendant in relation to a special reasons hearing, where a witness in the case was the defendant's 12-year-old son. The child was a witness entitled to and requiring special measures, and consideration would need to be given to video-interviewing the young witness in order to ensure best evidence was given; such measures would be outside the competence and resources of the defendant.

A25.3 Transfer of representation

In *Ashgar Khan* (unreported, 10 July 2001, Birmingham Crown Court), the court emphasized the requirement to satisfy the Criminal Defence Service (General) (No 2) Regulations 2001, reg 16(2), and in particular, the need to show good cause for the transfer:

> It will not generally be sufficient to allege a lack of care or competence of existing representatives. As from 2nd April 2001 only those solicitors who have obtained a criminal franchise contract with the Legal Services Commission (LSC) are able to undertake work and obtain a representations order in criminal proceedings. Those franchises are only obtained after rigorous audit, inspection and control by the LSC, the Commission thereby satisfying itself that the professional standard of solicitors with franchises is of a high order. The court will infer from that fact that such solicitors do provide representation of good quality. Only in extremely rare circumstances, and where full particulars are given in the application, will a general ground of loss of confidence or incompetence be entertained. It must be further pointed out that it will not be sufficient simply to say that there is a breakdown in the relationship between solicitor and client. Many breakdowns are imagined rather than real or as the result of proper advice. This court will want to look to see what the cause of that is.

 See *Blackstone's Criminal Practice 2012* D31

A26 **Mental Disorder**

A26.1 **Fitness to plead**

In a strict legal sense the issue of fitness to plead does not arise in the magistrates' court as the relevant legislation does not provide for any summary procedures. However, if the accused is being tried for an either-way or indictable offence, and it is shown that the accused did the act or made the omission charged, he can be made subject to a hospital order. The same provisions apply to the youth court (*R (on the application of P) v Barking Youth Court* (2002) EWHC 734 (Admin)).

Stages:

- Issue of mental disorder raised.
- Prove that the accused did the act or made the omission charged.
- Obtain requisite medical assessment.
- Make hospital order.

The prosecution will only be required to prove the actus reus of the offence (*R v Antoine* [2000] 2 All ER 208, HL). If the prosecution cannot prove the act or omission the defendant must be discharged. Insanity is available as a defence in the magistrates' court, but the defendant does not have an absolute right to having the issue determined at trial if the court feels that a disposal under section 37(3) of the Mental Health Act 1983 might be more appropriate (*R (Singh) v Stratford Magistrates' Court* [2007] EWHC 1582 (Admin)).

In order to decide whether the person should be tried or made subject to the fitness to plead procedure the court may need to consider the report of a medical practitioner, and a remand to hospital under section 11 of the Powers of Criminal Courts (Sentencing) Act 2000 will be necessary in most cases:

Powers of Criminal Courts (Sentencing) Act 2000, s 11

(1) If, on the trial by a magistrates' court of an offence punishable on summary conviction with imprisonment, the court—
 (a) is satisfied that the accused did the act or made the omission charged, but
 (b) is of the opinion that an inquiry ought to be made into his physical or mental condition before the method of dealing with him is determined,
 the court shall adjourn the case to enable a medical examination and report to be made, and shall remand him.

---

(2) An adjournment under subsection (1) above shall not be for more than three weeks at a time where the court remands the accused in custody, nor for more than four weeks at a time where it remands him on bail.

(3) Where on an adjournment under subsection (1) above the accused is remanded on bail, the court shall impose conditions under paragraph (d) of section 3(6) of the Bail Act 1976 and the requirements imposed as conditions under that paragraph shall be or shall include requirements that the accused—

    (a) undergo medical examination by a registered medical practitioner or, where the inquiry is into his mental condition and the court so directs, two such practitioners; and

    (b) for that purpose attend such an institution or place, or on such practitioner, as the court directs and, where the inquiry is into his mental condition, comply with any other directions which may be given to him for that purpose by any person specified by the court or by a person of any class so specified.

Subject to having obtained two satisfactory reports (the court can remand under section 35 for that purpose) the court can then go on to make a hospital order under section 37(3):

Mental Health Act 1983, s 37(3)

(3) Where a person is charged before a magistrates' court with any act or omission as an offence and the court would have power, on convicting him of that offence, to make an order under subsection (1) above in his case, then, if the court is satisfied that the accused did the act or made the omission charged, the court may, if it thinks fit, make such an order without convicting him.

A26.2 Diversion

The Crown Prosecution Service has issued the following guidance which is to be considered before prosecuting an offender (or if the prosecution has commenced, before dealing further with the offender):

The Code for Crown Prosecutors states that alternatives to prosecution should be considered when deciding whether a case should be prosecuted. Rehabilitative, reparative and restorative processes can be considered, and alternatives to prosecution for adult offenders include a simple caution and conditional caution.

The National Standards for Cautioning require that the following conditions are met before a simple caution may be administered by the police:
- there is a realistic prospect of conviction;
- the offender admits the offence; and
- the offender (or appropriate adult) understands the significance of a caution and gives informed consent to being cautioned.

A26 Mental Disorder

The National Standards for Conditional Cautioning require that the following conditions are met before a conditional caution may be administered:

- there is enough evidence to bring charges and it is in the public interest to do so;
- the offender has admitted the offence and is aged 18 or over;
- the offender agrees to accept the caution and to carry out the conditions;
- the most likely outcome of attending court would have been a small fine, compensation, conditional discharge or a community penalty at the lower end of the scale; and
- the use of reparative or rehabilitative conditions is felt to be the most effective way of dealing with the offending behaviour and/or recompensing the victim.

A caution or conditional caution will not be appropriate if there is any doubt about the reliability of any admissions made or if the defendant's level of understanding prevents him or her from understanding the significance of the caution or conditional caution and giving informed consent. It should not be assumed that all mentally disordered offenders are ineligible for cautioning or conditional cautioning, but there is no definition of or restriction on the particular form of mental or psychological condition or disorder that may make an admission unreliable (*R v Walker* [1998] Crim L.R. 211).

Where a caution or conditional caution is inappropriate, the only alternative to prosecution is to take no further action. In considering whether the public interest requires a prosecution, prosecutors should inquire whether:

- the police or Social Services have used their powers under sections 135 or 136 Mental Health Act 1983;
- the defendant has been admitted to hospital for assessment or treatment under sections 2 or 3 Mental Health Act 1983;
- the defendant is receiving supervised community treatment under a Community Treatment Order made under section 17A Mental Health Act 1983;
- the offender has been admitted to hospital as an informal patient under section 131 Mental Health Act 1983; or
- an order for guardianship under section 7 Mental Health Act 1983 has been made.

However, the existence of a mental disorder is only one of the factors to be taken into account when deciding whether the public interest requires a prosecution. The seriousness or the persistence of the offending behaviour, the views of the victim and any responsible clinician should also be considered.

The fact that a person is receiving compulsory treatment under the Mental Health Act 1983, or as an informal patient under section 131 Mental Health Act 1983, does not prevent a prosecution. However, a prosecution must not be pursued solely to treat and manage a mental disorder. The decision to prosecute or divert a patient receiving treatment under the Mental Health Act 1983 should be informed by additional information, including:

medical reports from the responsible clinician to explain the nature and degree of the disorder or disability, and any relationship between the disorder and the treatment and behaviour of the offender; and any other relevant information from hospital staff about the treatment and behaviour of the patient, including the treatment regime and any history of similar and recent behaviour.

Where the patient is alleged to have assaulted a member of staff, prosecutors should refer to the NHS/SMS/CPS Memorandum of Understanding on the Effective Prosecution of cases involving Violence and Abuse Against any Member of NHS staff.

 See *Blackstone's Criminal Practice 2012* **E22**

A27 **Misbehaviour at Court**

A27.1 **Misbehaviour during committal proceedings**

Section 4(4)(a) of the Magistrates' Courts Act 1980 provides:

Magistrates' Courts Act 1980, s 4(4)(a)

(4) Examining justices may allow evidence to be tendered before them in the absence of the accused if—
  (a) they consider that by reason of his disorderly conduct before them it is not practicable for the evidence to be tendered in his presence . . .

A27.2 **Misbehaviour during mode of trial and summary trial**

Section 18(3) of the Magistrates' Courts Act 1980 provides:

Magistrates' Courts Act 1980, s 18(3)

(3) The court may proceed in the absence of the accused in accordance with such of the provisions of sections 19 to 22 below as are applicable in the circumstances if the court considers that by reason of his disorderly conduct before the court it is not practicable for the proceedings to be conducted in his presence; and subsections (3) to (5) of section 23 below, so far as applicable, shall have effect in relation to proceedings conducted in the absence of the accused by virtue of this subsection (references in those subsections to the person representing the accused being for this purpose read as references to the person, if any, representing him).

A27.3 **Contempt of Court Act 1981**

Section 12 of the Contempt of Court Act 1981 provides:

Contempt of Court Act 1981, s 12

(1) A magistrates' court has jurisdiction under this section to deal with any person who—
  (a) wilfully insults the justice or justices, any witness before or officer of the court or any solicitor or counsel having business in the court, during his or their sitting or attendance in court or in going to or returning from the court; or
  (b) wilfully interrupts the proceedings of the court or otherwise misbehaves in court.
(2) In any such case the court may order any officer of the court, or any constable, to take the offender into custody and detain him until the rising of the

court; and the court may, if it thinks fit, commit the offender to custody for a specified period not exceeding one month or impose on him a fine not exceeding £2,500, or both.

(2A) A fine imposed under subsection (2) above shall be deemed, for the purposes of any enactment, to be a sum adjudged to be paid by a conviction.

(4) A magistrates' court may at any time revoke an order of committal made under subsection (2) and, if the offender is in custody, order his discharge.

(5) Section 135 of the Powers of Criminal Courts (Sentencing) Act 2000 (limit on fines in respect of young persons) and the following provisions of the Magistrates' Courts Act 1980 apply in relation to an order under this section as they apply in relation to a sentence on conviction or finding of guilty of an offence; and those provisions of the Magistrates' Courts Act 1980 are section 36 (restriction on fines in respect of young persons); sections 75 to 91 (enforcement); section 108 (appeal to Crown Court); section 136 (overnight detention in default of payment); and section 142(1) (power to rectify mistakes).

A27.4 Consolidated Criminal Practice Direction: Contempt

Consolidated Criminal Practice Direction, part V.54

General

(V.54.1)

Section 12 of the Contempt of Court Act 1981 gives magistrates' courts the power to detain until the court rises, someone, whether a defendant or another person present in court, who wilfully insults anyone specified in section 12 or who interrupts proceedings. In any such case, the court may order any officer of the court, or any constable, to take the offender into custody and detain him until the rising of the court; and the court may, if it thinks fit, commit the offender to custody for a specified period not exceeding one month or impose a fine not exceeding level 4 on the standard scale or both. This power can be used to stop disruption of their proceedings. Detention is until the person can be conveniently dealt with without disruption of the proceedings. Prior to the court using the power the offender should be warned to desist or face the prospect of being detained.

(V.54.2)

Magistrates' courts also have the power to commit to custody any person attending or brought before a magistrates' court who refuses without just cause to be sworn or to give evidence under section 97(4) of the Magistrates' Courts Act 1980, until the expiration of such period not exceeding one month as may be specified in the warrant or until he sooner gives evidence or produces the document or thing, or impose on him a fine not exceeding £2,500, or both.

(V.54.3)

In the exercise of any of these powers, as soon as is practical, and in any event prior to an offender being proceeded against, an offender should be told of the conduct which it is alleged to constitute his offending in clear terms. When making an order under section 12 the justices should state their findings of fact as to the contempt.

(V.54.4)

Exceptional situations require exceptional treatment. While this direction deals with the generality of situations, there will be a minority of situations where the application of the direction will not be consistent with achieving justice in the special circumstances of the particular case. Where this is the situation, the compliance with the direction should be modified so far as is necessary so as to accord with the interests of justice.

(V.54.5)

The power to bind persons over to be of good behaviour in respect of their conduct in court should cease to be exercised.

Contempt consisting of wilfully insulting anyone specified in section 12 or interrupting proceedings

(V.54.6)

In the case of someone who wilfully insults anyone specified in section 12 or interrupts proceedings, if an offender expresses a willingness to apologise for his misconduct, he should be brought back before the court at the earliest convenient moment in order to make the apology and to give undertakings to the court to refrain from further misbehaviour.

(V.54.7)

In the majority of cases, an apology and a promise as to future conduct should be sufficient for justices to order an offender's release. However, there are likely to be certain cases where the nature and seriousness of the misconduct requires the justices to consider using their powers under section 12(2) of the Contempt of Court 1981 Act either to fine or to order the offender's committal to custody.

Where an offender is detained for contempt of court

(V.54.8)

Anyone detained under either of these provisions in paragraphs V.54.1 or V.54.2 should be seen by the duty solicitor or another legal representative and be represented in proceedings if they so wish. Public funding should generally be granted to cover representation. The offender must be afforded adequate time and facilities in order to prepare his case. The matter should be resolved the same day if at all possible.

(V.54.9)

The offender should be brought back before the court before the justices conclude their daily business. The justices should ensure that he understands the nature of the proceedings, including his opportunity to apologise or give evidence and the alternative of them exercising their powers.

(V.54.10)

Having heard from the offender's solicitor, the justices should decide whether to take further action.

Sentencing of an offender who admits being in contempt
(V.54.11)

If an offence of contempt is admitted the justices should consider whether they are able to proceed on the day or whether to adjourn to allow further reflection. The matter should be dealt with on the same day if at all possible. If the justices are of the view to adjourn they should generally grant the offender bail unless one or more of the exceptions to the right to bail in the Bail Act 1976 are made out.

(V.54.12)

When they come to sentence the offender where the offence has been admitted, the justices should first ask the offender if he has any objection to them dealing with the matter. If there is any objection to the justices dealing with the matter a differently constituted panel should hear the proceedings. If the offender's conduct was directed to the justices, it will not be appropriate for the same bench to deal with the matter.

(V.54.13)

The justices should consider whether an order for the offender's discharge is appropriate, taking into account any time spent on remand, whether the offence was admitted and the seriousness of the contempt. Any period of committal should be for the shortest time commensurate with the interests of preserving good order in the administration of justice.

Trial of the issue where the contempt is not admitted
(V.54.14)

Where the contempt is not admitted the justices' powers are limited to making arrangements for a trial to take place. They should not at this stage make findings against the offender.

(V.54.15)

In the case of a contested contempt the trial should take place at the earliest opportunity and should be before a bench of justices other than those before whom the alleged contempt took place. If a trial of the issue can take place on the day such arrangements should be made taking into account the offender's rights under Article 6 of the European Convention for the Protection of Human Rights and Fundamental Freedoms (Rome, 4 November 1950; TS 71 (1953); Cmd 8969). If the trial cannot take place that day the justices should again bail the offender unless there are grounds under the Bail Act 1976 to remand him in custody.

(V.54.16)

The offender is entitled to call and examine witnesses where evidence is relevant. If the offender is found by the court to have committed contempt the court should again consider first whether an order for his discharge from custody is sufficient to bring proceedings to an end. The justices should also allow the offender a further opportunity to apologise for his contempt or to make representations. If the justices are of the view that they must exercise their powers to commit to custody under section 12(2) of the 1981 Act, they must take into account any time spent on remand and the nature and seriousness of the contempt. Any period of committal should be for the shortest period of time commensurate with the interests of preserving good order in the administration of justice.

 See *Blackstone's Criminal Practice 2012* **B14.69–B14.111**

A28 **Mode of Trial, Allocation, and Plea Before Venue**

A28.1 Overview

The court must determine venue for either-way offences. Some either-way offences have venue dictated by value (criminal damage, save arson and aggravated vehicle-taking). If the value of damage is less than £5,000, only summary trial will be offered. For multiple offences, the aggregate value must be considered (Magistrates' Courts Act 1980, s 22(11)). A court has a discretion but not a duty to hear evidence in relation to value (*R v Canterbury Justices, ex p Klisiak* [1981] 2 All ER 129). Value does not include consequential loss flowing from destruction (*R v Colchester Magistrates' Court, ex p Abbott* [2001] Crim LR 564). Where it is not clear whether or not the value exceeds £5,000, the defendant will be permitted if he so wishes to elect Crown Court trial.

Section 22 of the Magistrates' Courts Act 1980 provides:

Magistrates' Courts Act 1980, s 22(1)–(11)

(1) If the offence charged by the information is one of those mentioned in the first column of Schedule 2 to this Act (in this section referred to as 'scheduled offences') then, subject to subsection 7 below, the court shall, before proceeding in accordance with section 19 above, consider whether, having regard to any representations made by the prosecutor or the accused, the value involved (as defined in subsection (10) below) appears to the court to exceed the relevant sum. For the purposes of this section the relevant sum is £5,000.

(2) If, where subsection (1) above applies, it appears to the court clear that, for the offence charged, the value involved does not exceed the relevant sum, the court shall proceed as if the offence were triable only summarily, and sections 19 to 21 above shall not apply.

(3) If, where subsection (1) above applies, it appears to the court clear that, for the offence charged, the value involved exceeds the relevant sum, the court shall thereupon proceed in accordance with section 19 above in the ordinary way without further regard to the provisions of this section.

(4) If, where subsection (1) above applies, it appears to the court for any reason not clear whether, for the offence charged, the value involved does or does not exceed the relevant sum, the provisions of subsections (5) and (6) below shall apply.

(5) The court shall cause the charge to be written down, if this has not already been done, and read to the accused, and shall explain to him in ordinary language—

    (a) that he can, if he wishes, consent to be tried summarily for the offence and that if he consents to be so tried, he will definitely be tried in that way; and

---

(b) that if he is tried summarily and is convicted by the court, his liability to imprisonment or a fine will be limited as provided in section 33 below.

(6) After explaining to the accused as provided by subsection (5) above the court shall ask him whether he consents to be tried summarily and—

    (a) if he so consents, shall proceed in accordance with subsection (2) above as if that subsection applied;

    (b) if he does not so consent, shall proceed in accordance with subsection (3) above as if that subsection applied.

(7) [repealed]

(8) Where a person is convicted by a magistrates' court of a scheduled offence, it shall not be open to him to appeal to the Crown Court against the conviction on the ground that the convicting court's decision as to the value involved was mistaken.

(9) If, where subsection (1) above applies, the offence charged is one with which the accused is charged jointly with a person who has not attained the age of 17, the reference in that subsection to any representations made by the accused shall be read as including any representations made by the person under 18.

(10) In this section 'the value involved', in relation to any scheduled offence, means the value indicated in the second column of Schedule 2 to this Act, measured as indicated in the third column of that Schedule; and in that Schedule 'the material time' means the time of the alleged offence.

(11) Where—

    (a) the accused is charged on the same occasion with two or more scheduled offences and it appears to the court that they constitute or form part of a series of two or more offences of the same or a similar character; or

    (b) the offence charged consists in incitement to commit two or more scheduled offences,

this section shall have effect as if any reference in it to the value involved were a reference to the aggregate of the values involved.

A28.2 Plea before venue

The charge is read to the defendant and if he pleads guilty then a guilty plea will be recorded. If he indicates a not guilty plea or refuses to indicate, the court goes on to deal with mode of trial. An advocate can indicate a plea on a defendant's behalf if that defendant has been removed for unruly behaviour, or the defendant is a company.

Section 17A of the Magistrates' Courts Act 1980 provides:

Magistrates' Courts Act 1980, s 17A

(1) This section shall have effect where a person who has attained the age of 18 years appears or is brought before a magistrates' court on an information charging him with an offence triable either way.

(2) Everything that the court is required to do under the following provisions of this section must be done with the accused present in court.

(3) The court shall cause the charge to be written down, if this has not already been done, and to be read to the accused.

(4) The court shall then explain to the accused in ordinary language that he may indicate whether (if the offence were to proceed to trial) he would plead guilty or not guilty, and that if he indicates that he would plead guilty—

   (a) the court must proceed as mentioned in subsection (6) below; and

   (b) he may be committed for sentence to the Crown Court under section 3 of the Powers of Criminal Courts (Sentencing) Act 2000 below if the court is of such opinion as is mentioned in subsection (2) of that section.

(5) The court shall then ask the accused whether (if the offence were to proceed to trial) he would plead guilty or not guilty.

(6) If the accused indicates that he would plead guilty the court shall proceed as if—

   (a) the proceedings constituted from the beginning the summary trial of the information; and

   (b) section 9(1) above was complied with and he pleaded guilty under it.

(7) If the accused indicates that he would plead not guilty section 18(1) below shall apply.

(8) If the accused in fact fails to indicate how he would plead, for the purposes of this section and section 18(1) below he shall be taken to indicate that he would plead not guilty.

(9) Subject to subsection (6) above, the following shall not for any purpose be taken to constitute the taking of a plea—

   (a) asking the accused under this section whether (if the offence were to proceed to trial) he would plead guilty or not guilty;

   (b) an indication by the accused under this section of how he would plead.

A28.3 Sentence discount for early indication of plea

It is arguable that an early plea at plea before venue will attract a greater reduction in sentence. Such an approach is endorsed in sentencing guidelines and in the case of *R v Rafferty* [1998] 2 Cr App R (S) 449:

> when a defendant pleads guilty before venue at the Magistrates' Court, as the appellant did in this case, the judge at the Crown Court must have regard to the fact that the plea has been made at that early stage. In the usual case therefore a defendant who enters a plea of guilty before venue should be entitled to a greater discount than a person who delays making that plea until he pleads to the indictment in respect of those offences at the Crown Court. In our view it is no longer appropriate for counsel to say, as is common at the Crown Court, that a defendant, who could have pleaded guilty at the plea before venue, has pleaded at the earliest opportunity, if he only pleads to the indictment at the Crown Court. A defendant delaying his plea until that stage should not, unless there is a proper reason put before the Crown Court which satisfactorily explains the delay in making the plea, be entitled to the larger discount which has hitherto usually been given for making a plea at that

stage in the Crown Court. The discount for plea made at the Crown Court should, in the absence of good cause being shown as to why it was delayed until the Crown Court, be less than if it had been made at the plea before venue, and therefore less than that which he has hitherto received.

A28.4 Mode of trial procedure

The court must hear representations from all parties before considering whether jurisdiction ought to be accepted or declined. In a case with more than one defendant, each defendant has an individual right of election (*R v Wigan Magistrates' Court, ex p Layland* (1995) 160 JP 223). A court can change its election decision, provided the defendant consents (Magistrates' Courts Act 1980, s 25). A defendant can only change from summary trial to committal proceedings if he can establish that he did not understand the nature and significance of the election decision (*R v Birmingham Justices, ex p Hodgson and another* [1985] 2 WLR 630).

Section 19 of the Magistrates' Courts Act 1980 provides:

Magistrates' Courts Act 1980, s 19(1)–(3)

(1) The court shall consider whether, having regard to the matters mentioned in subsection (3) below and any representations made by the prosecutor or the accused, the offence appears to the court more suitable for summary trial or for trial on indictment.

(2) Before so considering, the court . . .
   (b) shall afford first the prosecutor and then the accused an opportunity to make representations as to which mode of trial would be more suitable.

(3) The matters to which the court is to have regard under subsection (1) above are the nature of the case; whether the circumstances make the offence one of serious character; whether the punishment which a magistrates' court would have power to inflict for it would be adequate; and any other circumstances which appear to the court to make it more suitable for the offence to be tried in one way rather than the other.

A28.5 Allocation guidelines and legislative changes

Following the publication of definitive guidelines dealing with sentencing in the magistrates' court, and for many offences in the Crown Court, the national mode of trial guidelines are now rendered otiose and no regard should be had to them. At the time of writing, the Sentencing Guidelines Council had not issued its guideline in relation to allocation, nor had the modified mode of trial provisions in the Criminal Justice Act 2003 been enacted. It is anticipated, however, that during the life of this edition the new allocation regime may be in force.

A28.5.1 *Modified mode of trial procedure*

Section 19 of the Magistrates' Courts Act 1980 will be amended so as to allow for the prosecution to inform the court of the offender's antecedent record (if he has one). There will be a presumption in favour of summary trial, but generally speaking the magistrates' court sentencing guidelines will be used to determine whether the court's sentencing powers are sufficient. Both prosecution and defence will make representations in the usual way.

If the defendant has the option of trial before the magistrates' court or Crown Court, he can if he wishes seek a binding indication of sentence, but only in the sense of whether or not a custodial sentence is the likely outcome of a guilty plea. If the offender pleads following such an indication then that indication will be binding on the court—but not otherwise.

 See *Blackstone's Criminal Practice 2012* **D6**

A29 **Presence of Defendant in Court**

A29.1 **General principles**

If a defendant has been bailed to attend court his presence is mandatory unless and until it is excused by the court. Where a defendant on bail fails to appear a warrant can be issued for his arrest.

On summons and certain other matters the defendant may be represented by a legal representative.

Section 122 of the Magistrates' Courts Act 1980 provides:

Magistrates' Courts Act 1980, s 122

(1) A party to any proceedings before a magistrates' court may be represented by a legal representative.
(2) Subject to subsection (3) below, an absent party so represented shall be deemed not to be absent.
(3) Appearance of a party by legal representative shall not satisfy any provision of any enactment or any condition of a recognizance expressly requiring his presence.

A29.2 **Defendant's presence at trial**

Section 11 of the Magistrates' Courts Act 1980 details the court's powers when a defendant does not appear for trial:

Magistrates' Courts Act 1980, s 11

(1) Subject to the provisions of this Act, where at the time and place appointed for the trial or adjourned trial of an information the prosecutor appears but the accused does not—
  (a) if the accused is under 18 years of age, the court may proceed in his absence; and
  (b) if the accused has attained the age of 18 years, the court shall proceed in his absence unless it appears to the court to be contrary to the interests of justice to do so.
  This is subject to subsections (2), (2A), (3) and (4).
(2) Where a summons has been issued, the court shall not begin to try the information in the absence of the accused unless either it is proved to the satisfaction of the court, on oath or in such other manner as may be prescribed, that the summons was served on the accused within what appears to the court to be a reasonable time before the trial or adjourned trial or the accused has appeared on a previous occasion to answer to the information.

(2A) The court shall not proceed in the absence of the accused if it considers that there is an acceptable reason for his failure to appear.

(3) In proceedings to which this subsection applies, the court shall not in a person's absence sentence him to imprisonment or detention in a detention centre or make a detention and training order or an order under paragraph 8(2)(a) or (b) of Schedule 12 to the Criminal Justice Act 2003 that a suspended sentence passed on him shall take effect.

(3A) But where a sentence or order of a kind mentioned in subsection (3) is imposed or given in the absence of the offender, the offender must be brought before the court before being taken to a prison or other institution to begin serving his sentence (and the sentence or order is not to be regarded as taking effect until he is brought before the court).

(4) In proceedings to which this subsection applies, the court shall not in a person's absence impose any disqualification on him, except on resumption of the hearing after an adjournment under section 10(3) above; and where a trial is adjourned in pursuance of this subsection the notice required by section 10(2) above shall include notice of the reason for the adjournment.

(5) Subsections (3) and (4) apply to—
   (a) proceedings instituted by an information, where a summons has been issued; and
   (b) proceedings instituted by a written charge.

(6) Nothing in this section requires the court to enquire into the reasons for the accused's failure to appear before deciding whether to proceed in his absence.

(7) The court shall state in open court its reasons for not proceeding under this section in the absence of an accused who has attained the age of 18 years; and the court shall cause those reasons to be entered in its register of proceedings.

In deciding whether or not to proceed in the defendant's absence, the court has to have regard to the following principles (*R v Jones and others* [2001] QB 862; *Shirzadeh v Maidstone Magistrates' Court* [2003] EWHC 2216 (Admin)):

- the nature and circumstances of the defendant's behaviour in absenting himself from the trial or disrupting it, as the case may be and, in particular, whether his behaviour was deliberate, voluntary, and such as plainly waived his right to appear;
- [in the case of a defendant aged under 18 years] whether an adjournment might result in the defendant being caught or attending voluntarily and/or not disrupting the proceedings;
- [in the case of a defendant aged under 18 years] the likely length of such an adjournment;
- whether the defendant, though absent, is, or wishes to be, legally represented at the trial or has, by his conduct, waived his right to representation;

- whether an absent defendant's legal representatives are able to receive instructions from him during the trial and the extent to which they are able to present his defence;
- the extent of the disadvantage to the defendant in not being able to give his account of events, having regard to the nature of the evidence against him;
- the risk of the jury reaching an improper conclusion about the absence of the defendant;
- the seriousness of the offence, which affects defendant, victim, and public;
- the general public interest and the particular interest of victims and witnesses that a trial should take place within a reasonable time of the events to which it relates;
- the effect of delay on the memories of witnesses;
- where there is more than one defendant and not all have absconded, the undesirability of separate trials, and the prospects of a fair trial for the defendants who are present.

The court in *Shirzadeh* identified four additional factors relevant to trial in the magistrates' court:

> that there ought to be less risk from either a trained lay justice or a district judge in drawing an impermissible inference from a defendant's absence; secondly, in a magistrates' court the finder of fact may ask its own questions and test the evidence of prosecution witnesses; thirdly, a defendant in summary proceedings can apply to set aside any resulting conviction under section 142 of the Magistrates' Courts Act 1980; and fourthly, a defendant in summary proceedings has an automatic right of appeal to the Crown Court.

A29.3 Statutory declarations

Where a defendant is convicted in absence, having not known of the summons or proceedings, he may apply to the court for the conviction to be set aside. Section 14 Magistrates' Courts Act 1980 provides:

Magistrates' Courts Act 1980, s 14

(1) Where a summons has been issued under section 1 above and a magistrates' court has begun to try the information to which the summons relates, then, if—

    (a) the accused, at any time during or after the trial, makes a statutory declaration that he did not know of the summons or the proceedings until a date specified in the declaration, being a date after the court has begun to try the information; and

    (b) within 21 days of that date the declaration is served on the designated officer for the court,

without prejudice to the validity of the information, the summons and all subsequent proceedings shall be void.

---

(2) For the purposes of subsection (1) above a statutory declaration shall be deemed to be duly served on the designated officer if it is delivered to him, or left at his office, or is sent in a registered letter or by the recorded delivery service addressed to him at his office.

(3) If on the application of the accused it appears to a magistrates' court (which for this purpose may be composed of a single justice) that it was not reasonable to expect the accused to serve such a statutory declaration as is mentioned in subsection (1) above within the period allowed by that subsection, the court may accept service of such a declaration by the accused after that period has expired; and a statutory declaration accepted under this subsection shall be deemed to have been served as required by that subsection.

(4) Where any proceedings have become void by virtue of subsection (1) above, the information shall not be tried again by any of the same justices.

 See *Blackstone's Criminal Practice 2012* D22

A30 **Remand Periods**

A30.1 **Prior to conviction**

- Remand to police cells for three days.
- Remand to custody for maximum of eight clear days on first remand.
- Subsequent remand to custody for up to 28 clear days provided the next stage in the proceedings will be dealt with. If it is known that the next stage cannot be dealt with in that period, then eight-day remands will have to follow until such time as completion of the next stage within 28 days is achievable.
- Subsequent remand to custody for 28 clear days if the defendant is already in custody serving a sentence and will not be released before that date.
- Remand on bail for eight days, or longer if the defendant consents.
- Following a committal or sending to the Crown Court, the magistrates have the power to adjourn for a period up to the date of trial (so the normal eight-day limit on first remand does not apply). It is important to note that the expression 'remand' has a particular meaning within the 1980 Act, and the court is not remanding a person when it commits or sends someone for trial—therefore when a court sends a person for trial during their first appearance it can do so in custody for a period in excess of eight days.

Section 129 of the Magistrates' Courts Act 1980 allows for the remands of persons not produced before the court due to illness or accident. The court must have 'solid grounds' to justify an opinion that failure to be produced was due to illness or accident (*R v Liverpool Justices, ex p Grogan* The Times, 8 October 1990).

A30.2 **Post conviction**

- Maximum three weeks if in custody, four weeks if on bail.

 See *Blackstone's Criminal Practice 2011* **D5.14–D5.26**

A31 **Reporting Restrictions**

A31.1 **Youths**

Proceedings in youth courts are protected under section 39 of the Children and Young Persons Act 1933. Section 39 of that Act is a discretionary power that exists for other courts to protect the identity of children (whether a party or otherwise connected with the proceedings).

Children and Young Persons Act 1933, s 39

(1) In relation to any proceedings in any court, the court may direct that—
   (a) no newspaper report of the proceedings shall reveal the name, address or school, or include any particulars calculated to lead to the identification, of any child or young person concerned in the proceedings, either as being the person by or against or in respect of whom the proceedings are taken, or as being a witness therein:
   (b) no picture shall be published in any newspaper as being or including a picture of any child or young person so concerned in the proceedings as aforesaid;
   except in so far (if at all) as may be permitted by the direction of the court.
(2) Any person who publishes any matter in contravention of any such direction shall on summary conviction be liable in respect of each offence to a fine not exceeding level 5 on the standard scale.

The Judicial College (formerly the Judicial Studies Board) has issued the following guidance in its *ASBO Guidance for the Judiciary* (3rd edn):

- The court has the discretion to hear media representations on whether it should make or lift a section 39 order. Courts have discretion to hear reporters in person, as well as their legal representatives. Indeed, many courts have formally reconsidered orders or purported restrictions after media representations by letter or discussion with the clerk to the justices.
- There must be good reason to make a section 39 order. There is a clear distinction between the automatic ban on identification of children involved in youth court proceedings under section 49 and the discretion to impose an order under section 39 of the 1933 Act. *R v Lee* [1993] 1 WLR 103, *R v Central Criminal Court, ex p W, B, and C* [2001] Cr App R 2. Age alone is insufficient to justify the order. Courts have accepted that very young children cannot be harmed by publicity of which they will be unaware and therefore section 39 orders are unnecessary. Orders cannot be made in respect of dead children. Naming a young offender who has been convicted

might act as a deterrent to others or the public might wish to know the outcome of the trial in serious cases.

- The order must be restricted to the terms of section 39. The court cannot ban the naming of any adult, nor make any order relating to any child or young person who is not involved in the proceedings. The court can give guidance on the practical effect of the order and what, in its view, might and might not be caught by the order. However, this can only be guidance, which is not binding on the media.

- If a reporting restriction is imposed, the justices must make it clear in court that a formal order has been made. The order should use the words of section 39 and identify the child or children involved with clarity. A written copy should be drawn up as soon as possible after the order has been made orally.

- The order only applies to the proceedings in the court by which it was made, but is not limited as to time.

In its *ASBO Guidance for the Judiciary* (3rd edn), the Judicial College outlines that in relation to anti-social behaviour orders, the following considerations apply:

> Applications for anti-social behaviour orders (ASBOs) pursuant to section 1 of the Crime and Disorder Act 1998 are civil proceedings (*R (McCann) v Crown Court at Manchester* [2001] 1 WLR 1084 (CA); *B v Chief Constable of Avon and Somerset Constabulary* [2001] 1 WLR 340). Since the Youth Court has no civil jurisdiction, all such applications will be heard by the Magistrates' Court. The Magistrates' Court is open to the general public; no automatic restrictions will apply to prevent public and press access or to prevent reporting of the proceedings or to protect the identity of any adult or juvenile who are defendants as the subject of an application.

> The court would have to have good reason, aside from age alone, to impose any discretionary order under section 39 of the Children and Young Persons Act 1933 to prevent the identification of any child or young person concerned in the proceedings (see *R v Lee* (1993) 96 Cr App R 188 applied by the Divisional Court in *R v Central Criminal Court, ex p W, B, and C* [2001] Cr App R 2).

Although any request for reporting restrictions to be imposed is for the court to decide, the applicant may resist a call from the defendant's representatives for such restrictions if the effectiveness of the ASBO will largely depend on a wider community knowing the details. Given the nature of the proceedings, that is, that the under-18-year-old is being accused of anti-social behaviour in the community, it is in the community interest that any order will be enforced in order to protect the community. Unless the nuisance is extremely localized, enforcement of the order will normally depend upon the general public being aware of the order and of the identity of the person against whom it is made.

Effective enforcement may require the publication of photographs of the subjects, as well as their names and addresses. The magistrates dealing with a youth in ASBO proceedings may be called upon to balance the interests of the community with that of the young person against whom the order has been made.

Breach of an ASBO without reasonable excuse is an offence, punishable on conviction on indictment with five years' imprisonment and/or fine and on summary conviction by six months' imprisonment and/or fine up to the statutory maximum. Again, no automatic restrictions upon press and public access or upon media reporting will apply to criminal proceedings before the magistrates' court (or the Crown Court). There would have to be good reason to impose any restrictions to prevent media reports' identification of any under-18-year-old involved in the proceedings under section 39 of the Children and Young Persons Act 1933 or its replacement, section 45 of the Youth Justice and Criminal Evidence Act 1999, when in force.

If the defendant is under 18 and is the subject of criminal proceedings before the youth court for the alleged breach of an ASBO, then the automatic restrictions upon public, but not press, access to the proceedings and upon identification of the alleged offender will apply. The press will have the right to attend the proceedings under section 47 of the Children and Young Persons Act 1933 and the right to report the proceedings, subject to the automatic restrictions upon identification of the under-18-year-old involved under section 49 of the Children and Young Persons Act 1933. As outlined in the two Home Office/Lord Chancellor's Department's publications, Circular 1998, *Opening Up the Youth Court* and *Youth Court 2001—The Changing Culture of the Youth Court: Good Practice Guide*, the youth court has the discretion to admit the public and to lift the automatic reporting restrictions. The joint publications suggest relevant considerations.

The High Court in *McKerry v Teesdale and Wear Justices* [2000] Crim LR 594 considered factors to be taken into account by youth courts in lifting section 49 restrictions. (Note that this case did not directly relate to imposition of discretionary restrictions under section 39 and the court was not referred to the Court of Appeal's judgment in *R v Lee—McKerry* was considered but not followed by the Divisional Court in *R v Central Crown Court, ex p W, B, and C* [2001] Cr App R 2 which re-emphasized Parliament's distinction between treatment of juveniles appearing in youth courts and juveniles appearing in adult courts.)

The factors included the great care, caution, and circumspection which had to be exercised; the need for the statutory public interest test to be satisfied; the background of international law and practice, including the competing principles of Articles 8 and 10 of the

European Convention on Human Rights; and the collision between the hallowed principle that justice was administered in public, open to full and fair reporting of court proceedings so that the public might be informed about the justice administered in their name and the important principle of protection of juveniles' privacy in legal proceedings, great weight being given to their welfare; and inappropriateness of dispensing with a juvenile's prima facie right to privacy as an additional punishment.

The High Court also made clear that there was nothing to preclude the justices from hearing a representative of the press either orally or in writing on whether reporting restrictions should be lifted and that could be a valuable process since the reporter might well have a legitimate point to make and one which would save the court from falling into error.

A31.2 Adults

Section 4(2) of the Contempt of Court Act 1981 provides:

> **Contempt of Court Act 1981, s 4(2)**
>
> (2) In any such proceedings the court may, where it appears to be necessary for avoiding a substantial risk of prejudice to the administration of justice in those proceedings, or in any other proceedings pending or imminent, order that the publication of any report of the proceedings, or any part of the proceedings, be postponed for such period as the court thinks necessary for that purpose.

A32 Special Measures and Vulnerable Witnesses

A32.1 Special measures

Sections 16 and 17 of the Youth Justice and Criminal Evidence Act 1999 provide for special measures. Particular regard should be had to the forthcoming changes outlined in **A32.2** as they are likely to be implemented during the lifetime of this book.

Youth Justice and Criminal Evidence Act 1999, s 16

16 Witnesses eligible for assistance on grounds of age or incapacity

(1) For the purposes of this Chapter a witness in criminal proceedings (other than the accused) is eligible for assistance by virtue of this section—

    (a) if under the age of 17 [see **A32.2** below] at the time of the hearing; or

    (b) if the court considers that the quality of evidence given by the witness is likely to be diminished by reason of any circumstances falling within subsection (2).

(2) The circumstances falling within this subsection are—

    (a) that the witness—

        (i) suffers from mental disorder within the meaning of the Mental Health Act 1983, or

        (ii) otherwise has a significant impairment of intelligence and social functioning;

    (b) that the witness has a physical disability or is suffering from a physical disorder.

(3) In subsection (1)(a) 'the time of the hearing', in relation to a witness, means the time when it falls to the court to make a determination for the purposes of section 19(2) in relation to the witness.

(4) In determining whether a witness falls within subsection (1)(b) the court must consider any views expressed by the witness.

(5) In this Chapter references to the quality of a witness's evidence are to its quality in terms of completeness, coherence and accuracy; and for this purpose 'coherence' refers to a witness's ability in giving evidence to give answers which address the questions put to the witness and can be understood both individually and collectively.

17 Witnesses eligible for assistance on grounds of fear or distress about testifying [see A32.2 below]

(1) For the purposes of this Chapter a witness in criminal proceedings (other than the accused) is eligible for assistance by virtue of this subsection if the court is satisfied that the quality of evidence given by the witness is likely to be diminished by reason of fear or distress on the part of the witness in connection with testifying in the proceedings.

---

(2) In determining whether a witness falls within subsection (1) the court must take into account, in particular—

    (a) the nature and alleged circumstances of the offence to which the proceedings relate;

    (b) the age of the witness;

    (c) such of the following matters as appear to the court to be relevant, namely—

        (i) the social and cultural background and ethnic origins of the witness,

        (ii) the domestic and employment circumstances of the witness, and

        (iii) any religious beliefs or political opinions of the witness;

    (d) any behaviour towards the witness on the part of—

        (i) the accused,

        (ii) members of the family or associates of the accused, or

        (iii) any other person who is likely to be an accused or a witness in the proceedings.

(3) In determining that question the court must in addition consider any views expressed by the witness.

(4) Where the complainant in respect of a sexual offence is a witness in proceedings relating to that offence (or to that offence and any other offences), the witness is eligible for assistance in relation to those proceedings by virtue of this subsection unless the witness has informed the court of the witness's wish not to be so eligible by virtue of this subsection.

The following special measures are available in the magistrates' court:

	Section 16 witnesses (children and vulnerable adults)	Section 17 witnesses (intimidated/fear or distress)
Section 23 screening witness from accused	Full availability	Full availability
Section 24 evidence via live link [see **B1.5** for young defendants, and **A32.2**]	Full availability	Full availability
Section 25 evidence given in private	Full availability	Full availability
Section 26 removal of wigs/gowns	Not applicable	Not applicable
Section 27 video recorded evidence in chief [see **A32.2**]	Available for 'child witnesses in need of special protection' (defined by section 21 of the 1999 Act) only since 24 July 2002	Not available
Section 28 video recorded cross-examination and re-examination	Not available	Not available

Section 29 examination through an intermediary [see **A32.2** and **B1.6**]	Full availability	Not applicable
Section 30 aids to communication	Full availability	Not applicable.

A32.2 Coroners and Justice Act 2009

Seven sections of the 2009 Act, not in force at the time of writing, make amendment to the law above.

Section 98 of the Act will amend section 16(1)(a) of the 1999 Act to read '18 years' instead of '17 years'.

Section 99 of the Act amends section 17 to provide for automatic eligibility for special measures in relation to relevant offences. Relevant offences are listed in Schedule 14 to the 2009 Act, and are detailed in **Appendix 5**.

Section 100 of the Act amends section 21 of the 1999 Act:

- to make special measures available to child witnesses in relation to all offences;
- to allow a child to opt out of special measures if the quality of that witnesse's evidence would not be diminished.

Section 102 of the Act allows for a witness to be accompanied while giving evidence via live link.

Section 103 of the Act relaxes the restriction on asking supplemental questions.

Section 104 of the Act provides for the examination of an accused, under the age of 18—to be through an intermediary—see **B1.6**.

Section 111 of the Act repeals section 138(1) of the Criminal Justice Act 2003 (a provision also not yet in force), to provide for oral evidence where a witness has given a video account.

A32.3 Witness anonymity

The Coroners and Justice Act 2009 provides for the making and discharge of witness anonymity orders:

> **Coroners and Justice Act 2009, ss 86–89, 91, 95, and 97**
>
> **86 Witness anonymity orders**
>
> (1) In this Chapter a 'witness anonymity order' is an order made by a court that requires such specified measures to be taken in relation to a witness in criminal proceedings as the court considers appropriate to ensure that

the identity of the witness is not disclosed in or in connection with the proceedings.

(2) The kinds of measures that may be required to be taken in relation to a witness include measures for securing one or more of the following—

(a) that the witness's name and other identifying details may be—

(i) withheld;

(ii) removed from materials disclosed to any party to the proceedings;

(b) that the witness may use a pseudonym;

(c) that the witness is not asked questions of any specified description that might lead to the identification of the witness;

(d) that the witness is screened to any specified extent;

(e) that the witness's voice is subjected to modulation to any specified extent.

(3) Subsection (2) does not affect the generality of subsection (1).

(4) Nothing in this section authorises the court to require—

(a) the witness to be screened to such an extent that the witness cannot be seen by—

(i) the judge or other members of the court (if any), or

(ii) the jury (if there is one);

(b) the witness's voice to be modulated to such an extent that the witness's natural voice cannot be heard by any persons within paragraph (a)(i) or (ii).

(5) In this section 'specified' means specified in the witness anonymity order concerned.

87 Applications

(1) An application for a witness anonymity order to be made in relation to a witness in criminal proceedings may be made to the court by the prosecutor or the defendant.

(2) Where an application is made by the prosecutor, the prosecutor—

(a) must (unless the court directs otherwise) inform the court of the identity of the witness, but

(b) is not required to disclose in connection with the application—

(i) the identity of the witness, or

(ii) any information that might enable the witness to be identified, to any other party to the proceedings or his or her legal representatives.

(3) Where an application is made by the defendant, the defendant—

(a) must inform the court and the prosecutor of the identity of the witness, but

(b) (if there is more than one defendant) is not required to disclose in connection with the application—

(i) the identity of the witness, or

(ii) any information that might enable the witness to be identified, to any other defendant or his or her legal representatives.

(4) Accordingly, where the prosecutor or the defendant proposes to make an application under this section in respect of a witness, any relevant material which is disclosed by or on behalf of that party before the determination of the application may be disclosed in such a way as to prevent—

(a) the identity of the witness, or

(b) any information that might enable the witness to be identified, from being disclosed except as required by subsection (2)(a) or (3)(a).

(5) 'Relevant material' means any document or other material which falls to be disclosed, or is sought to be relied on, by or on behalf of the party concerned in connection with the proceedings or proceedings preliminary to them.

(6) The court must give every party to the proceedings the opportunity to be heard on an application under this section.

(7) But subsection (6) does not prevent the court from hearing one or more parties in the absence of a defendant and his or her legal representatives, if it appears to the court to be appropriate to do so in the circumstances of the case.

(8) Nothing in this section is to be taken as restricting any power to make rules of court.

88 Conditions for making order

(1) This section applies where an application is made for a witness anonymity order to be made in relation to a witness in criminal proceedings.

(2) The court may make such an order only if it is satisfied that Conditions A to C below are met.

(3) Condition A is that the proposed order is necessary—
   (a) in order to protect the safety of the witness or another person or to prevent any serious damage to property, or
   (b) in order to prevent real harm to the public interest (whether affecting the carrying on of any activities in the public interest or the safety of a person involved in carrying on such activities, or otherwise).

(4) Condition B is that, having regard to all the circumstances, the effect of the proposed order would be consistent with the defendant receiving a fair trial.

(5) Condition C is that the importance of the witness's testimony is such that in the interests of justice the witness ought to testify and—
   (a) the witness would not testify if the proposed order were not made, or
   (b) there would be real harm to the public interest if the witness were to testify without the proposed order being made.

(6) In determining whether the proposed order is necessary for the purpose mentioned in subsection (3)(a), the court must have regard (in particular) to any reasonable fear on the part of the witness—
   (a) that the witness or another person would suffer death or injury, or
   (b) that there would be serious damage to property, if the witness were to be identified.

89 Relevant considerations

(1) When deciding whether Conditions A to C in section 88 are met in the case of an application for a witness anonymity order, the court must have regard to—
   (a) the considerations mentioned in subsection (2) below, and
   (b) such other matters as the court considers relevant.

(2) The considerations are—
   (a) the general right of a defendant in criminal proceedings to know the identity of a witness in the proceedings;
   (b) the extent to which the credibility of the witness concerned would be a relevant factor when the weight of his or her evidence comes to be assessed;

   (c) whether evidence given by the witness might be the sole or decisive evidence implicating the defendant;

   (d) whether the witness's evidence could be properly tested (whether on grounds of credibility or otherwise) without his or her identity being disclosed;

   (e) whether there is any reason to believe that the witness—

      (i) has a tendency to be dishonest, or

      (ii) has any motive to be dishonest in the circumstances of the case, having regard (in particular) to any previous convictions of the witness and to any relationship between the witness and the defendant or any associates of the defendant;

   (f) whether it would be reasonably practicable to protect the witness by any means other than by making a witness anonymity order specifying the measures that are under consideration by the court.

90 . . .

91 Discharge or variation of order

(1) A court that has made a witness anonymity order in relation to any criminal proceedings may in those proceedings subsequently discharge or vary (or further vary) the order if it appears to the court to be appropriate to do so in view of the provisions of sections 88 and 89 that apply to the making of an order.

(2) The court may do so—

   (a) on an application made by a party to the proceedings if there has been a material change of circumstances since the relevant time, or

   (b) on its own initiative.

(3) The court must give every party to the proceedings the opportunity to be heard—

   (a) before determining an application made to it under subsection (2);

   (b) before discharging or varying the order on its own initiative.

(4) But subsection (3) does not prevent the court hearing one or more of the parties to the proceedings in the absence of a defendant in the proceedings and his or her legal representatives, if it appears to the court to be appropriate to do so in the circumstances of the case.

(5) 'The relevant time' means—

   (a) the time when the order was made, or

   (b) if a previous application has been made under subsection (2), the time when the application (or the last application) was made.

92 . . .

93 . . .

94 . . .

95 Public interest immunity

Nothing in this Chapter affects the common law rules as to the withholding of information on the grounds of public interest immunity.

See *Blackstone's Criminal Practice 2012* D14

A33 **Submission of No Case**

A33.1 **Test for no case to answer**

In *R v Galbraith* (1981) 73 Cr App R 124 the court laid down the following test:

(1) If there is no evidence that the crime alleged has been committed by the defendant, there is no difficulty. The judge will of course stop the case.

(2) The difficulty arises where there is some evidence but it is of a tenuous character, for example because of inherent weakness or vagueness or because it is inconsistent with other evidence. (a) Where the judge comes to the conclusion that the prosecution evidence, taken at its highest, is such that a jury properly directed could not properly convict upon it, it is his duty, upon a submission being made, to stop the case. (b) Where however the prosecution evidence is such that its strength or weakness depends on the view to be taken of a witness's reliability, or other matters which are generally speaking within the province of the jury and where on one possible view of the facts there is evidence upon which a jury could properly come to the conclusion that the defendant is guilty, then the judge should allow the matter to be tried by the jury. It follows that we think the second of the two schools of thought is to be preferred.

 See *Blackstone's Criminal Practice 2012* **D16.51–D16.69**

A34 **Transfer of Criminal Cases**

Section 27A of the Magistrates' Courts Act 1980 provides:

Magistrates' Courts Act 1980, s 27A

(1) Where a person appears or is brought before a magistrates' court—
   (a) to be tried by the court for an offence, or
   (b) for the court to inquire into the offence as examining justices,
   the court may transfer the matter to another magistrates' court.
(2) The court may transfer the matter before or after beginning the trial or inquiry.
(3) But if the court transfers the matter after it has begun to hear the evidence and the parties, the court to which the matter is transferred must begin hearing the evidence and the parties again.
(4) The power of the court under this section to transfer any matter must be exercised in accordance with any directions given under section 30(3) of the Courts Act 2003.

 See *Blackstone's Criminal Practice 2012* **D21.12**

A35 **Video Links**

Sections 57A–57F of the Crime and Disorder Act 1998 provide for the use of live links in relation to preliminary hearings and sentence (see **A32** for special measure provisions):

Crime and Disorder Act 1998, ss 57A–57F

57A Introductory

(1) This Part—

    (a) applies to preliminary hearings and sentencing hearings in the course of proceedings for an offence and enforcement hearings relating to confiscation orders; and

    (b) enables the court in the circumstances provided for in sections 57B, 57C, 57E and 57F to direct the use of a live link for securing the accused's attendance at a hearing to which this Part applies.

(2) The accused is to be treated as present in court when, by virtue of a live link direction under this Part, he attends a hearing through a live link.

(3) In this Part—

    'confiscation order' means an order made under—

        (a) section 71 of the Criminal Justice Act 1988;

        (b) section 2 of the Drug Trafficking Act 1994; or

        (c) section 6 of the Proceeds of Crime Act 2002;

    'custody'—

        (a) includes local authority accommodation to which a person is remanded or committed by virtue of section 23 of the Children and Young Persons Act 1969; but

        (b) does not include police detention;

    'enforcement hearing' means a hearing under section 82 of the Magistrates' Courts Act 1980 to consider the issuing of a warrant of committal or to inquire into a person's means;

    'live link' means an arrangement by which a person (when not in the place where the hearing is being held) is able to see and hear, and to be seen and heard by, the court during a hearing (and for this purpose any impairment of eyesight or hearing is to be disregarded);

    'police detention' has the meaning given by section 118(2) of the Police and Criminal Evidence Act 1984;

    'preliminary hearing' means a hearing in the proceedings held before the start of the trial (within the meaning of subsection (11A) or (11B) of section 22 of the 1985 Act) including, in the case of proceedings in the Crown Court, a preparatory hearing held under—

        (a) section 7 of the Criminal Justice Act 1987 (cases of serious or complex fraud); or

        (b) section 29 of the Criminal Procedure and Investigations Act 1996 (other serious, complex or lengthy cases);

'sentencing hearing' means any hearing following conviction which is held for the purpose of—

(a) proceedings relating to the giving or rescinding of a direction under section 57E;

(b) proceedings (in a magistrates' court) relating to committal to the Crown Court for sentencing; or

(c) sentencing the offender or determining how the court should deal with him in respect of the offence.

57B Use of live link at preliminary hearings where accused is in custody

(1) This section applies in relation to a preliminary hearing in a magistrates' court or the Crown Court.

(2) Where it appears to the court before which the preliminary hearing is to take place that the accused is likely to be held in custody during the hearing, the court may give a live link direction under this section in relation to the attendance of the accused at the hearing.

(3) A live link direction under this section is a direction requiring the accused, if he is being held in custody during the hearing, to attend it through a live link from the place at which he is being held.

(4) If a hearing takes place in relation to the giving or rescinding of such a direction, the court may require or permit a person attending the hearing to do so through a live link.

(5) The court shall not give or rescind such a direction (whether at a hearing or otherwise) unless the parties to the proceedings have been given the opportunity to make representations.

(6) If in a case where it has power to do so a magistrates' court decides not to give a live link direction under this section, it must—

(a) state in open court its reasons for not doing so; and

(b) cause those reasons to be entered in the register of its proceedings.

(7) The following functions of a magistrates' court under this section may be discharged by a single justice—

(a) giving a live link direction under this section;

(b) rescinding a live link direction before a preliminary hearing begins; and

(c) requiring or permitting a person to attend by live link a hearing about a matter within paragraph (a) or (b).

57C Use of live link at preliminary hearings where accused is at police station

(1) This section applies in relation to a preliminary hearing in a magistrates' court.

(2) Where subsection (3) or (4) applies to the accused, the court may give a live link direction in relation to his attendance at the preliminary hearing.

(3) This subsection applies to the accused if—

(a) he is in police detention at a police station in connection with the offence; and

(b) it appears to the court that he is likely to remain at that station in police detention until the beginning of the preliminary hearing.

(4) This subsection applies to the accused if he is at a police station in answer to live link bail in connection with the offence.

(5) A live link direction under this section is a direction requiring the accused to attend the preliminary hearing through a live link from the police station.

(6) But a direction given in relation to an accused to whom subsection (3) applies has no effect if he does not remain in police detention at the police station until the beginning of the preliminary hearing.

(6A) A live link direction under this section may not be given unless the court is satisfied that it is not contrary to the interests of justice to give the direction.

(8) A magistrates' court may rescind a live link direction under this section at any time during a hearing to which it relates.

(9) A magistrates' court may require or permit—

    [. . .]

    (b) any party to the proceedings who wishes to make representations in relation to the giving or rescission of a live link direction under this section to do so through a live link.

(10) Where a live link direction under this section is given in relation to an accused person who is answering to live link bail he is to be treated as having surrendered to the custody of the court (as from the time when the direction is given).

(11) In this section, 'live link bail' means bail granted under Part 4 of the Police and Criminal Evidence Act 1984 subject to the duty mentioned in section 47(3)(b) of that Act.

57D Continued use of live link for sentencing hearing following a preliminary hearing

(1) Subsection (2) applies where—

    (a) a live link direction under section 57B or 57C is in force;

    (b) the accused is attending a preliminary hearing through a live link by virtue of the direction;

    (c) the court convicts him of the offence in the course of that hearing (whether by virtue of a guilty plea or an indication of an intention to plead guilty); and

    (d) the court proposes to continue the hearing as a sentencing hearing in relation to the offence.

(2) The accused may continue to attend through the live link by virtue of the direction if—

    (a) the hearing is continued as a sentencing hearing in relation to the offence; and

    (c) the court is satisfied that the accused continuing to attend through the live link is not contrary to the interests of justice.

(3) But the accused may not give oral evidence through the live link during a continued hearing under subsection (2) unless—

    [. . .]

    (b) the court is satisfied that it is not contrary to the interests of justice for him to give it in that way.

57E Use of live link in sentencing hearings

(1) This section applies where the accused is convicted of the offence.

(2) If it appears to the court by or before which the accused is convicted that it is likely that he will be held in custody during any sentencing hearing for the offence, the court may give a live link direction under this section in relation to that hearing.

(3) A live link direction under this section is a direction requiring the accused, if he is being held in custody during the hearing, to attend it through a live link from the place at which he is being held.

(4) Such a direction—
   (a) may be given by the court of its own motion or on an application by a party; and
   (b) may be given in relation to all subsequent sentencing hearings before the court or to such hearing or hearings as may be specified or described in the direction.

(5) The court may not give such a direction unless—
   [. . .]
   (b) the court is satisfied that it is not contrary to the interests of justice to give the direction.

(6) The court may rescind such a direction at any time before or during a hearing to which it relates if it appears to the court to be in the interests of justice to do so (but this does not affect the court's power to give a further live link direction in relation to the offender).
   The court may exercise this power of its own motion or on an application by a party.

(7) The offender may not give oral evidence while attending a hearing through a live link by virtue of this section unless—
   [. . .]
   (b) the court is satisfied that it is not contrary to the interests of justice for him to give it in that way.

(8) The court must—
   (a) state in open court its reasons for refusing an application for, or for the rescission of, a live link direction under this section; and
   (b) if it is a magistrates' court, cause those reasons to be entered in the register of its proceedings.

57F Use of live link in certain enforcement hearings

(1) This section applies where—
   (a) a confiscation order is made against a person; and
   (b) the amount required to be paid under the order is not paid when it is required to be paid.

(2) If it appears to the court before which an enforcement hearing relating to the confiscation order is to take place that it is likely that the person will be held in custody at the time of the hearing, the court may give a live link direction under this section in relation to that hearing.

(3) A live link direction under this section is a direction requiring the person, if the person is being held in custody at the time of the hearing, to attend it through a live link from the place at which the person is being held.

(4) Such a direction—
  (a) may be given by the court of its own motion or on an application by a party; and
  (b) may be given in relation to all subsequent enforcement hearings before the court or to such hearing or hearings as may be specified or described in the direction.

(5) The court may rescind a live link direction under this section at any time before or during a hearing to which it relates.

(6) The court may not give or rescind a live link direction under this section (whether at a hearing or otherwise) unless the parties to the proceedings have been given the opportunity to make representations.

(7) If a hearing takes place in relation to the giving or rescinding of such a direction, the court may require or permit any party to the proceedings who wishes to make representations in relation to the giving or rescission of a live link direction under this section to do so through a live link.

(8) The person may not give oral evidence while attending a hearing through a live link by virtue of this section unless the court is satisfied that it is not contrary to the interests of justice for the person to give it that way.

(9) If in a case where it has power to do so a court decides not to give a live link direction under this section, it must—
  (a) state in open court its reasons for not doing so; and
  (b) cause those reasons to be entered in the register of its proceedings.

(10) The following functions of a magistrates' court under this section may be discharged by a single justice—
  (a) giving a live link direction under this section;
  (b) rescinding a live link direction before a preliminary hearing begins; and
  (c) requiring or permitting a person to attend by live link a hearing about a matter within paragraph (a) or (b).

 See *Blackstone's Criminal Practice 2012* **D14.34**

A36 **Warrants**

Sections 1 and 13 of the Magistrates' Courts Act 1980 provide for the issue of warrants to secure a person's attendance before the court:

Magistrates' Courts Act 1980, ss 1 and 13

1 Issue of summons to accused or warrant for his arrest

(1) On an information being laid before a justice of the peace that a person has, or is suspected of having, committed an offence, the justice may issue—

    (a) a summons directed to that person requiring him to appear before a magistrates' court to answer the information, or

    (b) a warrant to arrest that person and bring him before a magistrates' court.

(3) No warrant shall be issued under this section unless the information is in writing.

(4) No warrant shall be issued under this section for the arrest of any person who has attained the age of 18 years unless—

    (a) the offence to which the warrant relates is an indictable offence or is punishable with imprisonment, or

    (b) the person's address is not sufficiently established for a summons to be served on him.

(6) Where the offence charged is an indictable offence, a warrant under this section may be issued at any time notwithstanding that a summons has previously been issued.

(7) A justice of the peace may issue a summons or warrant under this section upon an information being laid before him notwithstanding any enactment requiring the information to be laid before two or more justices.

13 Non-appearance of accused: issue of warrant

(1) Subject to the provisions of this section, where the court, instead of proceeding in the absence of the accused, adjourns or further adjourns the trial, the court may issue a warrant for his arrest.

(2) Where a summons has been issued, the court shall not issue a warrant under this section unless the condition in subsection (2A) below or that in subsection (2B) below is fulfilled.

(2A) The condition in this subsection is that it is proved to the satisfaction of the court, on oath or in such other manner as may be prescribed, that the summons was served on the accused within what appears to the court to be a reasonable time before the trial or adjourned trial.

(2B) The condition in this subsection is that—

    (a) the adjournment now being made is a second or subsequent adjournment of the trial,

    (b) the accused was present on the last (or only) occasion when the trial was adjourned, and

   (c) on that occasion the court determined the time for the hearing at
      which the adjournment is now being made.

(3) A warrant for the arrest of any person who has attained the age of 18 shall
  not be issued under this section unless—
   (a) the offence to which the warrant relates is punishable with imprison-
      ment, or
   (b) the court, having convicted the accused, proposes to impose a disquali-
      fication on him.

(3A) A warrant for the arrest of any person who has not attained the age of 18
  shall not be issued under this section unless—
   (a) the offence to which the warrant relates is punishable, in the case of a
      person who has attained the age of 18, with imprisonment, or
   (b) the court, having convicted the accused, proposes to impose a disqualifi-
      cation on him.

(4) This section shall not apply to an adjournment on the occasion of the
  accused's conviction in his absence under subsection (5) of section 12
  above or to an adjournment required by subsection (9) of that section.

 See *Blackstone's Criminal Practice 2012* **D1**

A37 **Witnesses, Issue of Summons or Warrant**

A37.1 **Power to require attendance**

Magistrates' Courts Act 1980, s 97

97 Summons to witness and warrant for his arrest

(1) Where a justice of the peace is satisfied that—

    (a) any person in England or Wales is likely to be able to give material evidence, or produce any document or thing likely to be material evidence, at the summary trial of an information or hearing of a complaint or of an application under the Adoption and Children Act 2002 (c. 38) by a magistrates' court, and

    (b) it is in the interests of justice to issue a summons under this subsection to secure the attendance of that person to give evidence or produce the document or thing,

the justice shall issue a summons directed to that person requiring him to attend before the court at the time and place appointed in the summons to give evidence or to produce the document or thing.

(2) If a justice of the peace is satisfied by evidence on oath of the matters mentioned in subsection (1) above, and also that it is probable that a summons under that subsection would not procure the attendance of the person in question, the justice may instead of issuing a summons issue a warrant to arrest that person and bring him before such a court as aforesaid at a time and place specified in the warrant; but a warrant shall not be issued under this subsection where the attendance is required for the hearing of a complaint or of an application under the Adoption and Children Act 2002 (c. 38).

(2A) A summons may also be issued under subsection (1) above if the justice is satisfied that the person in question is outside the British Islands but no warrant shall be issued under subsection (2) above unless the justice is satisfied by evidence on oath that the person in question is in England or Wales.

(2B) A justice may refuse to issue a summons under subsection (1) above in relation to the summary trial of an information if he is not satisfied that an application for the summons was made by a party to the case as soon as reasonably practicable after the accused pleaded not guilty.

(2C) In relation to the summary trial of an information, subsection (2) above shall have effect as if the reference to the matters mentioned in subsection (1) above included a reference to the matter mentioned in subsection (2B) above.

(3) On the failure of any person to attend before a magistrates' court in answer to a summons under this section, if—

    (a) the court is satisfied by evidence on oath that he is likely to be able to give material evidence or produce any document or thing likely to be material evidence in the proceedings; and

(b) it is proved on oath, or in such other manner as may be prescribed, that he has been duly served with the summons, and that a reasonable sum has been paid or tendered to him for costs and expenses; and

(c) it appears to the court that there is no just excuse for the failure,

the court may issue a warrant to arrest him and bring him before the court at a time and place specified in the warrant.

(4) If any person attending or brought before a magistrates' court refuses without just excuse to be sworn or give evidence, or to produce any document or thing, the court may commit him to custody until the expiration of such period not exceeding one month as may be specified in the warrant or until he sooner gives evidence or produces the document or thing or impose on him a fine not exceeding £2,500 or both.

Conduct money should be served with any summons sufficient to enable the person to attend court.

The power to compel production of documents relates only to material evidence, and should not be used to compel the production of documents solely for the purpose of cross-examination (*R v Skegness Magistrates' Court, ex p Cardy* [1985] RTR 49).

 See *Blackstone's Criminal Practice 2012* **D21.21–D21.25**

Part B
Youth Court

B1 General Provisions

B1.1 Notifications pre-charge

Sections 5 and 34(2) of the Children and Young Persons Act 1969 stipulate that the local authority and probation service must be informed when a young person is to be prosecuted. A failure to so notify is not however fatal to the proceedings and the sections have been held to be discretionary, not mandatory (*Director of Public Prosecutions v Cottier* [1996] 3 All ER 126).

B1.2 The youth court

Save where otherwise provided for (eg youth appearing with an adult) the youth court enjoys exclusive jurisdiction over those aged under 18 years in regard to criminal matters (freestanding applications for anti-social behaviour orders (ASBOs) and other civil matters must be made to an adult magistrates' court). In law, a youth court is simply a magistrates' court constituted in a particular manner:

Children and Young Persons Act 1933, s 45(1)–(3)

(1) Magistrates' courts—
    (a) constituted in accordance with this section or section 66 of the Courts Act 2003 (judges having powers of District Judges (Magistrates' Courts)), and
    (b) sitting for the purpose of—
        (i) hearing any charge against a child or young person, or
        (ii) exercising any other jurisdiction conferred on youth courts by or under this or any other Act, are to be known as youth courts.
(2) A justice of the peace is not qualified to sit as a member of a youth court for the purpose of dealing with any proceedings unless he has an authorisation extending to the proceedings.
(3) He has an authorisation extending to the proceedings only if he has been authorised by the Lord Chief Justice, with the concurrence of the Lord Chancellor, to sit as a member of a youth court to deal with—
    (a) proceedings of that description, or
    (b) all proceedings dealt with by youth courts.

B1.3 Constitution

In the absence of unforeseen circumstances a youth court should be constituted either of a District Judge (sitting alone or exceptionally with lay justices) or of three magistrates one of whom must be male and one of whom must be female. If the court is proposing to sit in any other combination it should make that clear to the parties and invite representations (*R v Birmingham Justices, ex p F* (1999) 163 JP 523).

B1.4 Intellectual capacity to understand the proceedings

There have been a number of cases where the defence has sought to raise a capacissue, namely that the defendant whether due to immaturity or mental capacity, is unable to understand the proceedings such that it would be an abuse of process to continue on the ground that he could not have a fair trial.

The elements of a fair trial (in this regard) are:

- he had to understand what he is said to have done wrong;
- the court had to be satisfied that the claimant when he had done wrong by act or omission had the means of knowing that was wrong;
- he had to understand what, if any, defences were available to him;
- he had to have a reasonable opportunity to make relevant representations if he wished;
- he had to have the opportunity to consider what representation he wished to make once he understood the issues involved.

He had, therefore, to be able to give proper instructions and to participate by way of providing answers to questions and suggesting questions to his lawyers in the circumstances of the trial as they arose.

The following guidance on how to approach the issue was issued by the court in *Crown Prosecution Service v P* [2007] EWHC 946 (Admin):

- The fitness to plead procedure (in so far as it applies in the magistrates' court (see **A26.1**) does not provide a complete answer to the defendant who lacks capacity as there are fair trial issues under article 6 to consider.
- In an exceptional case there may be grounds to stay a case as an abuse of process if the child lacks capacity.
- Medical evidence on the issue is not decisive.
- Before considering a stay the court should consider conducting a fact-finding exercise with a view to a medical disposal under the Mental Health Act 1983 in appropriate cases.

It can be seen, therefore, that only in cases where the capacity issue is not linked to mental health, or a mental health disposal is not appropriate, will a court consider a stay of proceedings.

B1.5 Live link direction for vulnerable young defendants

The court has power to allow a vulnerable young defendant to give evidence via live link (Youth Justice and Criminal Evidence Act 1999, s 33A):

Youth Justice and Criminal Evidence Act 1999, s 33A

33A Live link directions

(1) This section applies to any proceedings (whether in a magistrates' court or before the Crown Court) against a person for an offence.

(2) The court may, on the application of the accused, give a live link direction if it is satisfied—
   (a) that the conditions in subsection (4) or, as the case may be, subsection (5) are met in relation to the accused, and
   (b) that it is in the interests of justice for the accused to give evidence through a live link.

(3) A live link direction is a direction that any oral evidence to be given before the court by the accused is to be given through a live link.

(4) Where the accused is aged under 18 when the application is made, the conditions are that—
   (a) his ability to participate effectively in the proceedings as a witness giving oral evidence in court is compromised by his level of intellectual ability or social functioning, and
   (b) use of a live link would enable him to participate more effectively in the proceedings as a witness (whether by improving the quality of his evidence or otherwise).

(5) Where the accused has attained the age of 18 at that time, the conditions are that—
   (a) he suffers from a mental disorder (within the meaning of the Mental Health Act 1983) or otherwise has a significant impairment of intelligence and social function,
   (b) he is for that reason unable to participate effectively in the proceedings as a witness giving oral evidence in court, and
   (c) use of a live link would enable him to participate more effectively in the proceedings as a witness (whether by improving the quality of his evidence or otherwise).

(6) While a live link direction has effect the accused may not give oral evidence before the court in the proceedings otherwise than through a live link.

(7) The court may discharge a live link direction at any time before or during any hearing to which it applies if it appears to the court to be in the interests of justice to do so (but this does not affect the power to give a further live link direction in relation to the accused).
   The court may exercise this power of its own motion or on an application by a party.

---

(8) The court must state in open court its reasons for—
  (a) giving or discharging a live link direction, or
  (b) refusing an application for or for the discharge of a live link direction,
  and, if it is a magistrates' court, it must cause those reasons to be entered in the register of its proceedings.

B1.6 Examination of accused through intermediary

Note: at the time of writing this provision was not in force.

Sections 33BA and 33BB of the Youth Justice and Criminal Evidence Act 1999 (as inserted by the Coroners and Justice Act 2009, s 104) provides:

Youth Justice and Criminal Evidence Act 1999, ss 33BA and 33BB

33BA Examination of accused through intermediary

(1) This section applies to any proceedings (whether in a magistrates' court or before the Crown Court) against a person for an offence.

(2) The court may, on the application of the accused, give a direction under subsection (3) if it is satisfied—
  (a) that the condition in subsection (5) is or, as the case may be, the conditions in subsection (6) are met in relation to the accused, and
  (b) that making the direction is necessary in order to ensure that the accused receives a fair trial.

(3) A direction under this subsection is a direction that provides for any examination of the accused to be conducted through an interpreter or other person approved by the court for the purposes of this section ('an intermediary').

(4) The function of an intermediary is to communicate—
  (a) to the accused, questions put to the accused, and
  (b) to any person asking such questions, the answers given by the accused in reply to them,
  and to explain such questions or answers so far as necessary to enable them to be understood by the accused or the person in question.

(5) Where the accused is aged under 18 when the application is made the condition is that the accused's ability to participate effectively in the proceedings as a witness giving oral evidence in court is compromised by the accused's level of intellectual ability or social functioning.

(6) Where the accused has attained the age of 18 when the application is made the conditions are that—
  (a) the accused suffers from a mental disorder (within the meaning of the Mental Health Act 1983) or otherwise has a significant impairment of intelligence and social function, and
  (b) the accused is for that reason unable to participate effectively in the proceedings as a witness giving oral evidence in court.

(7) Any examination of the accused in pursuance of a direction under subsection (3) must take place in the presence of such persons as Criminal Procedure Rules or the direction may provide and in circumstances in which—

    (a) the judge or justices (or both) and legal representatives acting in the proceedings are able to see and hear the examination of the accused and to communicate with the intermediary,

    (b) the jury (if there is one) are able to see and hear the examination of the accused, and

    (c) where there are two or more accused in the proceedings, each of the other accused is able to see and hear the examination of the accused.

For the purposes of this subsection any impairment of eyesight or hearing is to be disregarded.

(8) Where two or more legal representatives are acting for a party to the proceedings, subsection (7)(a) is to be regarded as satisfied in relation to those representatives if at all material times it is satisfied in relation to at least one of them.

(9) A person may not act as an intermediary in a particular case except after making a declaration, in such form as may be prescribed by Criminal Procedure Rules, that the person will faithfully perform the function of an intermediary.

(10) Section 1 of the Perjury Act 1911 (perjury) applies in relation to a person acting as an intermediary as it applies in relation to a person lawfully sworn as an interpreter in a judicial proceeding.

33BB Further provision as to directions under section 33BA(3)

(1) The court may discharge a direction given under section 33BA(3) at any time before or during the proceedings to which it applies if it appears to the court that the direction is no longer necessary in order to ensure that the accused receives a fair trial (but this does not affect the power to give a further direction under section 33BA(3) in relation to the accused).

(2) The court may vary (or further vary) a direction given under section 33BA(3) at any time before or during the proceedings to which it applies if it appears to the court that it is necessary for the direction to be varied in order to ensure that the accused receives a fair trial.

(3) The court may exercise the power in subsection (1) or (2) of its own motion or on an application by a party.

(4) The court must state in open court its reasons for—

    (a) giving, varying or discharging a direction under section 33BA(3), or

    (b) refusing an application for, or for the variation or discharge of, a direction under section 33BA(3),

. . .

In *C v Seven Oaks Youth Court* [2009] EWHC 3088 (Admin) the court held that an intermediary could be appointed under the court's common law power to ensure a fair trial process. The court has no power to order central funds costs, but it would appear that the Ministry of Justice considers funding on an ad hoc basis.

B1.7 **Doli incapax**

The presumption of doli incapax was abolished by section 34 of the Crime and Disorder Act 1998 (*R v T* [2008] 3 WLR 923).

B1.8 **Attendance of parent or guardian**

Section 34A of the Children and Young Persons Act 1933 provides:

Children and Young Persons Act 1933, s 34A

34A Attendance at court of parent or guardian

(1) Where a child or young person is charged with an offence or is for any other reason brought before a court, the court—

    (a) may in any case; and

    (b) shall in the case of a child or a young person who is under the age of sixteen years,

require a person who is a parent or guardian of his to attend at the court during all the stages of the proceedings, unless and to the extent that the court is satisfied that it would be unreasonable to require such attendance, having regard to the circumstances of the case.

(2) In relation to a child or young person for whom a local authority have parental responsibility and who—

    (a) is in their care; or

    (b) is provided with accommodation by them in the exercise of any functions (in particular those under the Children Act 1989) which are social services functions within the meaning of the Local Authority Social Services Act 1970,

the reference in subsection (1) above to a person who is a parent or guardian of his shall be construed as a reference to that authority or, where he is allowed to live with such a person, as including such a reference.

. . .

In the sentencing guideline, *Overarching Principles—Sentencing Youths* (to which the court must have regard), it is stated:

The statutory framework clearly envisages the attendance of an adult with a degree of responsibility for the young person; this obligation reflects the principal aim of reducing offending, recognising that that is unlikely to be achieved by the young person alone. A court must be aware of a risk that a young person will seek to avoid this requirement either by urging the court to proceed in the absence of an adult or in arranging for a person to come to court who purports to have (but in reality does not have) the necessary degree of responsibility.

Insistence on attendance may produce a delay in the case before the court; however, it is important that this obligation is maintained and that it is widely recognised that a court will require such attendance, especially when imposing sentence.

The court has the power to issue a summons and/or warrant for arrest, in relation to an absent parent or guardian.

B1.9 Restricted hearings

Access to the youth court is restricted under section 47(2) of the Children and Young Persons Act 1933:

Children and Young Persons Act 1933, s 47(2)

(2) No person shall be present at any sitting of a youth court except—
   (a) members and officers of the court;
   (b) parties to the case before the court, their solicitors and counsel, and witnesses and other persons directly concerned in that case;
   (c) bonâ fide representatives of newspapers or news agencies;
   (d) such other persons as the court may specially authorise to be present:

B1.10 Reporting restrictions

The reporting of youth court matters is regulated under section 49 of the Children and Young Persons Act 1933.

These automatic reporting restrictions may be lifted in three specific circumstances:

- the court may lift the restriction if satisfied that it is appropriate to do so for avoiding injustice to the child;
- the court may lift the restriction to assist in the search for a missing, convicted, or alleged young offender who has been charged with, or convicted of, a violent or sexual offence (or one punishable with a prison sentence of 14 years or more in the case of a 21-year-old offender);
- the restriction may be lifted in relation to a child or young person who has been convicted, if the court is satisfied that it is in the public interest.

Discretionary reporting restrictions can also apply, for example when a youth appears before a magistrates' court in relation to the making of an anti-social behaviour order (see **A28.1**).

Section 49 of the Children and Young Persons Act 1933 provides:

Children and Young Persons Act 1933, s 49(1)–(10)

(1) The following prohibitions apply (subject to subsection (5) below) in relation to any proceedings to which this section applies, that is to say—
   (a) no report shall be published which reveals the name, address or school of any child or young person concerned in the proceedings or includes

any particulars likely to lead to the identification of any child or young person concerned in the proceedings; and

(b) no picture shall be published or included in a programme service as being or including a picture of any child or young person concerned in the proceedings.

(2) The proceedings to which this section applies are—

(a) proceedings in a youth court;

(b) proceedings on appeal from a youth court (including proceedings by way of case stated);

(c) proceedings under Schedule 7 to the Powers of Criminal Courts (Sentencing) Act 2000 (proceedings for varying or revoking supervision orders); and

(d) proceedings on appeal from a magistrates' court arising out of proceedings under Schedule 7 to that Act (including proceedings by way of case stated).

(3) The reports to which this section applies are reports in a newspaper and reports included in a programme service; and similarly as respects pictures.

(4) For the purposes of this section a child or young person is 'concerned' in any proceedings whether as being the person against or in respect of whom the proceedings are taken or as being a witness in the proceedings.

(4A) If a court is satisfied that it is in the public interest to do so, it may, in relation to a child or young person who has been convicted of an offence, by order dispense to any specified extent with the requirements of this section in relation to any proceedings before it to which this section applies by virtue of subsection (2)(a) or (b) above, being proceedings relating to—

(a) the prosecution or conviction of the offender for the offence;

(b) the manner in which he, or his parent or guardian, should be dealt with in respect of the offence;

(c) the enforcement, amendment, variation, revocation or discharge of any order made in respect of the offence;

(d) where an attendance centre order is made in respect of the offence, the enforcement of any rules made under section 222(1)(d) or (e) of the Criminal Justice Act 2003; or

(e) where a detention and training order is made, the enforcement of any requirements imposed under section 103(6)(b) of the Powers of Criminal Courts (Sentencing) Act 2000.

(4B) A court shall not exercise its power under subsection (4A) above without—

(a) affording the parties to the proceedings an opportunity to make representations; and

(b) taking into account any representations which are duly made.

(5) Subject to subsection (7) below, a court may, in relation to proceedings before it to which this section applies, by order dispense to any specified extent with the requirements of this section in relation to a child or young person who is concerned in the proceedings if it is satisfied—

(a) that it is appropriate to do so for the purpose of avoiding injustice to the child or young person; or

(b) that, as respects a child or young person to whom this paragraph applies who is unlawfully at large, it is necessary to dispense with those requirements for the purpose of apprehending him and bringing him before a court or returning him to the place in which he was in custody.

(6) Paragraph (b) of subsection (5) above applies to any child or young person who is charged with or has been convicted of—

(a) a violent offence,

(b) a sexual offence, or

(c) an offence punishable in the case of a person aged 21 or over with imprisonment for fourteen years or more.

(7) The court shall not exercise its power under subsection (5)(b) above—

(a) except in pursuance of an application by or on behalf of the Director of Public Prosecutions; and

(b) unless notice of the application has been given by the Director of Public Prosecutions to any legal representative of the child or young person.

(8) The court's power under subsection (5) above may be exercised by a single justice.

(9) If a report or picture is published or included in a programme service in contravention of subsection (1) above, the following persons, that is to say—

(a) in the case of publication of a written report or a picture as part of a newspaper, any proprietor, editor or publisher of the newspaper;

(b) in the case of the inclusion of a report or picture in a programme service, any body corporate which provides the service and any person having functions in relation to the programme corresponding to those of an editor of a newspaper,

shall be liable on summary conviction to a fine not exceeding level 5 on the standard scale.

(10) In any proceedings under Schedule 7 to the Powers of Criminal Courts (Sentencing) Act 2000 (proceedings for varying or revoking supervision orders) before a magistrates' court other than a youth court or on appeal from such a court it shall be the duty of the magistrates' court or the appellate court to announce in the course of the proceedings that this section applies to the proceedings; and if the court fails to do so this section shall not apply to the proceedings.

B1.11 Age of offender

It is the duty of a youth court to determine age when a young person is brought before the court. In most cases there is no dispute and a simple confirmation of the youth's date of birth will suffice. The court is, however, able to hear evidence on the issue. If the age is later found to be incorrect this has no bearing on any orders made by the court. Section 99(1) of the Children and Young Persons Act 1933 provides:

Children and Young Persons Act 1933, s 99

(1) Where a person, whether charged with an offence or not, is brought before any court otherwise than for the purpose of giving evidence, and it appears to the court that he is a child or young person, the court shall make due inquiry as to the age of that person, and for that purpose shall take such evidence as may be forthcoming at the hearing of the case, but an order or judgment of the court shall not be invalidated by any subsequent proof that the age of that person has not been correctly stated to the court, and the age presumed or declared by the court to be the age of the person so brought before it shall, for the purposes of this Act, be deemed to be the true age of that person, and, where it appears to the court that the person so brought before it has attained the age of eighteen years, that person shall for the purposes of this Act be deemed not to be a child or young person.

(2) Where in any charge or indictment for any offence under this Act or any of the offences mentioned in the First Schedule to this Act except as provided in that Schedule, it is alleged that the person by or in respect of whom the offence was committed was a child or young person or was under or had attained any specified age, and he appears to the court to have been at the date of the commission of the alleged offence a child or young person, or to have been under or to have attained the specified age, as the case may be, he shall for the purposes of this Act be presumed at that date to have been a child or young person or to have been under or to have attained that age, as the case may be, unless the contrary is proved.

(3) Where, in any charge or indictment for any offence under this Act or any of the offences mentioned in the First Schedule to this Act, it is alleged that the person in respect of whom the offence was committed was a child or was a young person, it shall not be a defence to prove that the person alleged to have been a child was a young person or the person alleged to have been a young person was a child in any case where the acts constituting the alleged offence would equally have been an offence if committed in respect of a young person or child respectively.

(4) Where a person is charged with an offence under this Act in respect of a person apparently under a specified age it shall be a defence to prove that the person was actually of or over that age.

B1.12 Youth becoming an adult during course of proceedings

The following scenarios detail what happens when a youth becomes an adult post charge:

- D aged 17 years is bailed to the youth court on a date when he would be 18 years of age. In this instance the proceedings had not begun as he had not appeared before the court, accordingly the court lacked jurisdiction to try D (*R v Amersham Juvenile Court, ex p Wilson* [1981] 2 All ER 315).

- D aged 17 is bailed to the youth court on a date when he would still be 17. D fails to appear at court, and the arrest warrant is executed only later when he is 18 years of age. In this instance no court has jurisdiction, and D will have to be recharged to an adult court (*R v Uxbridge Youth Court, ex p H* [1998] EWHC Admin 342).

- D aged 17 appears before the youth court. After he has attained 18 years the prosecution lay an alternative charge against D arising out of the same facts. Any new charge, even one based on the same facts, must commence in an adult court if the defendant is aged 18 years or over (*R v Chelsea Justices, ex p Director of Public Prosecutions* [1963] 3 All ER 657).

- D aged 17 years appears before the youth court. Section 24(1) of the Magistrates' Courts Act 1980 (see **B2.1**) does not apply in his case, and before he is put to plea he attains 18 years. In this case D is entitled in an appropriate case to elect Crown Court trial (*R v Islington North Juvenile Court, ex p Daley* [1983] 1 AC 347; see also *R v Lewes Juvenile Court, ex p Turner* (1984) 149 JP 186).

- D aged 17 years appears before the youth court. During the proceedings he attains 18 years of age. In this instance the court may continue to deal with the case (Children and Young Persons Act 1963, s 29(1)). Crucially, section 29 extends to the imposition of any sentence that would have been available to the court had the defendant not turned 18, for example, a referral order (see *A v Director of Public Prosecutions* [2002] 2 Cr App R (S) 88. Provided that the court has not begun to hear prosecution evidence it can instead exercise its discretion to remit D to the adult court (Crime and Disorder Act 1998, s 47(1)). Section 29 provides:

Children and Young Persons Act 1969, s 29

(1) Where proceedings in respect of a young person are begun [under section 1 of the Children and Young Persons Act 1969 or for an offence] and he attains the age of seventeen before the conclusion of the proceedings, the court may deal with the case and make any order which it could have made if he had not attained that age.

 See *Blackstone's Criminal Practice 2012* **D24**

B2 **Mode of Trial and Allocation**

At the time of writing the Sentencing Council had not issued its guideline in relation to allocation, nor had the modified mode of trial provisions in the Criminal Justice Act 2003 been enacted.

B2.1 **Homicide and other offences that cannot be tried in the youth court**

- An offence of murder, attempted murder, manslaughter, causing or allowing the death of a child or vulnerable adult, or infanticide must be committed to the Crown Court for trial (Magistrates' Courts Act 1980, s 24(1)), along with any other offences with which he is charged at the same time if the charges for both offences could be joined in the same indictment (Magistrates' Courts Act 1980, s 24(1A)).
- Offences falling within section 51A of the Firearms Act 1968 provided the youth was aged at least 16 years at the date of offence (see below).
- Section 29(3) of the Violent Crime Reduction Act 2006 (minimum sentences in certain cases of using someone to mind a weapon) would apply if he were convicted of the offence (see below).

Firearms Act 1968, s 51A

(1) This section applies where—
  (a) an individual is convicted of—
    (i) an offence under section 5(1)(a), (ab), (aba), (ac), (ad), (ae), (af) or (c) of this Act,
    (ii) an offence under section 5(1A)(a) of this Act, or
    (iii) an offence under any of the provisions of this Act listed in subsection (1A) in respect of a firearm or ammunition specified in section 5(1)(a), (ab), (aba), (ac), (ad), (ae), (af) or (c) or section 5(1A) (a) of this Act, and
  (b) the offence was committed after the commencement of this section and at a time when he was aged 16 or over.
(1A) The provisions are—
  (a) section 16 (possession of firearm with intent to injure);
  (b) section 16A (possession of firearm with intent to cause fear of violence);
  (c) section 17 (use of firearm to resist arrest);
  (d) section 18 (carrying firearm with criminal intent);
  (e) section 19 (carrying a firearm in a public place);
  (f) section 20(1) (trespassing in a building with firearm).
(2) The court shall impose an appropriate custodial sentence (or order for detention) for a term of at least the required minimum term (with or

---

without a fine) unless the court is of the opinion that there are exceptional circumstances relating to the offence or to the offender which justify its not doing so.

(3) Where an offence is found to have been committed over a period of two or more days, or at some time during a period of two or more days, it shall be taken for the purposes of this section to have been committed on the last of those days.

(4) In this section 'appropriate custodial sentence (or order for detention)' means—

  (a) in relation to England and Wales—

    (i) in the case of an offender who is aged 18 or over when convicted, a sentence of imprisonment, and

    (iii) in the case of an offender who is aged under 18 at that time, a sentence of detention under section 91 of the Powers of Criminal Courts (Sentencing) Act 2000;

  (b) in relation to Scotland—

    (i) in the case of an offender who is aged 21 or over when convicted, a sentence of imprisonment,

    (ii) in the case of an offender who is aged under 21 at that time (not being an offender mentioned in sub-paragraph (iii)), a sentence of detention under section 207 of the Criminal Procedure (Scotland) Act 1995, and

    (iii) in the case of an offender who is aged under 18 at that time and is subject to a supervision requirement, an order for detention under section 44, or sentence of detention under section 208, of that Act.

(5) In this section 'the required minimum term' means—

  (a) in relation to England and Wales—

    (i) in the case of an offender who was aged 18 or over when he committed the offence, five years, and

    (ii) in the case of an offender who was under 18 at that time, three years, and

  (b) in relation to Scotland—

    (i) in the case of an offender who was aged 21 or over when he committed the offence, five years, and

    (ii) in the case of an offender who was aged under 21 at that time, three years.

Violent Crime Reduction Act 2006, s 29(3)

(3) Where—

  (a) at the time of the offence, the offender was aged 16 or over, and

  (b) the dangerous weapon in respect of which the offence was committed was a firearm mentioned in section 5(1)(a) to (af) or (c) or section 5(1A) (a) of the 1968 Act (firearms possession of which attracts a minimum sentence),

the offender shall be liable, on conviction on indictment, to imprisonment for a term not exceeding 10 years or to a fine, or to both.

 See *Blackstone's Criminal Practice 2012* **D24.17**

B2.2 Youth charged with an adult

If a youth is jointly charged with an indictable only offence, the youth will be sent to the Crown Court with the adult unless it is not in the interests of justice to do so (this will be rare). Note that the youth does not have to be charged, or appear at court, at the same time. Any related either-way or summary offences will be sent alongside.

If a youth is jointly charged with an either-way offence the venue will be dictated by the adult. If the adult pleads guilty, the charge will be put to the youth (the youth has no right to elect Crown Court trial). If the adult pleads not guilty, the youth will be tried at the same venue as the adult (unless on election it is not in the interests of justice to try the youth with the adult).

 See *Blackstone's Criminal Practice 2012* **D24.31**

B2.3 Youth charged alone (or only with other youths)

If the youth is charged alone he will appear for trial in the youth court unless the offence is one of homicide or is a grave crime.

B2.4 Grave crimes

Homicide etc: Is the defendant charged with offence of homicide or a firearms offence that carries a mandatory minimum sentence (see Firearms Act 1968, s 51A(1), at **B2.1**)?	Yes—proceed to committal proceedings	No—consider grave crimes
Grave crimes: Is the defendant charged with one of the offences listed below this table AND a sentence of more than two years' detention would be a real possibility if he was convicted?	Yes—proceed to committal proceedings	No—proceed to summary trial

List of potential grave crimes:

- an offence punishable in the case of a person aged 21 or over with imprisonment for 14 years or more, not being an offence the sentence for which is fixed by law; or
- an offence under section 3 of the Sexual Offences Act 2003 (in this section, 'the 2003 Act') (sexual assault); or
- an offence under section 13 of the 2003 Act (child sex offences committed by children or young persons); or
- an offence under section 25 of the 2003 Act (sexual activity with a child family member); or

- an offence under section 26 of the 2003 Act (inciting a child family member to engage in sexual activity); or
- under subsection (1)(a), (ab), (aba), (ac), (ad), (ae), (af), or (c) of section 5 of the Firearms Act 1968 (prohibited weapons); or
- under subsection (1A)(a) of that section; or
- under subsection (1)(a), (ab), (aba), (ac), (ad), (ae), (af), or (c) of section 5 of the Firearms Act 1968 (prohibited weapons); or under subsection (1A)(a) of that section; or
- under section 51A(1A)(b), (e), or (f) of that Act and was committed in respect of a firearm or ammunition specified in section 5(1) (a), (ab), (aba), (ac), (ad), (ae), (af), or (c) or section 5(1A)(a) of that Act; or
- an offence under section 28 of the Violent Crime Reduction Act 2006 (using someone to mind a weapon).

In determining whether a sentence of more than two years would be imposed the court should ask itself what sentence was realistically possible bearing in mind the sentencing range (*Crown Prosecution Service v Newcastle Upon Tyne Youth Court* [2010] EWHC 2773 (Admin)).

 See *Blackstone's Criminal Practice 2012* **D24.22**

B2.5 Dangerous offenders

A court can send the youth for trial at the Crown Court if it is believed that the dangerous offender provisions will apply.

 See *Blackstone's Criminal Practice 2012* **D24.30**

B3 Bail: Young Offenders

B3.1 Provision of bail for juveniles

The provision of bail for juveniles (below the age of 17) is almost exactly the same as for adults, save that age determines where the juvenile will be remanded to if bail is refused.

> **Overview**
>
> **Remand will be local authority accommodation unless**
>
> (1) boy or girl aged 10 or 11 and the local authority can apply for a secure accommodation order under section 25 of the Children Act 1989 (see B3.5);
> (2) girl aged 12-16 or boy aged 12-14 AND security requirement met. In that case remand will be to secure accommodation;
> (3) boy aged 15 or 16 AND security requirement met AND vulnerable AND place available in secure accommodation. In that case remand will be to secure accommodation;
> (4) boy aged 15 or 16 AND security requirement met AND either the boy is not vulnerable, or is vulnerable but there is no secure accommodation available. In that case remand will be to remand centre or prison.

B3.2 Security requirement

In order to impose a security requirement the following conditions must be met where the juvenile is:

- charged with a violent or sexual offence, or an offence which for an adult is punishable with imprisonment of 14 years or more; or
- charged with or has been convicted of one or more imprisonable offences, which, together with any other imprisonable offences of which he has been convicted in any proceedings, amount to (or would amount to if he were convicted for the offences with which he is charged) a recent history of repeatedly committing imprisonable offences while remanded on bail or to local authority accommodation.

AND, in either case where:

- the court is of the opinion, after considering all the options for the remand of the person, that only remanding him to local authority accommodation with a security requirement would be adequate—
  (a) to protect the public from really serious harm from him; or
  (b) to prevent the commission by him of imprisonable offences.

The juvenile must be legally represented (or have refused representation) before the court can impose a security requirement.

B3.3 Vulnerability criteria

Section 23(5A) of the Children and Young Persons Act 1969 provides:

Children and Young Persons Act 1969, s 23(5A)

This subsection applies to a person if the court is of opinion that, by reason of his physical or emotional immaturity or a propensity of his to harm himself, it would be undesirable for him to be remanded to a remand centre or a prison.

Advocates should insist on seeing the assessment of vulnerability carried out by the Youth Offending Team (an *Asset* assessment). The key factors from this assessment that determine the vulnerability of a young person, and therefore influence what type of custodial establishment they are placed in, include:

- risk of self-harm;
- having been bullied, abused, neglected, or depressed;
- separation, loss, or care episodes;
- risk-taking;
- substance misuse;
- other health-related needs;
- ability to cope in a young offender institution or other custodial establishment.

B3.4 Conditions

A court can impose the same conditions as it could in the case of an adult. Conditions can also be imposed on the local authority.

B3.5 Applications for secure accommodation

An application for secure remand under section 25 of the Children Act 1989 in relation to a ten- or 11-year-old must be made to the Family Proceedings Court and cannot be remunerated under criminal legal aid. Remand must not exceed 28 days (although subsequent applications can be made).

An application under this section is also available where the secure accommodation requirements set out in **B3.2** are not met in relation to a child 12 years or above (*Re G (A Child) (Secure Accommodation Order)* (2001) FLR 884). In this instance regulation 6(2) of the Children (Secure Accommodation) Regulations 1991 provides that a court cannot securely remand unless the child is likely to abscond from such accommodation or the child is likely to injure himself or other people if he is kept in any other accommodation.

B3 Bail: Young Offenders

Section 25 of the Children Act 1989 provides:

Children Act 1989, s 25

(1) Subject to the following provisions of this section, a child who is being looked after by a local authority may not be placed, and, if placed, may not be kept, in accommodation provided for the purpose of restricting liberty ('secure accommodation') unless it appears—

  (a) that—

    (i) he has a history of absconding and is likely to abscond from any other description of accommodation; and

    (ii) if he absconds, he is likely to suffer significant harm; or

  (b) that if he is kept in any other description of accommodation he is likely to injure himself or other persons.

(2) The appropriate national authority may by regulations—

  (a) specify a maximum period—

    (i) beyond which a child may not be kept in secure accommodation without the authority of the court; and

    (ii) for which the court may authorise a child to be kept in secure accommodation;

  (b) empower the court from time to time to authorise a child to be kept in secure accommodation for such further period as the regulations may specify; and

  (c) provide that applications to the court under this section shall be made only by local authorities.

(3) It shall be the duty of a court hearing an application under this section to determine whether any relevant criteria for keeping a child in secure accommodation are satisfied in his case.

(4) If a court determines that any such criteria are satisfied, it shall make an order authorising the child to be kept in secure accommodation and specifying the maximum period for which he may be so kept.

(5) On any adjournment of the hearing of an application under this section, a court may make an interim order permitting the child to be kept during the period of the adjournment in secure accommodation.

(6) No court shall exercise the powers conferred by this section in respect of a child who is not legally represented in that court unless, having been informed of his right to apply for representation funded by the Legal Services Commission as part of the Community Legal Service or Criminal Defence Service and having had the opportunity to do so, he refused or failed to apply.

(7) The appropriate national authority may by regulations provide that—

  (a) this section shall or shall not apply to any description of children specified in the regulations;

  (b) this section shall have effect in relation to children of a description specified in the regulations subject to such modifications as may be so specified;

  (c) such other provisions as may be so specified shall have effect for the purpose of determining whether a child of a description specified in the regulations may be placed or kept in secure accommodation.

(8) The giving of an authorisation under this section shall not prejudice any power of any court in England and Wales or Scotland to give directions relating to the child to whom the authorisation relates.

(9) This section is subject to section 20(8).

B3.6 Change of circumstances

See A8.2.

 See *Blackstone's Criminal Practice 2012* **D24.6**

B4 **Sentencing**

B4.1 **Overview**

The following sentencing options are available in relation to young offenders. Reference should be made to **Part D** for individual sentences.

Age (last birthday)	10–13	14	15	16–17
Absolute discharge	Y	Y	Y	Y
Conditional discharge (note that a conditional discharge cannot be imposed if the offender has received a final warning in the previous 24 months unless exceptional circumstances are found). A conditional discharge in respect to a youth can be for a maximum period of 3 years.	Y	Y	Y	Y
Referral order (for a period of between 3 and 12 months)	Y	Y	Y	Y
Fine	Y: maximum £250. Order must be made against parent/guardian unless unreasonable in the circumstances	Y: maximum £1,000. Order must be made against parent/guardian unless unreasonable in the circumstances	Y: maximum £1,000. Order must be made against parent/guardian unless unreasonable in the circumstances	Y: maximum £1,000
Compensation order	Y	Y	Y	Y
Costs	Y	Y	Y	Y
Reparation order (max 24 hours)	Y	Y	Y	Y
Youth rehabilitation order	Y (but cannot impose residence requirement or unpaid work). Can only impose ISSR or fostering if persistent offender	Y (but cannot impose residence requirement or unpaid work). Can only impose ISSR or fostering if persistent offender	Y (but cannot impose residence requirement or unpaid work).	Y

Age (last birthday)	10–13	14	15	16–17
Detention and training order (period of 4, 6, 8, 10, 12, 18, or 24 months)	10 or 11 years: No 12 or 13 years: Yes if persistent offender	14-year-old if persistent offender	Y	Y

B4.2 Orders in respect to parents and guardians

Regard should be had to the court's powers to:

- bind over a parent or guardian, and/or impose financial sanctions (see **D44**);
- make a parenting order (see **D43**).

 See *Blackstone's Criminal Practice 2012* **D24.63–D24.72**

Part C
Offences

C1 **Animal Offences**

C1.1 **Animal cruelty**

Animal Welfare Act 2006, ss 4, 5, 6, 7, 8, and 9

These sections provide for offences in relation to unnecessary suffering, mutilation, docking of dogs' tails, administration of poisons, and fighting.

Animal Welfare Act 2006, ss 4(1)–(2), 5(1)–(2), (6), 6(1)–(12), 7, 8, and 9

4 Unnecessary suffering

(1) A person commits an offence if—
    (a) an act of his, or a failure of his to act, causes an animal to suffer,
    (b) he knew, or ought reasonably to have known, that the act, or failure to act, would have that effect or be likely to do so,
    (c) the animal is a protected animal, and
    (d) the suffering is unnecessary.
(2) A person commits an offence if—
    (a) he is responsible for an animal,
    (b) an act, or failure to act, of another person causes the animal to suffer,
    (c) he permitted that to happen or failed to take such steps (whether by way of supervising the other person or otherwise) as were reasonable in all the circumstances to prevent that happening, and
    (d) the suffering is unnecessary. . . .

5 Mutilation

(1) A person commits an offence if—
    (a) he carries out a prohibited procedure on a protected animal;
    (b) he causes such a procedure to be carried out on such an animal.
(2) A person commits an offence if—
    (a) he is responsible for an animal,
    (b) another person carries out a prohibited procedure on the animal, and
    (c) he permitted that to happen or failed to take such steps (whether by way of supervising the other person or otherwise) as were reasonable in all the circumstances to prevent that happening.
[. . .]
(6) Nothing in this section applies to the removal of the whole or any part of a dog's tail.

6 Docking of dogs' tails

(1) A person commits an offence if—
    (a) he removes the whole or any part of a dog's tail, otherwise than for the purpose of its medical treatment;
    (b) he causes the whole or any part of a dog's tail to be removed by another person, otherwise than for the purpose of its medical treatment.
(2) A person commits an offence if—
    (a) he is responsible for a dog,

   (b) another person removes the whole or any part of the dog's tail, otherwise than for the purpose of its medical treatment, and
   (c) he permitted that to happen or failed to take such steps (whether by way of supervising the other person or otherwise) as were reasonable in all the circumstances to prevent that happening.
(3) Subsections (1) and (2) do not apply if the dog is a certified working dog that is not more than 5 days old.
(4) For the purposes of subsection (3), a dog is a certified working dog if a veterinary surgeon has certified, in accordance with regulations made by the appropriate national authority, that the first and second conditions mentioned below are met.
(5) The first condition referred to in subsection (4) is that there has been produced to the veterinary surgeon such evidence as the appropriate national authority may by regulations require for the purpose of showing that the dog is likely to be used for work in connection with—
   (a) law enforcement,
   (b) activities of Her Majesty's armed forces,
   (c) emergency rescue,
   (d) lawful pest control, or
   (e) the lawful shooting of animals.
(6) The second condition referred to in subsection (4) is that the dog is of a type specified for the purposes of this subsection by regulations made by the appropriate national authority.
(7) It is a defence for a person accused of an offence under subsection (1) or (2) to show that he reasonably believed that the dog was one in relation to which subsection (3) applies.
(8) A person commits an offence if—
   (a) he owns a subsection (3) dog, and
   (b) fails to take reasonable steps to secure that, before the dog is 3 months old, it is identified as a subsection (3) dog in accordance with regulations made by the appropriate national authority.
(9) A person commits an offence if—
   (a) he shows a dog at an event to which members of the public are admitted on payment of a fee,
   (b) the dog's tail has been wholly or partly removed (in England and Wales or elsewhere), and
   (c) removal took place on or after the commencement day.
(10) Where a dog is shown only for the purpose of demonstrating its working ability, subsection (9) does not apply if the dog is a subsection (3) dog.
(11) It is a defence for a person accused of an offence under subsection (9) to show that he reasonably believed—
   (a) that the event was not one to which members of the public were admitted on payment of an entrance fee,
   (b) that the removal took place before the commencement day, or
   (c) that the dog was one in relation to which subsection (10) applies.
(12) A person commits an offence if he knowingly gives false information to a veterinary surgeon in connection with the giving of a certificate for the purposes of this section.

7 Administration of poisons etc.

(1) A person commits an offence if, without lawful authority or reasonable excuse, he—

  (a) administers any poisonous or injurious drug or substance to a protected animal, knowing it to be poisonous or injurious, or

  (b) causes any poisonous or injurious drug or substance to be taken by a protected animal, knowing it to be poisonous or injurious.

(2) A person commits an offence if—

  (a) he is responsible for an animal,

  (b) without lawful authority or reasonable excuse, another person administers a poisonous or injurious drug or substance to the animal or causes the animal to take such a drug or substance, and

  (c) he permitted that to happen or, knowing the drug or substance to be poisonous or injurious, he failed to take such steps (whether by way of supervising the other person or otherwise) as were reasonable in all the circumstances to prevent that happening.

(3) In this section, references to a poisonous or injurious drug or substance include a drug or substance which, by virtue of the quantity or manner in which it is administered or taken, has the effect of a poisonous or injurious drug or substance.

8 Fighting etc.

(1) A person commits an offence if he—

  (a) causes an animal fight to take place, or attempts to do so;

  (b) knowingly receives money for admission to an animal fight;

  (c) knowingly publicises a proposed animal fight;

  (d) provides information about an animal fight to another with the intention of enabling or encouraging attendance at the fight;

  (e) makes or accepts a bet on the outcome of an animal fight or on the likelihood of anything occurring or not occurring in the course of an animal fight;

  (f) takes part in an animal fight;

  (g) has in his possession anything designed or adapted for use in connection with an animal fight with the intention of its being so used;

  (h) keeps or trains an animal for use for in connection with an animal fight;

  (i) keeps any premises for use for an animal fight.

(2) A person commits an offence if, without lawful authority or reasonable excuse, he is present at an animal fight.

(3) A person commits an offence if, without lawful authority or reasonable excuse, he—

  (a) knowingly supplies a video recording of an animal fight,

  (b) knowingly publishes a video recording of an animal fight,

  (c) knowingly shows a video recording of an animal fight to another, or

  (d) possesses a video recording of an animal fight, knowing it to be such a recording, with the intention of supplying it.

(4) Subsection (3) does not apply if the video recording is of an animal fight that took place—

  (a) outside Great Britain, or

  (b) before the commencement date.

(5) Subsection (3) does not apply—
  (a) in the case of paragraph (a), to the supply of a video recording for inclusion in a programme service;
  (b) in the case of paragraph (b) or (c), to the publication or showing of a video recording by means of its inclusion in a programme service;
  (c) in the case of paragraph (d), by virtue of intention to supply for inclusion in a programme service.

. . .

(7) In this section—
  'animal fight' means an occasion on which a protected animal is placed with an animal, or with a human, for the purpose of fighting, wrestling or baiting;
  . . .;
  'programme service' has the same meaning as in the Communications Act 2003 (c. 21);
  'video recording' means a recording, in any form, from which a moving image may by any means be reproduced and includes data stored on a computer disc or by other electronic means which is capable of conversion into a moving image.

(8) In this section—
  (a) references to supplying or publishing a video recording are to supplying or publishing a video recording in any manner, including, in relation to a video recording in the form of data stored electronically, by means of transmitting such data;
  (b) references to showing a video recording are to showing a moving image reproduced from a video recording by any means.

[Note. Subsections 3, 4, 5, and 6 were not in force at the time of writing.]

9 Duty of person responsible for animal to ensure welfare

(1) A person commits an offence if he does not take such steps as are reasonable in all the circumstances to ensure that the needs of an animal for which he is responsible are met to the extent required by good practice.

(2) For the purposes of this Act, an animal's needs shall be taken to include—
  (a) its need for a suitable environment,
  (b) its need for a suitable diet,
  (c) its need to be able to exhibit normal behaviour patterns,
  (d) any need it has to be housed with, or apart from, other animals, and
  (e) its need to be protected from pain, suffering, injury and disease.

(3) The circumstances to which it is relevant to have regard when applying subsection (1) include, in particular—
  (a) any lawful purpose for which the animal is kept, and
  (b) any lawful activity undertaken in relation to the animal.

(4) Nothing in this section applies to the destruction of an animal in an appropriate and humane manner.

SO But note that a magistrates' court may try an information relating to an offence under this Act if the information is laid—
   (a) before the end of the period of three years beginning with the date of the commission of the offence, and
   (b) before the end of the period of six months beginning with the date on which evidence which the prosecutor thinks is sufficient to justify the proceedings comes to his knowledge.

£20,000 fine and/or 6 months imprisonment (sections 4, 5, 6(1) and (2), 7, and 8)

Level 5 fine and/or 6 months imprisonment (section 9)

C1.1.1 *Sentencing*

Offence seriousness (culpability and harm)		
A. Identify the appropriate starting point Starting points based on first time offender pleading not guilty		
Examples of nature of activity	**Starting point**	**Range**
One impulsive act causing little or no injury; short-term neglect	Band C fine	Band B fine to medium level community order
Several incidents of deliberate ill-treatment/frightening animal(s); medium-term neglect	High level community order	Medium level community order to 12 weeks custody
Attempt to kill/torture; animal baiting/conducting or permitting cock-fighting etc; prolonged neglect	18 weeks custody	12 to 26 weeks custody

Offence seriousness (culpability and harm)	
B. Consider the effect of aggravating and mitigating factors (other than those within examples above) The following may be particularly relevant but **these lists are not exhaustive**	
Factors indicating higher culpability 1. Offender in position of special responsibility 2. Adult involves children in offending 3. Animal(s) kept for livelihood 4. Use of weapon 5. Offender ignored advice/warnings 6. Offence committed for commercial gain **Factors indicating greater degree of harm** 1. Serious injury or death 2. Several animals affected	**Factors indicating lower culpability** 1. Offender induced by others 2. Ignorance of appropriate care 3. Offender with limited capacity

C1.1.2 *Deprivation order*

Section 33 of the Animal Welfare Act 2006 provides for a convicted person to be deprived of their animals:

Animal Welfare Act 2006, s 33

(1) If the person convicted of an offence under any of sections 4, 5, 6(1) and (2), 7, 8 and 9 is the owner of an animal in relation to which the offence was committed, the court by or before which he is convicted may, instead of or in addition to dealing with him in any other way, make an order depriving him of ownership of the animal and for its disposal.

(2) Where the owner of an animal is convicted of an offence under section 34(9) because ownership of the animal is in breach of a disqualification under section 34(2), the court by or before which he is convicted may, instead of or in addition to dealing with him in any other way, make an order depriving him of ownership of the animal and for its disposal.

(3) Where the animal in respect of which an order under subsection (1) or (2) is made has any dependent offspring, the order may include provision depriving the person to whom it relates of ownership of the offspring and for its disposal.

(4) Where a court makes an order under subsection (1) or (2), it may—
   (a) appoint a person to carry out, or arrange for the carrying out of, the order;
   (b) require any person who has possession of an animal to which the order applies to deliver it up to enable the order to be carried out;
   (c) give directions with respect to the carrying out of the order;
   (d) confer additional powers (including power to enter premises where an animal to which the order applies is being kept) for the purpose of, or in connection with, the carrying out of the order;
   (e) order the offender to reimburse the expenses of carrying out the order.

(5) Directions under subsection (4)(c) may—
   (a) specify the manner in which an animal is to be disposed of, or
   (b) delegate the decision about the manner in which an animal is to be disposed of to a person appointed under subsection (4)(a).

(6) Where a court decides not to make an order under subsection (1) or (2) in relation to an offender, it shall—
   (a) give its reasons for the decision in open court, and
   (b) if it is a magistrates' court, cause them to be entered in the register of its proceedings.

(7) Subsection (6) does not apply where the court makes an order under section 34(1) in relation to the offender.

(8) In subsection (1), the reference to an animal in relation to which an offence was committed includes, in the case of an offence under section 8, an animal which took part in an animal fight in relation to which the offence was committed.

(9) In this section, references to disposing of an animal include destroying it.

C1.1.3 *Disqualification order*

Section 34 of the Animal Welfare Act 2006 provides for disqualification orders to be made against convicted persons, thereby making it an offence for them to be involved with owning, keeping, or otherwise being involved in the control of animals:

Animal Welfare Act 2006, s 34

(1) If a person is convicted of an offence to which this section applies, the court by or before which he is convicted may, instead of or in addition to dealing with him in any other way, make an order disqualifying him under any one or more of subsections (2) to (4) for such period as it thinks fit.

(2) Disqualification under this subsection disqualifies a person—
   (a) from owning animals,
   (b) from keeping animals,
   (c) from participating in the keeping of animals, and
   (d) from being party to an arrangement under which he is entitled to control or influence the way in which animals are kept.

(3) Disqualification under this subsection disqualifies a person from dealing in animals.

(4) Disqualification under this subsection disqualifies a person—
   (a) from transporting animals, and
   (b) from arranging for the transport of animals.

(5) Disqualification under subsection (2), (3) or (4) may be imposed in relation to animals generally, or in relation to animals of one or more kinds.

(6) The court by which an order under subsection (1) is made may specify a period during which the offender may not make an application under section 43(1) for termination of the order.

. . .

(10) This section applies to an offence under any of sections 4, 5, 6(1) and (2), 7, 8, 9 and 13(6) and subsection (9).

C1.1.4 *Destruction orders*

Sections 37 and 38 of the Animal Welfare Act 2006 allow for destruction orders to be made in appropriate cases:

Animal Welfare Act 2006, ss 37 and 38

37 Destruction in the interests of the animal

(1) The court by or before which a person is convicted of an offence under any of sections 4, 5, 6(1) and (2), 7, 8(1) and (2) and 9 may order the destruction of an animal in relation to which the offence was committed if it is satisfied, on the basis of evidence given by a veterinary surgeon, that it is appropriate to do so in the interests of the animal.

---

(2) A court may not make an order under subsection (1) unless—

    (a) it has given the owner of the animal an opportunity to be heard, or

    (b) it is satisfied that it is not reasonably practicable to communicate with the owner.

(3) Where a court makes an order under subsection (1), it may—

    (a) appoint a person to carry out, or arrange for the carrying out of, the order;

    (b) require a person who has possession of the animal to deliver it up to enable the order to be carried out;

    (c) give directions with respect to the carrying out of the order (including directions about how the animal is to be dealt with until it is destroyed);

    (d) confer additional powers (including power to enter premises where the animal is being kept) for the purpose of, or in connection with, the carrying out of the order;

    (e) order the offender or another person to reimburse the expenses of carrying out the order.

(4) Where a court makes an order under subsection (1), each of the offender and, if different, the owner of the animal may—

    (a) in the case of an order made by a magistrates' court, appeal against the order to the Crown Court;

    (b) in the case of an order made by the Crown Court, appeal against the order to the Court of Appeal.

(5) Subsection (4) does not apply if the court by which the order is made directs that it is appropriate in the interests of the animal that the carrying out of the order should not be delayed.

(6) In subsection (1), the reference to an animal in relation to which an offence was committed includes, in the case of an offence under section 8(1) or (2), an animal which took part in an animal fight in relation to which the offence was committed.

38 Destruction of animals involved in fighting offences

(1) The court by or before which a person is convicted of an offence under section 8(1) or (2) may order the destruction of an animal in relation to which the offence was committed on grounds other than the interests of the animal.

(2) A court may not make an order under subsection (1) unless—

    (a) it has given the owner of the animal an opportunity to be heard, or

    (b) it is satisfied that it is not reasonably practicable to communicate with the owner.

(3) Where a court makes an order under subsection (1), it may—

    (a) appoint a person to carry out, or arrange for the carrying out of, the order;

    (b) require a person who has possession of the animal to deliver it up to enable the order to be carried out;

    (c) give directions with respect to the carrying out of the order (including directions about how the animal is to be dealt with until it is destroyed);

    (d) confer additional powers (including power to enter premises where the animal is being kept) for the purpose of, or in connection with, the carrying out of the order;

(e) order the offender or another person to reimburse the expenses of carrying out the order.

(4) Where a court makes an order under subsection (1) in relation to an animal which is owned by a person other than the offender, that person may—

(a) in the case of an order made by a magistrates' court, appeal against the order to the Crown Court;

(b) in the case of an order made by the Crown Court, appeal against the order to the Court of Appeal.

(5) In subsection (1), the reference to an animal in relation to which the offence was committed includes an animal which took part in an animal fight in relation to which the offence was committed.

C1.1.5 Key points

- The six-month limitation period for summary offences under this Act can be disapplied in certain circumstances (see section 31 of the 2006 Act and *RSPCA v Johnson* [2009] EWHC 2702 (Admin)).
- References to a person responsible for an animal are to a person responsible for an animal whether on a permanent or a temporary basis.
- References to being responsible for an animal include being in charge of it.
- A person who owns an animal shall always be regarded as being a person who is responsible for it.
- A person shall be treated as responsible for any animal for which a person under the age of 16 years of whom he has actual care and control is responsible.
- Protected animal refers to an animal commonly domesticated in the British Isles, under the control of man, or not living in a wild state.

The considerations to which it is relevant to have regard when determining for the purposes of this section whether suffering is unnecessary include:

- whether the suffering could reasonably have been avoided or reduced;
- whether the conduct which caused the suffering was in compliance with any relevant enactment or any relevant provisions of a licence or code of practice issued under an enactment;
- whether the conduct which caused the suffering was for a legitimate purpose, such as:
  - the purpose of benefiting the animal, or
  - the purpose of protecting a person, property, or another animal;
- whether the suffering was proportionate to the purpose of the conduct concerned;
- whether the conduct concerned was in all the circumstances that of a reasonably competent and humane person.

Nothing in this section applies to the destruction of an animal in an appropriate and humane manner.

When considering making a disqualification order under section 4 of the Act, regard can be had to any previous convictions (*Ward v RSPCA*, unreported, 29 January 2010).

C1.1.6 *Animal welfare: section 9*

The welfare offence in this section extends to non-farmed animals; similar provisions as are found in the Welfare of Farmed Animals (England) Regulations 2000 (made under Part 1 of the Agriculture (Miscellaneous Provisions) Act 1968), which ensure the welfare of livestock situated on agricultural land. A duty to ensure welfare will therefore apply to all animals for which someone is responsible, as defined in section 3. Where someone is responsible for an animal, he has a duty to take steps that are reasonable in all the circumstances to ensure its needs are met to the extent required by good practice (subsection (1)).

Subsection (3) specifies certain matters to which the courts should have regard when considering whether a person has committed an offence under this section. The provision recognizes that some otherwise lawful practices may prevent or hinder a person from ensuring that all of the welfare needs specified in subsection (2) can be met, and requires the courts to take this into account when considering what is reasonable in the circumstances of the case.

C1.2 **Dangerous dogs**

Dangerous Dogs Act 1991, ss 1, 3

Dangerous Dogs Act 1991, s 1

(1) This section applies to—
   (a) any dog of the type known as the pit bull terrier;
   (b) any dog of the type known as the Japanese tosa; and
   (c) any dog of any type designated for the purposes of this section by an order of the Secretary of State, being a type appearing to him to be bred for fighting or to have the characteristics of a type bred for that purpose.
(2) No person shall—
   (a) breed, or breed from, a dog to which this section applies;
   (b) sell or exchange such a dog or offer, advertise or expose such a dog for sale or exchange;

(c) make or offer to make a gift of such a dog or advertise or expose such a dog as a gift;

(d) allow such a dog of which he is the owner or of which he is for the time being in charge to be in a public place without being muzzled and kept on a lead; or

(e) abandon such a dog of which he is the owner or, being the owner or for the time being in charge of such a dog, allow it to stray.

(3) After such day as the Secretary of State may by order appoint for the purposes of this subsection no person shall have any dog to which this section applies in his possession or custody except—

(a) in pursuance of the power of seizure conferred by the subsequent provisions of this Act; or

(b) in accordance with an order for its destruction made under those provisions;

but the Secretary of State shall by order make a scheme for the payment to the owners of such dogs who arrange for them to be destroyed before that day of sums specified in or determined under the scheme in respect of those dogs and the cost of their destruction.

(4) Subsection (2)(b) and (c) above shall not make unlawful anything done with a view to the dog in question being removed from the United Kingdom before the day appointed under subsection (3) above.

(5) The Secretary of State may by order provide that the prohibition in subsection (3) above shall not apply in such cases and subject to compliance with such conditions as are specified in the order and any such provision may take the form of a scheme of exemption containing such arrangements (including provision for the payment of charges or fees) as he thinks appropriate.

(6) A scheme under subsection (3) or (5) above may provide for specified functions under the scheme to be discharged by such persons or bodies as the Secretary of State thinks appropriate.

(7) Any person who contravenes this section is guilty of an offence and liable on summary conviction to imprisonment for a term not exceeding six months or a fine not exceeding level 5 on the standard scale or both except that a person who publishes an advertisement in contravention of subsection (2)(b) or (c)—

(a) shall not on being convicted be liable to imprisonment if he shows that he published the advertisement to the order of someone else and did not himself devise it; and

(b) shall not be convicted if, in addition, he shows that he did not know and had no reasonable cause to suspect that it related to a dog to which this section applies.

Dangerous Dogs Act 1991, s 3

(1) If a dog is dangerously out of control in a public place—

(a) the owner; and

(b) if different, the person for the time being in charge of the dog, is guilty of an offence, or, if the dog while so out of control injures any person, an aggravated offence, under this subsection.

C1 **Animal Offences**

(2) In proceedings for an offence under subsection (1) above against a person who is the owner of a dog but was not at the material time in charge of it, it shall be a defence for the accused to prove that the dog was at the material time in the charge of a person whom he reasonably believed to be a fit and proper person to be in charge of it.

(3) If the owner or, if different, the person for the time being in charge of a dog allows it to enter a place which is not a public place but where it is not permitted to be and while it is there—

    (a) it injures any person; or

    (b) there are grounds for reasonable apprehension that it will do so,

he is guilty of an offence, or, if the dog injures any person, an aggravated offence, under this subsection.

(4) A person guilty of an offence under subsection (1) or (3) above other than an aggravated offence is liable on summary conviction to imprisonment for a term not exceeding six months or a fine not exceeding level 5 on the standard scale or both; and a person guilty of an aggravated offence under either of those subsections is liable—

    (a) on summary conviction, to imprisonment for a term not exceeding six months or a fine not exceeding the statutory maximum or both;

    (b) on conviction on indictment, to imprisonment for a term not exceeding two years or a fine or both.

(5) It is hereby declared for the avoidance of doubt that an order under section 2 of the Dogs Act 1871 (order on complaint that dog is dangerous and not kept under proper control)—

    (a) may be made whether or not the dog is shown to have injured any person; and

    (b) may specify the measures to be taken for keeping the dog under proper control, whether by muzzling, keeping on a lead, excluding it from specified places or otherwise.

(6) If it appears to a court on a complaint under section 2 of the said Act of 1871 that the dog to which the complaint relates is a male and would be less dangerous if neutered the court may under that section make an order requiring it to be neutered.

(7) The reference in section 1(3) of the Dangerous Dogs Act 1989 (penalties) to failing to comply with an order under section 2 of the said Act of 1871 to keep a dog under proper control shall include a reference to failing to comply with any other order made under that section; but no order shall be made under that section by virtue of subsection (6) above where the matters complained of arose before the coming into force of that subsection.

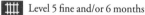 Level 5 fine and/or 6 months

Aggravated offence under either s 3(1) or (3) is either way— level 5 fine and/or 6 months/2 years on indictment.

An offence is aggravated if the dog injures a person.

In relation to an offence under s 1(2)(b) or (c) see section 1(7) which limits sentence in certain circumstances.

C1.2.1 *Sentencing*

There are no sentencing guidelines for this offence. A sentence of three months has been upheld for a person of good character on a guilty plea whose pack of dogs attacked a boy in a park (*R v Cox* [2004] EWCA Crim 282). A six-month sentence was imposed on appeal where two dogs attacked an elderly person and severely injured them (*R v Lee* [2009] EWCA Crim 2046).

On conviction there is power under section 4 of the 1991 Act to make destruction and disqualification orders:

Dangerous Dogs Act 1991, s 4(1)–(3)

(1) Where a person is convicted of an offence under section 1 or 3(1) or (3) above or of an offence under an order made under section 2 above the court—
   (a) may order the destruction of any dog in respect of which the offence was committed and, subject to subsection (1A) below, shall do so in the case of an offence under section 1 or an aggravated offence under section 3(1) or (3) above; and
   (b) may order the offender to be disqualified, for such period as the court thinks fit, for having custody of a dog.
(1A) Nothing in subsection (1)(a) above shall require the court to order the destruction of a dog if the court is satisfied—
   (a) that the dog would not constitute a danger to public safety; and
   (b) where the dog was born before 30th November 1991 and is subject to the prohibition in section 1(3) above, that there is a good reason why the dog has not been exempted from that prohibition.
(2) Where a court makes an order under subsection (1)(a) above for the destruction of a dog owned by a person other than the offender, the owner may appeal to the Crown Court against the order.
(3) A dog shall not be destroyed pursuant to an order under subsection (1)(a) above—
   (a) until the end of the period for giving notice of appeal against the conviction or, against the order; and
   (b) if notice of appeal is given within that period, until the appeal is determined or withdrawn,
   unless the offender and, in a case to which subsection (2) above applies, the owner of the dog give notice to the court that made the order that there is to be no appeal.

C1.2.2 Key points

- The appointed day for the purposes of section 1(3) was 30 November 1991.
- For 'type' see *Crown Court at Knightsbridge, ex p Dune* [1993] 4 All ER 491.
- 'Dangerously out of control' is defined under section 10(3) of the Act:

> For the purposes of this Act a dog shall be regarded as dangerously out of control on any occasion on which there are grounds for reasonable apprehension that it will injure any person, whether or not it actually does so, but references to a dog injuring a person or there being grounds for reasonable apprehension that it will do so do not include references to any case in which the dog is being used for a lawful purpose by a constable or a person in the service of the Crown.

- Regard must be had to the behaviour of the dog and the degree of control exercised by its handler. The fact that the dog has not displayed any previous bad traits was of relevance but not conclusive (*R v Gedmintaite* [2008] EWCA Crim 814).
- It is sufficient that the danger is only to other dogs (*Briscoe v Shattock* (1998) 163 JP 201), but a dog hunting and killing rabbits and other small animals is part of a dog's nature and does make it dangerous (*Sansom v Chief Constable of Kent* [1981] Crim LR 617).
- The owner of the dog has a defence under section 3(2) if another fit and proper person was in charge of the dog at the material time. Whether a person is a fit and proper person will depend on all of the circumstances. The dog must have been left with an identifiable person, it was not sufficient merely to say that different members of a family looked after the dog at different times (*R v Huddart* [1999] Crim LR 568).
- It is irrelevant that the owner did not anticipate the behaviour of the dog (*R v Bezzina* (1994) 158 JP 671).
- A person who relinquishes physical control of a dog by passing the lead to another may remain in joint control of the dog (*L v Crown Prosecution Service*, unreported, 10 February 2010). Plain evidence is required to demonstrate that control has been passed to another (*R v Huddart* (1999) Crim LR 568).
- Public place includes the inside of a vehicle which is itself in a public place (*Bates v Director of Public Prosecutions* (1993) 157 JP 1004).
- There are no defences in relation to section 1 (see *Director of Public Prosecutions v Kellett* (1994) 158 JP 1138 (intoxication) and *Cichon v Director of Public Prosecutions* [1994] Crim LR (welfare of the animal—unmuzzling to allow the dog to be sick).
- In relation to destruction orders all advocates should be aware of the guidance issued by the Court of Appeal in *R v Flack* [2008] 2 Cr App R (S) 395 and what was said in relation to suspended orders.

C1.3 **Dog worrying livestock**

Dogs (Protection of Livestock) Act 1953, s 1

(1) Subject to the provisions of this section, if a dog worries livestock on any agricultural land, the owner of the dog, and, if it is in the charge of a person other than its owner, that person also, shall be guilty of an offence under this Act.

(2) For the purposes of this Act worrying livestock means—
   (a) attacking livestock, or
   (b) chasing livestock in such a way as may reasonably be expected to cause injury or suffering to the livestock or, in the case of females, abortion, or loss of or diminution in their produce, or
   (c) being at large (that is to say not on a lead or otherwise under close control) in a field or enclosure in which there are sheep.

(2A) Subsection (2)(c) of this section shall not apply in relation to—
   (a) a dog owned by, or in the charge of, the occupier of the field or enclosure or the owner of the sheep or a person authorised by either of those persons; or
   (b) a police dog, a guide dog, trained sheep dog, a working gun dog or a pack of hounds.

(3) A person shall not be guilty of an offence under this Act by reason of anything done by a dog, if at the material time the livestock are trespassing on the land in question and the dog is owned by, or in the charge of, the occupier of that land or a person authorised by him, except in a case where the said person causes the dog to attack the livestock.

(4) The owner of a dog shall not be convicted of an offence under this Act in respect of the worrying of livestock by the dog if he proves that at the time when the dog worried the livestock it was in the charge of some other person, whom he reasonably believed to be a fit and proper person to be in charge of the dog.

 SO

 Fine level 3

 See *Blackstone's Criminal Practice 2012* **B20**

C1.4 **Guard dogs**

Guard Dogs Act 1975, ss 1, 7

1 Control of guard dogs

(1) A person shall not use or permit the use of a guard dog at any premises unless a person ("the handler") who is capable of controlling the dog is present on the premises and the dog is under the control of the handler at

all times while it is being so used except while it is secured so that it is not at liberty to go freely about the premises.

(2) The handler of a guard dog shall keep the dog under his control at all times while it is being used as a guard dog at any premises except—

    (a) while another handler has control over the dog; or

    (b) while the dog is secured so that it is not at liberty to go freely about the premises.

(3) A person shall not use or permit the use of a guard dog at any premises unless a notice containing a warning that a guard dog is present is clearly exhibited at each entrance to the premises.

7 Interpretation

In this Act, unless the context otherwise requires—

    "guard dog" means a dog which is being used to protect—

    (a) premises; or

    (b) property kept on the premises; or

    (c) a person guarding the premises or such property;

SO

Fine level 3

See *Blackstone's Criminal Practice 2012* **B20.8**

C2 Anti-Social Behaviour Order, Breach of

> **Crime and Disorder Act 1998, s 1(10)**
>
> If without reasonable excuse a person does anything which he is prohibited from doing by an anti-social behaviour order, he is guilty of an offence.

EW

 Level 5 fine and/or 6 months/5 years. When section 41 Crime and Security Act 2010 comes into force a parenting order must be made in certain circumstances following a conviction for breaching an anti-social behaviour order (see **D38.2**).

C2.1 *Sentencing*

Nature of failure and harm	Starting point	Sentencing range
Serious harassment, alarm, or distress has been caused or where such harm was intended	26 weeks custody	Custody threshold—2 years custody
Lesser degree of harassment, alarm, or distress, where such harm was intended, or where it would have been likely if the offender had not been apprehended	6 weeks custody	Medium level community order to 26 weeks custody
No harassment, alarm, or distress was actually caused by the breach and none was intended by the offender	Low level community order	Band B fine to medium level community order

Aggravating factors	Mitigating factors
1. Offender has a history of disobedience to court orders 2. Breach was committed immediately or shortly after the order was made 3. Breach was committed subsequent to earlier breach proceedings arising from the same order 4. Targeting of a person the order was made to protect or a witness in the original proceedings	1. Breach occurred after a long period of compliance 2. The prohibition(s) breached was not fully understood, especially where an interim order was made without notice

C2.2 Key points

- The prosecution must be in a position to prove that the person before the court is the person in respect of whom the order was made (*Barber v Crown Prosecution Service* [2004] EWHC 2605 (Admin)).

- In *R v Nicholson* [2006] EWCA Crim 1518 the offender took part in a demonstration within a prohibited distance of a named property. She admitted, too, that she had not carefully checked the terms of the order, in particular the scheduled inclusion of premises named Halifax House. However, she maintained that she had a reasonable excuse for breaching the terms of the order within the statutory provision because she had no recollection of ever having heard before, or at the demonstration, of any reference to Halifax House as the address of the proposed laboratory, and she had mistakenly believed that she was entitled to attend the demonstration as she did. Held: forgetfulness, misunderstanding, or ignorance could amount in law to a reasonable excuse.

- The fact that a person is appealing against the imposition of an order does not give rise to a reasonable excuse (*West Midlands Probation Board v Daly* [2008] EWHC 15 (Admin)).

- A belief that the order has come to an end is capable of amounting to a reasonable excuse (*Barber v Crown Prosecution Service* [2004] EWHC 2605 (Admin)).

- Where conduct forming the breach would also be a criminal offence in its own right, a court was not bound by the maximum sentence available for that offence, but should have regard to proportionality. It would be wrong for a prosecutor to proceed with a breach of an anti-social behaviour order simply because it was thought that the penalty for the substantive offence was too lenient (*R v Stevens* [2006] EWCA Crim 255).

The burden of negativing reasonable excuse falls on the prosecution (*R v Charles* [2009] EWCA Crim 1570).

See *Blackstone's Criminal Practice 2012* D25.17

C3 Bail, Failure to Surrender

Bail Act 1976, s 6(1)–(2)

(1) If a person who has been released on bail in criminal proceedings fails without reasonable cause to surrender to custody he shall be guilty of an offence.

(2) If a person who—

(a) has been released on bail in criminal proceedings, and

(b) having reasonable cause therefor [sic], has failed to surrender to custody, fails to surrender to custody at the appointed place as soon after the appointed time as is reasonably practicable he shall be guilty of an offence.

 Level 5 fine and/or 3 months/12 months

C3.1 *Sentencing*

Offence seriousness (culpability and harm) A. Identify the appropriate starting point Starting points based on first time offender pleading not guilty		
Example of nature of activity	**Starting point**	**Range**
Surrenders late on day but case proceeds as planned	Band A fine	Band A fine to band B fine
Negligent or non-deliberate failure to attend causing delay and/or interference with the administration of justice	Band C fine	Band B fine to medium level community order
Deliberate failure to attend causing delay and/or interference with the administration of justice The type and degree of harm actually caused will affect where in the range the case falls	14 days custody	Low level community order to 10 weeks custody

Offence seriousness (culpability and harm) **B. Consider the effect of aggravating and mitigating factors** **(other than those within examples above)** The following may be particularly relevant but **these lists are not exhaustive**	
Factors indicating higher culpability 1. Serious attempts to evade justice 2. Determined attempt seriously to undermine the course of justice 3. Previous relevant convictions and/or breach of court orders or court bail **Factor indicating greater degree of harm** 1. Lengthy absence	**Factors indicating lower culpability** Where not amounting to a defence: 1. Misunderstanding 2. Failure to comprehend bail significance or requirements 3. Caring responsibilities **Factor indicating lesser degree of harm** 1. Prompt voluntary surrender

Section 135 of the Magistrates' Courts Act (MCA) 1980 provides:

> **Magistrates' Courts Act 1980, s 135**
>
> (1) A magistrates' court that has power to commit to prison a person convicted of an offence, or would have that power but for section 82 or 88 above, may order him to be detained within the precincts of the court-house or at any police station until such hour, not later than 8 o'clock in the evening of the day on which the order is made, as the court may direct, and, if it does so, shall not, where it has power to commit him to prison [or detention if aged 18–20 years], exercise that power.
>
> (2) A court shall not make such an order under this section as will deprive the offender of a reasonable opportunity of returning to his abode on the day of the order.

C3.2 Key points

- In *R v Scott* [2007] EWCA Crim 2757 the court rejected an argument that surrendering to bail 30 minutes late was *de minimis* so as to make proceeding with a Bail Act charge Wednesbury unreasonable. The court held:

  > We are prepared for the sake of argument to accept the possibility that there could be circumstances where a defendant's late arrival at court was so truly marginal that it would be Wednesbury unreasonable to pursue it but it would be a rare case.

- In *R v Gateshead Justices, ex p Usher* [1981] Crim LR 491, DC, a period of seven minutes was held to be *de minimis*; however, in *Scott* the court said that no gloss should be placed on the clear wording in the Bail Act and *Usher* established no clear principle of law, observing that:

  > . . . there could be circumstances where a defendant's late arrival at court was so truly marginal that it would be Wednesbury unreasonable to pursue it but

it would be a rare case. . . Even if a delay is small it can still cause inconvenience and waste of time. If a culture of lateness is tolerated the results can be cumulative and bad for the administration of justice.

- Proof of *bail* conditions: section 6 of the MCA 1980 provides:

Magistrates' Courts Act 1980, s 6(8)–(9)

(8) In any proceedings for an offence under subsection (1) or (2) above a document purporting to be a copy of the part of the prescribed record which relates to the time and place appointed for the person specified in the record to surrender to custody and to be duly certified to be a true copy of that part of the record shall be evidence of the time and place appointed for that person to surrender to custody.

(9) For the purposes of subsection (8) above—

    (a) 'the prescribed record' means the record of the decision of the court, officer or constable made in pursuance of section 5(1) of this Act;

    (b) the copy of the prescribed record is duly certified if it is certified by the appropriate officer of the court or, as the case may be, by the constable who took the decision or a constable designated for the purpose by the officer in charge of the police station from which the person to whom the record relates was released.

- In *R v Liverpool Justices, ex p Santos* The Times, 23 January 1997 the court held that reliance on mistaken information provided by a solicitor may be found a reasonable excuse for failing to surrender. The court went on to say that all relevant factors would need to be considered and a mistake on the part of a solicitor in calculating the bail date did not automatically excuse the defendant's non-attendance.
- A failure to give the defendant a written bail notice does not amount to a reasonable excuse.
- A genuine, albeit mistaken, belief that bail was to another date would not amount to a reasonable excuse (*Laidlaw v Atkinson* The Times, 2 August 1986).
- A reasonable excuse need only be proved to the civil standard (*R v Carr-Bryant* (1944) 29 Cr App R 76).
- A person who had overtly [subjected] himself to the court's direction (see *R v Central Criminal Court, ex p Guney* [1995] 2 All ER 577), or reported to court officials as directed, had surrendered to custody (see *Director of Public Prosecutions v Richards* [1988] QB 701). If the defendant later left court, no offence would be committed (although the court could issue a warrant for arrest). It is not essential that there be a formal surrender to an official (*R v Rumble* [2003] EWCA Crim 770), but simply arriving at the court at the proper time may not be enough (*R v Render* (1987) 84 Cr App R 294).

- If a person is acquitted of the offence which he was on bail for, that does not mitigate the penalty for failing to surrender (*R v Maguire* [1993] RTR 306).

See *Blackstone's Criminal Practice 2012* **D7.74**

C4 **Communication Network Offences**

C4.1 **Improper use of public electronic communications network**

Communications Act 2003, s 127(1)–(2)

(1) A person is guilty of an offence if he—
  (a) sends by means of a public electronic communications network a message or other matter that is grossly offensive or of an indecent, obscene or menacing character; or
  (b) causes any such message or matter to be so sent.
(2) A person is guilty of an offence if, for the purpose of causing annoyance, inconvenience or needless anxiety to another, he—
  (a) sends by means of a public electronic communications network, a message that he knows to be false,
  (b) causes such a message to be sent; or
  (c) persistently makes use of a public electronic communications network.

SO

🏛 Level 5 fine/6 months

C4.1.1 *Sentencing*

Offence seriousness (culpability and harm)		
A. Identify the appropriate starting point Starting points based on first time offender pleading not guilty		
Sending grossly offensive, indecent, obscene, or menacing messages (s 127(1))		
Example of nature of activity	**Starting point**	**Range**
Single offensive, indecent, obscene, or menacing call of short duration, having no significant impact on receiver	Band B fine	Band A fine to band C fine
Single call where extreme language used, having only moderate impact on receiver	Medium level community order	Low level community order to high level community order
Single call where extreme language used and substantial distress or fear caused to receiver; OR One of a series of similar calls as described in box above	6 weeks custody	High level community order to 12 weeks custody

Sending false message/persistent use of communications network for purpose of causing annoyance, inconvenience, or needless anxiety (s 127(2))		
Examples of nature of activity	**Starting point**	**Range**
Persistent silent calls over short period to private individual, causing inconvenience or annoyance	Band B fine	Band A fine to band C fine
Single hoax call to public or private organization resulting in moderate disruption or anxiety	Medium level community order	Low level community order to high level community order
Single hoax call resulting in major disruption or substantial public fear or distress; OR One of a series of similar calls as described in box above	12 weeks custody	High level community order to 18 weeks custody

C4.1.2 Key points

- In *Director of Public Prosecutions v Collins* [2006] UKHL 40 the court held that to be guilty of an offence under section 127:

  (1) The defendant must have intended his words to be offensive to those to whom they related, or
  (2) be aware that they might be taken to be so.

- It does not matter if the material sent was not received. The question of whether something is in fact offensive is to be determined by reference to whether or not reasonable persons would find the message grossly offensive, judged by the standards of an open and just multiracial society.

- Parliament cannot have intended to criminalize the conduct of a person using language which is, for reasons unknown to him, grossly offensive to those to whom it relates, or which may even be thought, however wrongly, to represent a polite or acceptable usage. On the other hand, a culpable state of mind will ordinarily be found where a message is couched in terms showing an intention to insult those to whom the message relates or giving rise to the inference that a risk of doing so must have been recognized by the sender. The same will be true where facts known to the sender of a message about an intended recipient render the message peculiarly offensive to that recipient, or likely to be so, whether or not the message in fact reaches the recipient.

- European Convention rights to freedom of expression will rarely provide a defence (see *Connolly v Director of Public Prosecutions* [2007] EWHC 237 (Admin), a case concerned with a different statute).

See *Blackstone's Criminal Practice 2012* B18.23

C4.2 Sending indecent material through post

Postal Services Act 2000, s 85

85 Prohibition on sending certain articles by post

(1) A person commits an offence if he sends by post a postal packet which encloses any creature, article or thing of any kind which is likely to injure other postal packets in course of their transmission by post or any person engaged in the business of a postal operator.

(2) Subsection (1) does not apply to postal packets which enclose anything permitted (whether generally or specifically) by the postal operator concerned.

(3) A person commits an offence if he sends by post a postal packet which encloses—

   (a) any indecent or obscene print, painting, photograph, lithograph, engraving, cinematograph film or other record of a picture or pictures, book, card or written communication, or

   (b) any other indecent or obscene article (whether or not of a similar kind to those mentioned in paragraph (a)).

(4) A person commits an offence if he sends by post a postal packet which has on the packet, or on the cover of the packet, any words, marks or designs which are of an indecent or obscene character.

(5) A person who commits an offence under this section shall be liable—

   (a) on summary conviction, to a fine not exceeding the statutory maximum,

   (b) on conviction on indictment, to a fine or to imprisonment for a term not exceeding twelve months or to both.

EW

 Level 5 fine; 12 months imprisonment

C4.2.1 Key points

Whether something is obscene is to be judged objectively.

In relation to Article 10 considerations the court in *R v Kirk* [2006] EWCA Crim 725 held:

> We derive assistance, so far as the reference to the Convention is concerned, from the recent decision of the House of Lords in K v London Borough of Lambeth [2006] UKHL 10. We refer in particular to paragraph 110 of the opinion of Lord Hope. Article 10 protects the right of free speech; but the right is not absolute, and paragraph 2 of Article 10 permits restrictions on that right. It is not suggested, in the present case, that section 85 of the Postal Services Act 2000 is incompatible with the Convention. It follows that the restriction

---

created by section 85 is accepted to be a restriction that is permitted by the Convention. That being so, the statute falls to be applied in the normal way: if a matter which is sent through the post is of an indecent or obscene character, there will be an offence under the Act.

 See *Blackstone's Criminal Practice 2012* **B11.74** and **B18.21**

C4.3 **Indecent or offensive or threatening letters etc**

Malicious Communications Act 1988, s 1

1 Offence of sending letters etc. with intent to cause distress or anxiety

(1) Any person who sends to another person—
   (a) a letter, electronic communication or article of any description which conveys—
       (i) a message which is indecent or grossly offensive;
       (ii) a threat; or
       (iii) information which is false and known or believed to be false by the sender; or
   (b) any article or electronic communication which is, in whole or part, of an indecent or grossly offensive nature,

   is guilty of an offence if his purpose, or one of his purposes, in sending it is that it should, so far as falling within paragraph (a) or (b) above, cause distress or anxiety to the recipient or to any other person to whom he intends that it or its contents or nature should be communicated.

(2) A person is not guilty of an offence by virtue of subsection (1)(a)(ii) above if he shows—
   (a) that the threat was used to reinforce a demand made by him on reasonable grounds; and
   (b) that he believed, and had reasonable grounds for believing, that the use of the threat was a proper means of reinforcing the demand.

(2A) In this section "electronic communication" includes—
   (a) any oral or other communication by means of an electronic communications network; and
   (b) any communication (however sent) that is in electronic form.

(3) In this section references to sending include references to delivering or transmitting and to causing to be sent, delivered or transmitted and "sender" shall be construed accordingly.

SO

 6 months/fine level 5

SO Summary Only   Sentence

C4.3.1 Key points

See *Connolly v Director of Public Prosecutions* [2008] 1 WLR 276 for Articles 9 (religion) and 10 (free speech) considerations.

See *Blackstone's Criminal Practice 2012* **B18.24**

C5 Criminal Damage

C5.1 Destroying or damaging property

Criminal Damage Act 1971, s 1

(1) A person who without lawful excuse destroys or damages any property belonging to another intending to destroy or damage any such property or being reckless as to whether any such property would be destroyed or damaged shall be guilty of an offence.

(2) A person who without lawful excuse destroys or damages any property, whether belonging to himself or another—

    (a) intending to destroy or damage any property or being reckless as to whether any property would be destroyed or damaged; and

    (b) intending by the destruction or damage to endanger the life of another or being reckless as to whether the life of another would be thereby endangered;

shall be guilty of an offence.

(3) An offence committed under this section by destroying or damaging property by fire shall be charged as arson.

EW (Note: Venue dictated by value)

⊞ 3 months and/or fine level 4 (6 months if value > £5,000)/ 10 years

DO (Section 1(2) offence)

C5.1.1 *Sentencing: criminal damage*

Offence seriousness (culpability and harm)		
A. Identify the appropriate starting point		
Starting points bases on first time offender pleading not guilty		
Examples of nature of activity	**Starting point**	**Range**
Minor damage eg breaking small window; small amount of graffiti	Band B fine	Conditional discharge to band C fine
Moderate damage eg breaking large plate-glass or shop window; widespread graffiti	Low level community order	Band C fine to medium level community order
Significant damage up to £5,000 eg damage caused as part of a spree	High level community order	Medium level community order to 12 weeks custody
Damage between £5,000 and £10,000	12 weeks custody	6 to 26 weeks custody
Damage over £10,000	Crown Court	Crown Court

Offence seriousness (culpability and harm)
B. Consider the effect of aggravating and mitigating factors
(other than those within examples above)
The following may be particularly relevant but **these lists are not exhaustive**

Factors indicating higher culpability	Factors indicating lower culpability
1. Revenge attack	1. Damage caused recklessly
2. Targeting vulnerable victim	2. Provocation
Factors indicating greater degree of harm	
1. Damage to emergency equipment	
2. Damage to public amenity	
3. Significant public or private fear caused eg in domestic context	

C5.1.2 *Sentencing: arson*

Offence seriousness (culpability and harm)
A. Identify the appropriate starting point
Starting points based on first time offender pleading not guilty

Examples of nature of activity	Starting point	Range
Minor damage by fire	High level community order	Medium level community order to 12 weeks custody
Moderate damage by fire	12 weeks custody	6 to 26 weeks custody
Significant damage by fire	Crown Court	Crown Court

Offence seriousness (culpability and harm)
B. Consider the effect of aggravating and mitigating factors
(other than those within examples above)
The following may be particularly relevant but **these lists are not exhaustive**

Factors indicating higher culpability	Factor indicating lower culpability
1. Revenge attack	1. Damage caused recklessly
2. Targeting vulnerable victim	
Factors indicating greater degree of harm	
1. Damage to emergency equipment	
2. Damage to public amenity	
3. Significant public or private fear caused eg in domestic context	

C5.1.3 **Key points**

- There is no bar on charging attempted criminal damage where, due to value, the matter can be tried summarily only (*R v Bristol Justices, ex p E* [1999] 1 WLR 390).
- Lawful excuse is defined in section 5:

Criminal Damage Act 1971, s 5(2)–(5)

(2) A person charged with an offence to which this section applies, shall, whether or not he would be treated for the purposes of this Act as having a lawful excuse apart from this subsection, be treated for those purposes as having a lawful excuse—

    (a) if at the time of the act or acts alleged to constitute the offence he believed that the person or persons whom he believed to be entitled to consent to the destruction of or damage to the property in question had so consented, or would have so consented to it if he or they had known of the destruction or damage and its circumstances; or

    (b) if he destroyed or damaged or threatened to destroy or damage the property in question or, in the case of a charge of an offence under section 3 above, intended to use or cause or permit the use of something to destroy or damage it, in order to protect property belonging to himself or another or a right or interest in property which was or which he believed to be vested in himself or another, and at the time of the act or acts alleged to constitute the offence he believed—

        (i) that the property, right or interest was in immediate need of protection; and

        (ii) that the means of protection adopted or proposed to be adopted were or would be reasonable having regard to all the circumstances.

(3) For the purposes of this section it is immaterial whether a belief is justified or not if it is honestly held.

(4) For the purposes of subsection (2) above a right or interest in property includes any right or privilege in or over land, whether created by grant, licence or otherwise.

(5) This section shall not be construed as casting doubt on any defence recognised by law as a defence to criminal charges.

- A person can avail himself of the defence of lawful excuse notwithstanding the fact that he was intoxicated (*Jaggard v Dickinson* (1981) 72 Cr App R 33).
- It is clear that subsection (5) above is intended to cover the situation whereby damage is caused to protect life or prevent injury (*R v Baker* The Times, 26 November 1996).
- Damage does not need to be destruction and encompasses not permanent harm, such as graffiti. If expense or inconvenience is involved in putting right the matter then damage will have been caused (eg stamping on a policeman's helmet so that it had to be pushed back into shape). Damaging something that can be restored (eg deleting a computer program) constitutes damage (*Cox v Riley* (1986) 83 Cr App R 54). Spitting on a police officer's uniform is unlikely to cause damage (*A v R* [1978] Crim LR 689). The soaking of a blanket and the flooding of the floor of a police cell was held to amount to damage in *R v Fiak* [2005] EWCA 2381, and the daubing of water-soluble paint on a pavement was equally found to amount to

damage in *Hardman v Chief Constable of Avon and Somerset* [1986] Crim LR 330.

- Determining whether something has been damaged is a matter of fact and degree to be determined by the magistrates or jury (*Roe v Kingerlee* [1986] Crim LR 735).

- It is an offence to damage jointly owned property. Section 10 provides:

Criminal Damage Act 1971, s 10

(1) In this Act 'property' means of a tangible nature, whether real or personal, including money and—
   (a) including wild creatures which have been tamed or are ordinarily kept in captivity, and any other wild creatures or their carcasses if, but only if, they have been reduced into possession which has not been lost or abandoned or are in the course of being reduced into possession; but
   (b) not including mushrooms growing wild on any land or flowers, fruit or foliage of a plant growing wild on any land.
   For the purposes of this subsection 'mushroom' includes any fungus and 'plant' includes any shrub or tree.

(2) Property shall be treated for the purposes of this Act as belonging to any person—
   (a) having the custody or control of it;
   (b) having in it any proprietary right or interest (not being an equitable interest arising only from an agreement to transfer or grant an interest); or
   (c) having a charge on it.

(3) Where property is subject to a trust, the persons to whom it belongs shall be so treated as including any person having a right to enforce the trust.

(4) Property of a corporation sole shall be so treated as belonging to the corporation notwithstanding a vacancy in the corporation.

- The prosecution will have proved that the defendant was reckless if, having regard to all the available evidence the court is sure:
  - that he was aware of a risk that property would be destroyed/damaged; and
  - that in the circumstances which were known to him it was unreasonable for him to take that risk.

- This test allows for some of the personal characteristics of a defendant to be taken into account, see: *R v G* [2003] UKHL 50.

C5.1.4 *Criminal damage (by fire): Criminal Damage Act 1971, s 1(3)*

▥ 6 months and/or level 5 fine (regardless of value)—an offence under section 1(2) or 1(3) is triable only on indictment

See **C5.1**.

C5.1.5 *Racially or religiously aggravated criminal damage: Crime and Disorder Act 1998, s 30*

 EW

6 months and/or level 5/14 years

C5.2 **Threats to destroy or damage property**

> **Criminal Damage Act 1971, s 2**
>
> A person who without lawful excuse makes to another a threat, intending that that other would fear it would be carried out,—
> (a) to destroy or damage any property belonging to that other or a third person; or
> (b) to destroy or damage his own property in a way which he knows is likely to endanger the life of that other or third person;
> shall be guilty of an offence.

EW

Level 5 fine/6 months/10 years

C5.2.1 *Sentencing*

There are no sentencing guidelines for this offence.

C5.2.2 Key points

- Whether a threat has been made under s 2(a) is to be assessed objectively with reference to the words and actions of the defendant (*R v Cakmak* [2002] EWCA Crim 500).
- 'without lawful excuse' is defined in section 5 of the Act:

> **Criminal Damage Act 1971, s 5**
>
> (1) This section applies to any offence under section 1(1) above and any offence under section 2 or 3 above other than one involving a threat by the person charged to destroy or damage property in a way which he knows is likely to endanger the life of another or involving an intent by the person charged to use or cause or permit the use of something in his custody or under his control so to destroy or damage property.

(2) A person charged with an offence to which this section applies, shall, whether or not he would be treated for the purposes of this Act as having a lawful excuse apart from this subsection, be treated for those purposes as having a lawful excuse—

(a) if at the time of the act or acts alleged to constitute the offence he believed that the person or persons whom he believed to be entitled to consent to the destruction of or damage to the property in question had so consented, or would have so consented to it if he or they had known of the destruction or damage and its circumstances; or

(b) if he destroyed or damaged or threatened to destroy or damage the property in question or, in the case of a charge of an offence under section 3 above, intended to use or cause or permit the use of something to destroy or damage it, in order to protect property belonging to himself or another or a right or interest in property which was or which he believed to be vested in himself or another, and at the time of the act or acts alleged to constitute the offence he believed—

(i) that the property, right or interest was in immediate need of protection; and

(ii) that the means of protection adopted or proposed to be adopted were or would be reasonable having regard to all the circumstances.

(3) For the purposes of this section it is immaterial whether a belief is justified or not if it is honestly held.

(4) For the purposes of subsection (2) above a right or interest in property includes any right or privilege in or over land, whether created by grant, licence or otherwise.

(5) This section shall not be construed as casting doubt on any defence recognised by law as a defence to criminal charges.

C5.3 Possessing anything with intent to destroy or damage property

Criminal Damage Act 1971, s 3(a)

A person who has anything in his custody or under his control intending without lawful excuse to use it or cause or permit another to use it—

(a) to destroy or damage any property belonging to some other person; or

(b) to destroy or damage his own or the user's property in a way which he knows is likely to endanger the life of some other person;

shall be guilty of an offence.

 EW

 Level 5 fine/6 months/10 years

C5.3.1 Key points

A conditional intent will suffice (*R v Buckingham* (1976) 63 Cr App R 159).

📖 See *Blackstone's Criminal Practice 2012* **B8**

C6 **Drugs**

C6.1 **Drugs—Class A: fail to attend/ remain for initial assessment**

Drugs Act 2005, s 12(1)–(3)

(1) This section applies if a person is required to attend an initial assessment and remain for its duration by virtue of section 9(2).

(2) The initial assessor must inform a police officer or a police support officer if the person—
   (a) fails to attend the initial assessment at the specified time and place, or
   (b) attends the assessment at the specified time and place but fails to remain for its duration.

(3) A person is guilty of an offence if without good cause—
   (a) he fails to attend an initial assessment at the specified time and place, or
   (b) he attends the assessment at the specified time and place but fails to remain for its duration.

SO

▥ 3 months and/or level 4 fine

C6.1.1 *Sentencing*

Offence seriousness (culpability and harm) A. Identify the appropriate starting point Starting points based on first time offender pleading not guilty		
Examples of nature of activity	**Starting point**	**Range**
Failure to attend at the appointed place and time	Medium level community order	Band C fine to high level community order
Offence seriousness (culpability and harm) B. Consider the effect of aggravating and mitigating factors (other than those within examples above) The following may be particularly relevant but **these lists are not exhaustive**		
Factor indicating greater degree of harm	**Factors indicating lower culpability**	
1. Threats or abuse to assessor or other staff	1. Offender turns up but at wrong place or time or fails to remain for duration of appointment 2. Subsequent voluntary contact to rearrange appointment	

C6.2 **Drugs—Class A: fail/refuse to provide a sample**

Practitioners need to consider carefully section 63B before allowing a client to plead guilty to an offence under this section as there are a considerable number of condition precedents that need to be satisfied before a lawful request for a sample can be made.

Police and Criminal Evidence Act 1984, s 63B

(1) A sample of urine or a non-intimate sample may be taken from a person in police detention for the purpose of ascertaining whether he has any specified Class A drug in his body if—
   (a) either the arrest condition or the charge condition is met;
   (b) both the age condition and the request condition are met; and
   (c) the notification condition is met in relation to the arrest condition, the charge condition or the age condition (as the case may be).

(1A) The arrest condition is that the person concerned has been arrested for an offence but has not been charged with that offence and either—
   (a) the offence is a trigger offence; or
   (b) a police officer of at least the rank of inspector has reasonable grounds for suspecting that the misuse by that person of a specified Class A drug caused or contributed to the offence and has authorised the sample to be taken.

(2) The charge condition is either—
   (a) that the person concerned has been charged with a trigger offence; or
   (b) that the person concerned has been charged with an offence and a police officer of at least the rank of inspector, who has reasonable grounds for suspecting that the misuse by that person of any specified Class A drug caused or contributed to the offence and has authorised the sample to be taken.

(3) The age condition is—
   (a) if the arrest condition is met, that the person concerned has attained the age of 18;
   (b) if the charge condition is met, that he has attained the age of 14.

(4) The request condition is that a police officer has requested the person concerned to give the sample.

(4A) . . .

(4B) . . .

(5) Before requesting the person concerned to give a sample, an officer must—
   (a) warn him that if, when so requested, he fails without good cause to do so he may be liable to prosecution, and
   (b) in a case within subsection (1A)(b) or (2)(b) above, inform him of the giving of the authorisation and of the grounds in question.

(5A) In the case of a person who has not attained the age of 17—
  (a) the making of the request under subsection (4) above;
  (b) the giving of the warning and (where applicable) the information under subsection (5) above; and
  (c) the taking of the sample,
may not take place except in the presence of an appropriate adult.

(5B) ...

(5C) Despite subsection (1)(a) above, a sample may be taken from a person under this section if—
  (a) he was arrested for an offence (the first offence),
  (b) the arrest condition is met but the charge condition is not met,
  (c) before a sample is taken by virtue of subsection (1) above he would (but for his arrest as mentioned in paragraph (d) below) be required to be released from police detention,
  (d) he continues to be in police detention by virtue of his having been arrested for an offence not falling within subsection (1A) above, and
  (e) the sample is taken before the end of the period of 24 hours starting with the time when his detention by virtue of his arrest for the first offence began.

(5D) A sample must not be taken from a person under this section if he is detained in a police station unless he has been brought before the custody officer.

(6) A sample may be taken under this section only by a person prescribed by regulations made by the Secretary of State by statutory instrument.

(6A) ...

(6B) ...

(7) ...

(8) A person who fails without good cause to give any sample which may be taken from him under this section shall be guilty of an offence.

SO

 3 months and/or level 4 fine

C6.2.1 *Sentencing*

Offence seriousness (culpability and harm)		
A. Identify the appropriate starting point		
Starting points based on first time offender pleading not guilty		
Examples of nature of activity	**Starting point**	**Range**
Refusal to provide sample without good cause when required by police officer	Medium level community order	Band C fine to high level community order

Offence seriousness (culpability and harm)
B. Consider the effect of aggravating and mitigating factors
(other than those within examples above)
The following may be particularly relevant but **these lists are not exhaustive**

Factor indicating greater degree of harm	**Factors indicating lower culpability**
1. Threats or abuse to staff	1. Subsequent voluntary contact with drug workers
	2. Subsequent compliance with testing on arrest/charge

C6.3 **Drugs—Class A: possession**

Misuse of Drugs Act 1971, s 5(2)

It is an offence for a person to have a controlled drug in his possession.

 6 months and/or level 5 fine/7 years

C6.3.1 *Sentencing*

Offence seriousness (culpability and harm)		
A. Identify the appropriate starting point		
Starting points based on first time offender pleading not guilty		
Examples of nature of activity	**Starting point**	**Range**
Possession of a very small quantity of the drug eg one small wrap or tablet	Band C fine	Band B fine to medium level community order
More than a very small quantity of the drug eg up to six wraps or tablets	Medium level community order	Low level community order to high level community order
Larger amounts	High level community order	Medium level community order to Crown Court
Possession of drug in prison—whether by prisoner or another	Crown Court	Crown Court

Offence seriousness (culpability and harm) **B. Consider the effect of aggravating and mitigating factors** (other than those within examples above) The following may be particularly relevant but **these lists are not exhaustive**	
Factor indicating higher culpability 1. Offender exercising or acting in position of special responsibility **Factor indicating greater degree of harm** 1. Possession of drug in a public place or school	

C6.3.2 Key points

- A person must know that he is in possession of the drug, therefore a person holding drugs believing that they were something else would not be guilty (assuming the court believed the defendant). Note, however, that suspicion would be sufficient (see s 28 below).
- A person who 'forgot' that he had drugs would still be in possession of those drugs, but a person who had no knowledge at all would not (*R v Martindale* [1986] 3 All ER 25).
- A person need not be in physical possession of a drug provided he is in control (sole or joint): see Misuse of Drugs Act 1971, s 37(3). It is not sufficient that the defendant might have knowledge of a confederate's possession of drugs; the test is whether the drugs were part of a common pool from which all could draw (*R v Searle* [1971] Crim LR 592).
- The fact that the quantity of drug was so miniscule as to be incapable of being used does not amount to a defence (*R v Boyesen* [1982] AC 768), it is merely an indication that the defendant may not have knowledge of its presence.
- If a person is in possession of a container and he knows there is something inside, he will be in possession of the contents, even if he does not know their characteristics (*R v Lambert* [2002] 2 AC 545). If, however, the defendant had no right to open the container he may not be in possession of its contents (*Warner v Metropolitan Police Commissioner* [1969] 2 AC 256), nor if he believed the contents to be different from what in fact they were (*R v McNamara* (1988) 87 Cr App R 246).
- Defences are provided by sections 5 and 28 of the Act.

Misuse of Drugs Act 1971, s 5(4)

(4) In any proceedings for an offence under subsection (2) above in which it is proved that the accused had a controlled drug in his possession, it shall be a defence for him to prove—

   (a) that, knowing or suspecting it to be a controlled drug, he took possession of it for the purpose of preventing another from committing or continuing to commit an offence in connection with that drug and that as soon as possible after taking possession of it he took all such steps as were reasonably open to him to destroy the drug or to deliver it into the custody of a person lawfully entitled to take custody of it; or

   (b) that, knowing or suspecting it to be a controlled drug, he took possession of it for the purpose of delivering it into the custody of a person lawfully entitled to take custody of it and that as soon as possible after taking possession of it he took all such steps as were reasonably open to him to deliver it into the custody of such a person.

Section 28 provides:

Misuse of Drugs Act 1971, s 28

(1) This section applies to offences under any of the following provisions of this Act, that is to say section 4(2) and (3), section 5(2) and (3), section 6(2) and section 9.

(2) Subject to subsection (3) below, in any proceedings for an offence to which this section applies it shall be a defence for the accused to prove that he neither knew of nor suspected nor had reason to suspect the existence of some fact alleged by the prosecution which it is necessary for the prosecution to prove if he is to be convicted of the offence charged.

(3) Where in any proceedings for an offence to which this section applies it is necessary, if the accused is to be convicted of the offence charged, for the prosecution to prove that some substance or product involved in the alleged offence was the controlled drug which the prosecution alleges it to have been, and it is proved that the substance or product in question was that controlled drug, the accused—

   (a) shall not be acquitted of the offence charged by reason only of proving that he neither knew nor suspected nor had reason to suspect that the substance or product in question was the particular controlled drug alleged; but

   (b) shall be acquitted thereof—

      (i) if he proves that he neither believed nor suspected nor had reasons to suspect that the substance or product in question was a controlled drug; or

      (ii) if he proves that he believed the substance or product in question to be a controlled drug, or a controlled drug of a description, such that, if it had in fact been that controlled drug or a controlled drug of that description, he would not at the material time have been committing any offence to which this section applies.

(4) Nothing in this section shall prejudice any defence which it is open to a person charged with an offence to which this section applies to raise apart from this section.

- In considering a defence under section 28(3)(b), self-induced intoxication should not be considered (*R v Young* [1984] 2 All ER 164).
- The defence of necessity (commonly pleaded by sufferers of certain illnesses) is not a defence available in law for this charge (*R v Quayle and others* [2006] 1 All ER 988).
- Possession of drugs for religious purposes is not afforded any special protection under the European Convention (*R v Taylor* [2002] 1 Cr App R 519).

C6.4 **Drugs—Class A: produce, supply, possess with intent to supply**

Misuse of Drugs Act 1971, ss 4(2)–(3) and 5(3)

 6 months and/or level 5 fine/life imprisonment

C6.4.1 *Sentencing*

Offence seriousness (culpability and harm)
A. Identify the appropriate starting point
Starting points based on first time offender pleading not guilty

These offences should normally be dealt with in the Crown Court.
However, there may be very rare cases involving non-commercial supply (eg between equals) of a very small amount (eg one small wrap or tablet) in which a custodial sentence within the jurisdiction of a magistrates' court may be appropriate.

C6.5 **Drugs—Class B and C: possession**

Misuse of Drugs Act 1971, s 5(2)

 Level 4 fine and/or 3 months (Class B); level 3 fine and/or 3 months (Class C)/5 years (Class B); 2 years (Class C)

C6.5.1 *Sentencing*

Offence seriousness (culpability and harm) A. Identify the appropriate starting point Starting points based on first time offender pleading not guilty		
Examples of nature of activity	**Starting point**	**Range**
Possession of a small amount of Class B drug for personal use	Band B fine	Band A fine to low level community order
Possession of large amount of Class B drug for personal use	Band C fine	Band B fine to 12 weeks custody

Offence seriousness (culpability and harm) B. Consider the effect of aggravating and mitigating factors (other than those within examples above) The following may be particularly relevant but **these lists are not exhaustive**	
Factor indicating higher culpability 1. Offender exercising or acting in position of special responsibility **Factor indicating greater degree of harm** 1. Possession of drugs in a public place or school	**Factors indicating lower culpability** 1. Possession of Class C rather than Class B drug 2. Evidence that use was to help cope with a medical condition

See **C6.3** for meaning of possession and defences.

C6.6 Drugs—Class B and C: supply, possess with intent to supply

Misuse of Drugs Act 1971, ss 4(3) and 5(3)

 Level 5 fine and/or 6 months (Class B); level 4 fine and/or 3 months (Class C)/14 years (Class B and Class C)

C6.6.1 *Sentencing*

Offence seriousness (culpability and harm)		
A. Identify the appropriate starting point		
Starting points based on first time offender pleading not guilty		
Examples of nature of activity	**Starting point**	**Range**
Sharing minimal quantity between equals on a non-commercial basis eg a reefer	Band C fine	Band B fine to low level community order
Small scale retail supply to consumer	High level community order (Class C)	Low level community order to 6 weeks custody (Class C)
	6 weeks custody (Class B)	Medium level community order to 26 weeks custody (Class B)
Any other supply, including small scale supply in prison—whether by prisoner or another	Crown Court	Crown Court

Offence seriousness (culpability and harm)	
B. Consider the effect of aggravating and mitigating factors	
(other than those within examples above)	
The following may be particularly relevant but **these lists are not exhaustive**	
Factor indicating higher culpability	
1. Offender exercising or acting in position of special responsibility	
Factors indicating greater degree of harm	
1. Supply to vulnerable persons including children	
2. Offence committed on/in vicinity of school premises	
(Note: supply on or in the vicinity of school premises is a statutory aggravating factor: Misuse of Drugs Act 1971, s 4A. Consult your legal adviser for guidance.)	

C6.6.2 *Aggravation of offence of supply of controlled drug*

Section 4A provides:

Misuse of Drugs Act 1971, s 4A

(1) This section applies if—
 (a) a court is considering the seriousness of an offence under section 4(3) of this Act, and
 (b) at the time the offence was committed the offender had attained the age of 18.
(2) If either of the following conditions is met the court—
 (a) must treat the fact that the condition is met as an aggravating factor (that is to say, a factor that increases the seriousness of the offence), and
 (b) must state in open court that the offence is so aggravated.
(3) The first condition is that the offence was committed on or in the vicinity of school premises at a relevant time.
(4) The second condition is that in connection with the commission of the offence the offender used a courier who, at the time the offence was committed, was under the age of 18.
(5) In subsection (3), a relevant time is—
 (a) any time when the school premises are in use by persons under the age of 18;
 (b) one hour before the start and one hour after the end of any such time.
(6) For the purposes of subsection (4), a person uses a courier in connection with an offence under section 4(3) of this Act if he causes or permits another person (the courier)—
 (a) to deliver a controlled drug to a third person, or
 (b) to deliver a drug related consideration to himself or a third person.
(7) For the purposes of subsection (6), a drug related consideration is a consideration of any description which—
 (a) is obtained in connection with the supply of a controlled drug, or
 (b) is intended to be used in connection with obtaining a controlled drug.
(8) In this section—
 'school premises' means land used for the purposes of a school excluding any land occupied solely as a dwelling by a person employed at the school; and
 'school' has the same meaning—
 (a) in England and Wales, as in section 4 of the Education Act 1996.

C6.6.3 Key points

- See **C6.3** for meaning of possession and defences (but note that the defence under section 5(4) is not available for these offences).
- Purchasing drugs on behalf of a third party, and passing those drugs to that party, even for no profit, amounts to supply.

- So-called 'social supply' should be charged as simple possession, in *R v Denslow* [1998] Crim LR 566 the court observed:

> We wonder why it was thought necessary to charge supply in the circumstances of this case. How could it possibly serve the interests of the public that there should be either a trial or if not a trial as conventionally understood a hearing to determine this matter of law? It was inevitable that the appellant would be dealt with at worst as though he were in possession of the drugs and, as turned out in this case, as though he were without any criminal responsibility for that particular part of the transaction. We are told that a plea had been offered to a charge of possession. It ought to have been accepted. We hope that those words will be borne in mind by prosecuting authorities in the future.

- A person who places drugs in the hands of a third party merely for safekeeping does not supply drugs (*R v Maginnis* [1987] AC 303).
- An offer to supply can be made by words or conduct, and once made cannot be withdrawn.

C6.7 **Drugs: cultivation of cannabis**

C6.7.1 *Sentencing*

Misuse of Drugs Act 1971, s 6(2)

 6 months and/or level 5 fine/14 years

Offence seriousness (culpability and harm) A. Identify the appropriate starting point Starting points based on first time offender pleading not guilty		
Examples of nature of activity	**Starting point**	**Range**
Very small scale cultivation for personal use only ie one or two plants	Band C fine	Band B fine to low level community order
Small scale cultivation for personal use and non-commercial supply to small circle of friends	High level community order	Medium level community order to 12 weeks custody
Commercial cultivation	Crown Court	Crown Court

The above guideline needs to be read in conjunction with the later case of *R v Auton* [2011] EWCA Crim 76 where it was held that the following sentences should be considered starting points after trial:

i) where the cultivation will genuinely involve no element of supply of any kind, the sentence after trial is likely to be in the range 9 to 18 months, depending on the size of the operation, and the personal history of the defendant;

ii) where the cultivation is for the defendant's own use and is not a frankly commercial operation for profit, but will involve supply to others, the sentence after trial is likely to be in the range 18 months to 3 years; where any individual case will come within this range will depend on, inter alia, the scale of cultivation, the investment made, the number of parties involved, the nature of the likely supply and, in the upper reaches of the range, the level of any profit element; a previous history of directly relevant similar offending may take the case above this range.

iii) where the cultivation is a frankly commercial one designed with a view to sale for profit, and whether or not the defendant may use a limited quantity of the drug himself, the sentence will usually be somewhat below the Xu range because of the smaller size of operation, but is likely to be in the general range after trial of 3 to 6 years.

C6.7.2 Key points

- It is the plant that must be cultivated, not the cannabis produced from the plant.
- The accused does not need to know that the plant was in fact cannabis (*R v Champ* (1981) 73 Cr App R 267).
- The defence under section 28 of the Act is available (see **C6.3.2**).

Offence seriousness (culpability and harm) **B. Consider the effect of aggravating and mitigating factors** **(other than those within examples above)** The following may be particularly relevant but **these lists are not exhaustive**	
Factors indicating higher culpability 1. Use of sophisticated growing system 2. Use of sophisticated system of concealment 3. Persistent use/cultivation of cannabis **Factor indicating greater degree of harm** 1. Involvement of vulnerable/young person(s)	**Factors indicating lower culpability** 1. Evidence drug used to help with a medical condition 2. Original planting carried out by others

 See *Blackstone's Criminal Practice 2012* **B19**

C7 Education Act

C7.1 School Non-attendance

Education Act 1996, s 444(1), (1A), (1B), (2), (2A), and (3)

(1) If a child of compulsory school age who is a registered pupil at a school fails to attend regularly at the school, his parent is guilty of an offence.

(1A) If in the circumstances mentioned in subsection (1) the parent knows that his child is failing to attend regularly at the school and fails to cause him to do so, he is guilty of an offence.

(1B) It is a defence for a person charged with an offence under subsection (1A) to prove that he had a reasonable justification for his failure to cause the child to attend regularly at the school.

(2) Subsections (2A) to (6) below apply in proceedings for an offence under this section in respect of a child who is not a boarder at the school at which he is a registered pupil.

(2A) The child shall not be taken to have failed to attend regularly at the school by reason of his absence from the school at any time if the parent proves that at that time the child was prevented from attending by reason of sickness or any unavoidable cause.

(3) The child shall not be taken to have failed to attend regularly at the school by reason of his absence from the school—

    (a) with leave, or

    (b) [repealed]

    (c) on any day exclusively set apart for religious observance by the religious body to which his parent belongs.

SO

▥ Level 3 fine (s 444(1)); level 4 fine and/or 3 months (s 444(1A))

C7.1.1 *Sentencing*

Offence seriousness (culpability and harm) A. Identify the appropriate starting point Starting points based on first time offender pleading not guilty		
Example of nature of activity	**Starting point**	**Range**
Short period following previous good attendance (s 444(1))	Band A fine	Conditional discharge to band A fine
Erratic attendance for long period (s 444(1))	Band B fine	Band B fine to band C fine
Colluding in and condoning non-attendance or deliberately instigating non-attendance (s 444(1A))	Medium level community order	Low level community order to high level community order

Offence seriousness (culpability and harm) B. Consider the effect of aggravating and mitigating factors (other than those within examples above) The following may be particularly relevant but **these lists are not exhaustive**	
Factors indicating higher culpability 1. Parental collusion (s 444(1) only) 2. Lack of parental effort to ensure attendance (s 444(1) only) 3. Threats to teachers and/or officials 4. Refusal to cooperate with school and/or officials **Factors indicating greater degree of harm** 1. More than one child 2. Harmful effect on other children in family	**Factors indicating lower culpability** 1. Parent unaware of child's whereabouts 2. Parent tried to ensure attendance 3. Parent concerned by child's allegations of bullying/unable to get school to address bullying

C7.1.2 Key points

- The offence under section 444(1) is strict liability and the prosecution has the duty to prove all four limbs. This is not contrary to the ECHR (*Barnfather v Islington Education Authority* [2003] 1 WLR 2318).
- Difficulties in getting a child to school due to the child's behavioural and psychological difficulties did not equate to an unavoidable cause (s 444 (1)), nor did it provide a defence under section 444(2A) (*Islington London Borough Council v D*, unreported, 23 March 2011. Unavoidable cause had to relate to the child, not parent, and had to be something in the nature of an emergency.
- In relation to section 444(1A) the parent will have only an evidential burden to satisfy, the prosecution having then to prove to the criminal standard that the defence is not made out (*R (P) v Liverpool City Magistrates' Court* [2006] EWHC 2732 (Admin)).

C7.2 Education Act, failure to comply with school attendance order

Education Act 1996, s 443(1) and (2)

(1) If a parent on whom a school attendance order is served fails to comply with the requirements of the order, he is guilty of an offence, unless he proves that he is causing the child to receive suitable education otherwise than at school.

(2) If, in proceedings for an offence under this section, the parent is acquitted, the court may direct that the school attendance order shall cease to be in force.

 Level 3 fine

C7.2.1 Key points

- Where a parent asserts the defence contained in section 443(1) the burden of proving it remains with the parent (*Oxfordshire County Council v L*, unreported, 3 March 2010).

C8 Fail to Comply with Notification Requirements, Sex Offenders Register

Sexual Offences Act 2003, s 91(1)

(1) A person commits an offence if he—

   (a) fails, without reasonable excuse, to comply with section 83(1), 84(1), 4(4)(b), 85(1), 87(4) or 89(2)(b) or any requirement imposed by regulations made under section 86(1); or

   (b) notifies to the police, in purported compliance with section 83(1), 4(1) or 85(1) or any requirement imposed by regulations made under section 86(1), any information which he knows to be false.

Level 5 fine and/or 6 months/5 years

C8.1 *Sentencing*

Offence seriousness (culpability and harm)		
A. Identify the appropriate starting point		
Starting points based on first time offender (see note below) pleading not guilty		
Example of nature of activity	**Starting point**	**Range**
Negligent or inadvertent failure to comply with requirements	Medium level community order	Band C fine to high level community order
Deliberate failure to comply with requirements OR Supply of information known to be false	6 weeks custody	High level community order to 26 weeks custody
Conduct as described in box above AND Long period of non-compliance OR Attempts to avoid detection	18 weeks custody	6 weeks custody to Crown Court

Offence seriousness (culpability and harm)	
B. Consider the effect of aggravating and mitigating factors	
(other than those within examples above)	
The following may be particularly relevant but **these lists are not exhaustive**	
Factor indicating higher culpability	**Factor indicating lower culpability**
1. Long period of non-compliance (where not in the examples above)	1. Genuine misunderstanding
Factors indicating greater degree of harm	
1. Alarm or distress caused to victim	
2. Particularly serious original offence	

C8.2 Key points

- A person who is subject to the notification requirements commits a criminal offence if he fails, without reasonable excuse, to:
  - (a) make an initial notification in accordance with section 83(1)
  - (b) notify a change of details in accordance with section 84(1)
  - (c) make an annual renotification in accordance with section 85(1)
  - (d) comply with any requirement imposed by regulations concerned with the notification of foreign travel (s 86(1))
  - (e) notify the fact that a change did not happen as predicted when it had been notified in advance in accordance with section 84(4)(b)
  - (f) allow a police officer to take his photograph or fingerprints (s 87(4))
  - (g) ensure that a young offender on whose behalf he is required by a parental direction to comply with the notification requirements attends a police station when a notification is made (s 89(2)(b))
  - (h) in the first four cases set out above, if he knowingly provides false information.
- The offence occurs on the first day of breach and continues—only one breach can be prosecuted in such circumstances.
- A conditional discharge cannot be imposed on breach.

📖 See *Blackstone's Criminal Practice 2012* **E23**

C9 **Immigration Offences**

Illegal entry and deception (Immigration Act 1971, s 24, 24A)

24 Illegal entry and similar offences

(1) [It is an offence—]
   (a) if contrary to this Act he knowingly enters the United Kingdom in breach of a deportation order or without leave;
   (b) if, having only a limited leave to enter or remain in the United Kingdom, he knowingly either—
      (i) remains beyond the time limited by the leave; or
      (ii) fails to observe a condition of the leave;
   (c) if, having lawfully entered the United Kingdom without leave by virtue of section 8(1) above, he remains without leave beyond the time allowed by section 8(1);
   (d) if, without reasonable excuse, he fails to comply with any requirement imposed on him under Schedule 2 to this Act to report to a medical officer of health, or to attend, or submit to a test or examination, as required by such an officer;
   (e) if, without reasonable excuse, he fails to observe any restriction imposed on him under Schedule 2 or 3 to this Act as to residence , as to his employment or occupation or as to reporting to the police, to an immigration officer or to the Secretary of State;
   (f) if he disembarks in the United Kingdom from a ship or aircraft after being placed on board under Schedule 2 or 3 to this Act with a view to his removal from the United Kingdom;
   (g) if he embarks in contravention of a restriction imposed by or under an Order in Council under section 3(7) of this Act.

(1A) A person commits an offence under subsection (1)(b)(i) above on the day when he first knows that the time limited by his leave has expired and continues to commit it throughout any period during which he is in the United Kingdom thereafter; but a person shall not be prosecuted under that provision more than once in respect of the same limited leave.

(3) The extended time limit for prosecutions which is provided for by section 28 below shall apply to offences under subsection (1)(a) and (c) above.

(4) In proceedings for an offence against subsection (1)(a) above of entering the United Kingdom without leave,—
   (a) any stamp purporting to have been imprinted on a passport or other travel document by an immigration officer on a particular date for the purpose of giving leave shall be presumed to have been duly so imprinted, unless the contrary is proved;
   (b) proof that a person had leave to enter the United Kingdom shall lie on the defence if, but only if, he is shown to have entered within six months before the date when the proceedings were commenced.

24A Deception

(1) A person who is not a British citizen is guilty of an offence if, by means which include deception by him—

(a) he obtains or seeks to obtain leave to enter or remain in the United Kingdom; or

(b) he secures or seeks to secure the avoidance, postponement or revocation of enforcement action against him.

(2) "Enforcement action", in relation to a person, means—

(a) the giving of directions for his removal from the United Kingdom ("directions") under Schedule 2 to this Act or section 10 of the Immigration and Asylum Act 1999;

(b) the making of a deportation order against him under section 5 of this Act; or

(c) his removal from the United Kingdom in consequence of directions or a deportation order.

SO s 24

EW s 24A

▦ Fine level 5/6 months (s 24)

▦ 6 months/2 years (s 24A)

Assisting unlawful entry (Immigration Act 1971, ss 25, 25A, and 25B)

25 Assisting unlawful immigration to member State

(1) A person commits an offence if he—

(a) does an act which facilitates the commission of a breach of immigration law by an individual who is not a citizen of the European Union,

(b) knows or has reasonable cause for believing that the act facilitates the commission of a breach of immigration law by the individual, and

(c) knows or has reasonable cause for believing that the individual is not a citizen of the European Union.

25A Helping asylum-seeker to enter United Kingdom

(1) A person commits an offence if—

(a) he knowingly and for gain facilitates the arrival in, or the entry into, the United Kingdom of an individual, and

(b) he knows or has reasonable cause to believe that the individual is an asylum-seeker.

25B Assisting entry to United Kingdom in breach of deportation or exclusion order

(1) A person commits an offence if he—

(a) does an act which facilitates a breach of a deportation order in force against an individual who is a citizen of the European Union, and

(b) knows or has reasonable cause for believing that the act facilitates a breach of the deportation order.

EW

 Fine level 5/6 months/14 years

Possessing false passports, work permits, registration cards, etc (Immigration Act 1971, ss 26 and 26A)

26 General offences in connection with administration of Act

(1) A person shall be guilty of an offence punishable on summary conviction with a fine of not more than level 5 on the standard scale or with imprisonment for not more than six months, or with both, in any of the following cases—

(a) if, without reasonable excuse, he refuses or fails to submit to examination under Schedule 2 to this Act;

(b) if, without reasonable excuse, he refuses to fails to furnish or produce any information in his possession, or any documents in his possession or control, which he is on an examination under that Schedule required to furnish or produce;

(c) if on any such examination or otherwise he makes or causes to be made to an immigration officer or other person lawfully acting in the execution of a relevant enactment a return, statement or representation which he knows to be false or does not believe to be true;

(d) if, without lawful authority, he alters any certificate of entitlement, entry clearance, work permit or other document issued or made under or for the purposes of this Act, or uses for the purposes of this Act, or has in his possession for such use, any passport, certificate of entitlement, entry clearance, work permit or other document which he knows or has reasonable cause to believe to be false;

(e) if, without reasonable excuse, he fails to complete and produce a landing or embarkation card in accordance with any order under Schedule 2 to this Act;

(f) if, without reasonable excuse, he fails to comply with any requirement of regulations under section 4(3) or of an order under section 4(4) above;

(g) if, without reasonable excuse, he obstructs an immigration officer or other person lawfully acting in the execution of this Act.

(2) The extended time limit for prosecutions which is provided for by section 28 below shall apply to offences under subsection (1)(c) and (d) above.

26A Registration card

...

(3) A person commits an offence if he—

(a) makes a false registration card,

(b) alters a registration card with intent to deceive or to enable another to deceive,

(c) has a false or altered registration card in his possession without reasonable excuse,

(d) uses or attempts to use a false registration card for a purpose for which a registration card is issued,

> (e) uses or attempts to use an altered registration card with intent to deceive,
> (f) makes an article designed to be used in making a false registration card,
> (g) makes an article designed to be used in altering a registration card with intent to deceive or to enable another to deceive, or
> (h) has an article within paragraph (f) or (g) in his possession without reasonable excuse.
>
> (4) In subsection (3) "false registration card" means a document which is designed to appear to be a registration card.

 Fine level 5/6 months/10 years (subsection (3)(a), (b), (d), (e), (f) or (g)), 2 years (subsection (3)(c) or (h))

C9.1 Key points

- Refugees are protected under Article 31 of the UN Convention relating to the status of refugees. Regard should always be had to *R v Uxbridge Magistrates' Court, ex p Adimi* [2001] QB 667, and the Law Society Practice Note available at: <http://www.lawsociety.org.uk/productsandservices/practicenotes/victimsoftrafficking.page>.
- The six-month time limit does not apply to offences under section 26(1)(c), (d) or section 28(1)(a), (c).
- The burden of proving that entry was legal falls upon the defendant in relation to prosecutions commenced within six months of that entry (s 24(4)(b)).

See *Blackstone's Criminal Practice 2012* **B22**

C10 **Prison Offences**

C10.1 **Prison licence, breach of**

Criminal Justice Act 1991, s 40A(4)

If the person fails to comply with such conditions as may for the time being be specified in the licence, he shall be liable on summary conviction—
(a) to a fine not exceeding level 3 on the standard scale; or
(b) to a sentence of imprisonment for a term not exceeding the relevant period,
but not liable to be dealt with in any other way.
. . . 'the relevant period' means a period which is equal in length to the period between the date on which the failure occurred or began and the date of the expiry of the licence.

SO

 See above

C10.1.1 **Key points**

• In relation to proving the licence conditions see *West Midlands Probation Board v French* [2008] EWHC 2631 (Admin).

C11 **Protective Order, Breach of**

- Protection from Harassment Act 1997, s 5(5)
- Family Law Act 1996, s 42A
- Restraining order, breach of: Protection from Harassment Act 1997, s 5(5)

 EW

 Level 5 fine and/or 6 months/5 years

DO

C11.1 *Sentencing*

Offence seriousness (culpability and harm) A. Identify the appropriate starting point Starting points based on first time offender pleading not guilty		
Examples of nature of activity	**Starting point**	**Range**
Single breach involving no/minimal direct contact	Low level community order	Band C fine to medium level community order
More than one breach involving no/minimal contact or some direct contact	Medium level community order	Low level community order to high level community order
Single breach involving some violence and/or significant physical or psychological harm to the victim	18 weeks custody	13 to 26 weeks custody
More than one breach involving some violence and/or significant physical or psychological harm to the victim	Crown Court	26 weeks custody to Crown Court
Breach (whether one or more) involving significant physical violence and significant physical or psychological harm to the victim	Crown Court	Crown Court

C11 Protective Order, Breach of

Offence seriousness (culpability and harm)	
B. Consider the effect of aggravating and mitigating factors (other than those within examples above) The following may be particularly relevant but **these lists are not exhaustive**	
Factors indicating higher culpability 1. Proven history of violence or threats by the offender 2. Using contact arrangements with a child to instigate offence 3. Offence is a further breach, following earlier breach proceedings 4. Offender has history of disobedience to court orders 5. Breach committed immediately or shortly after order made **Factors indicating greater degree of harm** 1. Victim is particularly vulnerable 2. Impact on children 3. Victim is forced to leave home	**Factors indicating lower culpability** 1. Breach occurred after long period of compliance 2. Victim initiated contact

 See *Blackstone's Criminal Practice 2012* B14.115

C12 **Public Order**

C12.1 **Affray**

> **Public Order Act 1986, s 3(1), (2), and (4)**
>
> (1) A person is guilty of affray if he uses or threatens unlawful violence towards another and his conduct is such as would cause a person of reasonable firmness present at the scene to fear for his personal safety.
> (2) Where 2 or more persons use or threaten the unlawful violence, it is the conduct of them taken together that must be considered for the purposes of subsection (1).
> (3) . . .
> (4) No person of reasonable firmness need actually be, or be likely to be, present at the scene.

EW

⊞ 6 months and/or level 5 fine/3 years

DO

C12.1.1 *Sentencing*

Offence seriousness (culpability and harm) A. Identify the appropriate starting point Starting points based on first time offender pleading not guilty		
Example of nature of activity	**Starting point**	**Range**
Brief offence involving low level violence, no substantial fear created	Low level community order	Band C fine to medium level community order
Degree of fighting or violence that causes substantial fear	High level community order	Medium level community order to 12 weeks custody
Fight involving a weapon/throwing objects, or conduct causing risk of serious injury	18 weeks custody	12 weeks custody to Crown Court

Offence seriousness (culpability and harm)
B. Consider the effect of aggravating and mitigating factors
(other than those within examples above)
The following may be particularly relevant but **these lists are not exhaustive**

Factors indicating higher culpability	Factors indicating lower culpability
1. Group action	1. Did not start the trouble
2. Threats	2. Provocation
3. Lengthy incident	3. Stopped as soon as police arrived

Factors indicating greater degree of harm	
1. Vulnerable person(s) present	
2. Injuries caused	
3. Damage to property	

C12.1.2 Key points

- Section 6 provides:

  A person is guilty of violent disorder or affray only if he intends to use or threaten violence or is aware that his conduct may be violent or threaten violence.

- A threat cannot be made by the use of words alone.
- Affray may be committed in private as well as in public places. In *Leeson v Director of Public Prosecutions* [2010] EWHC 994 (Admin) a conviction was quashed where L, who was drunk, had threatened a person with a knife in the bathroom of a private dwelling. The court held that an hypothetical bystander would have viewed the threat as being restricted to the parties involved due to the turbulence of their relationship (para 17).
- In *R v Sanchez* (1996) 160 JP 321 the court approved the following academic commentary:

  The offence of affray envisages at least three persons: (i) the person using or threatening unlawful violence; (ii) a person towards whom the violence or threat is directed; and (iii) a person of reasonable firmness who need not actually be, or be likely to be, present at the scene. Thus the question in the present case was not whether a person of reasonable firmness in J's shoes would have feared for his personal safety but whether this hypothetical person, present in the room and seeing D's conduct towards J, would have so feared.

  The definition of affray is very wide and the court agreed with D's counsel that care has to be taken to avoid extending it so widely that it would cover every case of common assault. A common assault may be very trivial, so that it would not cause anyone to fear for his 'personal safety'. But where the assault threatens serious harm to the victim, there may be evidence of affray depending on the circumstances. The person of reasonable firmness present in a small room as in the present case might fear for his personal safety whereas the same person, observing the same conduct in an open space, would not.

  The common law offence which it was intended to replace was, said the Law Commission, 'typically charged in cases of pitched street battles between rival gangs, spontaneous fights in public houses, clubs and at seaside resorts, and revenge attacks on individuals'.

 See *Blackstone's Criminal Practice 2012* **B11.34–B11.41**

C12.2 **Alcohol sale offences**

> **Licensing Act 2003, s 141 (sale of alcohol to drunk person), s 146 (sale of alcohol to children), s 147 (allowing sale of alcohol to children), S147A (persistently selling alcohol to children)**

Section 147A of the Licensing Act 2003 makes it an offence if, on three or more different occasions within a period of three consecutive months, alcohol is unlawfully sold on the same premises to a person under 18.

SO

 Level 3 fine (s 141), level 5 fine (ss 146 and 147), £10,000 fine (s 147A)

C12.2.1 *Sentencing (for Licensing Act 2003 offences only)*

Offence seriousness (culpability and harm)		
A. Identify the appropriate starting point		
Starting points based on first time offender pleading not guilty		
Examples of nature of activity	**Starting point**	**Range**
Sale to a child (ie person under 18)/ to a drunk person	Band B fine	Band A fine to band C fine

Offence seriousness (culpability and harm)	
B. Consider the effect of aggravating and mitigating factors (other than those within examples above)	
The following may be particularly relevant but **these lists are not exhaustive**	
Factors indicating higher culpability	
1. No attempt made to establish age	
2. Spirits/high alcohol level of drink	
3. Drunk person highly intoxicated	
4. Large quantity of alcohol supplied	
5. Sale intended for consumption by group of children/drunk people	
6. Offender in senior or management position	
Factors indicating greater degree of harm	
1. Younger child/children	
2. Drunk person causing distress to others	
3. Drunk person aggressive	

C12.2.2 Key points

- Provided a person has the authority to sell alcohol, it is irrelevant that he is unpaid (s 141).
- Section 146 provides:

Licensing Act 2003, s 146(4)–(6)

(4) Where a person is charged with an offence under this section by reason of his own conduct it is a defence that—
   (a) he believed that the individual was aged 18 or over, and
   (b) either—
      (i) he had taken all reasonable steps to establish the individual's age, or
      (ii) nobody could reasonably have suspected from the individual's appearance that he was aged under 18.

(5) For the purposes of subsection (4), a person is treated as having taken all reasonable steps to establish an individual's age if—
   (a) he asked the individual for evidence of his age, and
   (b) the evidence would have convinced a reasonable person.

(6) Where a person ('the accused') is charged with an offence under this section by reason of the act or default of some other person, it is a defence that the accused exercised all due diligence to avoid committing it.

C12.3 **Alcohol on coaches and trains**

Sporting Events (Control of Alcohol etc.) Act 1985, s 1(1)–(4)

(1) This section applies to a vehicle which—
   (a) is a public service vehicle or railway passenger vehicle, and
   (b) is being used for the principal purpose of carrying passengers for the whole or part of a journey to or from a designated sporting event.

(2) A person who knowingly causes or permits alcohol to be carried on a vehicle to which this section applies is guilty of an offence—
   (a) if the vehicle is a public service vehicle and he is the operator of the vehicle or the servant or agent of the operator, or
   (b) if the vehicle is a hired vehicle and he is the person to whom it is hired or the servant or agent of that person.

(3) A person who has alcohol in his possession while on a vehicle to which this section applies is guilty of an offence.

(4) A person who is drunk on a vehicle to which this section applies is guilty of an offence.

(5) In this section 'public service vehicle' and 'operator' have the same meaning as in the Public Passenger Vehicles Act 1981.

Fine level 4 (s 1(2) offence), 3 months/fine level 3 (s 1(3) offence), fine level 2 (s 1(4) offence)

C12.4 **Bladed article or offensive weapon, possession of**

Criminal Justice Act 1988, s 139(1)–(3)

(1) Subject to subsections (4) and (5) below, any person who has an article to which this section applies with him in a public place shall be guilty of an offence.

(2) Subject to subsection (3) below, this section applies to any article which has a blade or is sharply pointed except a folding pocketknife.

(3) This section applies to a folding pocketknife if the cutting edge of its blade exceeds 3 inches.

Prevention of Crime Act 1953, s 1(1)

(1) Any person who without lawful authority or reasonable excuse, the proof whereof shall lie on him, has with him in any public place any offensive weapon shall be guilty of an offence.

Criminal Justice Act 1988, s 139A(1)–(2)

(1) Any person who has an article to which section 139 of this Act applies with him on school premises shall be guilty of an offence.

(2) Any person who has an offensive weapon within the meaning of section 1 of the Prevention of Crime Act 1953 with him on school premises shall be guilty of an offence.

 6 months and/or level 5 fine/4 years

C12.4.1 *Sentencing*

Offence seriousness (culpability and harm)		
A. Identify the appropriate starting point		
Starting points based on first time offender pleading not guilty		
Examples of nature of activity	**Starting point**	**Range**
Weapon not used to threaten or cause fear	High level community order	Band C fine to 12 weeks custody
Weapon not used to threaten or cause fear but offence committed in dangerous circumstances	6 weeks custody	High level community order to Crown Court
Weapon used to threaten or cause fear and offence committed in dangerous circumstances	Crown Court	Crown Court

Offence seriousness (culpability and harm)	
B. Consider the effect of aggravating and mitigating factors	
(other than those within examples above)	
The following may be particularly relevant but **these lists are not exhaustive**	
Factors indicating higher culpability	**Factors indicating lower culpability**
1. Particularly dangerous weapon 2. Specifically planned use of weapon to commit violence, threaten violence, or intimidate 3. Offence motivated by hostility towards minority individual or group 4. Offender under influence of drink or drugs 5. Offender operating in group or gang **Factors indicating greater degree of harm** 1. Offence committed at school, hospital, or other place where vulnerable persons may be present 2. Offence committed on premises where people carrying out public services 3. Offence committed on or outside licensed premises 4. Offence committed on public transport 5. Offence committed at large public gathering, especially where there may be risk of disorder	1. Weapon carried only on temporary basis 2. Original possession legitimate eg in course of trade or business

C12.4.2 Key points

- Section 139 (bladed articles) provides:

Criminal Justice Act 1988, s 139(4)–(5)

(4) It shall be a defence for a person charged with an offence under this section to prove that he had good reason or lawful authority for having the article with him in a public place.

(5) Without prejudice to the generality of subsection (4) above, it shall be a defence for a person charged with an offence under this section to prove that he had the article with him—

    (a) for use at work;

    (b) for religious reasons; or

    (c) as part of any national costume.

- A lock knife is not a folding knife, irrespective of the blade length (*Harris v Director of Public Prosecutions* [1993] 1 WLR 82).
- A screwdriver is not a bladed article (*R v Davis* [1998] Crim LR 564).
- A blade does not need to be sharp—a butter knife can be a bladed article (*Brooker v Director of Public Prosecutions* [2005] EWHC 1132).
- The fact that a defendant's employment was only casual was not a relevant consideration (*Chalal v Director of Public Prosecutions* [2010] EWHC 439 (Admin)).

Section 1 (offensive weapons) provides that lawful authority and reasonable excuses are capable of being a defence to this charge. Typical defences advanced, the success of which will be heavily fact-dependent, include: forgetfulness (*R v Tsap* [2008] EWCA Crim 2580—but note that 'mere' forgetfulness cannot amount to a defence); self-defence (eg *R v McAuley* [2009] EWCA Crim 2130).

- An offensive weapon means any article made or adapted for use for causing injury to the person, or intended by the person having it with him for such use by him, or by some other person.
- Weapons held by the appellate courts to be offensive per se include: a bayonet, a stiletto, a handgun, a butterfly knife, and a flickknife. Items that are inherently dangerous, but manufactured for a lawful purpose, are not offensive per se (eg razor blades, baseball bat, kitchen knives). It is submitted that items prohibited for sale in England and Wales by virtue of the Criminal Justice Act 1988 (Offensive Weapons) (Amendment) Order 1988 are offensive per se. It is necessary to show that the person knew that they were in possession of the offensive weapon (*R v Cugullere* [1961] 2 All ER 343).

- Section 139A weapons on school premises:
  - school premises extend to surrounding land, playing fields, and yards;
  - the offence can be committed when the school is closed;
  - private schools premises fall within the Act.

See *Blackstone's Criminal Practice 2012* B12.117–B12.142

C12.5 **Sale of knives and certain articles with blade or point to persons under 18**

Criminal Justice Act 1988, s 141A

141A Sale of knives and certain articles with blade or point to persons under eighteen

(1) Any person who sells to a person under the age of eighteen years an article to which this section applies shall be guilty of an offence and liable on summary conviction to imprisonment for a term not exceeding six months, or a fine not exceeding level 5 on the standard scale, or both.

(2) Subject to subsection (3) below, this section applies to—
   (a) any knife, knife blade or razor blade,
   (b) any axe, and
   (c) any other article which has a blade or which is sharply pointed and which is made or adapted for use for causing injury to the person.

(3) This section does not apply to any article described in—
   (a) section 1 of the Restriction of Offensive Weapons Act 1959.
   (b) an order made under section 141(2) of this Act, or
   (c) an order made by the Secretary of State under this section.

(4) It shall be a defence for a person charged with an offence under subsection (1) above to prove that he took all reasonable precautions and exercised all due diligence to avoid the commission of the offence.

SO

See above

C12.5.1 Key points

- A grapefruit knife is a knife for the purposes of section 141A (*R (Windsor and Maidenhead Royal Borough) v East Berkshire Justices* [2010] EWHC 3020 (Admin)).

C12.6 **Disorderly behaviour (harassment, alarm, or distress)**

Public Order Act 1986, s 5(1)

(1) A person is guilty of an offence if he—
   (a) uses threatening, abusive or insulting words or behaviour, or disorderly behaviour, or
   (b) displays any writing, sign or other visible representation which is threatening, abusive or insulting,
   within the hearing or sight of a person likely to be caused harassment, alarm or distress thereby.

SO

 Level 3 fine; level 4 fine if racially or religiously aggravated

C12.6.1 *Sentencing*

Offence seriousness (culpability and harm) A. Identify the appropriate starting point Starting points based on first time offender pleading not guilty		
Examples of nature of activity	**Starting point**	**Range**
Shouting, causing disturbance for some minutes	Band A fine	Conditional discharge to band B fine
Substantial disturbance caused	Band B fine	Band A fine to band C fine

Offence seriousness (culpability and harm)
B. Consider the effect of aggravating and mitigating factors
(other than those within examples above)
The following may be particularly relevant but **these lists are not exhaustive**

Factors indicating higher culpability	Factors indicating lower culpability
1. Group action	1. Stopped as soon as police arrived
2. Lengthy incident	2. Brief/minor incident
Factors indicating greater degree of harm	3. Provocation
1. Vulnerable person(s) present	
2. Offence committed at school, hospital, or other place where vulnerable persons may be present	
3. Victim providing public service	

C12.6.2　Key points

- Section 5 provides:

> **Public Order Act 1986, s 5(3)**
>
> (3) It is a defence for the accused to prove—
>   (a) that he had no reason to believe that there was any person within hearing or sight who was likely to be caused harassment, alarm or distress, or
>   (b) that he was inside a dwelling and had no reason to believe that the words or behaviour used, or the writing, sign or other visible representation displayed, would be heard or seen by a person outside that or any other dwelling, or
>   (c) that his conduct was reasonable.

- Section 6 provides:

> **Public Order Act 1986, s 6(4)**
>
> (4) A person is guilty of an offence under section 5 only if he intends his words or behaviour, or the writing, sign or other visible representation, to be threatening, abusive or insulting, or is aware that it may be threatening, abusive or insulting or (as the case may be) he intends his behaviour to be or is aware that it may be disorderly.

- An offence under this section may be committed in a public or a private place, except that no offence is committed where the words or behaviour are used, or the writing, sign, or other visible representation is displayed, by a person inside a dwelling and the other person is also inside that or another dwelling.
- A person can be harassed without emotional upset (*Southard v Director of Public Prosecutions* [2006] EWHC 3449 (Admin)).

In *Southard* the defendant intervened in his brother's arrest shouting 'fuck off' and 'fuck you' at the officer. The conviction was upheld. The harassment must not, however, be trivial (eg *R (R) v Director of Public Prosecutions* [2006] EWHC 1375 (Admin)—another case involving a police officer where the conviction was quashed).

- Concealing a video camera in a changing room can amount to disorderly behaviour (*Vigon v Director of Public Prosecutions* (1997) 162 JP 115).
- For ECHR considerations (and in particular Article 10) see *Abdul and Others v Crown Prosecution Service* [2011] EWHC 247 (Admin)).

 See *Blackstone's Criminal Practice 2012* B11.61–B11.72

C12.7 **Disorderly behaviour with intent to cause harassment, alarm, or distress**

Public Order Act 1986, s 4A(1)

(1) A person is guilty of an offence if, with intent to cause a person harassment, alarm or distress, he—
    (a) uses threatening, abusive or insulting words or behaviour, or disorderly behaviour, or
    (b) displays any writing, sign or other visible representation which is threatening, abusive or insulting,
    thereby causing that or another person harassment, alarm or distress.

SO

 6 months and/or level 5 fine

Note: racially or religiously aggravated offence is triable either way (2 years on indictment).

C12.7.1 *Sentencing*

Offence seriousness (culpability and harm) A. Identify the appropriate starting point Starting points based on first time offender pleading not guilty		
Examples of nature of activity	**Starting point**	**Range**
Threats, abuse, or insults made more than once but on same occasion against the same person eg while following down the street	Band C fine	Band B fine to low level community order
Group action or deliberately planned action against targeted victim	Medium level community order	Low level community order to 12 weeks custody
Weapon brandished or used or threats against vulnerable victim—course of conduct over longer period	12 weeks custody	High level community order to 26 weeks custody

Offence seriousness (culpability and harm) B. Consider the effect of aggravating and mitigating factors (other than those within examples above) The following may be particularly relevant but **these lists are not exhaustive**	
Factors indicating higher culpability 1. High degree of planning 2. Offender deliberately isolates victim **Factors indicating greater degree of harm** 1. Offence committed in vicinity of victim's home 2. Large number of people in vicinity 3. Actual or potential escalation into violence 4. Particularly serious impact on victim	**Factors indicating lower culpability** 1. Very short period 2. Provocation

C12.7.2 Key points

- Section 4A(3) provides:

> **Public Order Act 1986, s 4A(3)**
>
> (3) It is a defence for the accused to prove—
>   (a) that he was inside a dwelling and had no reason to believe that the words or behaviour used, or the writing, sign or other visible representation displayed, would be heard or seen by a person outside that or any other dwelling, or
>   (b) that his conduct was reasonable.

- An offence under this section may be committed in a public or a private place, except that no offence is committed where the words or behaviour are used, or the writing, sign or other visible representation is displayed, by a person inside a dwelling and the person who is harassed, alarmed, or distressed is also inside that or another dwelling.
- For ECHR considerations (and in particular Article 10) see *Abdul and Others v Crown Prosecution Service* [2011] EWHC 247 (Admin)).

See *Blackstone's Criminal Practice 2012* **B11.52–11.60**

C12.8 **Drunk and disorderly in a public place**

Criminal Justice Act 1967, s 91(1), (2), and (4)

(1) Any person who in any public place is guilty, while drunk, of disorderly behaviour . . . shall be liable on summary conviction to a fine not exceeding [level 3 on the standard scale].

(2) The foregoing subsection shall have effect instead of any corresponding provision contained in section 12 of the Licensing Act 1872, section 58 of the Metropolitan Police Act 1839, section 37 of the City of London Police Act 1839, and section 29 of the Town Police Clauses Act 1847 (being enactments which authorise the imposition of a short term of imprisonment or of a fine not exceeding £10 or both for the corresponding offence) and instead of any corresponding provision contained in any local Act.

(3) . . .

(4) In this section 'public place' includes any highway and any other premises or place to which at the material time the public have or are permitted to have access, whether on payment or otherwise.

SO Level 3 fine

C12.8.1 *Sentencing*

Offence seriousness (culpability and harm) A. Identify the appropriate starting point Starting points based on first time offender pleading not guilty		
Examples of nature of activity	**Starting point**	**Range**
Shouting, causing disturbance for some minutes	Band A fine	Conditional discharge to band B fine
Substantial disturbance caused	Band B fine	Band A fine to band C fine

Offence seriousness (culpability and harm)
B. Consider the effect of aggravating and mitigating factors
(other than those within examples above)
The following may be particularly relevant but **these lists are not exhaustive**

Factors indicating higher culpability	**Factors indicating lower culpability**
1. Brandishing firearm	1. Firearm not in sight
2. Carrying firearm in a busy place	2. No intention to use firearm
3. Planned illegal use	3. Firearm to be used for lawful purpose
Factors indicating greater degree	(not amounting to defence)
of harm	
1. Person or people put in fear	
2. Offender participating in violent incident	

C12.8.2 Key points

- In *Carroll v Director of Public Prosecutions* [2009] EWHC 554 (Admin) the court stated that:

> The offence requires proof of three elements, namely that (1) the defendant was drunk; (2) he was in a public place; and (3) he was guilty of disorderly behaviour. Only the first and third elements call for further comment:

> 9. As to the first element in *Neale v E (A Minor)* (1983) 80 Crim App R 20, this court (Robert Goff LJ and Mann J, as they each then were) decided that the word 'drunk' should be given its ordinary and natural meaning. In the end, therefore, whether a defendant was drunk is a simple question of fact in each case. On familiar principles it is the voluntary consumption of alcohol which is the requisite mens rea, such as it is, of this most basic offence. If that voluntary consumption results in the defendant becoming drunk then the first element of the offence is proved.

> 10. As to the third element, there is no requirement for mens rea at all. What is required is proof that objectively viewed the defendant was guilty of disorderly behaviour. Specific drunken intent and recklessness are nothing to the point. The words 'disorderly behaviour' are again to be given their ordinary and natural meaning. In the end, therefore, it is a simple question of fact in each case: whether the defendant is guilty of disorderly behaviour.

 See *Blackstone's Criminal Practice 2012* **B11.180–B11.184**

C12.9 **Firearm, carrying in public place**

Firearms Act 1968, s 19

A person commits an offence if, without lawful authority or reasonable excuse (the proof whereof lies on him) he has with him in a public place—

(a) a loaded shot gun,

(b) an air weapon (whether loaded or not),

(c) any other firearm (whether loaded or not) together with ammunition suitable for use in that firearm, or

(d) an imitation firearm.

 (Summary only if an air weapon)

 6 months and/or level 5 fine/7 years (12 months if imitation weapon)

C12.9.1 *Sentencing*

Offence seriousness (culpability and harm)		
A. Identify the appropriate starting point		
Starting points based on first time offender pleading not guilty		
Examples of nature of activity	**Starting point**	**Range**
Carrying an unloaded air weapon	Low level community order	Band B fine to medium level community order
Carrying loaded air weapon/imitation firearm/ unloaded shot gun without ammunition	High level community order	Medium level community order to 26 weeks custody (air weapon) Medium level community order to Crown Court (imitation firearm, unloaded shot gun)
Carrying loaded shot gun/ carrying shot gun or any other firearm together with ammunition for it	Crown Court	Crown Court

Offence seriousness (culpability and harm)
B. Consider the effect of aggravating and mitigating factors
(other than those within examples above)
The following may be particularly relevant but **these lists are not exhaustive**

Factors indicating higher culpability	Factors indicating lower culpability
1. Brandishing firearm	1. Firearm not in sight
2. Carrying firearm in a busy place	2. No intention to use firearm
3. Planned illegal use	3. Firearm to be used for lawful purpose
Factors indicating greater degree	(not amounting to defence)
of harm	
1. Person or people put in fear	
2. Offender participating in violent incident	

C12.9.2 **Key points**

- It is not necessary to show that the defendant knew that a gun was loaded (*R v Harrison* [1996] Crim LR 200).
- An item is an imitation firearm if it 'looked like' a firearm at the time of its use (*R v Morris and King* (1984) 149 JP 60).
- A part of the body (eg fingers pointed under clothing) could not constitute an imitation firearm (*R v Bentham* [2005] UKHL 18).

See *Blackstone's Criminal Practice 2012* **B12.89**

C12.10 **Air guns**

Firearms Act 1968, s 22(4)

It is an offence for a person under the age of eighteen to have with him an air weapon or ammunition for an air weapon.

SO

 Level 3 fine

C12.10.1 Key points

• Section 23 provides:

Firearms Act 1968, s 23

(1) It is not an offence under section 22(4) of this Act for a person to have with him an air weapon or ammunition while he is under the supervision of a person of or over the age of twenty-one; but where a person has with him an air weapon on any premises in circumstances where he would be prohibited from having it with him but for this subsection, it is an offence for the person under whose supervision he is to allow him to use it for firing any missile beyond those premises.

(1A) In proceedings against a person for an offence under subsection (1) it shall be a defence for him to show that the only premises into or across which the missile was fired were premises the occupier of which had consented to the firing of the missile (whether specifically or by way of a general consent).

(2) It is not an offence under section 22(4) of this Act for a person to have with him an air weapon or ammunition at a time when—

(a) being a member of a rifle club or miniature rifle club for the time being approved by the Secretary of State for the purposes of this section or section 15 of the Firearms (Amendment) Act 1988, he is engaged as such a member in connection with target shooting; or

(b) he is using the weapon or ammunition at a shooting gallery where the only firearms used are either air weapons or miniature rifles not exceeding .23 inch calibre.

(3) It is not an offence under section 22(4) of this Act for a person of or over the age of fourteen to have with him an air weapon or ammunition on private premises with the consent of the occupier.

 See *Blackstone's Criminal Practice 2012* **B12.42–B12.46**

C12.11 **Football related offences**

Sporting Events (Control of Alcohol etc.) Act 1985, s 2(1)

This concerns possession of alcohol whilst entering or trying to enter ground), s 2(1), (2) (being drunk in, or whilst trying to enter, ground); Football Offences Act 1991, s 2 (throwing missile), s 3 (indecent or racist chanting), s 4 (going onto prohibited areas); Criminal Justice and Public Order Act 1994, s 166 (unauthorized sale or attempted sale of tickets).

Sporting Events (Control of Alcohol etc.) Act 1985, s 2(1) and (2)

(1) A person who has alcohol or an article to which this section applies in his possession—

  (a) at any time during the period of a designated sporting event when he is in any area of a designated sports ground from which the event may be directly viewed, or

  (b) while entering or trying to enter a designated sports ground at any time during the period of a designated sporting event at that ground,

  is guilty of an offence.

(1A) Subsection (1)(a) above has effect subject to section 5A(1) of this Act.

(2) A person who is drunk in a designated sports ground at any time during the period of a designated sporting event at that ground or is drunk while entering or trying to enter such a ground at any time during the period of a designated sporting event at that ground is guilty of an offence.

(3) This section applies to any article capable of causing injury to a person struck by it, being—

  (a) a bottle, can or other portable container (including such an article when crushed or broken) which—

    (i) is for holding any drink, and

    (ii) is of a kind which, when empty, is normally discarded or returned to, or left to be recovered by, the supplier, or

  (b) part of an article falling within paragraph (a) above;

  but does not apply to anything that is for holding any medicinal product (within the meaning of the Medicines Act 1968) or any veterinary medicinal product (within the meaning of the Veterinary Medicines Regulations 2006).

Football Offences Act 1991, ss 2, 3, and 4

2 Throwing of missiles

It is an offence for a person at a designated football match to throw anything at or towards—

(a) the playing area, or any area adjacent to the playing area to which spectators are not generally admitted, or

(b) any area in which spectators or other persons are or may be present,

without lawful authority or lawful excuse (which shall be for him to prove).

3 Indecent or racialist chanting

(1) It is an offence to engage or take part in chanting of an indecent or racialist nature at a designated football match.

(2) For this purpose—

  (a) 'chanting' means the repeated uttering of any words or sounds (whether alone or in concert with one or more others); and

  (b) 'of a racialist nature' means consisting of or including matter which is threatening, abusive or insulting to a person by reason of his colour, race, nationality (including citizenship) or ethnic or national origins.

4 Going onto the playing area

It is an offence for a person at a designated football match to go onto the playing area, or any area adjacent to the playing area to which spectators are not generally admitted, without lawful authority or lawful excuse (which shall be for him to prove).

Criminal Justice and Public Order Act 1994, s 166

(1) It is an offence for an unauthorised person to—
   (a) sell a ticket for a designated football match, or
   (b) otherwise to dispose of such a ticket to another person.
(2) For this purpose—
   (a) a person is 'unauthorised' unless he is authorised in writing to sell or otherwise dispose of tickets for the match by the organisers of the match;
   (aa) a reference to selling a ticket includes a reference to—
      (i) offering to sell a ticket;
      (ii) exposing a ticket for sale;
      (iii) making a ticket available for sale by another;
      (iv) advertising that a ticket is available for purchase; and
      (v) giving a ticket to a person who pays or agrees to pay for some other goods or services or offering to do so.
   (b) a 'ticket' means anything which purports to be a ticket;

SO

 3 months/level 3 (s 2(1) offence), level 2 (s 2(2) offence)
Level 3 fine (throwing missile; indecent or racialist chanting; going onto prohibited areas)
Level 5 fine (unauthorized sale of tickets)
Level 3 fine and/or 3 months (possession of alcohol)

C12.11.1 *Sentencing*

Offence seriousness (culpability and harm) A. Identify the appropriate starting point Starting points based on first time offender pleading not guilty		
Examples of nature of activity	**Starting point**	**Range**
Being drunk in, or whilst trying to enter, ground	Band A fine	Conditional discharge to band B fine
Going onto playing or other prohibited area; unauthorized sale or attempted sale of tickets	Band B fine	Band A fine to band C fine
Throwing missile; indecent or racialist chanting	Band C fine	Band C fine
Possession of alcohol whilst entering or trying to enter ground	Band C fine	Band B fine to high level community order

Offence seriousness (culpability and harm)	
B. Consider the effect of aggravating and mitigating factors	
(other than those within examples above)	
The following may be particularly relevant but **these lists are not exhaustive**	
Factors indicating higher culpability 1. Commercial ticket operation; potential high cash value; counterfeit tickets 2. Inciting others to misbehave 3. Possession of large quantity of alcohol 4. Offensive language or behaviour (where not an element of the offence) **Factor indicating greater degree of harm** 1. Missile likely to cause serious injury eg coin, glass, bottle, stone	

 See *Blackstone's Criminal Practice 2012* B11.112–B11.116 and B11.192–B11.196

C12.12 **Threatening behaviour, fear, or provocation of violence**

Public Order Act 1986, s 4(1)

(1) A person is guilty of an offence if he—
  (a) uses towards another person threatening, abusive or insulting words or behaviour, or
  (b) distributes or displays to another person any writing, sign or other visible representation which is threatening, abusive or insulting,
  with intent to cause that person to believe that immediate unlawful violence will be used against him or another by any person, or to provoke the immediate use of unlawful violence by that person or another, or whereby that person is likely to believe that such violence will be used or it is likely that such violence will be provoked.

SO (Racially or religiously aggravated offence is triable either way)

▥ 6 months and/or level 5 fine. Racially or religiously aggravated offence carries a maximum 2 years on indictment

C12.12.1 *Sentencing*

Offence seriousness (culpability and harm) A. Identify the appropriate starting point Starting points based on first time offender pleading not guilty		
Examples of nature of activity	**Starting point**	**Range**
Fear or threat of low level immediate unlawful violence such as push, shove, or spit	Low level community order	Band B fine to medium level community order
Fear or threat of medium level immediate unlawful violence such as punch	High level community order	Low level community order to 12 weeks custody
Fear or threat of high level immediate unlawful violence such as use of weapon; missile thrown; gang involvement	12 weeks custody	6 to 26 weeks custody

Offence seriousness (culpability and harm) B. Consider the effect of aggravating and mitigating factors (other than those within examples above) The following may be particularly relevant but **these lists are not exhaustive**	
Factors indicating higher culpability 1. Planning 2. Offender deliberately isolates victim 3. Group action 4. Threat directed at victim because of job 5. History of antagonism towards victim **Factors indicating greater degree of harm** 1. Offence committed at school, hospital, or other place where vulnerable persons may be present 2. Offence committed on enclosed premises such as public transport 3. Vulnerable victim(s) 4. Victim needs medical help/counselling	**Factors indicating lower culpability** 1. Impulsive action 2. Short duration 3. Provocation

C12.12.2 Key points

- A person is guilty of an offence under section 4 only if he intends his words or behaviour, or the writing, sign, or other visible representation, to be threatening, abusive, or insulting, or is aware that it may be threatening, abusive, or insulting.
- An offence under this section may be committed in a public or a private place, except that no offence is committed where the words or behaviour are used, or the writing, sign, or other visible representation is distributed or displayed, by a person inside a dwelling and the other person is also inside that or another dwelling.
- For ECHR considerations (and in particular Article 10) see *Abdul and Others v Crown Prosecution Service* [2011] EWHC 247 (Admin)).

See *Blackstone's Criminal Practice 2012* **B11.42–B11.51**

C12.13 **Taxi touting/soliciting for hire**

Criminal Justice and Public Order Act 1994, s 167

 Level 4 fine

C12.13.1 *Sentencing*

Offence seriousness (culpability and harm) A. Identify the appropriate starting point Starting points based on first time offender pleading not guilty		
Examples of nature of activity	**Starting point**	**Range**
Licensed taxi-driver touting for trade (ie making approach rather than waiting for a person to initiate hiring)	Band A fine	Conditional discharge to band A fine and consider disqualification 1-3 months
PHV licence held but touting for trade rather than being booked through an operator; an accomplice to touting	Band B fine	Band A fine to band C fine and consider disqualification 3-6 months
No PHV licence held	Band C fine	Band B fine to band C fine and disqualification 6-12 months

Offence seriousness (culpability and harm) B. Consider the effect of aggravating and mitigating factors (other than those within examples above) The following may be particularly relevant but **these lists are not exhaustive**	
Factors indicating higher culpability 1. Commercial business/large scale operation 2. No insurance/invalid insurance 3. No driving licence and/or no MOT 4. Vehicle not roadworthy **Factors indicating greater degree of harm** 1. Deliberately diverting trade from taxi rank 2. PHV licence had been refused/offender ineligible for licence	**Factor indicating lower culpability** 1. Providing a service when no licensed taxi available

C12.14 **Violent disorder**

Public Order Act 1986, s 2(1)–(3)

(1) Where 3 or more persons who are present together use or threaten unlawful violence and the conduct of them (taken together) is such as would cause a person of reasonable firmness present at the scene to fear for his personal safety, each of the persons using or threatening unlawful violence is guilty of violent disorder.

(2) It is immaterial whether or not the 3 or more use or threaten unlawful violence simultaneously.

 EW

 6 months and/or level 5 fine/5 years

DO

C12.14.1 *Sentencing*

Offence seriousness (culpability and harm)
A. Identify the appropriate starting point
Starting points based on first time offender pleading not guilty

The offences should normally be dealt with in the Crown Court
However, there may be rare cases involving minor violence or threats of violence leading to no or minor injury, with few people involved and no weapon or missiles, in which a custodial sentence within the jurisdiction of a magistrates' court may be appropriate.

C12.14.2 **Key points**

- The expression means no more than being in the same place at the same time. Three or more people using or threatening violence in the same place at the same time, whether for the same purpose or different purposes, are capable of creating a daunting prospect for those who may encounter them simply by reason of the fact that they represent a breakdown of law and order which has unpredictable consequences. [The court is unable] to accept that the phrase requires any degree of cooperation between those who are using or threatening violence; all that is required is that they be present in the same place at the same time. The section is concerned with public disorder and is deliberately worded in a way that is apt to apply to anyone who uses or threatens violence of the requisite nature

---

in a particular context, namely, in a public place where others are engaged in the same activity. . . .the requirement that the conduct of the participants taken together should be such as to cause members of the public to fear for their safety was included in order to direct attention to the overall effect of what may otherwise be unrelated acts or threats of violence (*R v NW* [2010] EWCA Crim 404).

- No person of reasonable firmness need actually be, or be likely to be, present at the scene.
- The use of words alone is not sufficient.
- A fight in public does not automatically become an affray (*R v Plavecz* [2002] EWCA Crim 1802).
- Section 6 provides:

   A person is guilty of violent disorder or affray only if he intends to use or threaten violence or is aware that his conduct may be violent or threaten violence.

Violent disorder may be committed in private as well as in public places.

 See *Blackstone's Criminal Practice 2012* **B11.26–B11.33**

C13 **Road Traffic Offences, Definitions**

C13.1 *Accident*

Accident is to be given its ordinary meaning (*Chief Constable of West Midlands v Billingham* [1979] 1 WLR 747). A deliberate act can amount to an accident (*Chief Constable of Staffordshire v Lees* [1981] RTR 506). A physical impact is not necessary (*R v Currie* [2007] EWCA Crim 927), but the *de minimis* principle applies (*R v Morris* [1972] 1 WLR 228).

C13.2 *Causing*

Causing requires a positive act (*Ross Hillman Ltd v Bond* [1974] QB 435) committed with prior knowledge.

C13.3 *Driver*

Section 192 of the Road Traffic Act 1988 provides:

> **Road Traffic Act 1988, s 192(1)**
>
> . . . 'driver', where a separate person acts as a steersman of a motor vehicle, includes (except for the purposes of section 1 of this Act) that person as well as any other person engaged in the driving of the vehicle, and 'drive' is to be interpreted accordingly . . .

A person supervising a driver will not be a driver unless they exercise some control over the vehicle (dual controls, for example) (*Evans v Walkden* [1956] 1 WLR 1019).

C13.4 *Driving*

R v MacDonagh [1974] QB 448 defined driving as use of the driver's controls for the purpose of directing the movement of the vehicle. The court gave the following guidance:

> There are an infinite number of ways in which a person may control the movement of a motor vehicle, apart from the orthodox one of sitting in the driving seat and using the engine for propulsion. He may be coasting down a hill with the gears in neutral and the engine switched off; he may be steering a vehicle which is being towed by another. As has already been pointed out, he may be sitting in the driving seat whilst others push, or half sitting in the driving seat but keeping one foot on the road in order to induce the car to move. Finally, as in the present case, he may be standing in the road and

himself pushing the car with or without using the steering wheel to direct it. Although the word 'drive' must be given a wide meaning, the Courts must be alert to see that the net is not thrown so widely that it includes activities which cannot be said to be driving a motor vehicle in any ordinary use of that word in the English language.

As a person may be driving a stationary vehicle, it is a matter of fact to be decided in each case and factors such as the reason for the vehicle stopping and the duration of the stop will be relevant (*Planton v Director of Public Prosecutions* [2002] RTR 107).

Steering a vehicle being towed would amount to driving where there was an operational breaking system (*McQuaid v Anderton* [1981] 1 WLR 154), as would freewheeling a vehicle down a hill while steering (*Saycell v Bool* [1948] 2 All ER 83). A person steering from the passenger seat is driving (*Tyler v Whatmore* [1976] RTR 83).

C13.5 *In charge*

In cases where the matter is not clear, the case of *Director of Public Prosecutions v Watkins* (1989) 89 Cr App R 112 should be considered in detail. The court laid down the following broad guidance:

> Broadly there are two distinct classes of case. (1) If the defendant is the owner or lawful possessor of the vehicle or has recently driven it, he will have been in charge of it, and the question for the Court will be whether he is still in charge or whether he has relinquished his charge. Usually such a defendant will be prima facie in charge unless he has put the vehicle in someone else's charge. However he would not be so if in all the circumstances he has ceased to be in actual control and there is no realistic possibility of his resuming actual control while unfit: eg if he is at home in bed for the night, if he is a great distance from the car, or if it is taken by another.
>
> (2) If the defendant is not the owner, the lawful possessor, or recent driver but is sitting in the vehicle or is otherwise involved with it, the question for the Court is, as here, whether he has assumed being in charge of it. In this class of case the defendant will be in charge if, whilst unfit, he is voluntarily in de facto control of the vehicle or if, in the circumstances, including his position, his intentions and his actions, he may be expected imminently to assume control. Usually this will involve his having gained entry to the car and evinced an intention to take control of it. But gaining entry may not be necessary if he has manifested that intention some other way, eg by stealing the keys of a car in circumstances which show he means presently to drive it.
>
> The circumstances to be taken into account will vary infinitely, but the following will be usually relevant:
> (i)   Whether and where he is in the vehicle or how far he is from it.
> (ii) What he is doing at the relevant time.
> (iii) Whether he is in possession of a key that fits the ignition.
> (iv) Whether there is evidence of an intention to take or assert control of the car by driving or otherwise.

(v) Whether any other person is in, at or near the vehicle and if so, the like particulars in respect of that person.

It will be for the Court to consider all the above factors with any others which may be relevant and reach its decision as a question of fact and degree.

C13.6 *Motor vehicle*

There is no statutory definition of vehicle and therefore its ordinary meaning of a carriage or conveyance should apply. Where the statute uses the phrase 'motor vehicle', the definition to be found in section 185 of the Road Traffic Act 1988 states that it is a 'mechanically propelled vehicle intended or adapted for use on roads'. The maximum speed of the vehicle is not a relevant factor (*Director of Public Prosecutions v King* [2008] EWHC 447 (Admin)).

C13.7 *Owner*

This includes a person in possession of a vehicle under a hire or hire purchase agreement.

C13.8 *Permitting*

A person permits use when he allows or authorizes use, or fails to take reasonable steps to prevent use. For permitting no insurance the prosecution do not need to show that the person knew the driver to be uninsured. If, however, use is conditional (for example, on the person having insurance) the outcome would be different (*Newbury v Davis* [1974] RTR 367).

C13.9 *Public place*

This is a place to which the public have access. However, the law draws a distinction between general public access, and access for a defined group of persons. The law in this area is complex and voluminous and advocates should always seek an adjournment where the answer is not clear.

C13.10 *Road*

This is defined as any highway or road to which the public has access. The following have been held to be a road:

- Pedestrian pavement (*Randall v Motor Insurers' Bureau* [1968] 1 WLR 1900).
- Grass verge at the side of a road (*Worth v Brooks* [1959] Crim LR 855).

It will be a matter of fact and degree as to whether something is a road, and whether or not the public have access. A car park will not generally be a road, even if there are roads running through it. In *Barrett v Director of Public Prosecutions*, unreported, 10 February 2009 the court held that a roadway running through a private caravan park, and facilitating entry to a beach, constituted a road.

 See *Blackstone's Criminal Practice 2012* **C1**

C14 Road Traffic Offences, Suitable for Fine/Discharge

C14.1 Careless driving (drive without due care and attention)

Road Traffic Act 1988, s 3

If a person drives a mechanically propelled vehicle on a road or other public place without due care and attention, or without reasonable consideration for other persons using the road or place, he is guilty of an offence.

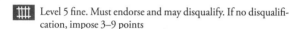 Level 5 fine. Must endorse and may disqualify. If no disqualification, impose 3–9 points

C14.1.1 *Sentencing*

Offence seriousness (culpability and harm) A. Identify the appropriate starting point Starting points based on first time offender pleading not guilty		
Example of nature of activity	**Starting point**	**Range**
Momentary lapse of concentration or misjudgement at low speed	Band A fine	Band A fine 3–4 points
Loss of control due to speed, mishandling or insufficient attention to road conditions, or carelessly turning right across oncoming traffic	Band B fine	Band B fine 5–6 points
Overtaking manoeuvre at speed resulting in collision of vehicles, or driving bordering on the dangerous	Band C fine	Band C fine Consider disqualification OR 7–9 points

 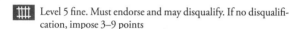

Offence seriousness (culpability and harm)
B. Consider the effect of aggravating and mitigating factors
(other than those within examples above)
The following may be particularly relevant but **these lists are not exhaustive**

Factors indicating higher culpability	Factors indicating lower culpability
1. Excessive speed	1. Minor risk
2. Carrying out other tasks while driving	2. Inexperience of driver
3. Carrying passengers or heavy load	3. Sudden change in road or weather conditions
4. Tiredness	
Factors indicating greater degree of harm	
1. Injury to others	
2. Damage to other vehicles or property	
3. High level of traffic or pedestrians in vicinity	
4. Location eg near school when children are likely to be present	

C14.1.2 Key points

- Careless driving is defined in the Act.
- Road Traffic Act 1988, section 3ZA provides:

> **Road Traffic Act 1988, s 3ZA**
>
> (2) A person is to be regarded as driving without due care and attention if (and only if) the way he drives falls below what would be expected of a competent and careful driver.
>
> (3) In determining for the purposes of subsection (2) above what would be expected of a careful and competent driver in a particular case, regard shall be had not only to the circumstances of which he could be expected to be aware but also to any circumstances shown to have been within the knowledge of the accused.
>
> (4) A person is to be regarded as driving without reasonable consideration for other persons only if those persons are inconvenienced by his driving.

- Examples of careless or inconsiderate driving:
  Careless driving
  - overtaking on the inside or driving inappropriately close to another vehicle
  - inadvertent mistakes such as driving through a red light or emerging from a side road into the path of another vehicle
  - short distractions such as tuning a car radio

  Inconsiderate driving
  - flashing of lights to force other drivers in front to give way
  - misuse of any lane to avoid queuing or gain some other advantage over other drivers

- driving that inconveniences other road users or causes unnecessary hazards such as unnecessarily remaining in an overtaking lane, unnecessarily slow driving or braking without good cause, driving with undipped headlights which dazzle oncoming drivers or driving through a puddle causing pedestrians to be splashed.
- If death has resulted from the driving any trial should await the conclusion of any inquest (*Smith v Director of Public Prosecutions* [2000] RTR 36).
- Failure to drive in accordance with the highway code will generally amount to careless driving.
- An offence of careless driving can be tried alongside an offence of dangerous driving as an alternative. However, it is not clear as to why this is done in the magistrates' court as the offence is a statutory alternative in any event.
- If the facts are such that in the absence of an explanation put forward by the defendant, or that explanation is objectively inadequate, and the only possible conclusion is that he was careless, he should be convicted (*Director of Public Prosecutions v Cox* (1993) 157 JP 1044).
- A court does not need to consider an alternative inference from facts, such as mechanical defect, without hearing evidence of the same (*Director of Public Prosecutions v Tipton* (1992) 156 JP 172).

 See *Blackstone's Criminal Practice 2012* **C6.1–C6.6**

C14.2 **Causing death by driving**

Road Traffic Act 1988 ss 2B and 3ZB

The Road Safety Act 2006 introduced new offences of causing death by:
- careless or inconsiderate driving
- unlicensed, disqualified, or uninsured drivers.

 EW

 5 years' imprisonment (2 years for unlicensed, disqualified, or uninsured), minimum disqualification of 12 months, discretionary re-test, 3–11 penalty points

---

C14.2.1 *Sentencing*

Death by careless or inconsiderate driving

Nature of offence	Starting point	Sentencing range
Careless or inconsiderate driving falling not far short of dangerous driving	15 months custody	36 weeks–3 years custody
Other cases of careless or inconsiderate driving	36 weeks custody	Community order (HIGH)–2 years custody
Careless or inconsiderate driving arising from momentary inattention with no aggravating factors	Community order (MEDIUM)	Community order (LOW)–Community order (HIGH)

Additional aggravating factors	Additional mitigating factors
1. Other offences committed at the same time, such as driving other than in accordance with the terms of a valid licence; driving while disqualified; driving without insurance; taking a vehicle without consent; driving a stolen vehicle 2. Previous convictions for motoring offences, particularly offences that involve bad driving 3. More than one person was killed as a result of the offence 4. Serious injury to one or more persons in addition to the death(s) 5. Irresponsible behaviour, such as failing to stop or falsely claiming that one of the victims was responsible for the collision	1. Offender was seriously injured in the collision 2. The victim was a close friend or relative 3. The actions of the victim or a third party contributed to the commission of the offence 4. The offender's lack of driving experience contributed significantly to the likelihood of a collision 5. The driving was in response to a proven and genuine emergency falling short of a defence

Causing death by unlicensed, disqualified or uninsured drivers

Nature of offence	Starting point	Sentencing range
The offender was disqualified from driving; OR The offender was unlicensed or uninsured plus two or more aggravating factors from the list below	12 months custody	36 weeks–2 years custody
The offender was unlicensed or uninsured plus at least one aggravating factor from the list below	26 weeks custody	Community order (HIGH)–36 weeks custody
The offender was unlicensed or uninsured—no aggravating factors	Community order (MEDIUM)	Community order (LOW)–Community order (HIGH)

Additional aggravating factors	Additional mitigating factors
1. Previous convictions for motoring offences, whether involving bad driving or involving an offence of the same kind that forms part of the present conviction (ie unlicensed, disqualified, or uninsured driving)	1. The decision to drive was brought about by a proven and genuine emergency falling short of a defence
2. More than one person was killed as a result of the offence	2. The offender genuinely believed that he or she was insured or licensed to drive
3. Serious injury to one or more persons in addition to the death(s)	3. The offender was seriously injured as a result of the collision
4. Irresponsible behaviour such as failing to stop or falsely claiming that someone else was driving	4. The victim was a close friend or relative

C14.2.2 Key points

- Death must result from the act of driving.
- The driving must be more than a minimal cause of the death.
- It is not necessary that the driver be culpable or blameworthy in respect of an offence under section 3ZB. Where, therefore, a pedestrian walked in front of a vehicle and a collision occurred through no fault of the driver, a conviction would follow in the event that the driver was uninsured, disqualified or driving otherwise than in accordance with a licence (*R v Williams* [2010] EWCA Crim 2552).
- For an early sentencing decision in relation to this Act see *R v Campbell* [2009] EWCA Crim 2459.
- See *R v Coe* [2009] EWCA Crim 1452 in relation to the admission of samples taken in relation to alcohol.

 See *Blackstone's Criminal Practice 2012* **C3**

C14.3 **Dangerous driving**

Road Traffic Act 1988, s 2

A person who drives a mechanically propelled vehicle dangerously on a road or other public place is guilty of an offence.

EW

 6 months and/or level 5 fine/2 years. Must endorse and disqualify for a minimum period of 12 months; must order extended re-test. Must disqualify for at least 2 years if offender has had two or more disqualifications for periods of 56 days or more in preceding 3 years

C14.3.1 *Sentencing*

Offence seriousness (culpability and harm) A. Identify the appropriate starting point Starting points based on first time offender pleading not guilty		
Example of nature of activity	**Starting point**	**Range**
Single incident where little or no damage or risk of personal injury	Medium level community order	Low level community order to high level community order Disqualify 12-15 months
Incident(s) involving excessive speed or showing off, especially on busy roads or in built-up area; OR Single incident where little or no damage or risk of personal injury but offender was disqualified driver	12 weeks custody	High level community order to 26 weeks custody Disqualify 15–24 months
Prolonged bad driving involving deliberate disregard for safety of others; OR Incident(s) involving excessive speed or showing off, especially on busy roads or in built-up area, by disqualified driver; OR Driving as described in box above while being pursued by police	Crown Court	Crown Court

Offence seriousness (culpability and harm) B. Consider the effect of aggravating and mitigating factors (other than those within examples above) The following may be particularly relevant but **these lists are not exhaustive**	
Factors indicating higher culpability	**Factors indicating lower culpability**
1. Disregarding warnings of others 2. Evidence of alcohol or drugs 3. Carrying out other tasks while driving 4. Carrying passengers or heavy load 5. Tiredness 6. Aggressive driving, such as driving much too close to vehicle in front, racing, inappropriate attempts to overtake, or cutting in after overtaking 7. Driving when knowingly suffering from a medical condition which significantly impairs the offender's driving skills 8. Driving a poorly maintained or dangerously loaded vehicle, especially where motivated by commercial concerns	1. Genuine emergency 2. Speed not excessive 3. Offence due to inexperience rather than irresponsibility of driver
Factors indicating greater degree of harm	
1. Injury to others 2. Damage to other vehicles or property	

C14.3.2 Key points

- Road Traffic Act 1988, s 2A, the meaning of dangerous driving, provides:

Road Traffic Act 1988, s 2A

(1) For the purposes of sections 1 and 2 above a person is to be regarded as driving dangerously if (and, subject to subsection (2) below, only if)—
    (a) the way he drives falls far below what would be expected of a competent and careful driver, and
    (b) it would be obvious to a competent and careful driver that driving in that way would be dangerous.

(2) A person is also to be regarded as driving dangerously for the purposes of sections 1 and 2 above if it would be obvious to a competent and careful driver that driving the vehicle in its current state would be dangerous.

(3) In subsections (1) and (2) above 'dangerous' refers to danger either of injury to any person or of serious damage to property; and in determining for the purposes of those subsections what would be expected of, or obvious to, a competent and careful driver in a particular case, regard shall be had not only to the circumstances of which he could be expected to be aware but also to any circumstances shown to have been within the knowledge of the accused.

(4) In determining for the purposes of subsection (2) above the state of a vehicle, regard may be had to anything attached to or carried on or in it and to the manner in which it is attached or carried.

- The special skill (or indeed lack of skill) of a driver is an irrelevant circumstance when considering whether the driving is dangerous (*R v Bannister* [2009] EWCA Crim 1571).
- The fact that the defendant had consumed alcohol is an admissible factor (*R v Webster* [2006] 2 Cr App R 103). Where drink is a major plank of the prosecution case, advocates should have regard to *R v McBride* [1962] 2 QB 167.
- Where a vehicle's dangerous state is due to its official design and not use, it will not usually be appropriate to prosecute (*R v Marchant* [2004] 1 All ER 1187).
- A vehicle is being driven in a dangerous state if the driver is aware that his ability to control the vehicle might be impaired such that the standard of his driving might fall below the requisite standard (*R v Marison* [1997] RTR 457).

 See *Blackstone's Criminal Practice 2012* **C3**

C14.4 **Drive whilst disqualified**

> ### Road Traffic Act 1988, s 103(1)
>
> (1) A person is guilty of an offence if, while disqualified for holding or obtaining a licence, he—
>   (a) obtains a licence, or
>   (b) drives a motor vehicle on a road.

SO

 6 months and/or level 5 fine. Must endorse and may disqualify. If no disqualification, impose 6 points

C14.4.1 *Sentencing*

Offence seriousness (culpability and harm) A. Identify the appropriate starting point Starting points based on first time offender pleading not guilty		
Example of nature of activity	**Starting point**	**Range**
Full period expired but re-test not taken	Low level community order	Band C fine to medium level community order 6 points or disqualify for 3-6 months
Lengthy period of ban already served	High level community order	Medium level community order to 12 weeks custody Lengthen disqualification for 6-12 months beyond expiry of current ban
Recently imposed ban	12 weeks custody	High level community order to 26 weeks custody Lengthen disqualification for 12-18 months beyond expiry of current ban

C14.4.2 **Key points**

- The prosecution do not need to prove that the defendant was aware of the prosecution that led to him being disqualified (*Taylor v Kenyon* [1952] 2 All ER 726), this is the case even where a driving licence has been returned to the defendant by mistake (*R v Bowsher* [1973] RTR 202).

- Strict proof that the person disqualified by the court is the person now charged is required. This will normally arise from (a) admission, (b) fingerprints, (c) evidence of identity from someone in court when the disqualification was made (*R v Derwentside Justices, ex p Heaviside* [1996] RTR 384). Other evidence such as an unusual name will at least raise a prima facie case that the defendant will need to answer in order to avoid conviction (*Olakunori v Director of Public Prosecutions* [1998] COD 443).

- An admission made whilst giving evidence is sufficient to prove a disqualification, even in the absence of a certificate of conviction (*Moran v Crown Prosecution Service* (2000) 164 JP 562).

- A defendant's silence in interview (where he did not later rely on any fact) and his general attitude to the management of the case in accordance with the Criminal Procedure Rules, could not provide sufficient proof (*Mills v Director of Public Prosecutions* [2008] EWHC 3304 (Admin)).

- Consistency of personal details will normally be sufficient to raise a prima facie case. If the defendant calls no evidence to contradict that prima facie case, it will be open to the court to be satisfied that identity is *proved* (*Pattison v Director of Public Prosecutions* [2006] RTR 13).

- A solicitor could be called as a witness to confirm identity (*R (Howe) v South Durham Magistrates' Court* [2005] RTR 4).

- A mistaken belief that he was not driving on a road will not amount to a defence (*R v Miller* [1975] 1 WLR 1222).

- The fact that a disqualification was later quashed on appeal does not provide a defence (*R v Thames Magistrates' Court, ex p Levy* The Times, 17 July 1997).

- A bad character application in relation to the disqualification is not necessary as it has to do with the facts of the alleged offence (Criminal Justice Act 2003, s 98) (*Director of Public Prosecutions v Agyemang* [2009] EWHC 1542 (Admin)).

 See *Blackstone's Criminal Practice 2012* C6.35–C6.39

C14.5 **Excess alcohol**

Road Traffic Act 1988, s 5(1)

(1) If a person—
   (a) drives or attempts to drive a motor vehicle on a road or other public place, or
   (b) is in charge of a motor vehicle on a road or other public place, after consuming so much alcohol that the proportion of it in his breath, blood, or urine exceeds the prescribed limit he is guilty of an offence.

SO

6 months and/or level 5. Must endorse and disqualify for at least 12 months. Must disqualify for at least 2 years if offender has had 2 or more disqualifications for periods of 56 days or more in preceding 3 years. Must disqualify for at least 3 years if offender has been convicted of a relevant offence in preceding 10 years

See **C14.15.2** for offence of being in charge.

C14.5.1 *Sentencing: driving*

			Offence seriousness (culpability and harm)			
			A. Identify the appropriate starting point			
			Starting points based on first time offender pleading not guilty			
Level of alcohol			Starting point	Range	Disqualification	Disqual. 2nd offence in 10 years—see note above
Breath (mg)	**Blood (ml)**	**Urine (ml)**				
36–59	81–137	108–183	Band C fine	Band C fine	12–16 months	36–40 months
60–89	138–206	184–274	Band C fine	Band C fine	17–22 months	36–46 months
90–119	207–275	275–366	Medium level community order	Low level community order to high level community order	23–28 months	36–52 months
120–150 and above	276–345 and above	367–459 and above	12 weeks custody	High level community order to 26 weeks custody	29–36 months	36–60 months

Offence seriousness (culpability and harm)
B. Consider the effect of aggravating and mitigating factors
(other than those within examples above)
The following may be particularly relevant but **these lists are not exhaustive**

Factors indicating higher culpability	Factors indicating lower culpability
1. LGV, HGV, PSV, etc 2. Poor road or weather conditions 3. Carrying passengers 4. Driving for hire or reward 5. Evidence of unacceptable standard of driving **Factors indicating greater degree of harm** 1. Involved in accident 2. Location eg near school 3. High level of traffic or pedestrians in the vicinity	1. Genuine emergency established* 2. Spiked drinks* 3. Very short distance driven* * even where not amounting to special reasons

C14.5.2 *Sentencing: in charge*

⊞ 3 months and/or level 4 fine. Must endorse and may disqualify. If no disqualification, impose 10 points

Offence seriousness (culpability and harm)
A. Identify the appropriate starting point
Starting points based on first time offender pleading not guilty

Level of alcohol			Starting point	Range
Breath (mg)	**Blood (ml)**	**Urine (ml)**	**Band B fine**	**Band B fine 10 points**
36–59	81–137	108–183		
60–89	138–206	184–274	Band B fine	Band B fine 10 points OR consider disqualification
90–119	207–275	275–366	Band C fine	Band C fine to medium level community order Consider disqualification up to 6 months OR 10 points
120–150 and above	276–345 and above	367–459 and above	Medium level community order	Low level community order to 6 weeks custody Disqualify 6–12 months

⊞ Sentence

Offence seriousness (culpability and harm)
B. Consider the effect of aggravating and mitigating factors
(other than those within examples above)
The following may be particularly relevant but **these lists are not exhaustive**

Factors indicating higher culpability	Factor indicating lower culpability
1. LGV, HGV, PSV, etc	1. Low likelihood of driving
2. Ability to drive seriously impaired	
3. High likelihood of driving	
4. Driving for hire or reward	

C14.5.3 Key points

- Section 5(2)–(3) provides:

> **Road Traffic Act 1988, s 5(2)–(3)**
>
> (2) It is a defence for a person charged with an offence under subsection (1) (b) above to prove that at the time he is alleged to have committed the offence the circumstances were such that there was no likelihood of his driving the vehicle whilst the proportion of alcohol in his breath, blood or urine remained likely to exceed the prescribed limit.
>
> (3) The court may, in determining whether there was such a likelihood as is mentioned in subsection (2) above, disregard any injury to him and any damage to the vehicle.

- The burden of proof falls on the defendant (*Sheldrake v Director of Public Prosecutions* [2005] RTR 2).
- Duress is available as a defence but only rarely will a driver be able to avail himself of it. The defence will only be available for so long as the threat is active and a sober and reasonable person would have driven (*Crown Prosecution Service v Brown* [2007] EWHC 3274 (Admin)).
- Automatism is available as a defence.
- Where there has been no consumption of alcohol between the incidence of driving and the testing, the alcohol reading is conclusive (Road Traffic Offences Act 1988, s 15(2), and *Griffiths v Director of Public Prosecutions* [2002] EWHC 792 (Admin)). However, the presumption in section 15(2) applies only to trials and does not extend to a Newton hearing (*Goldsmith v Director of Public Prosecutions* [2009] EWHC 3010 (Admin)).
- Where there is post driving consumption of alcohol the defendant is able to 'back calculate' to obtain a reading at the time of driving (Road Traffic Offences Act 1988, s 15(3)). The prosecution are also entitled to rely upon back calculations but in practice rarely do so (*Gumbley v Cunningham* [1989] RTR 49).

- There will be no prosecution unless the alcohol level is at least 40 microgrammes (Home Office Circular 46/1982); it should be noted that this 'allowance' is already built into any blood or urine analysis.

 See *Blackstone's Criminal Practice 2012* **C3**

C14.6 Fail to give information of driver's identity as required

Road Traffic Act 1988, s 172

(1) This section applies—
  (a) to any offence under the preceding provisions of this Act except—
    (i) an offence under Part V, or
    (ii) an offence under section 13, 16, 51(2), 61(4), 67(9), 68(4), 96 or 120, and to an offence under section 178 of this Act,
  (b) to any offence under sections 25, 26 or 27 of the Road Traffic Offenders Act 1988,
  (c) to any offence against any other enactment relating to the use of vehicles on roads, and
  (d) to manslaughter, or in Scotland culpable homicide, by the driver of a motor vehicle.
(2) Where the driver of a vehicle is alleged to be guilty of an offence to which this section applies—
  (a) the person keeping the vehicle shall give such information as to the identity of the driver as he may be required to give by or on behalf of a chief officer of police, and
  (b) any other person shall if required as stated above give any information which it is in his power to give and may lead to identification of the driver.
(3) Subject to the following provisions, a person who fails to comply with a requirement under subsection (2) above shall be guilty of an offence.
(4) . . .
(5) Where a body corporate is guilty of an offence under this section and the offence is proved to have been committed with the consent or connivance of, or to be attributable to neglect on the part of, a director, manager, secretary or other similar officer of the body corporate, or a person who was purporting to act in any such capacity, he, as well as the body corporate, is guilty of that offence and liable to be proceeded against and punished accordingly.
(6) Where the alleged offender is a body corporate, or in Scotland a partnership or an unincorporated association, or the proceedings are brought against him by virtue of subsection (5) above or subsection (11) below,

subsection (4) above shall not apply unless, in addition to the matters there mentioned, the alleged offender shows that no record was kept of the persons who drove the vehicle and that the failure to keep a record was reasonable.

(7) A requirement under subsection (2) may be made by written notice served by post; and where it is so made—

(a) it shall have effect as a requirement to give the information within the period of 28 days beginning with the day on which the notice is served, and

(b) the person on whom the notice is served shall not be guilty of an offence under this section if he shows either that he gave the information as soon as reasonably practicable after the end of that period or that it has not been reasonably practicable for him to give it.

(8) Where the person on whom a notice under subsection (7) above is to be served is a body corporate, the notice is duly served if it is served on the secretary or clerk of that body.

(9) For the purposes of section 7 of the Interpretation Act 1978 as it applies for the purposes of this section the proper address of any person in relation to the service on him of a notice under subsection (7) above is—

(a) in the case of the secretary or clerk of a body corporate, that of the registered or principal office of that body or (if the body corporate is the registered keeper of the vehicle concerned) the registered address, and

(b) in any other case, his last known address at the time of service.

(10) In this section—

'registered address', in relation to the registered keeper of a vehicle, means the address recorded in the record kept under the Vehicles Excise and Registration Act 1994 with respect to that vehicle as being that person's address, and 'registered keeper', in relation to a vehicle, means the person in whose name the vehicle is registered under that Act; and references to the driver of a vehicle include references to the rider of a cycle.

SO 6 points (no endorsement for limited companies)

C14.6.1 Key points

• Section 172(4) provides:

Road Traffic Act 1988, s 172(4)

(4) A person shall not be guilty of an offence by virtue of paragraph (a) of subsection (2) above if he shows that he did not know and could not with reasonable diligence have ascertained who the driver of the vehicle was.

- In *Duff v Director of Public Prosecutions* [2009] EWHC 675 (Admin), D's wife was served with a notice under section 172 of the Road Traffic Act 1988 requiring her to identify the name of the driver. D in fact replied to the notice, naming himself as the driver. As a result a further section 172 notice was then served on D. Following legal advice D did not respond to that notice and was subsequently convicted of failing to provide information. It was held that the conviction was sound as the request to which he had in fact responded was a request of D's wife, not D himself.

 See *Blackstone's Criminal Practice 2012* **C6**

C14.7 **Fail to provide specimen for analysis**

Road Traffic Act 1988, s 7(6)–(7)

(6) A person who, without reasonable excuse, fails to provide a specimen when required to do so in pursuance of this section is guilty of an offence.

(7) A constable must, on requiring any person to provide a specimen in pursuance of this section, warn him that a failure to provide it may render him liable to prosecution.

 SO

 Driving/attempting to drive: 6 months and/or level 5 fine. Must endorse and disqualify for at least 12 months. Must disqualify for at least 2 years if offender has had 2 or more disqualifications for periods of 56 days or more in preceding 3 years
Must disqualify for at least 3 years if offender has been convicted of a relevant offence in preceding 10 years

 In-charge: 3 months and/or level 4 fine. Must endorse and may disqualify. If no disqualification, impose 10 points

C14.7.1 *Sentencing: driving or attempting to drive*

Offence seriousness (culpability and harm) A. Identify the appropriate starting point Starting points based on first time offender pleading not guilty				
Examples of nature of activity	**Starting point**	**Range**	**Disqual.**	**Disqual. 2nd offence in 10 years**
Defendant refused test when had honestly held but unreasonable excuse	Band C fine	Band C fine	12–16 months	36–40 months
Deliberate refusal or deliberate failure	Low level community order	Band C fine to high level community order	17–28 months	36–52 months
Deliberate refusal or deliberate failure where evidence of serious impairment	12 weeks custody	High level community order to 26 weeks custody	29–36 months	36–60 months

Offence seriousness (culpability and harm) B. Consider the effect of aggravating and mitigating factors (other than those within examples above) The following may be particularly relevant but **these lists are not exhaustive**	
Factors indicating higher culpability 1. Evidence of unacceptable standard of driving 2. LGV, HGV, PSV, etc 3. Obvious state of intoxication 4. Driving for hire or reward **Factor indicating greater degree of harm** 1. Involved in accident	**Factor indicating lower culpability** 1. Genuine but unsuccessful attempt to provide specimen

C14.7.2 *Sentencing: in-charge*

Offence seriousness (culpability and harm)		
A. Identify appropriate starting point		
Starting points based on first time offender pleading not guilty		
Examples of nature of activity	**Starting point**	**Range**
Defendant refused test when had honestly held but unreasonable excuse	Band B fine	Band B fine 10 points
Deliberate refusal or deliberate failure	Band C fine	Band C fine to medium level community order Consider disqualification OR 10 points
Deliberate refusal or deliberate failure where evidence of serious impairment	Medium level community order	Low level community order to 6 weeks custody Disqualify 6–12 months

Offence seriousness (culpability and harm)	
B. Consider the effect of aggravating and mitigating factors	
(other than those within examples above)	
The following may be particularly relevant but **these lists are not exhaustive**	
Factors indicating higher culpability	**Factors indicating lower culpability**
1. Obvious state of intoxication 2. LGV, HGV, PSV, etc 3. High likelihood of driving 4. Driving for hire of reward	1. Genuine but unsuccessful attempt to provide specimen 2. Low likelihood of driving

C14.7.3 Key points

- A reasonable excuse for failing to provide must relate to inability due to physical or mental issues (*R v Lennard* [1973] RTR 252).
- Failure to mention a medical reason at the time of refusal does not preclude a court from finding that a reasonable excuse existed, although it was a factor to be taken into account (*Piggott v Director of Public Prosecutions* [2008] RTR 16).
- Once a reasonable excuse is raised it is for the prosecution to disprove it (*McKeon v Director of Public Prosecutions* [2008] RTR 14).
- A failure to understand the statutory warning relating to prosecution may amount to a reasonable excuse if the accused's understanding of English is poor. Failure to understand due to intoxication will not suffice.
- The taking of a specimen does not have to be delayed (over and above a couple of minutes) for the purpose of taking legal advice (*R v Gearing* [2008] EWHC 1695 (Admin)).

📖 See *Blackstone's Criminal Practice 2012* C5

C14.8 **Fail to stop/report road accident**

Road Traffic Act 1988, s 170

(1) This section applies in a case where, owing to the presence of a mechanically propelled vehicle on a road or other public place, an accident occurs by which—

    (a) personal injury is caused to a person other than the driver of that mechanically propelled vehicle, or

    (b) damage is caused—

        (i) to a vehicle other than that mechanically propelled vehicle or a trailer drawn by that mechanically propelled vehicle, or

        (ii) to an animal other than an animal in or on that mechanically propelled vehicle or a trailer drawn by that mechanically propelled vehicle, or

        (iii) to any other property constructed on, fixed to, growing in or otherwise forming part of the land on which the road or place in question is situated or land adjacent to such land.

(2) The driver of the mechanically propelled vehicle must stop and, if required to do so by any person having reasonable grounds for so requiring, give his name and address and also the name and address of the owner and the identification marks of the vehicle.

(3) If for any reason the driver of the mechanically propelled vehicle does not give his name and address under subsection (2) above, he must report the accident.

(4) A person who fails to comply with subsection (2) or (3) above is guilty of an offence.

(5) If, in a case where this section applies by virtue of subsection (1)(a) above, the driver of a motor vehicle does not at the time of the accident produce such a certificate of insurance or security, or other evidence, as is mentioned in section 165(2)(a) of this Act—

    (a) to a constable, or

    (b) to some person who, having reasonable grounds for so doing, has required him to produce it,

the driver must report the accident and produce such a certificate or other evidence.

This subsection does not apply to the driver of an invalid carriage.

(6) To comply with a duty under this section to report an accident or to produce such a certificate of insurance or security, or other evidence, as is mentioned in section 165(2)(a) of this Act, the driver—

    (a) must do so at a police station or to a constable, and

    (b) must do so as soon as is reasonably practicable and, in any case, within twenty-four hours of the occurrence of the accident.

(7) A person who fails to comply with a duty under subsection (5) above is guilty of an offence, but he shall not be convicted by reason only of a failure to produce a certificate or other evidence if, within seven days after the occurrence of the accident, the certificate or other evidence is produced

at a police station that was specified by him at the time when the accident was reported.

(8) In this section 'animal' means horse, cattle, ass, mule, sheep, pig, goat or dog.

SO

6 months and/or level 5 fine. Must endorse and may disqualify. If no disqualification, impose 5–10 points

C14.8.1 *Sentencing*

Offence seriousness (culpability and harm) A. Identify the appropriate starting point Starting points based on first time offender pleading not guilty		
Examples of nature of activity	**Starting point**	**Range**
Minor damage/injury or stopped at scene but failed to exchange particulars or report	Band B fine	Band B fine 5–6 points
Moderate damage/injury or failed to stop and failed to report	Band C fine	Band C fine 7–8 points Consider disqualification
Serious damage/injury and/or evidence of bad driving	High level community order	Band C fine to 26 weeks custody Disqualify 6–12 months OR 9–10 points

Offence seriousness (culpability and harm) B. Consider the effect of aggravating and mitigating factors (other than those within examples above) The following may be particularly relevant but **these lists are not exhaustive**	
Factors indicating higher culpability	**Factors indicating lower culpability**
1. Evidence of drink or drugs/evasion of test	1. Believed identity known
2. Knowledge/suspicion that personal injury caused (where not an element of the offence)	2. Genuine fear of retribution
3. Leaving injured party at scene	3. Subsequently reported
4. Giving false details	

See *Blackstone's Criminal Practice 2012* **C6.44–C6.46**

C14.9 **No insurance, using, causing, or permitting**

Road Traffic Act 1988, s 143

 Fine level 5/discretionary disqualification/ 6–8 penalty points

C14.9.1 *Sentencing*

Offence seriousness (culpability and harm) A. Identify the appropriate starting point Starting points based on first time offender pleading not guilty		
Examples of nature of activity	**Starting point**	**Range**
Using a motor vehicle on a road or other public place without insurance	Band C fine	Band C fine 6 points–12 months disqualification—see notes below

Offence seriousness (culpability and harm) B. Consider the effect of aggravating and mitigating factors (other than those within examples above) The following may be particularly relevant but **these lists are not exhaustive**	
Factors indicating higher culpability 1. Never passed test 2. Gave false details 3. Driving LGV, HGV, PSV etc 4. Driving for hire or reward 5. Evidence of sustained uninsured use **Factors indicating greater degree of harm** 1. Involved in accident 2. Accident resulting in injury	**Factors indicating lower culpability** 1. Responsibility for providing insurance rests with another 2. Genuine misunderstanding 3. Recent failure to renew or failure to transfer vehicle details where insurance was in existence 4. Vehicle not being driven

C14.9.2 Key points

- See **C13** for definitions.
- Proceedings may be brought within six months of a prosecutor forming the opinion that there is sufficient evidence of an offence having been committed (subject to an overall three-year time bar).
- It is for a defendant to show that he was insured once it is established that a motor vehicle was used on a road or other public place.
- It is not necessary that the vehicle be capable of being driven (*Pumbien v Vines* [1996] RTR 37).
- Employed drivers have the following defence available to them:
  A person charged with using a motor vehicle in contravention of this section shall not be convicted if he proves—
  (a) that the vehicle did not belong to him and was not in his possession under a contract of hiring or of loan,
  (b) that he was using the vehicle in the course of his employment, and
  (c) that he neither knew nor had reason to believe that there was not in force in relation to the vehicle such a policy of insurance or security as is mentioned in subsection (1) above.

 See *Blackstone's Criminal Practice 2012* **C6.40–C6.44**

C14.10 Motorway offences

Offence	Maximum	Points	Starting point	Special considerations
Drive in reverse or wrong way on slip road	L4	3	B	
Drive in reverse or wrong way on motorway	L4	3	C	
Drive off carriageway (central reservation or hard shoulder)	L4	3	B	
Make U turn	L4	3	C	
Learner driver or excluded vehicle	L4	3	B	
Stop on hard shoulder	L4	–	A	
Vehicle in prohibited lane	L4	3	A	
Walk on motorway, slip road or hard shoulder	L4	–	A	

C14.11 **Offences concerning the driver**

Offence	Maximum	Points	Starting point	Special considerations
Fail to cooperate with preliminary (roadside) breath test	L3	4	B	
Fail to give information of driver's identity as required	L3	6	C	For limited companies, endorsement is not available; a fine is the only available penalty
Fail to produce insurance certificate	L4	–	A	Fine per offence, not per document
Fail to produce test certificate	L3	–	A	
Drive otherwise than in accordance with licence (where could be covered)	L3	–	A	
Drive otherwise than in accordance with licence	L3	3–6	A	Aggravating factor if no licence ever held

 See *Blackstone's Criminal Practice 2012* **C6**

C14.12 **Offences concerning the vehicle**

- The guidelines for some of the offences below differentiate between three types of offender when the offence is committed in the course of business: driver, owner-driver, and owner-company. For owner-driver, the starting point is the same as for driver; however, the court should consider an uplift of at least 25 per cent.

Offence	Maximum	Points	Starting point	Special considerations
No excise licence	L3 or 5 times annual duty, whichever is greater	–	A (1–3 months unpaid) B (4–6 months unpaid) C (7–12 months unpaid)	Add duty lost
Fail to notify change of ownership to DVLA	L3	–	A	If offence committed in course of business: A (driver) A* (owner-driver) B (owner-company)
No test certificate	L3	–	A	If offence committed in course of business: A (driver) A* (owner-driver) B (owner-company)
Brakes defective Key points: It is sufficient only to prove that *any* part of the braking system is defective (*Kennett v British Airports Authority* [1975] Crim LR 106). The fact that everything possible (eg servicing) has been done in order to ensure that the vehicle is in good condition does not amount to a defence (*Hawkins v Holmes* [1974] RTR 436), as maintenance of the braking system is an absolute obligation on the driver (*Green v Burnett* [1954] 3 All ER 273).	L4	3	B	If offence committed in course of business: B (driver) B* (owner-driver) C (owner-company) L5 if goods vehicle
Steering defective	L4	3	B	If offence committed in course of business: B (driver) B* (owner-driver) C (owner-company) L5 if goods vehicle

Offence	Maximum	Points	Starting point	Special considerations
Tyres defective. It is a defence if the vehicle is not being used and there was no intention to use when the tyres were defective, regardless of the fact that the vehicle was on a road (*Eden v Mitchell* [1975] RTR 425). There is no requirement for the prosecution to have had the tyre examined by an authorized examiner as the issue was a simple question of fact (*Phillips v Thomas* [1974] RTR 28).	L4	3	B	If offence committed in course of business: B (driver) B* (owner-driver) C (owner-company) L5 if goods vehicle Penalty per tyre
Condition of vehicle/accessories/ equipment involving danger of injury (Road Traffic Act 1988, s 40A)	L4	3	B	Must disqualify for at least 6 months if offender has one or more previous convictions for same offence within three years If offence committed in course of business: B (driver) B* (owner-driver) C (owner-company) L5 if goods vehicle
Exhaust defective	L3	–	A	If offence committed in course of business: A (driver) A* (owner-driver) B (owner-company)
Lights defective	L3	–	A	If offence committed in course of business: A (driver) A* (owner-driver) B (owner-company)

See *Blackstone's Criminal Practice 2012* **C6**

C14.13 **Offences concerning use of the vehicle**

The guidelines for some of the offences below differentiate between three types of offender when the offence is committed in the course of business: driver, owner-driver and owner-company. For owner-driver, the starting point is the same as for driver; however, the court should consider an uplift of at least 25 per cent.

Offence	Maximum	Points	Starting point	Special considerations
Weight, position, or distribution of load or manner in which load secured involving danger of injury (Road Traffic Act 1988, s 40A) . Many cases involve unsecured passengers on the back of vehicles which is objectively often viewed as involving danger of injury (eg *Gray v Director of Public Prosecutions* [1999] RTR 339)	L4	3	B	Must disqualify for at least 6 months if offender has one or more previous convictions for same offence within three years If offence committed in course of business: A (driver) A* (owner-driver) B (owner-company) L5 if goods vehicle
Number of passengers or way carried involving danger of injury (Road Traffic Act 1988, s 40A)	L4	3	B	If offence committed in course of business: A (driver) A* (owner-driver) B (owner-company) L5 if goods vehicle
Position or manner in which load secured (not involving danger) (Road Traffic Act 1988, s 42)	L3	–	A	L4 if goods vehicle

See *Blackstone's Criminal Practice 2012* **C6**

C14.14 Offences re buses/goods vehicles over 3.5 tonnes (GVW)

Offence	Maximum	Points	Starting point	Special considerations
No goods vehicle plating certificate	L3		A (driver) A* (owner-driver) B (owner-company)	
No goods vehicle test certificate	L4		B (driver) B* (owner-driver) C (owner-company)	
Brakes defective	L5	3	B (driver) B* (owner-driver) C (owner-company)	
Steering defective	L5	3	B (driver) B* (owner-driver) C (owner-company)	
Tyres defective	L5	3	B (driver) B* (owner-driver) C (owner-company)	Penalty per tyre
Exhaust emission	L4	–	B (driver) B* (owner-driver) C (owner-company)	
Condition of vehicle/accessories/ equipment involving danger of injury (Road Traffic Act 1988, s 40A)	L5	3	B (driver) B* (owner-driver) C (owner-company)	Must disqualify for at least 6 months if offender has one or more previous convictions for same offence within three years
Number of passengers or way carried involving danger of injury (Road Traffic Act 1988, s 40A)	L5	3	B (driver) B* (owner-driver) C (owner-company)	Must disqualify for at least 6 months if offender has one or more previous convictions for same offence within three years
Weight, position, or distribution of load or manner in which load secured involving danger of injury (Road Traffic Act 1988, s 40A)	L5	3	B (driver) B* (owner-driver) C (owner-company)	Must disqualify for at least 6 months if offender has one or more previous convictions for same offence within three years

Offence	Maximum	Points	Starting point	Special considerations
Position or manner in which load secured (not involving danger) (Road Traffic Act 1988, s 42)	L4	–	B (driver) B*(owner-driver) C (owner-company)	
Overloading/ exceeding axle weight	L5	–	B (driver) B* (owner-driver) C (owner-company)	Starting points cater for cases where the overload is up to and including 10%. Thereafter, 10% should be added to the penalty for each additional 1% of overload. Penalty per axle

Offence	Maximum	Points	Starting point	Special considerations
No operators licence	L4	–	B (driver) B* (owner-driver) C (owner-company)	
Speed limiter not used or incorrectly calibrated	L4	–	B (driver) B* (owner-driver) C (owner-company)	
Tachograph not used/ not working	L5	–	B (driver) B* (owner-driver) C (owner-company)	
Exceed permitted driving time/periods of duty	L4	–	B (driver) B* (owner-driver) C (owner-company)	
Fail to keep/return written record sheets	L4	–	B (driver) B* (owner-driver) C (owner-company)	
Falsify or alter records with intent to deceive	L5/2 years	–	B (driver) B* (owner-driver) C (owner-company)	Either-way offence

C14.15 **Speeding**

Road Traffic Regulation Act 1984, s 89(10)

SO Level 3 fine (level 4 if motorway)

C14.15.1 *Sentencing*

Offence seriousness (culpability and harm) A. Identify the appropriate starting point Starting points based on first time offender pleading not guilty			
Speed limit (mph)	**Recorded speed (mph)**		
20	21–30	31–40	41–50
30	31–40	41–50	51–60
40	41–55	56–65	66–75
50	51–65	66–75	76–85
60	61–80	81–90	91–100
70	71–90	91–100	101–110
Starting point	Band A fine	Band B fine	Band B fine
Range	Band A fine	Band B fine	Band B fine
Points/ disqualification	3 points	4–6 points OR Disqualify 7–28 days	Disqualify 7–56 days OR 6 points

Offence seriousness (culpability and harm) B. Consider the effect of aggravating and mitigating factors (other than those within examples above) The following may be particularly relevant but **these lists are not exhaustive**	
Factors indicating higher culpability 1. Poor road or weather conditions 2. LGV, HGV, PSV, etc 3. Towing caravan/trailer 4. Carrying passengers or heavy load 5. Driving for hire or reward 6. Evidence of unacceptable standard of driving over and above speed **Factors indicating greater degree of harm** 1. Location eg near school 2. High level of traffic or pedestrians in the vicinity	**Factor indicating lower culpability** 1. Genuine emergency established

C14.15.2 Key points

- Necessity is available as a defence (*Moss v Howdle* 1997 SLT 782).
- Check that a notice of intended prosecution has been served in time.
- Save where the road is a restricted road, there needs to be signage in accordance with the regulations. A failure to provide adequate signage is fatal to any conviction. In *Jones v Director of Public Prosecutions*, unreported, 27 January 2011, the court held that the relevant question to be answered by the court was:

> Whether by the point on the road where the alleged offence took place (the point of enforcement) the driver by reference to the route taken thereto has been given (or drivers generally have been given) adequate guidance of the speed limit to be observed at that point on the road by the signs on the relevant part of parts of the road *in so far as (and thus to the extent that)* those traffic signs comply with the 2002 Regulations?

 See *Blackstone's Criminal Practice 2012* C6.51–C6.53

C14.16 **Unfit through drink or drugs**

Road Traffic Act 1988, s 4(1)–(2), and (5)

(1) A person who, when driving or attempting to drive a mechanically propelled vehicle on a road or other public place, is unfit to drive through drink or drugs is guilty of an offence.

(2) Without prejudice to subsection (1) above, a person who, when in charge of a mechanically propelled vehicle which is on a road or other public place, is unfit to drive through drink or drugs is guilty of an offence.

. . .

(5) . . . a person shall be taken to be unfit to drive if his ability to drive properly is for the time being impaired.

SO

 Drive/attempt to drive: 6 months and/or level 5 fine. Must endorse and disqualify for at least 12 months. Must disqualify for at least 2 years if offender has had 2 or more disqualifications for periods of 56 days or more in preceding 3 years

Must disqualify for at least 3 years if offender has been convicted of a relevant offence in preceding 10 years

 In-charge: 3 months and/or level 4 fine. Must endorse and may disqualify. If no disqualification, impose 10 points

C14.16.1 *Sentencing: driving or attempting to drive*

Offence seriousness (culpability and harm) A. Identify the appropriate starting point Starting points based on first time offender pleading not guilty				
Examples of nature of activity	**Starting point**	**Range**	**Disqual.**	**Disqual. 2nd offence in 10 years**
Evidence of moderate level of impairment and no aggravating factors	Band C fine	Band C fine	12–16 months	36–40 months
Evidence of moderate level of impairment and presence of one or more aggravating factors listed below	Band C fine	Band C fine	17–22 months	36–46 months
Evidence of high level of impairment and no aggravating factors	Medium level community order	Low level community order to high level community order	23–28 months	36–52 months
Evidence of high level of impairment and presence of one or more aggravating factors listed below	12 weeks custody	High level community order to 26 weeks custody	29–36 months	36–60 months

Offence seriousness (culpability and harm) B. Consider the effect of aggravating and mitigating factors (other than those within examples above) The following may be particularly relevant but **these lists are not exhaustive**	
Factors indicating higher culpability 1. LGV, HGV, PSV, etc 2. Poor road or weather conditions 3. Carrying passengers 4. Driving for hire or reward 5. Evidence of unacceptable standard of driving **Factors indicating greater degree of harm** 1. Involved in accident 2. Location eg near school 3. High level of traffic or pedestrians in the vicinity	**Factors indicating lower culpability** 1. Genuine emergency established* 2. Spike drinks* 3. Very short distance driven* * even where not amounting to special reasons

C14.16.2 *Sentencing: in-charge*

Offence seriousness (culpability and harm) A. Identify the appropriate starting point Starting points based on first time offender pleading not guilty		
Examples of nature of activity	**Starting point**	**Range**
Evidence of moderate level of impairment and no aggravating factors	Band B fine	Band B fine 10 points
Evidence of moderate level of impairment and presence of one or more aggravating factors listed below	Band B fine	Band B fine 10 points or consider disqualification
Evidence of high level of impairment and no aggravating factors	Band C fine	Band C fine to medium level community order 10 points OR consider disqualification
Evidence of high level of impairment and presence of one or more aggravating factors listed below	High level community order	Medium level community order to 12 weeks custody Consider disqualification OR 10 points

Offence seriousness (culpability and harm) B. Consider the effect of aggravating and mitigating factors (other than those within examples above) The following may be particularly relevant but **these lists are not exhaustive**	
Factors indicating higher culpability 1. LGV, HGV, PSV, etc 2. High likelihood of driving 3. Driving for hire or reward	**Factor indicating lower culpability** 1. Low likelihood of driving

C14.16.3 Key points

- No likelihood of driving whilst unfit provides a defence in law to the in-charge offence. Section 4(3), (4) provides:

Road Traffic Act 1988, s 4(3)–(4)

(3) For the purposes of subsection (2) above, a person shall be deemed not to have been in charge of a mechanically propelled vehicle if he proves that at the material time the circumstances were such that there was no likelihood of his driving it so long as he remained unfit to drive through drink or drugs.

(4) The court may, in determining whether there was such a likelihood as is mentioned in subsection (3) above, disregard any injury to him and any damage to the vehicle.

- Drugs include normal medicines.
- Evidence of impairment to drive may be provided by both expert and lay witnesses. Note, however, that a lay witness can give evidence as to a person's demeanour (and how much he drank, for example) but not on the ultimate question of whether the person was 'fit' to drive.
- The results of any evidential specimens are admissible (Road Traffic Offenders Act 1988, ss 15 and 16).

 See *Blackstone's Criminal Practice 2012* C5

C15 **Sexual Offences**

C15.1 **Child prostitution and pornography**

Sexual Offences Act 2003, ss 48, 49, and 50

EW

 6 months and/or level 5 fine/14 years

SO

C15.1.1 *Sentencing*

Offence seriousness (culpability and harm)
A. Identify the appropriate starting point
Starting points based on first time offender pleading not guilty

These offences should normally be dealt with in the Crown Court.
However, there may be rare cases of non-penetrative activity involving a victim aged 16 or 17 where the offender's involvement is minimal and not perpetrated for gain in which a custodial sentence within the jurisdiction of a magistrates' court may be appropriate.

Offence seriousness (culpability and harm)
B. Consider the effect of aggravating and mitigating factors
The following may be particularly relevant but **these lists are not exhaustive**

Factors indicating higher culpability	Factor indicating lower culpability
1. Background of threats or intimidation	1. Offender also being controlled in prostitution or pornography and subject to threats or intimidation
2. Large-scale commercial operation	
3. Use of drugs, alcohol, or other substance to secure the victim's compliance	
4. Forcing a victim to violate another person	
5. Abduction or detention	
6. Threats to prevent the victim reporting the activity	
7. Threats to disclose victim's activity to friends/ relatives	
8. Image distributed to other children or persons known to the victim	
9. Financial or other gain	

Factors indicating greater degree of harm	
1. Induced dependency on drugs 2. Victim has been manipulated into physical and emotional dependence on the offender 3. Storing, making available, or distributing images in such a way that they can be inadvertently accessed by others	

 See *Blackstone's Criminal Practice 2012* B3.193–B3.206

C15.2 **Exposure**

Sexual Offences Act 2003, s 66(1)

(1) A person commits an offence if—
  (a) he intentionally exposes his genitals, and
  (b) he intends that someone will see them and be caused alarm or distress.

EW

 6 months and/or level 5 fine/2 years

SO

C15.2.1 *Sentencing*

Offence seriousness (culpability and harm) A. Identify the appropriate starting point Starting points based on first time offender pleading not guilty		
Examples of nature of activity	**Starting point**	**Range**
Basic offence as defined in the Act, assuming no aggravating or mitigating factors	Low level community order	Band B fine to medium level community order
Offence with an aggravating factor	Medium level community order	Low level community order to high level community order
Two or more aggravating factors	12 weeks custody	6 weeks custody to Crown Court

Offence seriousness (culpability and harm)	
B. Consider the effect of aggravating and mitigating factors	
(other than those within examples above)	
The following may be particularly relevant but **these lists are not exhaustive**	
Factors indicating higher culpability	
1. Threats to prevent the victim reporting an offence	
2. Intimidating behaviour/threats of violence	
Factor indicating greater degree of harm	
1. Victim is a child	

C15.2.2 Key points

- This offence is committed where an offender intentionally exposes his or her genitals and intends that someone will see them and be caused alarm or distress. It is gender neutral, covering exposure of male or female genitalia to a male or female witness.
- The Sentencing Guidelines Council guideline provides that, when dealing with a repeat offender, the starting point should be 12 weeks custody with a range of four to 26 weeks custody. The presence of aggravating factors may suggest that a sentence above the range is appropriate and that the case should be committed to the Crown Court.
- In accordance with section 80 of and Schedule 3 to the Sexual Offences Act 2003, automatic notification requirements apply upon conviction to an offender aged 18 or over where:
  - the victim was under 18; or
  - a term of imprisonment or a community sentence of at least 12 months is imposed.
- This guideline may be relevant by way of analogy to conduct charged as the common law offence of outraging public decency; the offence is triable either way and has a maximum penalty of a level 5 fine and/or 6 months' imprisonment when tried summarily.

 See *Blackstone's Criminal Practice 2012* **B3.260–B3.263**

C15.3 **Indecent photographs of children**

Protection of Children Act 1978, s 1

1 Indecent photographs of children

(1) Subject to sections 1A and 1B, it is an offence for a person—

    (a) to take, or permit to be taken or to make, any indecent photograph or pseudo-photograph of a child; or

    (b) to distribute or show such indecent photographs or pseudo-photographs; or

    (c) to have in his possession such indecent photographs or pseudo-photographs, with a view to their being distributed or shown by himself or others; or

    (d) to publish or cause to be published any advertisement likely to be understood as conveying that the advertiser distributes or shows such indecent photographs or pseudo-photographs, or intends to do so.

(2) For purposes of this Act, a person is to be regarded as distributing an indecent photograph or pseudo-photograph if he parts with possession of it to, or exposes or offers it for acquisition by, another person.

(3) Proceedings for an offence under this Act shall not be instituted except by or with the consent of the Director of Public Prosecutions.

(4) Where a person is charged with an offence under subsection (1)(b) or (c), it shall be a defence for him to prove—

    (a) that he had a legitimate reason for distributing or showing the photographs or pseudo-photographs or (as the case may be) having them in his possession; or

    (b) that he had not himself seen the photographs or pseudo-photographs and did not know, nor had any cause to suspect, them to be indecent.

Criminal Justice Act 1988, s 160

160 Summary offence of possession of indecent photograph of child

(1) Subject to section 160A, it is an offence for a person to have any indecent photograph or pseudo-photograph of a child in his possession.

(2) Where a person is charged with an offence under subsection (1) above, it shall be a defence for him to prove—

    (a) that he had a legitimate reason for having the photograph or pseudo-photograph in his possession; or

    (b) that he had not himself seen the photograph or pseudo-photograph and did not know, nor had any cause to suspect, it to be indecent; or

    (c) that the photograph or pseudo-photograph was sent to him without any prior request made by him or on his behalf and that he did not keep it for an unreasonable time.

EW

 6 months and/or level 5 fine/10 years (5 if s 160)

C15.3.1 *Sentencing*

- The levels of seriousness (in ascending order) for sentencing for offences involving pornographic images are:
  - Level 1: Images depicting erotic posing with no sexual activity.
  - Level 2: Non-penetrative sexual activity between children, or solo masturbation by a child.
  - Level 3: Non-penetrative sexual activity between adults and children.
  - Level 4: Penetrative sexual activity involving a child or children, or both children and adults.
  - Level 5: Sadism or penetration of, or by, an animal.
- Pseudo-photographs generally should be treated less seriously than real photographs.
- Starting points should be higher where the subject of the indecent photograph(s) is a child under 13.
- In accordance with section 80 of and Schedule 3 to the Sexual Offences Act 2003, automatic notification requirements apply upon conviction to an offender aged 18 or over where the offence involved photographs of children aged under 16.

Offence seriousness (culpability and harm) A. Identify the appropriate starting point Starting points based on first time offender pleading not guilty		
Examples of nature of activity	**Starting point**	**Range**
Possession of a large amount of level 1 material and/or no more than a small amount of level 2, and the material is for personal use and has not been distributed or shown to others	Medium level community order	Band C fine to high level community order
Offender in possession of a large amount of material at level 2 or a small amount at level 3 Offender has shown or distributed material at level 1 on a limited scale Offender has exchanged images at level 1 or 2 with other collectors, but with no element of financial gain	12 weeks custody	4 to 26 weeks custody
Possession of a large quantity of level 3 material for personal use Possession of a small number of images at level 4 or 5 Large number of level 2 images shown or distributed Small number of level 3 images shown or distributed	26 weeks custody	4 weeks custody to Crown Court
Possession of a large quantity of level 4 or 5 material for personal use only Large number of level 3 images shown or distributed Offender traded material at levels 1–3 Level 4 or 5 images shown or distributed	Crown Court	26 weeks custody to Crown Court
Offender involved in the production of material of any level	Crown Court	Crown Court

Offence seriousness (culpability and harm)	
B. Consider the effect of aggravating and mitigating factors	
(other than those within examples above)	
The following may be particularly relevant but **these lists are not exhaustive**	
Factors indicating higher culpability	**Factors indicating lower culpability**
1. Collection is systematically stored or organized, indicating a sophisticated approach to trading or a high level of personal interest	1. A few images held solely for personal use
2. Use of drugs, alcohol, or other substance to facilitate the offence of making or taking	2. Images viewed but not stored
3. Background of intimidation or coercion	3. A few images held solely for personal use and it is established that the subject is aged 16 or 17 and that he or she was consenting
4. Threats to prevent victim reporting the activity	
5. Threats to disclose victim's activity to friends/relatives	
6. Financial or other gain	
Factors indicating greater degree of harm	
1. Images shown or distributed to others, especially children	
2. Images stored, made available, or distributed in such a way that they can be inadvertently accessed by others	

C15.3.2 Key points

- Photograph includes tracing or other image derived in whole or part from a photograph or pseudo-photograph.
- Whether a photograph is indecent depends on normally recognized standards of propriety.
- The age of the child may be relevant to the issue of indecency (*R v Owen* (1988) 88 Cr App R 291).
- The opening of an email, or viewing of an image on the screen would amount to the making of an image if the defendant has the requisite knowledge of what he is doing.
- A child is a person under 18 years of age (Sexual Offences Act 2003, s 45).

 See *Blackstone's Criminal Practice 2012* **B3.285–B3.291**

C15.4 **Kerb crawling, loitering, and soliciting**

Sexual Offences Act 1985, ss 1(1) and 2(1)

1 Kerb-crawling

(1) A person commits an offence if he solicits another person (or different persons) for the purpose of prostitution—

(a) from a motor vehicle while it is in a street or public place; or

(b) in a street or public place while in the immediate vicinity of a motor vehicle that he has just got out of or off,

persistently or in such manner or in such circumstances as to be likely to cause annoyance to the person (or any of the persons) solicited, or nuisance to other persons in the neighbourhood.

2 Persistent soliciting

(1) A person commits an offence if in a street or public place he persistently solicits another person (or different persons) for the purpose of prostitution.

Street Offences Act 1959, s 1

(1) It shall be an offence for a person (whether male or female) persistently to loiter or solicit in a street or public place for the purpose of prostitution.

 Fine level 3 (for a first offence under s 1 Street Offences Act 1959 the fine is level 2)

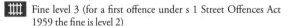 See *Blackstone's Criminal Practice 2012* B3.281–B3.284

C15.5 **Prohibited images of children**

Coroners and Justice Act 2009, s 63

(1) It is an offence for a person to be in possession of a prohibited image of a child.

(2) A prohibited image is an image which—

(a) is pornographic,

(b) falls within subsection (6), and

(c) is grossly offensive, disgusting or otherwise of an obscene character.

---

(3) An image is 'pornographic' if it is of such a nature that it must reasonably be assumed to have been produced solely or principally for the purpose of sexual arousal.

(4) Where (as found in the person's possession) an image forms part of a series of images, the question whether the image is of such a nature as is mentioned in subsection (3) is to be determined by reference to—

   (a) the image itself, and

   (b) (if the series of images is such as to be capable of providing a context for the image) the context in which it occurs in the series of images.

(5) So, for example, where—

   (a) an image forms an integral part of a narrative constituted by a series of images, and

   (b) having regard to those images as a whole, they are not of such a nature that they must reasonably be assumed to have been produced solely or principally for the purpose of sexual arousal, the image may, by virtue of being part of that narrative, be found not to be pornographic, even though it might have been found to be pornographic if taken by itself.

(6) An image falls within this subsection if it—

   (a) is an image which focuses solely or principally on a child's genitals or anal region, or

   (b) portrays any of the acts mentioned in subsection (7).

(7) Those acts are—

   (a) the performance by a person of an act of intercourse or oral sex with or in the presence of a child;

   (b) an act of masturbation by, of, involving or in the presence of a child;

   (c) an act which involves penetration of the vagina or anus of a child with a part of a person's body or with anything else;

   (d) an act of penetration, in the presence of a child, of the vagina or anus of a person with a part of a person's body or with anything else;

   (e) the performance by a child of an act of intercourse or oral sex with an animal (whether dead or alive or imaginary);

   (f) the performance by a person of an act of intercourse or oral sex with an animal (whether dead or alive or imaginary) in the presence of a child.

(8) For the purposes of subsection (7), penetration is a continuing act from entry to withdrawal.

(9) Proceedings for an offence under subsection (1) may not be instituted—

   (a) in England and Wales, except by or with the consent of the Director of Public Prosecutions;

EW

6 months and/or unlimited fine/3 years

C15.5.1 **Key points**

- Section 64 of the Act provides for the following defence:

Coroners and Justice Act 2009, s 64

(1) Where a person is charged with an offence under section 62(1), it is a defence for the person to prove any of the following matters—

   (a) that the person had a legitimate reason for being in possession of the image concerned;

   (b) that the person had not seen the image concerned and did not know, nor had any cause to suspect, it to be a prohibited image of a child;

   (c) that the person—

      (i) was sent the image concerned without any prior request having been made by or on behalf of the person, and

      (ii) did not keep it for an unreasonable time.

- Section 65 of the Act defines the meaning of image and child.

 See *Blackstone's Criminal Practice 2012* **B3.291–B3.296**

C15.6 **Extreme pornography**

Criminal Justice and Immigration Act 2008, s 63

(1) It is an offence for a person to be in possession of an extreme pornographic image.

(2) An 'extreme pornographic image' is an image which is both—

   (a) pornographic, and

   (b) an extreme image.

(3) An image is 'pornographic' if it is of such a nature that it must reasonably be assumed to have been produced solely or principally for the purpose of sexual arousal.

(4) Where (as found in the person's possession) an image forms part of a series of images, the question whether the image is of such a nature as is mentioned in subsection (3) is to be determined by reference to—

   (a) the image itself, and

   (b) (if the series of images is such as to be capable of providing a context for the image) the context in which it occurs in the series of images.

(5) So, for example, where—

   (a) an image forms an integral part of a narrative constituted by a series of images, and

   (b) having regard to those images as a whole, they are not of such a nature that they must reasonably be assumed to have been produced solely or principally for the purpose of sexual arousal, the image may, by virtue of being part of that narrative, be found not to be pornographic, even though it might have been found to be pornographic if taken by itself.

(6) An 'extreme image' is an image which—
   (a) falls within subsection (7), and
   (b) is grossly offensive, disgusting or otherwise of an obscene character.
(7) An image falls within this subsection if it portrays, in an explicit and realistic way, any of the following—
   (a) an act which threatens a person's life,
   (b) an act which results, or is likely to result, in serious injury to a person's anus, breasts or genitals,
   (c) an act which involves sexual interference with a human corpse, or
   (d) a person performing an act of intercourse or oral sex with an animal (whether dead or alive),and a reasonable person looking at the image would think that any such person or animal was real.
(8) In this section 'image' means—
   (a) a moving or still image (produced by any means); or
   (b) data (stored by any means) which is capable of conversion into an image within paragraph (a).
(9) In this section references to a part of the body include references to a part surgically constructed (in particular through gender reassignment surgery).
(10) Proceedings for an offence under this section may not be instituted—
   (a) in England and Wales, except by or with the consent of the Director of Public Prosecutions;

EW

6 months and/or level 5 fine/3 years (2 years if the offence relates to an image that does not portray any act within section 63(7)(a) or (b))

See *Blackstone's Criminal Practice 2012* **B3.297–B3.302**

C15.7 **Prostitution, exploitation of**

Sexual Offences Act 2003, ss 52 and 53

EW

▦ 6 months and/or level 5 fine/7 years

DO

C15.7.1 *Sentencing*

Offence seriousness (culpability and harm) A. Identify the appropriate starting point Starting points based on first time offender pleading not guilty		
Examples of nature of activity	**Starting point**	**Range**
No evidence victim was physically coerced or corrupted, and the involvement of the offender was minimal	Medium level community order	Band C fine to high level community order
No coercion or corruption but the offender is closely involved in the victim's prostitution	Crown Court	26 weeks custody to Crown Court
Evidence of physical and/or mental coercion	Crown Court	Crown Court

Offence seriousness (culpability and harm) B. Consider the effect of aggravating and mitigating factors (other than those within examples above)	
Factors indicating higher culpability 1. Background of threats, intimidation or coercion 2. Large-scale commercial operation 3. Substantial gain (in the region of £5,000 and up) 4. Use of drugs, alcohol, or other substance to secure the victim's compliance 5. Abduction or detention 6. Threats to prevent the victim reporting the activity 7. Threats to disclose victim's activity to friends/relatives **Factor indicating greater degree of harm** 1. Induced dependency on drugs	**Factor indicating lower culpability** 1. Offender also being controlled in prostitution and subject to threats or intimidation

📖 See *Blackstone's Criminal Practice 2012* B3.207–B3.220

C15.8 **Prostitution, keeping a brothel used for**

Sexual Offences Act 1956, ss 33 and 33A

 6 months and/or level 5 fine/7 years

C15.8.1 *Sentencing*

Offence seriousness (culpability and harm) A. Identify the appropriate starting point Starting points based on first time offender pleading not guilty		
Examples of nature of activity	**Starting point**	**Range**
Involvement of the offender was minimal	Medium level community order	Band C fine to high level community order
Offender is the keeper of a brothel and is personally involved in its management	Crown Court	26 weeks to Crown Court
Offender is the keeper of a brothel and has made substantial profits in the region of £5,000 and upwards	Crown Court	Crown Court

Offence seriousness (culpability and harm) B. Consider the effect of aggravating and mitigating factors (other than those within examples above) The following may be particularly relevant but **these lists are not exhaustive**	
Factors indicating higher culpability	**Factors indicating lower culpability**
1. Background of threats, intimidation, or coercion 2. Large-scale commercial operation 3. Personal involvement in the prostitution of others 4. Abduction or detention 5. Financial or other gain	1. Using employment as a route out of prostitution and not actively involved in exploitation 2. Coercion by third party

 See *Blackstone's Criminal Practice 2012* **B3.309–B3.324**

C15.9 **Sexual activity in a public lavatory**

Sexual Offences Act 2003, s 71(1)–(2)

(1) A person commits an offence if—
   (a) he is in a lavatory to which the public or a section of the public has or is permitted to have access, whether on payment or otherwise,
   (b) he intentionally engages in an activity, and,
   (c) the activity is sexual.
(2) For the purposes of this section, an activity is sexual if a reasonable person would, in all the circumstances but regardless of any person's purpose, consider it to be sexual.

 SO

 6 months and/or level 5 fine

C15.9.1 *Sentencing*

Offence seriousness (culpability and harm)		
A. Identify the appropriate starting point		
Starting points based on first time offender pleading not guilty		
Examples of nature of activity	**Starting point**	**Range**
Basic offence as defined in the Act, assuming no aggravating or mitigating factors	Band C fine	Band C fine
Offence with aggravating factors	Low level community order	Band C fine to medium level community order
Offence seriousness (culpability and harm)		
B. Consider the effect of aggravating and mitigating factors		
(other than those within examples above)		
The following may be particularly relevant but **these lists are not exhaustive**		
Factors indicating higher culpability 1. Intimidating behaviour/threats of violence to member(s) of the public 2. Blatant behaviour		

C15.9.2 Key points

- This offence is committed where an offender intentionally engages in sexual activity in a public lavatory. It was introduced to give adults and children the freedom to use public lavatories for the purpose for which they are designed, without the fear of being an unwilling witness to overtly sexual behaviour of a kind that most people would not expect to be conducted in public. It is primarily a public order offence rather than a sexual offence.

- When dealing with a repeat offender, the starting point should be a low level community order with a range of B and C fine to medium level community order. The presence of aggravating factors may suggest that a sentence above the range is appropriate.

- This guideline may be relevant by way of analogy to conduct charged as the common law offence of outraging public decency; the offence is triable either way and has a maximum penalty of a level 5 fine and/or 6 months' imprisonment when tried summarily.

 See *Blackstone's Criminal Practice 2012* B3.277–B3.279

C15.10 **Sexual assault**

Sexual Offences Act 2003, ss 3(1)–(3), 4, 7(1), 8, and 9

3 Sexual assault

(1) A person (A) commits an offence if—
   (a) he intentionally touches another person (B),
   (b) the touching is sexual,
   (c) B does not consent to the touching, and
   (d) A does not reasonably believe that B consents.
(2) Whether a belief is reasonable is to be determined having regard to all the circumstances, including any steps A has taken to ascertain whether B consents.
(3) Sections 75 and 76 apply to an offence under this section.

4 Causing a person to engage in sexual activity without consent

(1) A person (A) commits an offence if—
   (a) he intentionally causes another person (B) to engage in an activity,
   (b) the activity is sexual,
   (c) B does not consent to engaging in the activity, and
   (d) A does not reasonably believe that B consents.
(2) Whether a belief is reasonable is to be determined having regard to all the circumstances, including any steps A has taken to ascertain whether B consents.

(3) Sections 75 and 76 apply to an offence under this section.

(4) A person guilty of an offence under this section, if the activity caused involved—

   (a) penetration of B's anus or vagina,

   (b) penetration of B's mouth with a person's penis,

   (c) penetration of a person's anus or vagina with a part of B's body or by B with anything else, or

   (d) penetration of a person's mouth with B's penis,

is liable, on conviction on indictment, to imprisonment for life.

7 Sexual assault of a child under 13

(1) A person commits an offence if—

   (a) he intentionally touches another person,

   (b) the touching is sexual, and

   (c) the other person is under 13.

8 Causing or inciting a child under 13 to engage in sexual activity

(1) A person commits an offence if—

   (a) he intentionally causes or incites another person (B) to engage in an activity,

   (b) the activity is sexual, and

   (c) B is under 13.

(2) A person guilty of an offence under this section, if the activity caused or incited involved—

   (a) penetration of B's anus or vagina,

   (b) penetration of B's mouth with a person's penis,

   (c) penetration of a person's anus or vagina with a part of B's body or by B with anything else, or

   (d) penetration of a person's mouth with B's penis,

is liable, on conviction on indictment, to imprisonment for life.

9 Sexual activity with a child

(1) A person aged 18 or over (A) commits an offence if—

   (a) he intentionally touches another person (B),

   (b) the touching is sexual, and

   (c) either—

      (i) B is under 16 and A does not reasonably believe that B is 16 or over, or

      (ii) B is under 13.

(2) A person guilty of an offence under this section, if the touching involved—

   (a) penetration of B's anus or vagina with a part of A's body or anything else,

   (b) penetration of B's mouth with A's penis,

   (c) penetration of A's anus or vagina with a part of B's body, or

   (d) penetration of A's mouth with B's penis.

C15 Sexual Offences

EW Save for sections 4, 8 and 9 where penetration is involved and the offences become triable only on indictment with maximum sentences of life for both sections 4 and 8 and 14 years for section 9

▦ 6 months and/or level 5 fine/10 years (ss 3, 4) 14 years (ss 7, 8) 14 years (s 9), save for section 4 and 8 where penetration is involved and the offence is triable only on indictment with a maximum of life imprisonment)

DO

C15.10.1 *Sentencing*

Offence seriousness (culpability and harm) A. Identify the appropriate starting point Starting points based on first time offender pleading not guilty		
Examples of nature of activity	**Starting point**	**Range**
Contact between part of offender's body (other than the genitalia) with part of the victim's body (other than the genitalia)	26 weeks custody if the victim is under 13 Medium level community order if the victim is aged 13 or over	4 weeks custody to Crown Court Band C fine to 6 weeks custody
Contact between naked genitalia of offender and another part of victim's body Contact with naked genitalia of victim by offender using part of his or her body other than the genitalia, or an object Contact between either the clothed genitalia of offender and naked genitalia of victim or naked genitalia of offender and clothed genitalia of victim	Crown Court if the victim is under 13 Crown Court if the victim is aged 13 or over	Crown Court 26 weeks custody to Crown Court
Contact between naked genitalia of offender and naked genitalia, face, or mouth of the victim	Crown Court	Crown Court

Offence seriousness (culpability and harm)	
B. Consider the effect of aggravating and mitigating factors	
(other than those within examples opposite)	
The following may be particularly relevant but **these lists are not exhaustive**	
Factors indicating higher culpability	**Factors indicating lower culpability**
1. Background of intimidation or coercion	1. Youth and immaturity of the offender
2. Use of drugs, alcohol, or other substance to facilitate the offence	2. Minimal or fleeting contact
3. Threats to prevent the victim reporting the incident	*Where the victim is aged 16 or over*
4. Abduction or detention	3. Victim engaged in consensual activity with the offender on the same occasion and immediately before the offence
5. Offender aware that he or she is suffering from a sexually transmitted infection	
6. Prolonged activity or contact	*Where the victim is under 16*
Factors indicating greater degree of harm	4. Sexual activity between two children (one of whom is the offender) was mutually agreed and experimental
1. Offender ejaculated or caused victim to ejaculate	
2. Physical harm caused	

C15.10.2   Key points

- If a defendant does not reasonably know, or is mistaken about the age of the child, it affords a defence to a section 7 offence (*B v Director of Public Prosecutions* [2000] AC 428).
- A person under 16 years of age cannot in law consent.

  See *Blackstone's Criminal Practice 2012* B3.30–B3.43 and B3.51–B3.76

C15.11 Sex offenders register—fail to comply with notification requirements

Sexual Offences Act 2003, ss 91(1)(a) and 91(1)(b)

EW

6 months and/or level 5 fine/5 years

C15.11.1 *Sentencing*

Offence seriousness (culpability and harm)		
A. Identify the appropriate starting point		
Starting points based on first time offender (see note below) pleading not guilty		
Examples of nature of activity	**Starting point**	**Range**
Negligent or inadvertent failure to comply with requirements	Medium level community order	Band C fine to high level community order
Deliberate failure to comply with requirements OR Supply of information known to be false	6 weeks custody	High level community order to 26 weeks custody
Conduct as described in box above AND Long period of non-compliance OR Attempts to avoid detection	18 weeks custody	6 weeks custody to Crown Court

Offence seriousness (culpability and harm)	
B. Consider the effect of aggravating and mitigating factors	
(other than those within examples above)	
The following may be particularly relevant but **these lists are not exhaustive**	
Factor indicating higher culpability	**Factor indicating lower culpability**
1. Long period of non-compliance (where not in the examples above)	1. Genuine misunderstanding
Factors indicating greater degree of harm	
1. Alarm or distress caused to victim	
2. Particularly serious original offence	

 See *Blackstone's Criminal Practice 2012* **E23.4**

C15.12 **Voyeurism**

Sexual Offences Act 2003, s 67(1)–(4)

(1) A person commits an offence if—
   (a) for the purpose of obtaining sexual gratification, he observes another person doing a private act, and
   (b) he knows that the other person does not consent to being observed for his sexual gratification.

(2) A person commits an offence if—
   (a) he operates equipment with the intention of enabling another person to observe, for the purpose of obtaining sexual gratification, a third person (B) doing a private act, and
   (b) he knows that B does not consent to his operating equipment with that intention.

(3) A person commits an offence if—
  (a) he records another person (B) doing a private act,
  (b) he does so with the intention that he or a third person will, for the purpose of obtaining sexual gratification, look at an image of B doing the act, and
  (c) he knows that B does not consent to his recording the act with that intention.
(4) A person commits an offence if he installs equipment, or constructs or adapts a structure or part of a structure, with the intention of enabling himself or another person to commit an offence under subsection (1).

EW

🏛 6 months and/or level 5 fine/2 years

DO

15.12.1 *Sentencing*

Offence seriousness (culpability and harm)		
A. Identify the appropriate starting point		
Starting points based on first time offender pleading not guilty		
Examples of nature of activity	**Starting point**	**Range**
Basic offence as defined in the Act, assuming no aggravating or mitigating factors, eg the offender spies through a hole he or she has made in a changing room wall	Low level community order	Band B fine to high level community order
Offence with aggravating factors such as recording sexual activity and showing it to others	26 weeks custody	4 weeks custody to Crown Court
Offence with serious aggravating factors such as recording sexual activity and placing it on a website or circulating it for commercial gain	Crown Court	26 weeks to Crown Court

Offence seriousness (culpability and harm)
B. Consider the effect of aggravating and mitigating factors
(other than those within examples above)
The following may be particularly relevant but **these lists are not exhaustive**

Factors indicating higher culpability	
1. Threats to prevent the victim reporting an offence	
2. Recording activity and circulating pictures/videos	
3. Circulating pictures or videos for commercial gain— particularly if victim is vulnerable eg a child or a person with a mental or physical disorder	
Factor indicating greater degree of harm	
1. Distress to victim eg where the pictures/videos are circulated to people known to the victim	

C15.12.2 Key points

- Section 68 provides for the interpretation of key phrases:

> **Sexual Offences Act 2003, s 68**
>
> (1) For the purposes of section 67, a person is doing a private act if the person is in a place which, in the circumstances, would reasonably be expected to provide privacy, and—
>   (a) the person's genitals, buttocks or breasts are exposed or covered only with underwear,
>   (b) the person is using a lavatory, or
>   (c) the person is doing a sexual act that is not of a kind ordinarily done in public.
> (2) In section 67, 'structure' includes a tent, vehicle or vessel or other temporary or movable structure.

- Consent is defined under section 74 of the Act:

  For the purposes of this Part, a person consents if he agrees by choice, and has the freedom and capacity to make that choice.

- Sections 75 and 76 deal with evidential presumptions in relation to consent.

 See *Blackstone's Criminal Practice 2012* **B3.264–B3.268**

C16 **Theft, Fraud, and Evasion**

C16.1 **Aggravated vehicle-taking**

Theft Act 1968, s 12A(1)–(3)

(1) Subject to subsection (3) below, a person is guilty of aggravated taking of a vehicle if—

   (a) he commits an offence under section 12(1) above (in this section referred to as a 'basic offence') in relation to a mechanically propelled vehicle; and

   (b) it is proved that, at any time after the vehicle was unlawfully taken (whether by him or another) and before it was recovered, the vehicle was driven, or injury or damage was caused, in one or more of the circumstances set out in paragraphs (a) to (d) of subsection (2) below.

(2) The circumstances referred to in subsection (1)(b) above are—

   (a) that the vehicle was driven dangerously on a road or other public place;

   (b) that, owing to the driving of the vehicle, an accident occurred by which injury was caused to any person;

   (c) that, owing to the driving of the vehicle, an accident occurred by which damage was caused to any property, other than the vehicle;

   (d) that damage was caused to the vehicle.

(3) A person is not guilty of an offence under this section if he proves that, as regards any such proven driving, injury or damage as is referred to in subsection (1)(b) above, either—

   (a) the driving, accident or damage referred to in subsection (2) above occurred before he committed the basic offence; or

   (b) he was neither in nor on nor in the immediate vicinity of the vehicle when that driving, accident or damage occurred.

EW Summary if damage under £5,000

Ⅲ Section 12A(2)(a) and (b): 6 months and/or level 5 fine/2 years (14 years if accident caused death). Must endorse and disqualify for at least 12 months. Must disqualify for at least 2 years if offender has had 2 or more disqualifications for periods of 56 days or more in preceding 3 years

Ⅲ Section 12A(2)(c) and (d): 6 months and/or level 5 fine/2 years. Must endorse and disqualify for at least 12 months. Must disqualify for at least 2 years if offender has had 2 or more disqualifications for periods of 56 days or more in preceding 3 years

---

C16.1.1 *Sentencing: dangerous driving or accident causing injury*

Offence seriousness (culpability and harm) A. Identify the appropriate starting point Starting points based on first time offender pleading not guilty		
Example of nature of activity	**Starting point**	**Range**
Taken vehicle involved in single incident of bad driving where little or no damage or risk of personal injury	High level community order	Medium community order to 12 weeks custody
Taken vehicle involved in incident(s) involving excessive speed or showing off, especially on busy roads or in built-up area	18 weeks custody	12 to 26 weeks custody
Taken vehicle involved in prolonged bad driving involving deliberate disregard for safety of other	Crown Court	Crown Court

Offence seriousness (culpability and harm) B. Consider the effect of aggravating and mitigating factors (other than those within examples above) The following may be particularly relevant but **these lists are not exhaustive**	
Factors indicating higher culpability 1. Disregarding warnings of others 2. Evidence of alcohol or drugs 3. Carrying out other tasks while driving 4. Tiredness 5. Trying to avoid arrest 6. Aggressive driving, such as driving much too close to vehicle in front, inappropriate attempts to overtake, or cutting in after overtaking **Factors indicating greater degree of harm** 1. Injury to others 2. Damage to other vehicle or property	

C16.1.2 *Sentencing: damage caused*

Offence seriousness (culpability and harm) A. Identify the appropriate starting point Starting points based on first time offender pleading not guilty		
Examples of nature of activity	**Starting point**	**Range**
Exceeding authorized use of eg employer's or relative's vehicle; retention of hire car beyond return date; minor damage to taken vehicle	Medium level community order	Low level community order to high level community order
Greater damage to taken vehicle and/or moderate damage to another vehicle and/or moderate damage to another vehicle and/or property	High level community order	Medium level community order to 12 weeks custody
Vehicle taken as part of burglary or from private premises; severe damage	18 weeks custody	12 to 26 week custody (Crown Court if damage over £5,000)

Offence seriousness (culpability and harm) B. Consider the effect of aggravating and mitigating factors (other than those within examples above) The following may be particularly relevant but **these lists are not exhaustive**	
Factors indicating higher culpability 1. Vehicle deliberately damaged/destroyed 2. Offender under influence of alcohol/drugs **Factors indicating greater degree of harm** 1. Passenger(s) carried 2. Vehicle belonging to elderly or disabled person 3. Emergency services vehicle 4. Medium to large goods vehicle 5. Damage caused in moving traffic accident	**Factors indicating lower culpability** 1. Misunderstanding with owner 2. Damage resulting from actions of another (where this does not provide a defence)

C16.1.3 Key points

- If aggravating factor is solely damage, then the offence is triable summarily only if the damage does not exceed £5,000.
- A magistrates' court can convict a defendant of the alternative offence of vehicle taking if it does not find the aggravating feature(s) (*H v Liverpool Youth Court* [2001] Crim LR 897).

See *Blackstone's Criminal Practice 2012* **B4.101–B4.107**

C16.2 **Alcohol/tobacco, fraudulently evade duty**

Customs and Excise Management Act 1979, s 170

 6 months and/or 3 times the duty evaded or level 5 fine, whichever is the greater/7 years

C16.2.1 *Sentencing*

See **Appendix 6**.

C16.2.2 Key points

- It is not sufficient for the prosecution to show that the defendant was merely reckless (*R v Panayi* [1989] 1 WLR 187).
- It is irrelevant that the defendant does not know the precise nature of the goods being imported (*R v Shivpuri* [1987] AC 1).
- The burden of proving that duty has been paid falls on the defendant (s 154).
- The court may make a financial reporting order on conviction (see **D32**).
- The prosecution has the right to appeal sentence (*Customs and Excise Commissioners v Brunt* (1998) 163 JP 161).

See *Blackstone's Criminal Practice 2012* **B16.34–B16.43**

C16.3 **Burglary**

> **Theft Act 1968, s 9(1)–(2)**
>
> (1) A person is guilty of burglary if—
>   (a) he enters any building or part of a building as a trespasser and with intent to commit any such offence as is mentioned in subsection (2) below; or
>   (b) having entered any building or part of a building as a trespasser he steals or attempts to steal anything in the building or that part of it or inflicts or attempts to inflict on any person therein any grievous bodily harm.
> (2) The offences referred to in subsection (1) (a) above are offences of stealing anything in the building or part of a building in question, of inflicting on any person therein any grievous bodily harm therein, and of doing unlawful damage to the building or anything therein.

EW

 6 months and/or level 5 fine/10 years (14 if dwelling)

Offence is indictable only and must be sent to the Crown Court if:

(1)
- was 18 or over when he committed the offence;
- committed the offence on or after 1 December 1999;
- had previously been convicted of two other domestic burglary offences in England and Wales; one of those offences has been committed after conviction for the other; and
- both of the previous domestic burglaries had been committed on or after 1 December 1999.

(2) Any person was subjected to violence or the threat of violence: Magistrates' Courts Act 1980, Sch 1.

C16.3.1 *Sentencing: non-dwelling*

Type/nature of activity	Starting point	Range
Where the effect on the victim is particularly severe, the goods are of particularly high value, the cost of damage or consequential losses is significant, or there is evidence of a professional burglary and/or significant planning, a sentence of more than 7 years custody may be appropriate		
Burglary involving goods valued at £20,000 or more	2 years custody	12 months—7 years custody
Burglary involving goods valued at £2,000 or more but less than £20,000	18 weeks custody	Community order (HIGH)—12 months custody
Burglary involving goods valued at less than £2,000	Community order (MEDIUM)	Fine—26 weeks custody

Additional aggravating factors:
Targeting premises containing property of high value
Targeting vulnerable community premises
Targeting premises which have been burgled on prior occasion(s)
Possession of a weapon (where this is not charged separately)

C16.3.2 *Sentencing: dwelling*

Offence seriousness (culpability and harm)		
A. Identify the appropriate starting point		
Starting points based on first time offender pleading not guilty		
Examples of nature of activity	**Starting point**	**Range**
Unforced entry and low value theft with no aggravating features	Medium level community order	Low level community order to 12 weeks custody
Forced entry, goods stolen not high value, no aggravating features	12 weeks custody	High level community order to Crown Court
Goods stolen high value or any aggravating feature present	Crown Court	Crown Court

Offence seriousness (culpability and harm)	
B. Consider the effect of aggravating and mitigating factors	
(other than those within examples above)	
The following may be particularly relevant but **these lists are not exhaustive**	
Factors indicating higher culpability	**Factors indicating lower culpability**
1. Ransacking property	1. Offender played only a minor role in the burglary
2. Professionalism	2. Offence committed on impulse
3. Victim deliberately targeted eg out of spite	**Factor indicating lesser degree of harm**
4. Housebreaking implements or weapons carried	1. No damage or disturbance to property
Factors indicating greater degree of harm	
1. Occupier at home or returns home while offender present	
2. Goods stolen of sentimental value	

The Sentencing Guidelines Council has issued the following guidance in light of recent case law:

Burglary in a dwelling

In the Magistrates' Court Sentencing Guidelines, pages 34/35 provide a summary of the effect of the Court of Appeal guideline judgment in *McInerney and Keating* as it applies both to mode of trial (allocation) and to sentencing decisions in a magistrates' court. In the light of experience and pending any fuller consideration by the Sentencing Guidelines Council, that judgment has been reviewed and clarified by the Court of Appeal in *R. v. Saw and others* [2009] EWCA Crim 1.

The purpose of this note is to clarify the effect of the decision on the application of this part of the Magistrates' Court Sentencing Guidelines.

Approach to sentencing—Key points

1. The aim of the judgment is to achieve consistency of approach, clearly recognising the seriousness of this offence—not only is it an offence against property but it is also an offence against the person. Particular focus is required on the impact of the offence on those living in the burgled house; sentences should reflect the level of harmful consequences even when not intended by the offender.

2. The sentence must reflect the criminality of the offender. Previous convictions and the record of an offender are of more significance than in the case of some other crimes. Burglary of a dwelling should be treated as more serious when committed by an offender with previous convictions for relevant dishonesty than an identical offence committed by a first offender.

3. The judgment states that it does not add anything to the Magistrates' Court Sentencing Guidelines, emphasising the importance of addressing the aggravating and mitigating factors referred to in the judgment. The Magistrates' Court Sentencing Guidelines currently provide for committal to the Crown Court where an aggravating feature is present and sentence within the powers of the Crown Court is included within the range in some other circumstances.

4. A non-exhaustive list of aggravating and mitigating features commonly encountered in burglary is provided in the judgment; this is more extensive than the list in the Magistrates' Court Sentencing Guidelines derived from *McInerney and Keating*. They are summarised at the end of this note. The importance of the aggravating features derives from the *increase in the impact* of the offence that results from them, or from the *increase in the culpability* of the offender that they demonstrate, or from a combination of the two.

The guideline—categories of seriousness

The Magistrates' Court Sentencing Guidelines set out three categories of offence seriousness:

Category 1—Offences likely to be able to be sentenced within the jurisdiction of a magistrates' court (when committed by a first time offender) are those where the entry to the premises was unforced, the property stolen of low value and there were no aggravating features; the starting point is a community sentence. In determining whether an aggravating feature was present, the court should refer to the list set out in *Saw and others*.

Category 2—Where the entry was forced, the goods were not of high value, and there were no aggravating features, the sentencing range commences within the jurisdiction of a magistrates' court but ends within the jurisdiction of the Crown Court; the starting point is 12 weeks custody. In determining whether an aggravating feature was present, the court should refer to the list set out in *Saw and others*.

Although *Saw and others* requires particular focus on the impact of the offence on the victim, it confirms that a low level burglary with minimal loss and minimal damage and without raised culpability or raised impact, page no: 264 committed by a first time offender, may be dealt with by way of a community order rather than an immediate custodial penalty.

Category 3—An offence would be expected to be committed to the Crown Court where the goods stolen were of high value or any aggravating feature was present. *Saw and others* provides that the court must address the overall criminality of the offender (in the light of previous convictions) and the impact of the offence on the victim(s):

- where there is *limited raised culpability and/or impact*, it is likely that the sentence will be within a general range of 9 to18 months custody; a shorter sentence (including the making of a community order) may be appropriate where it is established that the offender played a subsidiary role or was exploited by other offenders;
- where there is *seriously raised culpability and/or serious impact*, the starting point should be a custodial sentence in excess of 18 months; a community order should be considered only in the most extreme and exceptional circumstances. As noted on page 34 of the Magistrates' Court Sentencing Guidelines, where a case otherwise appropriate for sentence in the Crown Court is, on its own particular facts likely to attract a community order, it should nonetheless be sentenced in the Crown Court so that any sanction for non-compliance can be imposed with the powers of that court rather than within the more limited powers of a magistrates' court.

Aggravating and mitigating features (not exhaustive)
Aggravating features:

- the use or threat of force on or against the victim (NB: this would make the offence triable on indictment only),
- trauma to the victim beyond that normally associated with this type of offence,
- pre-meditation and professional planning or organisation, such as by offenders,
- working in groups or when housebreaking implements are carried,
- vandalism of the premises burgled,
- deliberate targeting of any vulnerable victim,
- deliberate targeting of any victim,
- the presence of the occupier whether at night or during the day,
- high economic or sentimental value of the property stolen or damaged,
- offence committed on bail or shortly after imposition of a non-custodial sentence,
- two or more burglaries of homes rather than a single offence,
- the offender's previous convictions.

Mitigating features:

- nothing, or only property of very low value is taken,
- offender played a minor part in the burglary, and treated by others in group as if he were on the fringes,

- exploited by others,
- offence committed on impulse,
- age and state of health (mental and physical),
- good character,
- evidence of genuine regret and remorse,
- ready co-operation with the police,
- positive response to previous sentences.

C16.3.3   Key points

- Entry can be partial (*R v Brown* [1985] Crim LR 212), and can be effected without any part of the body entering the building (for example, cane and hook burglaries).
- 'Building' is a factual not a legal issue and will depend on all of the circumstances (*Brutus v Cozens* [1973] AC 854).
- Trespass can be committed knowingly or recklessly (*R v Collins* [1973] QB 100).

See *Blackstone's Criminal Practice 2012* B4.55–B4.71

C16.4 Electricity, abstract/use without authority

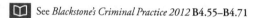

Theft Act 1968, s 13

A person who dishonestly uses without due authority, or dishonestly causes to be wasted or diverted, any electricity shall be guilty of an offence.

EW

6 months and/or level 5 fine/5 years

C16.4.1 *Sentencing*

Offence seriousness (culpability and harm)		
A. Identify the appropriate starting point		
Starting points based on first time offender pleading not guilty		
Examples of nature of activity	**Starting point**	**Range**
Where the offence results in substantial commercial gain, a custodial sentence may be appropriate		
Offence involving evidence of planning and indication that the offending was intended to be continuing, such as using a device to interfere with the electricity meter or rewiring to bypass the meter	Medium level community order	Band A fine to high level community order

Offence seriousness (culpability and harm)	
B. Consider the effect of aggravating and mitigating factors	
(other than those within examples above)	
The following may be particularly relevant but **these lists are not exhaustive**	
Factor indicating greater degree of harm 1. Risk of danger caused to property and/or life	

 See *Blackstone's Criminal Practice 2012* **B4.113–B4.118**

C16.5 **False accounting**

Theft Act 1968, s 17(1)

(1) Where a person dishonestly, with a view to gain for himself or another or with intent to cause loss to another,—

    (a) destroys, defaces, conceals or falsifies any account or any record or document made or required for any accounting purpose; or

    (b) in furnishing information for any purpose produces or makes use of any account, or any such record or document as aforesaid, which to his knowledge is or may be misleading, false or deceptive in a material particular, . . .

EW

 6 months and/or level 5 fine /7 years

C16.5.1 *Sentencing*

See **Appendix 6**.

📖 See *Blackstone's Criminal Practice 2012* B6.3–B6.13

C16.6 **Found on enclosed premises**

Vagrancy Act 1824, s 4

SO

🎚️ Level 3 fine/3 months

📖 See *Blackstone's Criminal Practice 2012* B4.71

C16.7 **Fraud**

Fraud Act 2006, ss 1(1)–(2), 2, 3, and 4

1 Fraud

(1) A person is guilty of fraud if he is in breach of any of the sections listed in subsection (2) (which provide for different ways of committing the offence).

(2) The sections are—

    (a) section 2 (fraud by false representation),

    (b) section 3 (fraud by failing to disclose information), and

    (c) section 4 (fraud by abuse of position).

2 Fraud by false representation

(1) A person is in breach of this section if he—

    (a) dishonestly makes a false representation, and

    (b) intends, by making the representation—

        (i) to make a gain for himself or another, or

        (ii) to cause loss to another or to expose another to a risk of loss.

(2) A representation is false if—

    (a) it is untrue or misleading, and

    (b) the person making it knows that it is, or might be, untrue or misleading.

---

(3) 'Representation' means any representation as to fact or law, including a representation as to the state of mind of—
  (a) the person making the representation, or
  (b) any other person.
(4) A representation may be express or implied.
(5) For the purposes of this section a representation may be regarded as made if it (or anything implying it) is submitted in any form to any system or device designed to receive, convey or respond to communications (with or without human intervention).

3 Fraud by failing to disclose information

(1) A person is in breach of this section if he—
  (a) dishonestly fails to disclose to another person information which he is under a legal duty to disclose, and
  (b) intends, by failing to disclose the information—
    (i) to make a gain for himself or another, or
    (ii) to cause loss to another or to expose another to a risk of loss.

4 Fraud by abuse of position

(1) A person is in breach of this section if he—
  (a) occupies a position in which he is expected to safeguard, or not to act against, the financial interests of another person,
  (b) dishonestly abuses that position, and
  (c) intends, by means of the abuse of that position—
    (i) to make a gain for himself or another, or
    (ii) to cause loss to another or to expose another to a risk of loss.
(2) A person may be regarded as having abused his position even though his conduct consisted of an omission rather than an act.

EW

 6 months and/or level 5 fine /10 years

C16.7.1 *Sentencing*

See **Appendix 6**.

C16.7.2 **Key points**

- See *R v Goldsmith* [2009] EWCA Crim 1840 for difficulties in relation to the commencement date of these offences.

 See *Blackstone's Criminal Practice 2012* **B5.3–B5.17**

C16.8 **Handling stolen goods**

Theft Act 1968, s 22(1)

(1) A person handles stolen goods if (otherwise than in the course of the stealing) knowing or believing them to be stolen goods he dishonestly receives the goods, or dishonestly undertakes or assists in their retention, removal, disposal or realisation by or for the benefit of another person, or if he arranges to do so.

 EW

 6 months and/or level 5 fine/14 years

C16.8.1 *Sentencing*

Offence seriousness (culpability and harm)		
A. Identify the appropriate starting point		
Starting points based on first time offender pleading not guilty		
Examples of nature of activity	**Starting point**	**Range**
Property worth £1,000 or less acquired for offender's own use	Band B fine	Band B fine to low level community order
Property worth £1,000 or less acquired for resale; or Property worth more than £1,000 acquired for offender's own use; or Presence of at least one aggravating factor listed below—regardless of value	Medium level community order	Low level community order to 12 weeks custody Note: the custody threshold is likely to be passed if the offender has a record of dishonesty offences
Sophisticated offending; or Presence of at least two aggravating factors listed below	12 weeks custody	6 weeks custody to Crown Court
Offence committed in context of Offender acts as organizer/distributor of proceeds of crime; or Offender makes self available to other criminals as willing to handle the proceeds of thefts or burglaries; or Offending highly organized, professional; or Particularly serious original offence, such as armed robbery	Crown Court	Crown Court

---

Offence seriousness (culpability and harm)	
B. Consider the effect of aggravating and mitigating factors	
(other than those within examples above)	
The following may be particularly relevant but **these lists are not exhaustive**	

Factors indicating higher culpability	**Factors indicating lower culpability**
1. Closeness of offender to primary offence Closeness may be geographical, arising from presence at or near the primary offence when it was committed, or temporal, where the handler instigated or encouraged the primary offence beforehand, or, soon after, provided a safe haven or route or disposal	1. Little or no benefit to offender
2. High level of profit made or expected by offender	2. Voluntary restitution to victim
Factors indicating greater degree of harm	**Factor indicating lower degree of harm**
1. Seriousness of the primary offence, including domestic burglary	1. Low value of goods
2. High value of goods to victim, including sentimental value	
3. Threats of violence or abuse of power by offender over others, such as an adult commissioning criminal activity by children, or a drug dealer pressurizing addicts to steal in order to pay for their habit	

C16.8.2 Key points

- Mere suspicion that goods are stolen will not suffice.
- In *R v Hall* (1985) 81 Cr App R 260, belief was said to be present when someone thought: 'I cannot say for certain that those goods are stolen, but there can be no other reasonable conclusion in the light of all the circumstances of all I have heard and seen'. Similarly, if the person admits that 'my brain is telling me [they are stolen] despite what I have heard'.
- If the defendant argues that he has paid an adequate consideration for the goods, it falls upon the prosecution to disprove (*Hogan v Director of Public Prosecutions* [2007] EWHC 978 (Admin)).

 See *Blackstone's Criminal Practice 2012* B4.128–B4.145

C16.9 Possession of false identity documents etc without reasonable excuse

Identity Documents Act 2010, s 6

(1) It is an offence for a person ("P"), without reasonable excuse, to have in P's possession or under P's control—
  (a) an identity document that is false,
  (b) an identity document that was improperly obtained,
  (c) an identity document that relates to someone else,
  (d) any apparatus which, to P's knowledge, is or has been specially designed or adapted for the making of false identity documents, or
  (e) any article or material which, to P's knowledge, is or has been specially designed or adapted to be used in the making of such documents.

7 Meaning of "identity document"

(1) For the purposes of sections 4 to 6 "identity document" means any document that is or purports to be—
  (a) an immigration document,
  (b) a United Kingdom passport (within the meaning of the Immigration Act 1971),
  (c) a passport issued by or on behalf of the authorities of a country or territory outside the United Kingdom or by or on behalf of an international organisation,
  (d) a document that can be used (in some or all circumstances) instead of a passport,
  (e) a licence to drive a motor vehicle granted under Part 3 of the Road Traffic Act 1988 or under Part 2 of the Road Traffic (Northern Ireland) Order 1981, or
  (f) a driving licence issued by or on behalf of the authorities of a country or territory outside the United Kingdom.
(2) In subsection (1)(a) "immigration document" means—
  (a) a document used for confirming the right of a person under the EU Treaties in respect of entry or residence in the United Kingdom,
  (b) a document that is given in exercise of immigration functions and records information about leave granted to a person to enter or to remain in the United Kingdom, or
  (c) a registration card (within the meaning of section 26A of the Immigration Act 1971).
(3) In subsection (2)(b) "immigration functions" means functions under the Immigration Acts (within the meaning of the Asylum and Immigration (Treatment of Claimants, etc.) Act 2004).
(4) References in subsection (1) to the issue of a document include its renewal, replacement or re-issue (with or without modifications).
(5) In this section "document" includes a stamp or label.
(6) The Secretary of State may by order amend the definition of "identity document".

C16.9.1 *Sentencing*

Offence seriousness (culpability and harm) A. Identify the appropriate starting point Starting points based on first time offender pleading not guilty		
Examples of nature of activity	**Starting point**	**Range**
Single document possessed	Medium level community order	Band C fine to high level community order
Small number of documents, no evidence of dealing	12 weeks custody	6 weeks custody to Crown Court
Considerable number of documents possessed, evidence of involvement in larger operation	Crown Court	Crown Court

Offence seriousness (culpability and harm) B. Consider the effect of aggravating and mitigating factors (other than those within examples above) The following may be particularly relevant but **these lists are not exhaustive**	
Factors indicating higher culpability 1. Clear knowledge that documents false 2. Number of documents possessed (where not in offence descriptions above) **Factor indicating greater degree of harm** 1. Genuine mistake or ignorance	**Factors indicating lower culpability** 1. Group activity 2. Potential impact of use (where not in offence descriptions above)

C16.9.2 Key points

- The offence under section 6 of the Identity Documents Act 2010 replaces the offence formally charged under section 25 of the Identity Cards Act 2006. Sentencing guidelines have effect in relation to the new offence (s 13(2) of the 2010 Act).
- If the document itself is false then it is no defence in a case where the document was being used for establishing a registrable fact, that it bore the correct details of the defendant (*R v Jamalov* The Times, 17 March 2010).

See *Blackstone's Criminal Practice 2012* **B6.48–B6.59**

C16.10 **Making off without payment**

> **Theft Act 1978, s 3**
>
> (1) Subject to subsection (3) below, a person who, knowing that payment on the spot for any goods supplied or service done is required or expected from him, dishonestly makes off without having paid as required or expected and with intent to avoid payment of the amount due shall be guilty of an offence.
> (2) For purposes of this section 'payment on the spot' includes payment at the time of collecting goods on which work has been done or in respect of which service has been provided.
> (3) Subsection (1) above shall not apply where the supply of the goods or the doing of the service is contrary to law, or where the service done is such that payment is not legally enforceable.

EW

 6 months and/or level 5 fine/2 years

C16.10.1 *Sentencing*

Offence seriousness (culpability and harm)		
A. Identify the appropriate starting point		
Starting points based on first time offender pleading not guilty		
Examples of nature of activity	**Starting point**	**Range**
Single offence committed by an offender acting alone with evidence of little or no planning, goods or services worth less than £200	Band C fine	Band A fine to high level community order
Offence displaying one or more of the following: – offender acting in unison with others – evidence of planning – offence part of a 'spree' – intimidation of victim – goods or services worth £200 or more	Medium level community order	Low level community order to 12 weeks custody

C16.10.2 Key points

• The intention to avoid making payment means a permanent intention not to pay, so a person who genuinely disputes a bill and challenges someone to bring legal action, cannot be said to have committed an offence.

See *Blackstone's Criminal Practice 2012* **B5.30–B5.37**

C16.11 **Obtaining services dishonestly**

Fraud Act 2006, s 11(1)–(2)

(1) A person is guilty of an offence under this section if he obtains services for himself or another—
    (a) by a dishonest act, and
    (b) in breach of subsection (2).
(2) A person obtains services in breach of this subsection if—
    (a) they are made available on the basis that payment has been, is being or will be made for or in respect of them,
    (b) he obtains them without any payment having been made for or in respect of them or without payment having been made in full, and
    (c) when he obtains them, he knows—
        (i) that they are being made available on the basis described in paragraph (a), or
        (ii) that they might be,
but intends that payment will not be made, or will not be made in full.

EW

 6 months and/or level 5 fine/5 years

C16.11.1 *Sentencing*

The offence of *obtaining services dishonestly* may be committed in circumstances that otherwise could be charged as an offence contrary to section 1 of the Fraud Act 2006 or may be more akin to *making off without payment*, contrary to section 3 of the Theft Act 1978. For this reason, it has not been included specifically within any of the guidelines for fraud, and one of the following approaches should be used:

- where it involves conduct which can be characterized as a fraud offence (such as obtaining credit through fraud or payment card fraud), the court should apply the guideline for the relevant type of fraud (see **Appendix 6**); or
- where the conduct could be characterized as *making off without payment* (ie, where an offender, knowing that payment on the spot for any goods supplied or service done is required or expected, dishonestly makes off without having paid and with intent to avoid payment), the guideline for that offence should be used (see **C16.10**).

See *Blackstone's Criminal Practice 2012* **B5.25–B5.29**

C16.12 **Possession of articles for fraud**

Fraud Act 2006, s 6

A person is guilty of an offence if he has in his possession or under his control any article for use in the course of or in connection with any fraud.

 EW

 Level 5 fine/6 months/5 years

C16.12.1 *Sentencing*
See **Appendix 6**.

C16.12.2 **Key points**
• Section 8 provides:

Fraud Act 2006, s 8

For the purposes of—
(a) sections 6 and 7, and
(b) the provisions listed in subsection (2), so far as they relate to articles for use in the course of or in connection with fraud,
'article' includes any program or data held in electronic form.

See *Blackstone's Criminal Practice 2012* B5.18–B5.19

C16.13 **Making, adapting, supplying, or offering to supply articles for fraud**

Fraud Act 2006, s 7

(1) A person is guilty of an offence if he makes, adapts, supplies or offers to supply any article—
   (a) knowing that it is designed or adapted for use in the course of or in connection with fraud, or intending it to be used to commit, or assist in the commission of, fraud.

EW

 Level 5 fine/6 months/10 years

C16.13.1 *Sentencing*

See **Appendix 6**.

C16.13.2 Key points

• Section 8 provides:

Fraud Act 2006, s 8

For the purposes of—
(a) sections 6 and 7, and
(b) the provisions listed in subsection (2), so far as they relate to articles for use in the course of or in connection with fraud,
'article' includes any program or data held in electronic form.

 See *Blackstone's Criminal Practice 2012* **B5.20–B5.21**

C16.14 **Income tax evasion**

Finance Act 2000, s 144

A person commits an offence if he is knowingly concerned in the fraudulent evasion of income tax by him or any other person.

EW

 Level 5 fine/6 months/7 years

C16.14.1 *Sentencing*

See **Appendix 6**.

See *Blackstone's Criminal Practice 2012* **B16.4**

EW Either Way   Sentence

C16.15 **Railway fare evasion**

Regulation of Railways Act 1889, s 5(1) and (3)

SO

Level 3 fine or 3 months (s 5(3)); level 2 fine (s 5(1))

C16.15.1 *Sentencing*

Offence seriousness (culpability and harm) A. Identify the appropriate starting point Starting points based on first time offender pleading not guilty		
Examples of nature of activity	**Starting point**	**Range**
Failing to produce ticket or pay fare on request	Band A fine	Conditional discharge to band B fine
Travelling on railway without having paid the fare or knowingly and wilfully travelling beyond the distance paid for, with intent to avoid payment	Band B fine	Band A fine to band C fine

Offence seriousness (culpability and harm) B. Consider the effect of aggravating and mitigating factors (other than those within examples above) The following may be particularly relevant but **these lists are not exhaustive**	
Factor indicating higher culpability 1. Offensive or intimidating language or behaviour towards railway staff **Factor indicating greater degree of harm.** 1. High level of loss caused or intended to be caused	

C16.16 **Social security benefit, false statement/representation to obtain**

Social Security Administration Act 1992, ss 111A and 112

111A Dishonest representations for obtaining benefit etc

(1) If a person dishonestly—

    (a) makes a false statement or representation; or

    (b) produces or furnishes, or causes or allows to be produced or furnished, any document or information which is false in a material particular;

with a view to obtaining any benefit or other payment or advantage under the relevant social security legislation (whether for himself or for some other person), he shall be guilty of an offence.

(1A) A person shall be guilty of an offence if—

    (a) there has been a change of circumstances affecting any entitlement of his to any benefit or other payment or advantage under any provision of the relevant social security legislation;

    (b) the change is not a change that is excluded by regulations from the changes that are required to be notified;

    (c) he knows that the change affects an entitlement of his to such a benefit or other payment or advantage; and

    (d) he dishonestly fails to give a prompt notification of that change in the prescribed manner to the prescribed person.

(1B) A person shall be guilty of an offence if—

    (a) there has been a change of circumstances affecting any entitlement of another person to any benefit or other payment or advantage under any provision of the relevant social security legislation;

    (b) the change is not a change that is excluded by regulations from the changes that are required to be notified;

    (c) he knows that the change affects an entitlement of that other person to such a benefit or other payment or advantage; and

    (d) he dishonestly causes or allows that other person to fail to give a prompt notification of that change in the prescribed manner to the prescribed person.

(1C) This subsection applies where—

    (a) there has been a change of circumstances affecting any entitlement of a person ('the claimant') to any benefit or other payment or advantage under any provision of the relevant social security legislation;

    (b) the benefit, payment or advantage is one in respect of which there is another person ('the recipient') who for the time being has a right to receive payments to which the claimant has, or (but for the arrangements under which they are payable to the recipient) would have, an entitlement; and

    (c) the change is not a change that is excluded by regulations from the changes that are required to be notified.

(1D) In a case where subsection (1C) above applies, the recipient is guilty of an offence if—

    (a) he knows that the change affects an entitlement of the claimant to a benefit or other payment or advantage under a provision of the relevant social security legislation;

    (b) the entitlement is one in respect of which he has a right to receive payments to which the claimant has, or (but for the arrangements under which they are payable to the recipient) would have, an entitlement; and

    (c) he dishonestly fails to give a prompt notification of that change in the prescribed manner to the prescribed person.

(1E) In a case where that subsection applies, a person other than the recipient is guilty of an offence if—

    (a) he knows that the change affects an entitlement of the claimant to a benefit or other payment or advantage under a provision of the relevant social security legislation;

    (b) the entitlement is one in respect of which the recipient has a right to receive payments to which the claimant has, or (but for the arrangements under which they are payable to the recipient) would have, an entitlement; and

    (c) he dishonestly causes or allows the recipient to fail to give a prompt notification of that change in the prescribed manner to the prescribed person.

(1F) In any case where subsection (1C) above applies but the right of the recipient is confined to a right, by reason of his being a person to whom the claimant is required to make payments in respect of a dwelling, to receive payments of housing benefit—

    (a) a person shall not be guilty of an offence under subsection (1D) or (1E) above unless the change is one relating to one or both of the following—

        (i) the claimant's occupation of that dwelling;

        (ii) the claimant's liability to make payments in respect of that dwelling; but

    (b) subsections (1D)(a) and (1E)(a) above shall each have effect as if after 'knows' there were inserted 'or could reasonably be expected to know'.

(1G) For the purposes of subsections (1A) to (1E) above a notification of a change is prompt if, and only if, it is given as soon as reasonably practicable after the change occurs.

112 False representations for obtaining benefit etc

(1) If a person for the purpose of obtaining any benefit or other payment under the relevant social security legislation whether for himself or some other person, or for any other purpose connected with that legislation—

    (a) makes a statement or representation which he knows to be false; or

    (b) produces or furnishes, or knowingly causes or knowingly allows to be produced or furnished, any document or information which he knows to be false in a material particular, he shall be guilty of an offence.

(1A) A person shall be guilty of an offence if—

    (a) there has been a change of circumstances affecting any entitlement of his to any benefit or other payment or advantage under any provision of the relevant social security legislation;

    (b) the change is not a change that is excluded by regulations from the changes that are required to be notified;

    (c) he knows that the change affects an entitlement of his to such a benefit or other payment or advantage; and

    (d) he fails to give a prompt notification of that change in the prescribed manner to the prescribed person.

(1B) A person is guilty of an offence under this section if—

    (a) there has been a change of circumstances affecting any entitlement of another person to any benefit or other payment or advantage under any provision of the relevant social security legislation;

    (b) the change is not a change that is excluded by regulations from the changes that are required to be notified;

    (c) he knows that the change affects an entitlement of that other person to such a benefit or other payment or advantage; and

    (d) he causes or allows that other person to fail to give a prompt notification of that change in the prescribed manner to the prescribed person.

(1C) In a case where subsection (1C) of section 111A above applies, the recipient is guilty of an offence if—

    (a) he knows that the change affects an entitlement of the claimant to a benefit or other payment or advantage under a provision of the relevant social security legislation;

    (b) the entitlement is one in respect of which he has a right to receive payments to which the claimant has, or (but for the arrangements under which they are payable to the recipient) would have, an entitlement; and

    (c) he fails to give a prompt notification of that change in the prescribed manner to the prescribed person.

(1D) In a case where that subsection applies, a person other than the recipient is guilty of an offence if—

    (a) he knows that the change affects an entitlement of the claimant to a benefit or other payment or advantage under a provision of the relevant social security legislation;

    (b) the entitlement is one in respect of which the recipient has a right to receive payments to which the claimant has, or (but for the arrangements under which they are payable to the recipient) would have, an entitlement; and

    (c) he causes or allows the recipient to fail to give a prompt notification of that change in the prescribed manner to the prescribed person.

(1E) Subsection (1F) of section 111A above applies in relation to subsections (1C) and (1D) above as it applies in relation to subsections (1D) and (1E) of that section.

> (1F) For the purposes of subsections (1A) to (1D) above a notification of a change is prompt if, and only if, it is given as soon as reasonably practicable after the change occurs.

EW

SO 6 months and/or level 5 fine/7 years

Section 112:

SO

⊞ 3 months and/or level 3 fine

C16.16.1 *Sentencing*

For offences under section 111A, refer to guideline Fraud—banking and insurance fraud and obtaining credit through fraud, benefit fraud, and revenue fraud at **Appendix 6**.

Offence seriousness (culpability and harm) A. Identify the appropriate starting point Starting points based on first time offender pleading not guilty		
Examples of nature of activity	**Starting point**	**Range**
Claim fraudulent from the start, up to £5,000 obtained (s 111A or s 112)	Medium level community order	Band B fine to high level community order
Claim fraudulent from the start, more than £5,000 but less than £20,000 obtained	12 weeks custody	Medium level community order to Crown Court
Claim fraudulent from the start, large-scale, professional offending	Crown Court	Crown Court

Offence seriousness (culpability and harm)
B. Consider the effect of aggravating and mitigating factors
(other than those within examples above)
The following may be particularly relevant but **these lists are not exhaustive**

Factors indicating higher culpability	**Factors indicating lower culpability**
1. Offending carried out over a long period	1. Pressurized by others
2. Offender acting in unison with one or more others	2. Claim initially legitimate
3. Planning	**Factor indicating lesser degree of harm**
4. Offender motivated by greed or desire to live beyond his/her means	1. Voluntary repayment of amounts overpaid
5. False identities or other personal details used	
6. False or forged documents used	
7. Official documents altered or falsified	

C16.16.2 Key points

- In *R v Laku*, unreported, 16 July 2008 (Court of Appeal), L made false representations in order to claim benefits and was prosecuted under sections 111A and 111A(1A) of the Social Security Administration Act 1992. On subsequent claims he did not correct the falsehoods. Held: Convictions under section 111A(1A) quashed; he had not failed to notify a change in circumstances as the same false circumstances that founded the convictions under section 111A continued.
- An offence under section 111A(1B) requires a positive act on the part of the defendant. Sitting back and doing nothing does not amount to (allowing) an offence (*R v T* [2009] EWCA Crim 1426).

See *Blackstone's Criminal Practice 2012* **B5.7** and **B16.45–B16.46**

C16.17 **Tax credit fraud**

Tax Credits Act 2002, s 35

A person commits an offence if he is knowingly concerned in any fraudulent activity undertaken with a view to obtaining payments of a tax credit by him or any other person.

 EW

 6 months and/or level 5 fine/7 years

C16.17.1 *Sentencing*

See **Appendix 6**.

C16.17.2 Key points

- Disposing of the proceeds of fraud amounts to a fraudulent activity (*R v Kolapo* [2009] EWCA Crim 545).

 See *Blackstone's Criminal Practice 2012* **B5.7** and
B16.45–B16.46

C16.18 **Theft**

Theft Act 1968, s 1(1)–(2)

(1) A person is guilty of theft if he dishonestly appropriates property belonging to another with the intention of permanently depriving the other of it; and 'thief' and 'steal' shall be construed accordingly.

(2) It is immaterial whether the appropriation is made with a view to gain, or is made for the thief's own benefit.

EW

C16.18.1 *Sentencing: theft, breach of trust*

Type/nature of activity	Starting point	Sentencing range
Theft of less than £2,000	Medium level community order	Band B fine to 26 weeks custody
Theft of £2,000 or more but less than £20,000 OR Theft of less than £2,000 in breach of a high degree of trust	18 weeks custody	High level community order to Crown Court
Theft of £20,000 or more OR Theft of £2,000 or more in breach of a high degree of trust	Crown Court	Crown Court

---

Additional aggravating factors:

1. Long course of offending
2. Suspicion deliberately thrown on others
3. Offender motivated by intention to cause harm or out of revenge

---

C16.18.2 *Sentencing: theft from the person*

Type/nature of activity	Starting point	Sentencing range
Where the effect on the victim is particularly severe, the stolen property is of high value, or substantial consequential loss results, a sentence higher than the range into which the offence would fall may be appropriate.		
Theft from a vulnerable victim involving intimidation or the use or threat of force (falling short of robbery)	18 months custody	12 months–3 years custody
Theft from a vulnerable victim	18 weeks custody	Community order (HIGH)—12 months custody
Theft from the person not involving vulnerable victim	Community order (MEDIUM)	Fine Band B—18 weeks custody

Additional aggravating factors:

1. Offender motivated by intention to cause harm or out of revenge
2. Intimidation or face-to-face confrontation with victim [except where this raises offence into the higher sentencing range]
3. Use of force, or threat of force, against victim (not amounting to robbery) [except where this raises the offence into a higher sentencing range]
4. High level of inconvenience caused to victim, eg replacing house keys, credit cards, etc

C16.18.3 *Sentencing: theft from shop*

Type/nature of activity	Starting point	Sentencing range
Organized gang/group and Intimidation or the use or threat of force (short of robbery)	12 months custody	36 weeks–4 years custody
Significant intimidation or threats OR Use of force resulting in slight injury OR Very high level of planning OR Significant related damage	6 weeks custody	Community order (HIGH)—36 weeks custody
Low level intimidation or threats OR Some planning eg a session of stealing on the same day or going equipped OR Some related damage	Community order (LOW)	Fine—Community order (MEDIUM)
Little or no planning or sophistication AND Goods stolen of low value	Fine	Conditional discharge—Community order (LOW)

Additional aggravating factors:

1. Child accompanying offender is involved in or aware of theft
2. Offender is subject to a banning order that includes the store targeted
3. Offender motivated by intention to cause harm or out of revenge
4. Professional offending
5. Victim particularly vulnerable (eg small independent shop)
6. Offender targeted high value goods

C16.18.4 Key points

- Dishonesty is a two-part test:
    (1) Were the accused's actions dishonest according to the ordinary standards of reasonable and honest people? and if so,
    (2) Did the accused know that those actions were dishonest according to those standards?

C16.19 **Theft, going equipped for**

Theft Act 1968, s 25

(1) A person shall be guilty of an offence if, when not at his place of abode, he has with him any article for use in the course of or in connection with any burglary or theft.

(2) A person guilty of an offence under this section shall on conviction on indictment be liable to imprisonment for a term not exceeding three years.

(3) Where a person is charged with an offence under this section, proof that he had with him any article made or adapted for use in committing a burglary or theft shall be evidence that he had it with him for such use.

(4) ...

(5) For purposes of this section an offence under section 12(1) of this Act of taking a conveyance shall be treated as theft.

EW

 6 months and/or level 5 fine/3 years

C16.19.1 *Sentencing*

Offence seriousness (culpability and harm) A. Identify the appropriate starting point Starting points based on first time offender pleading not guilty		
Examples of nature of activity	**Starting point**	**Range**
Possession of items for theft from shop or of vehicle	Medium level community order	Band C fine to high level community order
Possession of items for burglary, robbery	High level community order	Medium level community order to Crown Court

Offence seriousness (culpability and harm) B. Consider the effect of aggravating and mitigating factors (other than those within examples above) The following may be particularly relevant but **these lists are not exhaustive**	
Factors indicating higher culpability 1. Circumstances suggest offender equipped for particularly serious offence 2. Items to conceal identity	

 See *Blackstone's Criminal Practice 2012* **B4.120–B4.127**

C16.20 **Trade mark, unauthorized use of etc**

Trade Marks Act 1994, s 92(1)–(4)

(1) A person commits an offence who with a view to gain for himself or another, or with intent to cause loss to another, and without the consent of the proprietor—

    (a) applies to goods or their packaging a sign identical to, or likely to be mistaken for, a registered trade mark, or

    (b) sells or lets for hire, offers or exposes for sale or hire or distributes goods which bear, or the packaging of which bears, such a sign, or

    (c) has in his possession, custody or control in the course of a business any such goods with a view to the doing of anything, by himself or another, which would be an offence under paragraph (b).

(2) A person commits an offence who with a view to gain for himself or another, or with intent to cause loss to another, and without the consent of the proprietor—
- (a) applies a sign identical to, or likely to be mistaken for, a registered trade mark to material intended to be used—
  - (i) for labelling or packaging goods,
  - (ii) as a business paper in relation to goods, or
  - (iii) for advertising goods, or
- (b) uses in the course of a business material bearing such a sign for labelling or packaging goods, as a business paper in relation to goods, or for advertising goods, or
- (c) has in his possession, custody or control in the course of a business any such material with a view to the doing of anything, by himself or another, which would be an offence under paragraph (b).

(3) A person commits an offence who with a view to gain for himself or another, or with intent to cause loss to another, and without the consent of the proprietor—
- (a) makes an article specifically designed or adapted for making copies of a sign identical to, or likely to be mistaken for, a registered trade mark, or
- (b) has such an article in his possession, custody or control in the course of a business,

knowing or having reason to believe that it has been, or is to be, used to produce goods, or material for labelling or packaging goods, as a business paper in relation to goods, or for advertising goods.

(4) A person does not commit an offence under this section unless—
- (a) the goods are goods in respect of which the trade mark is registered, or
- (b) the trade mark has a reputation in the United Kingdom and the use of the sign takes or would take unfair advantage of, or is or would be detrimental to, the distinctive character or the repute of the trade mark.

EW

 6 months and/or level 5 fine/10 years

C16.20.1 *Sentencing*

Offence seriousness (culpability and harm)		
A. Identify the appropriate starting point		
Starting points based on first time offender pleading not guilty		
Examples of nature of activity	**Starting point**	**Range**
Small number of counterfeit items	Band C fine	Band B fine to low level community order
Larger number of counterfeit items but no involvement in wider operation	Medium level community order, plus fine*	Low level community order to 12 weeks custody, plus fine*
High number of counterfeit items or involvement in wider operation eg manufacture or distribution	12 weeks custody	6 weeks custody to Crown Court
Central role in large-scale operation	Crown Court	Crown Court

* this may be an offence where it is appropriate to combine a fine with a community order.

Offence seriousness (culpability and harm)	
B. Consider the effect of aggravating and mitigating factors	
(other than those within examples above)	
The following may be particularly relevant but **these lists are not exhaustive**	
Factors indicating higher culpability	**Factor indicating lower culpability**
1. High degree of professionalism	1. Mistake or ignorance about provenance of goods
2. High level of profit	
Factor indicating greater degree of harm	
1. Purchasers at risk of harm eg from counterfeit drugs	

C16.20.2 Key points

- It is a defence for a person charged with an offence under this section to show that he believed on reasonable grounds that the use of the sign in the manner in which it was used, or was to be used, was not an infringement of the registered trade mark. In order to be able to satisfy the statutory defence under section 95(2) of the Trade Marks Act 1994, the defendant must show that not only did he have an honest belief that the trade marks did not infringe registered trade marks, but also that he had reasonable grounds for so believing (*Essex Trading Standards v Singh*, unreported, 3 March 2009).

- It is not a defence to argue that the trade marks were of such poor quality that no confusion would be caused (*R v Boulter*, unreported, 7 October 2008).

📖 See *Blackstone's Criminal Practice 2012* B6.95–B6.102

C16.21 **TV licence payment evasion**

Communications Act 2003, s 363

 Level 3 fine

C16.21.1 *Sentencing*

Offence seriousness (culpability and harm) A. Identify the appropriate starting point Starting points based on first time offender pleading not guilty		
Examples of nature of activity	**Starting point**	**Range**
Up to 6 months unlicensed use	Band A fine	Band A fine
Over 6 months unlicensed use	Band B fine	Band A fine to band B fine

Offence seriousness (culpability and harm) B. Consider the effect of aggravating and mitigating factors (other than those within examples above) The following may be particularly relevant but **these lists are not exhaustive**	
	Factors indicating lower culpability 1. Accidental oversight or belief licence held 2. Confusion of responsibility 3. Licence immediately obtained

C16.22 **TWOC (vehicle-taking without consent)**

Theft Act 1968, s 12(1), (5), (6), and (7)

(1) Subject to subsections (5) and (6) below, a person shall be guilty of an offence if, without having the consent of the owner or other lawful authority, he takes any conveyance for his own or another's use or knowing that any conveyance has been taken without such authority, drives it or allows himself to be carried in or on it.

(5) Subsection (1) above shall not apply in relation to pedal cycles; but, subject to subsection (6) below, a person who, without having the consent of the owner or other lawful authority, takes a pedal cycle for his own or another's use, or rides a pedal cycle knowing it to have been taken without such authority, shall on summary conviction be liable to a fine not exceeding level 3 on the standard scale.

(6) A person does not commit an offence under this section by anything done in the belief that he has lawful authority to do it or that he would have the owner's consent if the owner knew of his doing it and the circumstances of it.

(7) For purposes of this section—

    (a) 'conveyance' means any conveyance constructed or adapted for the carriage of a person or persons whether by land, water or air, except that it does not include a conveyance constructed or adapted for use only under the control of a person not carried in or on it, and 'drive' shall be construed accordingly; and

    (b) 'owner', in relation to a conveyance which is the subject of a hiring agreement or hire-purchase agreement, means the person in possession of the conveyance under that agreement.

SO

 6 months and/or level 5 fine

C16.22.1 *Sentencing*

Offence seriousness (culpability and harm) A. Identify the appropriate starting point Starting points based on first time offender pleading not guilty		
Examples of nature of activity	**Starting point**	**Range**
Exceeding authorized use of eg employer's or relative's vehicle; retention of hire car beyond return date	Low level community order	Band B fine to medium level community order
As above with damage caused to lock/ignition; OR Stranger's vehicle involved but no damage caused	Medium level community order	Low level community order to high level community order
Taking vehicle from private premises; OR Causing damage to eg lock/ignition of stranger's vehicle	High level community order	Medium level community order to 26 weeks custody

Offence seriousness (culpability and harm)
B. Consider the effect of aggravating and mitigating factors
(other than those within examples above)
The following may be particularly relevant but **these lists are not exhaustive**

Factors indicating greater degree of harm	Factor indicating lower culpability
1. Vehicle later burnt	1. Misunderstanding with owner
2. Vehicle belonging to elderly/ disabled person	**Factor indicating lesser degree**
3. Emergency services vehicle	**of harm**
4. Medium to large goods vehicle	1. Offender voluntarily returned vehicle
5. Passengers carried	to owner

C16.22.2 Key points

- This offence is summary only but subject to the following exception in relation to limitation period. Section 12(4A) to (4C) of the Act provides:

Theft Act 1968, s 12(4A)–(4C)

(4A) Proceedings for an offence under subsection (1) above (but not proceedings of a kind falling within subsection (4) above) in relation to a
mechanically propelled vehicle—
  (a) shall not be commenced after the end of the period of three years
    beginning with the day on which the offence was committed; but
  (b) subject to that, may be commenced at any time within the period of six
    months beginning with the relevant day.

(4B) In subsection (4A)(b) above 'the relevant day' means—
  (a) in the case of a prosecution for an offence under subsection (1) above
    by a public prosecutor, the day on which sufficient evidence to justify
    the proceedings came to the knowledge of any person responsible for
    deciding whether to commence any such prosecution;
  (b) in the case of a prosecution for an offence under subsection (1) above
    which is commenced by a person other than a public prosecutor after
    the discontinuance of a prosecution falling within paragraph (a) above
    which relates to the same facts, the day on which sufficient evidence to
    justify the proceedings came to the knowledge of the person who has
    decided to commence the prosecution or (if later) the discontinuance
    of the other prosecution;
  (c) in the case of any other prosecution for an offence under subsection (1)
    above, the day on which sufficient evidence to justify the proceedings
    came to the knowledge of the person who has decided to commence
    the prosecution.

(4C) For the purposes of subsection (4A)(b) above a certificate of a person
responsible for deciding whether to commence a prosecution of a kind
mentioned in subsection (4B)(a) above as to the date on which such evidence as is mentioned in the certificate came to the knowledge of any
person responsible for deciding whether to commence any such prosecution shall be conclusive evidence of that fact.

See *Blackstone's Criminal Practice 2012* B4.92–B4.100

C16.23 **VAT evasion**

Value Added Tax Act 1994, s 72(1)

If any person is knowingly concerned in, or in the taking of steps with a view to, the fraudulent evasion of VAT by him or any other person.

EW

 Fine level 5 and/or 6 months/7 years

C16.23.1 *Sentence*

See **Appendix 6**.

C16.23.2 Key points

• Section 72(2) provides that:

Value Added Tax Act 1999, s 72(2)

Evasion of VAT includes a reference to the obtaining of—
(a) the payment of a VAT credit; or
(b) a refund under sections 35, 36 or 40 of this Act or section 22 of the 1983 Act; or
(c) a refund under any regulations made by virtue of section 13(5); or
(d) a repayment under section 39;
and any reference in those subsections to the amount of the VAT shall be construed—
(i) in relation to VAT itself or a VAT credit, as a reference to the aggregate of the amount (if any) falsely claimed by way of credit for input tax and the amount (if any) by which output tax was falsely understated, and
(ii) in relation to a refund or repayment falling within paragraph (b), (c) or (d) above, as a reference to the amount falsely claimed by way of refund or repayment.

- Turning a blind eye is sufficient to establish that a person 'knowingly' did one of the prohibited acts (*Ross v Moss* [1965] 2 QB 396).
- For an evasion there does not need to be any intention permanently to avoid payment (*R v Dealy* [1995] 1 WLR 658).

C16.24 Vehicle interference

Criminal Attempts Act 1981, s 9(1)–(2)

(1) A person is guilty of the offence of vehicle interference if he interferes with a motor vehicle or trailer or with anything carried in or on a motor vehicle or trailer with the intention that an offence specified in subsection (2) below shall be committed by himself or some other person.

(2) The offences mentioned in subsection (1) above are—
  (a) theft of the motor vehicle or trailer or part of it;
  (b) theft of anything carried in or on the motor vehicle or trailer; and
  (c) an offence under section 12(1) of the Theft Act 1968 (taking and driving away without consent);

  and, if it is shown that a person accused of an offence under this section intended that one of those offences should be committed, it is immaterial that it cannot be shown which it was.

SO

▦ 3 months and/or fine level 4

C16.24.1 *Sentencing*

Offence seriousness (culpability and harm)		
A. Identify the appropriate starting point		
Starting points based on first time offender pleading not guilty		
Examples of nature of activity	**Starting point**	**Range**
Trying door handles; no entry gained to vehicle; no damage caused	Band C fine	Band A fine to low level community order
Entering vehicle, little or no damage caused	Medium level community order	Band C fine to high level community order
Entering vehicle, with damage caused	High level community order	Medium level community order to 12 weeks custody

Offence seriousness (culpability and harm)
B. Consider the effect of aggravating and mitigating factors
(other than those within examples above)
The following may be particularly relevant but **these lists are not exhaustive**

Factor indicating higher culpability 1. Targeting vehicle in dark/isolated location **Factors indicating greater degree of harm** 1. Emergency services vehicle 2. Disabled driver's vehicle 3. Part of series	

 See *Blackstone's Criminal Practice 2012* **B4.109–B4.112**

C16.25 **Vehicle licence/registration fraud**

Vehicle Excise and Registration Act 1994, s 44

 EW

 Level 5 fine/2 years

C16.25.1 *Sentencing*

Offence seriousness (culpability and harm)		
A. Identify the appropriate starting point		
Starting points based on first time offender pleading not guilty		
Examples of nature of activity	**Starting point**	**Range**
Use of unaltered licence from another vehicle	Band B fine	Band B fine
Forged licence bought for own use, or forged/altered for own use	Band C fine	Band C fine
Use of number plates from another vehicle; OR Licence/number plates forged or altered for sale to another	High level community order (in Crown Court)	Medium level community order to Crown Court (Note: community order and custody available only in Crown Court)

Offence seriousness (culpability and harm)
B. Consider the effect of aggravating and mitigating factors
(other than those within examples above)
The following may be particularly relevant but **these lists are not exhaustive**

Factors indicating higher culpability	Factors indicating lower culpability
1. LGV, PSV, taxi, etc	1. Licence/registration mark from
2. Long-term fraudulent use	another vehicle owned by defendant
Factors indicating greater degree of harm	2. Short-term use
1. High financial gain	
2. Innocent victim deceived	
3. Legitimate owner inconvenienced	

 See *Blackstone's Criminal Practice 2012* **C4**

C17 **Violence Against the Person**

C17.1 **Assault occasioning actual bodily harm**

> **Offences Against the Person Act 1861, s 47**
> Any assault occasioning actual bodily harm.

EW

SO Maximum sentence

▦ Level 5 fine and/or 6 months/5 years (7 years if racially aggravated)

C17.1.1 *Sentencing*

See **Appendix 7**.

C17.1.2 **Key points**

- Action or words causing the person to apprehend imminent unlawful force. A conditional threat amounts to an assault, as does a threat to do something in the future (how far into the future is a matter of debate, see *R v Constanza* [1997] 2 Cr App R 492). Words in themselves could suffice as could a gesture (for example using fingers to imitate a gun being fired, or a slashing action across the throat). An extreme example can be found in *R v Ireland* [1998] AC 147, a case where the appellant made silent phone calls to the victim. Conditional actions, for example 'get out of my house or I will hurt you' will amount to an assault. The words may also indicate that no assault is going to happen, as in the famous case of *Tuberville v Savage* (1669) 1 Mod Rep 3—'if it were not assize time, I would not take such language from you.' Creating a danger can amount to an assault, for example, if a prisoner knows that he has a needle secreted on him and dishonestly does not inform a police officer carrying out a search, he may be liable if the officer injures himself on that needle, such a risk being reasonably forseeable (*Director of Public Prosecutions v Santana-Bermudez* [2003] EWHC 2908 (Admin)).
- A battery involves the use of actual force being applied to the victim.

- Harm, which must be more than merely transient or trifling, encompasses not only injury, but also hurt and damage. The concept of bodily harm is wide-ranging, and includes the cutting off of someone's hair *DPP v Smith* [2006] 2 Cr App R 1. Psychiatric injury, in a medically diagnosed form, can amount to bodily harm, but anything short of this, for example, upset or distress will not.
- Mens rea is intention or recklessness. Note that the mens rea relates to the act of assault or battery, there is no requirement to prove that harm was intended, or that the defendant was reckless as to whether or not harm would be caused.

 See *Blackstone's Criminal Practice 2012* **B2.22–B2.28**

C17.2 **Assault with intent to resist arrest**

> **Offences Against the Person Act 1861, s 38**
>
> Whosoever shall assault any person with intent to resist or prevent the lawful apprehension or detainer of himself or of any other person for any offence, shall be guilty of an offence.

EW

 6 months and/or level 5 fine/2 years

DO

C17.2.1 *Sentencing*

See **Appendix** 7.

C17.2.2 Key points

- The arrest must be a lawful one, and the defendant's honest but mistaken belief in that regard does not afford a defence (*R v Lee* (2001) 165 JP 344).
- The prosecution does not need to prove that the defendant knew (in the case of a police officer) that the person was a police officer (*R v Brightling* [1991] Crim LR 364).

 See *Blackstone's Criminal Practice 2012* **B2.17–B2.21**

C17.3 **Assaulting a police constable or resisting or obstructing a police constable**

Police Act 1996, s 89(1)–(2)

(1) Any person who assaults a constable in the execution of his duty, or a person assisting a constable in the execution of his duty, shall be guilty of an offence . . .

(2) Any person who resists or wilfully obstructs a constable in the execution of his duty, or a person assisting a constable in the execution of his duty, shall be guilty of an offence . . .

SO

 6 months and/or level 5 fine (assaults), 1 month and/or level 3 fine (resist/obstruct)

C17.3.1 *Sentencing*

See **Appendix 7**.

C17.3.2 **Key points**

- The constable must be acting lawfully (ie in execution of his duty).
- The prosecution does not need to prove that the defendant knew that the person was a police officer (*R v Brightling* [1991] Crim LR 364).
- If officer A is not acting lawfully in arresting a suspect, officer B who in good faith seeks to assist officer A will not be acting lawfully (*Cumberbatch v Crown Prosecution Service* [2009] EWHC 3353 (Admin)).
- If a suspect is accused of trying to impede the arrest of a third party, it must be shown that the arrest of that third party was lawful (*Riley v Director of Public Prosecutions* 91 Cr App R 14).
- The court is entitled to convict on the basis of recklessness even where the Crown puts its case on the basis of an intentional assault (*D v Director of Public Prosecutions* [2005] Crim LR 962).
- For the lawfulness of a police officer entering premises to save life or limb, see *Baker v Crown Prosecution Service* [2009] EWHC 299 (Admin).
- For the situation where a police officer has had a licence to remain on property revoked, see *R (Fullard) v Woking Magistrates' Court* [2005] EWHC 2922 (Admin).

- An officer who had not yet established grounds for arrest was acting unlawfully in restraining a suspect (*Wood v Director of Public Prosecutions* [2008] EWHC 1056 (Admin)).

 See *Blackstone's Criminal Practice 2012* **B2.29–B2.36**

C17.4 **Assaulting a court security officer**

Courts Act 2003, s 57

SO

 6 months and/or level 5 fine

C17.4.1 Key points

- A court officer must be appointed by the Lord Chancellor, and designated in that role (Courts Act 2003, s 51).
- Section 51(3) provides that '… a court security officer who is not readily identifiable as such (whether by means of his uniform or badge or otherwise), is not to be regarded as acting in the execution of his duty'.

C17.5 **Offences against designated and accredited persons**

Police Reform Act 2002, s 46

(1) Any person who assaults—
   (a) a designated person in the execution of his duty,
   (b) an accredited person in the execution of his duty,
   (ba) an accredited inspector in the execution of his duty, or
   (c) a person assisting a designated or accredited person or an accredited inspector in the execution of his duty,

   is guilty of an offence and shall be liable, on summary conviction, to imprisonment for a term not exceeding six months or to a fine not exceeding level 5 on the standard scale, or to both.

(2) Any person who resists or wilfully obstructs—
   (a) a designated person in the execution of his duty,
   (b) an accredited person or an accredited inspector in the execution of his duty,

---

(ba) an accredited inspector in the execution of his duty, or

(c) a person assisting a designated or accredited person in the execution of his duty,

is guilty of an offence and shall be liable, on summary conviction, to imprisonment for a term not exceeding one month or to a fine not exceeding level 3 on the standard scale, or to both.

(3) Any person who, with intent to deceive—

(a) impersonates a designated person, an accredited person or an accredited inspector,

(b) makes any statement or does any act calculated falsely to suggest that he is a designated person, that he is an accredited person or that he is an accredited inspector, or

(c) makes any statement or does any act calculated falsely to suggest that he has powers as a designated or accredited person or as an accredited inspector that exceed the powers he actually has,

is guilty of an offence and shall be liable, on summary conviction, to imprisonment for a term not exceeding six months or to a fine not exceeding level 5 on the standard scale, or to both.

(4) In this section references to the execution by a designated person, accredited person or accredited inspector of his duty are references to his exercising any power or performing any duty which is his by virtue of his designation or accreditation.

SO

▥ See above

C17.6 **Common assault**

Criminal Justice Act 1988, s 39

SO (Racially or religiously aggravated: either way)

▥ 6 months and/or level 5 fine (racially or religiously aggravated: 2 years)

DO (Racially or religiously aggravated: common assault)

C17.6.1 *Sentencing*

See **Appendix 7**.

C17.6.2 Key points

- Evidence of a lack of consent can be inferred from evidence in the case and need not come from the complainant (see *Director of Public Prosecutions v Shabbir* [2009] EWHC 2754 (Admin), where the court was scathing as to the raising of lack of consent as being an arguable point).

 See *Blackstone's Criminal Practice 2012* **B2.1–B2.16**

C17.7 **Cruelty to a child**

Children and Young Persons Act 1933, s 1(1)

(1) If any person who has attained the age of sixteen years and has responsibility for any child or young person under that age, wilfully assaults, ill-treats, neglects, abandons, or exposes him, or causes or procures him to be assaulted, ill-treated, neglected, abandoned, or exposed, in a manner likely to cause him unnecessary suffering or injury to health (including injury to or loss of sight, or hearing, or limb, or organ of the body, and any mental derangement), that person shall be guilty of an offence.

 EW

 6 months and/or level 5 fine/10 years

 DO

C17.7.1 *Sentencing*

- The same starting point and sentencing range are proposed for offences which might fall into the four categories (assault, ill-treatment or neglect, abandonment, and failure to protect). These are designed to take into account the fact that the victim is particularly vulnerable, assuming an abuse of trust or power and the likelihood of psychological harm, and are designed to reflect the seriousness with which society as a whole regards these offences.
- As noted above, the starting points have been calculated to reflect the likelihood of psychological harm and this cannot be treated as

---

an aggravating factor. Where there is an especially serious physical or psychological effect on the victim, even if unintended, this should increase sentence.

- The normal sentencing starting point for an offence of child cruelty should be a custodial sentence. The length of that sentence will be influenced by the circumstances in which the offence took place.
- However, in considering whether a custodial sentence is the most appropriate disposal, the court should take into account any available information concerning the future care of the child.
- Where the offender is the sole or primary carer of the victim or other dependants, this potentially should be taken into account for sentencing purposes, regardless of whether the offender is male or female. In such cases, an immediate custodial sentence may not be appropriate.
- The most relevant areas of personal mitigation are likely to be:
  - mental illness/depression;
  - inability to cope with pressures of parenthood;
  - lack of support;
  - sleep deprivation;
  - offender dominated by an abusive or stronger partner;
  - extreme behavioural difficulties in the child, often coupled with a lack of support;
  - inability to secure assistance or support services in spite of every effort having been made by the offender.
- Some of the factors identified above, in particular sleep deprivation, lack of support, and an inability to cope, could be regarded as an inherent part of caring for children, especially when a child is very young and could be put forward as mitigation by most carers charged with an offence of child cruelty. It follows that, before being accepted as mitigation, there must be evidence that these factors were present to a high degree and had an identifiable and significant impact on the offender's behaviour.

Offence seriousness (culpability and harm)		
A. Identify the appropriate starting point		
Starting points based on first time offender pleading not guilty		
Example of nature of activity	**Starting point**	**Range**
(i) Short-term neglect or ill-treatment (ii) Single incident of short-term abandonment (iii) Failure to protect a child from any of the above	12 weeks custody	Low level community order to 26 weeks custody

(i) Assault(s) resulting in injuries consistent with ABH (ii) More than one incident of neglect or ill-treatment (but not amounting to long-term behaviour) (iii) Single incident of long-term abandonment OR regular incidents of short-term abandonment (the longer the period of long-term abandonment or the greater the number of incidents of short-term abandonment, the more serious the offence) (iv) Failure to protect a child from any of the above	Crown Court	26 weeks custody to Crown Court
(i) Series of assaults (ii) Protracted neglect or ill-treatment (iii) Serious cruelty over a period of time (iv) Failure to protect a child from any of the above	Crown Court	Crown Court

Offence seriousness (culpability and harm) **B. Consider the effect of aggravating and mitigating factors** **(other than those within examples above)** The following may be particularly relevant but **these lists are not exhaustive**	
Factors indicating higher culpability 1. Targeting one particular child from the family 2. Sadistic behaviour 3. Threats to prevent the victim from reporting the offence 4. Deliberate concealment of the victim from the authorities 5. Failure to seek medical help	**Factor indicating lower culpability** 1. Seeking medical help or bringing the situation to the notice of the authorities

C17.7.2 Key points

- A parent or other person legally liable to maintain a child or young person, or the legal guardian of a child or young person, shall be deemed to have neglected him in a manner likely to cause injury to his health if he has failed to provide adequate food, clothing, medical aid, or lodging for him, or if, having been unable otherwise to provide such food, clothing, medical aid, or lodging, he has failed to take steps to procure it to be provided under the enactments applicable in that behalf.

- Where it is proved that the death of an infant under three years of age was caused by suffocation (not being suffocation caused by disease or the presence of any foreign body in the throat or air passages of the infant) while the infant was in bed with some other person who has attained the age of 16 years, that other person shall, if he was, when he went to bed, under the influence of drink, be deemed to have neglected the infant in a manner likely to cause injury to its health.

- A person may be convicted of an offence under this section:
  - notwithstanding that actual suffering or injury to health, or the likelihood of actual suffering or injury to health, was obviated by the action of another person;
  - notwithstanding the death of the child or young person in question.

See *Blackstone's Criminal Practice 2012* B2.114–B2.124

C17.8 Grievous bodily harm/unlawful wounding

Offences Against the Person Act 1861, s 20

Whosoever shall unlawfully and maliciously wound or inflict any grievous bodily harm upon any other person, either with or without any weapon or instrument, shall be guilty of an offence.

6 months and/or level 5 fine/5 years (7 years if racially or religiously aggravated)

DO

C17.8.1 *Sentencing*

See **Appendix 7**.

See *Blackstone's Criminal Practice 2012* B2.37–B2.49

C17.9 **Harassment, putting people in fear of violence**

Protection from Harassment Act 1997, s 4(1)

(1) A person whose course of conduct causes another to fear, on at least two occasions, that violence will be used against him is guilty of an offence if he knows or ought to know that his course of conduct will cause the other so to fear on each of those occasions.

 6 months and/or level 5 fine/5 years (7 years if racially or religiously aggravated)

DO

C17.9.1 *Sentencing*

Offence seriousness (culpability and harm)		
A. Identify the appropriate starting point		
Starting points based on first time offender pleading not guilty		
Examples of nature of activity	**Starting point**	**Range**
A pattern of two or more incidents of unwanted contact	6 weeks custody	High level community order to 18 weeks custody
Deliberate threats, persistent action over a longer period; or Intention to cause fear of violence	18 weeks custody	12 weeks custody to Crown Court
Sexual threats, vulnerable person targeted	Crown Court	Crown Court

Offence seriousness (culpability and harm)	
B. Consider the effect of aggravating and mitigating factors	
(other than those within examples above)	
The following may be particularly relevant but **these lists are not exhaustive**	
Factors indicating higher culpability	**Factors indicating lower capability**
1. Planning	1. Limited understanding of effect on victim
2. Offender ignores obvious distress	2. Initial provocation
3. Visits in person to victim's home or workplace	
4. Offender involves others	
5. Using contact arrangements with a child to instigate offence	
Factors indicating greater degree of harm	
1. Victim needs medical help/counselling	
2. Physical violence used	
3. Victim aware that offender has history of using violence	
4. Grossly violent or offensive material sent	
5. Children frightened	
6. Evidence that victim changed lifestyle to avoid contact	

C17.9.2 Key points

- The question of what constitutes a course of conduct has been considered in a number of cases, and the answer will always be fact-sensitive. In *R v Curtis* [2010] EWCA 123 the court allowed an appeal where the defendant, in the context of there being a volatile relationship, had been responsible for six incidents over a period of nine months. The court held that the conduct must be unacceptable to a degree which would sustain criminal liability and also must be oppressive, and went on to say:

  > Courts are well able to separate the wheat from the chaff at an early stage of the proceedings. They should be astute to do so. In most cases courts should have little difficulty in applying the 'close connection' test. Where the claim meets that requirement, and the quality of the conduct said to constitute harassment is being examined, courts will have in mind that irritations, annoyances, even a measure of upset, arise at times in everybody's day-to-day dealings with other people. Courts are able to recognise the boundary between conduct which is unattractive, even unreasonable, and conduct which is oppressive and unacceptable. To cross the boundary from the regrettable to the unacceptable the gravity of the misconduct must be of an order which would sustained (sic) criminal liability under section 2.

- The person whose course of conduct is in question ought to know that it will cause another to fear that violence will be used against him on any occasion if a reasonable person in possession of the same information would think the course of conduct would cause the other so to fear on that occasion.

- It is a defence for a person charged with an offence under this section to show that:
  - his course of conduct was pursued for the purpose of preventing or detecting crime,
  - his course of conduct was pursued under any enactment or rule of law or to comply with any condition or requirement imposed by any person under any enactment, or
  - the pursuit of his course of conduct was reasonable for the protection of himself or another or for the protection of his or another's property.
- The naming of two complainants in one charge is not duplicitous, but at least one of the complainants must have feared violence on at least two occasions (*Caurti v Director of Public Prosecutions* [2002] EWHC 867 (Admin)).

 See *Blackstone's Criminal Practice 2012* **B2.145–B2.152**

C17.10 **Harassment (without violence)**

Protection from Harassment Act 1997, s 2

SO (Either way if racially or religiously motivated)

▦ 6 months and/or level 5 fine/(2 years if racially or religiously motivated)

C17.10.1 *Sentencing*

Offence seriousness (culpability and harm) A. Identify the appropriate starting point Starting points based on first time offender pleading not guilty		
Examples of nature of activity	**Starting point**	**Range**
Small number of incidents	Medium level community order	Band C fine to high level community order
Constant contact at night, trying to come into workplace or home, involving others	6 weeks custody	Medium level community order to 12 weeks custody
Threatening violence, taking personal photographs, sending offensive material	18 weeks custody	12 to 26 weeks custody

Offence seriousness (culpability and harm)	
B. Consider the effect of aggravating and mitigating factors	
(other than those within examples above)	
The following may be particularly relevant but **these lists are not exhaustive**	
Factors indicating higher culpability	**Factors indicating lower culpability**
1. Planning	1. Limited understanding of effect on victim
2. Offender ignores obvious distress	2. Initial provocation
3. Offender involves others	
4. Using contact arrangements with a child to instigate offence	
Factors indicating greater degree of harm	
1. Victim needs medical help/counselling	
2. Action over long period	
3. Children frightened	
4. Use or distribution of photographs	

C17.10.2 Key points

- See **C17.9.2** above.
- The naming of two complainants in one charge is not duplicitous, but unlike the charge under section 4 there need only be conduct against at least two people on at least one occasion each (*Director of Public Prosecutions v Dunn* (2008) 165 JP 130).

📖 See *Blackstone's Criminal Practice 2012* **B2.133–B2.144**

C17.11 **Threats to kill**

Offences Against the Person Act 1861, s 16

A person who without lawful excuse makes to another a threat, intending that that other would fear it would be carried out, to kill that other or a third person shall be guilty of an offence.

EW

 6 months and/or level 5 fine/10 years

DO

C17.11.1 *Sentencing*

Offence seriousness (culpability and harm)		
A. Identify the appropriate starting point		
Starting points based on first time offender pleading not guilty		
Examples of nature of activity	**Starting point**	**Range**
One threat uttered in the heat of the moment, no more than fleeting impact on victim	Medium level community order	Low level community order to high level community order
Single calculated threat or victim fears that threat will be carried out	12 weeks custody	6 to 26 weeks custody
Repeated threats or visible weapon	Crown Court	Crown Court

Offence seriousness (culpability and harm)	
B. Consider the effect of aggravating and mitigating factors	
(other than those within examples above)	
The following may be particularly relevant but **these lists are not exhaustive**	
Factors indicating higher culpability 1. Planning 2. Offender deliberately isolates victim 3. Group action 4. Threat directed at victim because of job 5. History of antagonism towards victim **Factors indicating greater degree of harm** 1. Vulnerable victim 2. Victim needs medical help/counselling	**Factor indicating lower culpability** 1. Provocation

 See *Blackstone's Criminal Practice 2012* **B5.30–B5.37**

C17.12 **Witness intimidation**

Criminal Justice and Public Order Act 1994, s 51(1)–(5)

(1) A person commits an offence if—
  (a) he does an act which intimidates, and is intended to intimidate, another person ('the victim'),
  (b) he does the act knowing or believing that the victim is assisting in the investigation of an offence or is a witness or potential witness or a juror or potential juror in proceedings for an offence, and

> (c) he does it intending thereby to cause the investigation or the course of justice to be obstructed, perverted or interfered with.
> (2) A person commits an offence if—
>   (a) he does an act which harms, and is intended to harm, another person or, intending to cause another person to fear harm, he threatens to do an act which would harm that other person,
>   (b) he does or threatens to do the act knowing or believing that the person harmed or threatened to be harmed ('the victim'), or some other person, has assisted in an investigation into an offence or has given evidence or particular evidence in proceedings for an offence, or has acted as a juror or concurred in a particular verdict in proceedings for an offence, and
>   (c) he does or threatens to do it because of that knowledge or belief.
> (3) For the purposes of subsections (1) and (2) it is immaterial that the act is or would be done, or that the threat is made—
>   (a) otherwise than in the presence of the victim, or
>   (b) to a person other than the victim.
> (4) The harm that may be done or threatened may be financial as well as physical (whether to the person or a person's property) and similarly as respects an intimidatory act which consists of threats.
> (5) The intention required by subsection (1)(c) and the motive required by subsection (2)(c) above need not be the only or the predominating intention or motive with which the act is done or, in the case of subsection (2), threatened.

 EW

 6 months and/or level 5 fine/5 years

C17.12.1 *Sentencing*

Offence seriousness (culpability and harm) A. Identify the appropriate starting point Starting points based on first time offender pleading not guilty		
Examples of nature of activity	**Starting point**	**Range**
Sudden outburst in chance encounter	6 weeks custody	Medium level community order to 18 weeks custody
Conduct amounting to a threat; staring at, approaching, or following witnesses; talking about the case; trying to alter or stop evidence	18 weeks custody	12 weeks custody to Crown Court
Threats of violence to witnesses and/or their families; deliberately seeking out witnesses	Crown Court	Crown Court

Offence seriousness (culpability and harm)	
B. Consider the effect of aggravating and mitigating factors	
(other than those within examples above)	
The following may be particularly relevant but **these lists are not exhaustive**	
Factors indicating higher culpability	
1. Breach of bail conditions	
2. Offender involves others	
Factors indicating greater degree of harm	
1. Detrimental impact on administration of justice	
2. Contact made at or in vicinity of victim's home	

 See *Blackstone's Criminal Practice 2012* **B14.41** and **F16.10**

Part D
Sentencing

D1 Age of Offender

D1.1 General principles

The age of the offender is important in relation to the court's power to impose different types of sentence. If age is in doubt the court should consider all available evidence and make a determination before proceeding to sentence.

Generally speaking the relevant age is the age of the offender on the date of conviction, not the date of offence. As a matter of public policy, however, the courts have been willing to sentence in relation to offence date, as opposed to conviction date. In *R v Ghafoor* [2003] 2 Cr App R (S) 89 the court said:

> The approach to be adopted where a defendant crosses a relevant age threshold between the date of the commission of the offence and date of conviction should now be clear. The starting point is the sentence that the defendant would have been likely to receive if he had been sentenced at the date of the commission of the offence. It has been described as a 'powerful factor'. That is for the obvious reason that as Mr Emmerson points out, the philosophy of restricting sentencing powers in relation to young persons reflects both (a) society's acceptance that young offenders are less responsible for their actions and therefore less culpable than adults, and (b) the recognition that, in consequence, sentencing them should place greater emphasis on rehabilitation and less on retribution and deterrence than in the case of adults. It should be noted that the 'starting point' is not the maximum sentence that could lawfully have been imposed, but the sentence that the offender would have been likely to receive.

However, in *R v Bowker* (2008) 1 Cr App R (S) 72 the court said that *Ghafoor* was a powerful starting point, but other factors (such as the need for deterrent sentencing), may justify departing from it.

 See *Blackstone's Criminal Practice 2012* **D24**

D1.2 Exceptions to general rule

Where a court revokes one of the following orders the relevant age for the purpose of resentencing is determined by the date on which the offender appears before the court (ie the date of revocation):

- community rehabilitation and/or punishment;
- curfew;
- drug abstinence;
- drug treatment and testing;
- exclusion.

D1 Age of Offender

Where a court revokes one of the following orders the relevant age for the purpose of resentencing is the age of the offender when the order was made:

• community orders made pursuant to the Criminal Justice Act 2003.

Where a court activates a conditional discharge, the relevant age for the purpose of resentencing is determined by the date on which the offender appears for sentence.

Where a court is considering a minimum sentence under section 51A of the Firearms Act 1968, the relevant age is determined by reference to the date of offence.

 See *Blackstone's Criminal Practice 2011* **D24**

D2 **Alteration of Sentence**

D2.1 **Section 142 Magistrates' Courts Act 1980**

Section 142 of the Magistrates' Courts Act 1980 gives the court power to reopen sentence. There are no time restrictions but a court must have regard to the principle of finality of sentence, meaning that in many cases it will not be proper to interfere (*R (Trigger) v Northampton Magistrates' Court*, unreported, 2 February 2011. Section 142(1) provides:

Magistrates' Courts Act 1980, s 142(1)

(1) A magistrates' court may vary or rescind a sentence or other order imposed or made by it when dealing with an offender if it appears to the court to be in the interests of justice to do so, and it is hereby declared that this power extends to replacing a sentence or order which for any reason appears to be invalid by another which the court has power to impose or make.

 See *Blackstone's Criminal Practice 2012* **D23.19**

D3 **Anti-Social Behaviour Orders**

D3.1 **Age requirements**

An offender aged ten years or over.

D3.2 **Notice**

Criminal procedure rule 50.3 requires the prosecutor to give notice on a prescribed form, of his intention to apply for an anti-social behaviour order. There are therefore no circumstances under which a defence lawyer should feel pressurized into dealing with what can be a complex area of law without adequate notice.

D3.3 **Criteria**

Anti-social behaviour orders may be made either on a freestanding basis or following conviction. This book concentrates solely on the latter.

Section 1C of the Crime and Disorder Act 1998 provides:

> **Crime and Disorder Act 1998, s 1C**
>
> (1) This section applies where a person (the 'offender') is convicted of a relevant offence.
> (2) If the court considers—
>   (a) that the offender has acted, at any time since the commencement date, in an anti-social manner, that is to say in a manner that caused or was likely to cause harassment, alarm or distress to one or more persons not of the same household as himself, and
>   (b) that an order under this section is necessary to protect persons in any place in England and Wales from further anti-social acts by him,
>   it may make an order which prohibits the offender from doing anything described in the order.
> (3) The court may make an order under this section—
>   (a) if the prosecutor asks it to do so, or
>   (b) if the court thinks it is appropriate to do so.
> (3A) For the purpose of deciding whether to make an order under this section the court may consider evidence led by the prosecution and the defence.
> (3B) It is immaterial whether evidence led in pursuance of subsection (3A) would have been admissible in the proceedings in which the offender was convicted.
> (4) An order under this section shall not be made except—
>   (a) in addition to a sentence imposed in respect of the relevant offence; or
>   (b) in addition to an order discharging him conditionally.

(4A) The court may adjourn any proceedings in relation to an order under this section even after sentencing the offender.

(4B) If the offender does not appear for any adjourned proceedings, the court may further adjourn the proceedings or may issue a warrant for his arrest.

(4C) But the court may not issue a warrant for the offender's arrest unless it is satisfied that he has had adequate notice of the time and place of the adjourned proceedings.

(5) An order under this section takes effect on the day on which it is made, but the court may provide in any such order that such requirements of the order as it may specify shall, during any period when the offender is detained in legal custody, be suspended until his release from that custody.

. . .

(9) Subsections (7), (10), (10C), (10D), (10E) and (11) of section 1 apply for the purposes of the making and effect of orders made by virtue of this section as they apply for the purposes of the making and effect of anti-social behaviour orders.

(9A) The council for the local government area in which a person in respect of whom an anti-social behaviour order has been made resides or appears to reside may bring proceedings under section 1(10) (as applied by subsection (9) above) for breach of an order under subsection (2) above.

(9AA) Sections 1AA and 1AB apply in relation to orders under this section, with any necessary modifications, as they apply in relation to anti-social behaviour orders.

(9AB) In their application by virtue of subsection (9AA), sections 1AA(1A)(b) and 1AB(6) have effect as if the words 'by complaint' were omitted.

(9AC) In its application by virtue of subsection (9AA), section 1AA(1A)(b) has effect as if the reference to the relevant authority which applied for the anti-social behaviour order were a reference to the chief officer of police, or other relevant authority, responsible under section 1K(2)(a) or (b) for carrying out a review of the order under this section.

(9B) Subsection (9C) applies in relation to proceedings in which an order under subsection (2) is made against a child or young person who is convicted of an offence.

(9C) In so far as the proceedings relate to the making of the order—

    (a) section 49 of the Children and Young Persons Act 1933 (c 12) (restrictions on reports of proceedings in which children and young persons are concerned) does not apply in respect of the child or young person against whom the order is made;

    (b) section 39 of that Act (power to prohibit publication of certain matter) does so apply.

(10) In this section—

'child' and 'young person' have the same meaning as in the Children and Young Persons Act 1933 (c 12);

'the commencement date' has the same meaning as in section 1 above;

'the court' in relation to an offender means—

    (a) the court by or before which he is convicted of the relevant offence; or

    (b) if he is committed to the Crown Court to be dealt with for that offence, the Crown Court; and

'relevant offence' means an offence committed after the coming into force of section 64 of the Police Reform Act 2002 (c 30).

D3.4 Relevant case law

Evidence of post-complaint behaviour is admissible both to show whether a person has acted in an anti-social manner and whether an order is necessary (*Birmingham City Council v Dixon* [2009] EWHC 761 (Admin)).

The following case studies and guidance are reproduced from *Anti-Social Behaviour Orders: A Guide for the Judiciary*, available from <http://www.judiciary.gov.uk>.

In *R v Gowan* [2007] EWCA Crim 1360 the court made an ASBO against the defendant's wife. The order was quashed because, the defendant's wife being of the same household as him, there was no power to make it. ASBOs are properly made for the protection of the general public.

In *S v Poole Borough Council* [2002] EWHC 244 (Admin) a youth aged 15 had been engaged in anti-social behaviour for 18 months up to the date of the application. The magistrates' court hearing was concluded five months later and the Crown Court appeal seven and a half months after that. The defendant argued that there was no necessity for an order as there had been no anti-social behaviour for over a year. Describing this argument as hopeless, Simon Brown LJ said:

> It must be expected that, once an application of this sort is made, still more obviously once an ASBO has been made, its effect will be likely to deter future misconduct. That, indeed, is the justification for such orders in the first place . . . The conduct on which the magistrates' court, and in turn the Crown Court, should concentrate in determining whether such an order is necessary is that which underlay the authority's application for the order in the first place.

No prohibition may be imposed unless it is *necessary* for the purpose of protecting persons, whether relevant persons or persons elsewhere in England and Wales, from further anti-social acts by the defendant. The leading case is *R v Boness* [2005] EWCA Crim 2395. From that and other cases (notably *R v P (Shane Tony)* [2004] EWCA Crim 287, *R v McGrath* [2005] EWCA Crim 353, and *W v Director of Public Prosecutions* [2005] EWCA Civ 1333) the following principles emerge:

(1) The requirement that a prohibition must be necessary to protect persons from further anti-social acts by the defendant means that the use of an ASBO to punish a defendant is unlawful.

(2) Each separate prohibition must be targeted at the individual and the specific form of anti-social behaviour it is intended to prevent. The order must be tailored to the defendant and not designed on a word processor for generic use. Therefore the court must ask itself when considering a specific order, 'Is this order necessary to protect persons in any place in England and Wales from further anti-social acts by the defendant?'

(3) Each prohibition must be precise and capable of being understood by the defendant. Therefore the court should ask itself before making an order: 'Are the terms of this order clear so that the defendant will know precisely what it is that he is prohibited from doing?' (So that unfamiliar words like 'curtilage' and 'environs' should be avoided, as should vague ones like 'implement' or 'paraphernalia'.) For example, a prohibition should clearly delineate any exclusion zone by reference to a map and clearly identify those whom the defendant must not contact or associate with.

(4) Each prohibition must be prohibitory and not mandatory: this means substantially and not just formally prohibitory.

(5) The terms of the order must be proportionate in the sense that they must be commensurate with the risk to be guarded against. This is particularly important where an order may interfere with an ECHR right protected by the Human Rights Act 1998, eg articles 8, 10, and 11.

(6) There is no requirement that the prohibited acts should by themselves give rise to harassment, alarm, or distress.

(7) An ASBO should not be used merely to increase the sentence of imprisonment which an offender is liable to receive.

(8) Different considerations may apply if the maximum sentence is only a fine, but the court must still go through all the steps to make sure that an ASBO is necessary.

The fact that an order prohibits a defendant from committing a specified criminal offence does not automatically invalidate it. However, the court should not make such an order if the sentence which could be passed following conviction for the offence would be a sufficient deterrent. In addition, the Court of Appeal has indicated that prohibiting behaviour that is in any event a crime does not necessarily address the aim of an ASBO, which is to prevent anti-social behaviour. The better course is to make an anticipatory form of order, namely an order which prevents a defendant from doing an act preparatory to the commission of the offence, thereby helping to prevent the criminal offence from being committed in the first place. For example, an order might prevent a defendant from entering a shopping centre rather than stealing from shops.

In *Boness*, Hooper LJ gave other examples, drawing an analogy with bail conditions designed to prevent a defendant from committing further offences. He said:

> If, for example, a court is faced by an offender who causes criminal damage by spraying graffiti then the order should be aimed at facilitating action to be taken to prevent graffiti spraying by him and/or his associates before it takes place. An order in clear and simple terms preventing the offender from being in possession of a can of spray paint in a public place gives the police or others responsible for protecting the property an opportunity to take action in advance of the actual spraying and makes it clear to the offender that he has lost the right to carry such a can for the duration of the order.

> If a court wishes to make an order prohibiting a group of youngsters from racing cars or motor bikes on an estate or driving at excessive speed

(anti-social behaviour for those living on the estate), then the order should not (normally) prohibit driving whilst disqualified. It should prohibit, for example, the offender whilst on the estate from taking part in, or encouraging, racing or driving at an excessive speed. It might also prevent the group from congregating with named others in a particular area of the estate. Such an order gives those responsible for enforcing order on the estate the opportunity to take action to prevent the anti-social conduct, it is to be hoped, before it takes place.

In *R (Cooke) v Director of Public Prosecutions* [2008] EWHC 2703 (Admin) the court held that an order was not appropriate in relation to an offender who due to mental incapacity was not able to understand its terms, as such an order would fail to protect the public and could therefore not be said to be necessary to protect others.

In *R (McGarrett) v Kingston Crown Court*, unreported, 8 June 2009, the court quashed an indefinite anti-social behaviour order made against a defendant who had been convicted of a single offence of breaching a noise abatement notice. There were no other relevant offences or behaviour that had been considered by the court, and accordingly the test of necessity was not made out.

A condition not to cause harassment, alarm, or distress was too imprecise; conditions to be clear as to what behaviour the order was seeking to discourage (*Heron v Plymouth City Council* [2009] EWHC 3562 (Admin)).

See *Blackstone's Criminal Practice 2012* D25.1–D25.22

D4 **Banning Orders (Football)**

Imposed under section 14A of the Football Spectators Act 1989.

D4.1 **Criteria**

Banning orders can be imposed when an offender is convicted of a relevant offence and if the court is satisfied that there are reasonable grounds to believe that making a banning order would help to prevent violence or disorder at or in connection with any regulated football matches, it must make such an order in respect of the offender.

The core requirements of such an order are to prohibit the offender from attending regulated football matches in England and Wales. When matches are being played abroad, the order will require the offender to report to a police station and surrender his passport (unless there are exceptional circumstances certified by the court as to why this should not be done). Other requirements can be imposed, eg not to go within a certain distance of a football ground.

The order must be for a period of between three and five years, or six and ten years if a custodial sentence (including a sentence of detention) is imposed for the original offence.

In *Newman v Commissioner of Police for the Metropolis*, [2009] EWHC 1642 (Admin), the court held that police were entitled to rely upon compilation witness statements and compilation video footage, and had no duty to disclose the underlying material from which it was drawn. There is no statutory disclosure regime applicable to the making of banning orders and a court should apply normal principles of 'fairness'. Advocates seeking disclosure should be careful to specify the material that they wish to view and the reasons why. An application that amounts to nothing more than a 'fishing expedition' ought to be refused.

D4.2 **Relevant offences**

Relevant offences are listed in Schedule 1 to the 1989 Act. For some offences, the court will need to make a declaration of relevance (see below).

> ### Football Spectators Act 1989, Sch 1
>
> 1. This Schedule applies to the following offences:
>   (a) any offence under section 14J(1) or 21C(2) of this Act,

(b) any offence under section 2 or 2A of the Sporting Events (Control of Alcohol etc.) Act 1985 (alcohol, containers, and fireworks) committed by the accused at any football match to which this Schedule applies or while entering or trying to enter the ground,

(c) any offence under section 4A or 5 of the Public Order Act 1986 (harassment, alarm, or distress) or any provision of Part III of that Act (racial hatred) committed during a period relevant to a football match to which this Schedule applies at any premises while the accused was at, or was entering or leaving or trying to enter or leave, the premises,

(d) any offence involving the use or threat of violence by the accused towards another person committed during a period relevant to a football match to which this Schedule applies at any premises while the accused was at, or was entering or leaving or trying to enter or leave, the premises,

(e) any offence involving the use or threat of violence towards property committed during a period relevant to a football match to which this Schedule applies at any premises while the accused was at, or was entering or leaving or trying to enter or leave, the premises,

(f) any offence involving the use, carrying or possession of an offensive weapon or a firearm committed during a period relevant to a football match to which this Schedule applies at any premises while the accused was at, or was entering or leaving or trying to enter or leave, the premises,

(g) any offence under section 12 of the Licensing Act 1872 (persons found drunk in public places, etc) of being found drunk in a highway or other public place committed while the accused was on a journey to or from a football match to which this Schedule applies being an offence as respects which the court makes a declaration that the offence related to football matches,

(h) any offence under section 91(1) of the Criminal Justice Act 1967 (disorderly behaviour while drunk in a public place) committed in a highway or other public place while the accused was on a journey to or from a football match to which this Schedule applies being an offence as respects which the court makes a declaration that the offence related to football matches,

(j) any offence under section 1 of the Sporting Events (Control of Alcohol etc.) Act 1985 (alcohol on coaches or trains to or from sporting events) committed while the accused was on a journey to or from a football match to which this Schedule applies being an offence as respects which the court makes a declaration that the offence related to football matches,

(k) any offence under section 4A or 5 of the Public Order Act 1986 (harassment, alarm, or distress) or any provision of Part III of that Act (racial hatred) committed while the accused was on a journey to or from a football match to which this Schedule applies being an offence as respects which the court makes a declaration that the offence related to football matches,

(l) any offence under section 4 or 5 of the Road Traffic Act 1988 (driving etc when under the influence of drink or drugs or with an alcohol concentration above the prescribed limit) committed while the accused was on a journey to or from a football match to which this Schedule applies being an offence as respects which the court makes a declaration that the offence related to football matches,

(m) any offence involving the use or threat of violence by the accused towards another person committed while one or each of them was on a journey to or from a football match to which this Schedule applies being an offence as respects which the court makes a declaration that the offence related to football matches,

(n) any offence involving the use or threat of violence towards property committed while the accused was on a journey to or from a football match to which this Schedule applies being an offence as respects which the court makes a declaration that the offence related to football matches,

(o) any offence involving the use, carrying or possession of an offensive weapon or a firearm committed while the accused was on a journey to or from a football match to which this Schedule applies being an offence as respects which the court makes a declaration that the offence related to football matches,

(p) any offence under the Football (Offences) Act 1991,

(q) any offence under section 4A or 5 of the Public Order Act 1986 (harassment, alarm, or distress) or any provision of Part 3 or 3A of that Act (hatred by reference to race etc)—
   (i) which does not fall within paragraph (c) or (k) above,
   (ii) which was committed during a period relevant to a football match to which this Schedule applies, and
   (iii) as respects which the court makes a declaration that the offence related to that match or to that match and any other football match which took place during that period,

(r) any offence involving the use or threat of violence by the accused towards another person—
   (i) which does not fall within paragraph (d) or (m) above,
   (ii) which was committed during a period relevant to a football match to which this Schedule applies, and
   (iii) as respects which the court makes a declaration that the offence related to that match or to that match and any other football match which took place during that period,

(s) any offence involving the use or threat of violence towards property—
   (i) which does not fall within paragraph (e) or (n) above,
   (ii) which was committed during a period relevant to a football match to which this Schedule applies, and
   (iii) as respects which the court makes a declaration that the offence related to that match or to that match and any other football match which took place during that period,

(t) any offence involving the use, carrying or possession of an offensive weapon or a firearm—
   (i) which does not fall within paragraph (f) or (o) above,
   (ii) which was committed during a period relevant to a football match to which this Schedule applies, and

(iii) as respects which the court makes a declaration that the offence related to that match or to that match and any other football match which took place during that period.

(u) any offence under section 166 of the Criminal Justice and Public Order Act 1994 (sale of tickets by unauthorised persons) which relates to tickets for a football match.

D4.3 Declaration of relevance

The prosecution must give five days' notice that it intends to invite a court to make a declaration of relevance. That notice period can be waived by the defence; it can also be dispensed with by the court if the interests of justice do not require a longer notice period to be given. Note that the court can grant an adjournment to facilitate the five-day notice period.

The declaration is that the offence related to that match or to that match and any other football match which took place during that period.

Each of the following periods is 'relevant to' a football match to which Schedule 1 applies:

(a) in the case of a match which takes place on the day on which it is advertised to take place, the period:
   (i) beginning 24 hours before whichever is the earlier of the start of the match and the time at which it was advertised to start; and
   (ii) ending 24 hours after it ends;
(b) in the case of a match which does not take place on the day on which it was advertised to take place, the period:
   (i) beginning 24 hours before the time at which it was advertised to start on that day; and
   (ii) ending 24 hours after that time.

In *R v Arbery* [2008] EWCA Crim 702 the offenders were drinking in a public house following a football match, waiting for their train home when violence broke out with rival supporters. A football banning order was quashed on appeal as the court held that the offence arose out of a disagreement in the pub, completely unrelated to football.

In *R v Eliot* [2007] EWCA Crim 1002 the court gave a helpful insight into how the issue of 'relevance' might be approached:

Did the offences committed in the present case relate to the match? Clearly, the presence of the applicants in London and indeed at Leicester Square related to the match. But it is not their presence, or their allegiance, which is the touchstone of the declaration; it is the relationship between the offence and the match. Here, the offences were sparked by the presence of a group of football supporters in London. The spark, however, had nothing to do with the match itself on the facts as found by the judge. The violence took place, not because of anything that had happened at the football match, or between supporters but because of disparaging remarks made to a lady who had nothing to do with the football match and remarks which had nothing to do with the football match. In those circumstances, we do not consider that, in this case, the statutory requirement was satisfied.

In *Director of Public Prosecutions v Beaumont* [2008] EWHC 523 (Admin) the court rejected an argument that there was a temporal limit to the making of a banning order. In that case the violence erupted more than one hour after the end of the match.

A travel restriction, imposed as part of a banning order, does not infringe European Community Law, or the European Convention on Human Rights (*Gough v Chief Constable of Derbyshire* [2002] EWCA Civ 351).

D4.4 Appeals

An appeal lies to the Crown Court in respect to the making of a banning order, or dismissal of prosecution application (Football Spectators Act 1989, s 14D).

 See *Blackstone's Criminal Practice 2012* **E21.3–E21.7**

D5 **Bind Over**

D5.1 **Criteria**

Any person before the court, as defendant or witness (provided that they have given evidence), can be bound over.

A bind over can only be made by consent and the court should, as a matter of good practice, hear representations (but see *R v Woking Justices, ex p Gossage* [1973] QB 448 where the court held that there was no duty to hear representations if the court was binding over a person in their own recognizance for a 'just and suitable' sum); refusal can result in committal to prison. There is, however, no sanction for a person under 18 years of age, so query whether consent should be given. The order is to keep the peace and be of good behaviour; further conditions are not permitted.

The court will set a recognizance to be forfeit on breach. If the sum set is more than trivial, enquiry should be made in relation to means; a failure to do so may give rise to a successful challenge (*R v Lincoln Crown Court, ex p Jude* The Times, 30 April 1997).

Generally, a binding over to keep the peace is typically only warranted where there is evidence of likely personal danger to others involving violence or the threat of violence (see, for example, *Percy v Director of Public Prosecutions* [1995] 3 All ER 124).

In *R v Middlesex Crown Court, ex p Khan* (1997) 161 JP 240 the court held:

> . . . if a judge is going to require a man to be bound over in circumstances where he has been acquitted, it is particularly important that he should be satisfied beyond a reasonable doubt that the man poses a potential threat to other persons and that he is a man of violence.

D5.2 **Practice direction**

The Consolidated Criminal Practice Direction at paragraph III.31 states:

Consolidated Criminal Practice Direction para III.31.2, III.31.3, III.31.4, and III.31.8

Binding over to keep the peace

III.31.2

Before imposing a binding over order, the court must be satisfied that a breach of the peace involving violence, or an imminent threat of violence, has occurred, or that there is a real risk of violence in the future.

Such violence may be perpetrated by the individual who will be subject to the order, or by a third party as a natural consequence of the individual's conduct.

III.31.3

In light of the judgment in Hashman and Harrup, courts should no longer bind an individual over 'to be of good behaviour'. Rather than binding an individual over to 'keep the peace' in general terms, the court should identify the specific conduct or activity from which the individual must refrain.

Written order

III.31.4

When making an order binding an individual over to refrain from specified types of conduct or activities, the details of that conduct or those activities should be specified by the court in a written order served on all relevant parties. The court should state its reasons for the making of the order, its length and the amount of the recognisance. The length of the order should be proportionate to the harm sought to be avoided and should not generally exceed 12 months.

. . .

Burden of proof

III.31.8

The court should be satisfied beyond reasonable doubt of the matters complained of before a binding over order may be imposed. Where the procedure has been commenced on complaint, the burden of proof rests on the complainant. In all other circumstances the burden of proof rests on the prosecution.

 See *Blackstone's Criminal Practice 2012* **E13**

D6 **Breach of Community Order**

D6.1 **Criteria**

Breach of community orders imposed under the Criminal Justice Act 2003 are dealt with in accordance with Schedule 8 to that Act. A general defence of reasonable excuse is open to the defendant who must establish it on the balance of probabilities. The fact that a person is appealing against a community order does not give them a reasonable excuse not to comply (*West Midlands Probation Board v Sutton Coldfield Magistrates' Court* [2008] EWHC 15 (Admin)).

On breach of a community order due to having failed to comply with the terms of the order, the court has three options open to it:

* impose more onerous requirements than the original order (having taken into account the offender's level of cooperation with the order), and let the order continue; or
* if the order was made by the Crown Court, commit the offender for sentence, or
* revoke the order and deal with the offender in any manner in which it could deal with him if he had just been convicted by the court of the offence (having taken into account the offender's level of cooperation with the order). It should be noted that in respect to an offender aged 18 years or older, imprisonment can be imposed following a wilful and persistent failure to comply, even if the original offence is not in itself imprisonable.

If the offender has committed a further offence during the life of the community order and is convicted whilst that order is in force, the court has three options open to it in respect to the original order:

* do nothing, and sentence for the new offence; or
* if the order was made by the Crown Court, commit the offender for sentence; or
* revoke the order and deal with the offender in any manner in which it could deal with him if he had just been convicted by the court of the offence (having taken into account the offender's level of cooperation with the order).

A court must be 'satisfied' that a breach has occurred to the criminal standard of proof (*West Yorkshire Probation Board v Boulter* (2005) 169 JP 601).

If the breach has occurred due to the offender's ill-health, a court should not resentence (*R v Bishop* [2004] EWCA Crim 2956).

There is no power to commence breach proceedings once the operational period has expired (*West Yorkshire Probation Board v Cruickshanks* [2010] EWHC 615 (Admin)).

D6.2 Approach to be taken by the court

The Sentencing Guidelines Council has issued guidance (*Guideline: New Sentences: Criminal Justice Act 2003*), which is binding on all courts:

- Where an offender fails, without reasonable excuse, to comply with one or more requirements, the 'responsible officer' can either give a warning or initiate breach proceedings. Where the offender fails to comply without reasonable excuse for the second time within a 12-month period, the 'responsible officer' must initiate proceedings.
- In such proceedings the court must either increase the severity of the existing sentence (ie impose more onerous conditions, including requirements aimed at enforcement, such as a curfew or supervision requirement) or revoke the existing sentence and proceed as though sentencing for the original offence. The court is required to take account of the circumstances of the breach, which will inevitably have an impact on its response.
- In certain circumstances (where an offender has wilfully and persistently failed to comply with an order made in respect of an offence that is not itself punishable by imprisonment), the court can impose a maximum of six months custody.
- When increasing the onerousness of requirements, the court must consider the impact on the offender's ability to comply and the possibility of precipitating a custodial sentence for further breach. For that reason, and particularly where the breach occurs towards the end of the sentence, the court should take account of compliance to date and may consider that extending the supervision or operational periods will be more sensible; in other cases it might choose to add punitive or rehabilitative requirements instead. In making these changes the court must be mindful of the legislative restrictions on the overall length of community sentences and on the supervision and operational periods allowed for each type of requirement.
- The court dealing with breach of a community sentence should have as its primary objective ensuring that the requirements of the sentence are finished, and this is important if the court is to have regard to the statutory purposes of sentencing. A court that imposes a custodial sentence for breach without giving adequate consideration to alternatives is in danger of imposing a sentence that is not commensurate with the seriousness of the original offence and is

solely a punishment for breach. This risks undermining the purposes it has identified as being important. Nonetheless, courts will need to be vigilant to ensure that there is a realistic prospect of the purposes of the order being achieved.

- A court sentencing for breach must take account of the extent to which the offender has complied with the requirements of the community order, the reasons for breach, and the point at which the breach has occurred. Where a breach takes place towards the end of the operational period and the court is satisfied that the offender's appearance before the court is likely to be sufficient in itself to ensure future compliance, then given that it is not open to the court to make no order, an approach that the court might wish to adopt could be to resentence in a way that enables the original order to be completed properly—for example, a differently constructed community sentence that aims to secure compliance with the purposes of the original sentence.
- If the court decides to make the order more onerous, it must give careful consideration, with advice from the Probation Service, to the offender's ability to comply. A custodial sentence should be the last resort, where all reasonable efforts to ensure that an offender completes a community sentence have failed.

See *Blackstone's Criminal Practice 2012* E8

D7 **Breach of Supervision Order**

D7.1 **Criteria**

A breach can only be found in relation to the terms of the order; an offence committed during the supervision order does not put the offender in breach. The court has the following options open to it following a breach:

- If the order was made by a Crown Court it may commit the offender for sentence to the Crown Court that made the order.
- It may impose a fine not exceeding £1,000.
- It may impose an attendance centre order, or curfew order.
- It may revoke the order and deal with the offender in any manner in which it could deal with him if he had just been convicted by the court of the offence (note that this option is not available if the order was made by the Crown Court).

 See *Blackstone's Criminal Practice 2012* **E8**

D8 Committal for Sentence

D8.1 Age requirements

Offender is aged 18 years or over.

D8.2 Criteria

A magistrates' court may commit an offender for sentence post conviction (Powers of Criminal Courts (Sentencing) Act 2000, s 3 (PCC(S)A 2000)). When a magistrates' court has retained jurisdiction for an offence and the offender is convicted, it may commit the offender for sentence regardless of whether or not there is a change of circumstances.

A magistrates' court will commit for sentence if the court is of the opinion:

- that the offence or the combination of the offence and one or more offences associated with it was so serious that greater punishment should be inflicted for the offence than the court has power to impose; or
- in the case of a violent or sexual offence, that a custodial sentence for a term longer than the court has power to impose is necessary to protect the public from serious harm from him.

Additional committal powers are provided for under sections 4 and 6 PCC(S)A 2000.

Powers of Criminal Courts (Sentencing) Act 2000, ss 3–6

3 Committal for sentence on summary trial of offence triable either way

(1) Subject to subsection (4) below, this section applies where on the summary trial of an offence triable either way a person aged 18 or over is convicted of the offence.

(2) If the court is of the opinion—

  (a) that the offence or the combination of the offence and one or more offences associated with it was so serious that greater punishment should be inflicted for the offence than the court has power to impose, or

  (b) in the case of a violent or sexual offence, that a custodial sentence for a term longer than the court has power to impose is necessary to protect the public from serious harm from him,

---

the court may commit the offender in custody or on bail to the Crown Court for sentence in accordance with section 5(1) below.

(3) Where the court commits a person under subsection (2) above, section 6 below (which enables a magistrates' court, where it commits a person under this section in respect of an offence, also to commit him to the Crown Court to be dealt with in respect of certain other offences) shall apply accordingly.

(4) This section does not apply in relation to an offence as regards which this section is excluded by section 33 of the Magistrates' Courts Act 1980 (certain offences where value involved is small).

(5) The preceding provisions of this section shall apply in relation to a corporation as if—
  (a) the corporation were an individual aged 18 or over; and
  (b) in subsection (2) above, paragraph (b) and the words 'in custody or on bail' were omitted.

4 Committal for sentence on indication of guilty plea to offence triable either way

(1) This section applies where—
  (a) a person aged 18 or over appears or is brought before a magistrates' court ('the court') on an information charging him with an offence triable either way ('the offence');
  (b) he or his representative indicates that he would plead guilty if the offence were to proceed to trial; and
  (c) proceeding as if section 9(1) of the Magistrates' Courts Act 1980 were complied with and he pleaded guilty under it, the court convicts him of the offence.

(2) If the court has committed the offender to the Crown Court for trial for one or more related offences, that is to say, one or more offences which, in its opinion, are related to the offence, it may commit him in custody or on bail to the Crown Court to be dealt with in respect of the offence in accordance with section 5(1) below.

(3) If the power conferred by subsection (2) above is not exercisable but the court is still to inquire, as examining justices, into one or more related offences—
  (a) it shall adjourn the proceedings relating to the offence until after the conclusion of its inquiries; and
  (b) if it commits the offender to the Crown Court for trial for one or more related offences, it may then exercise that power.

(4) Where the court—
  (a) under subsection (2) above commits the offender to the Crown Court to be dealt with in respect of the offence, and
  (b) does not state that, in its opinion, it also has power so to commit him under section 3(2) above,

section 5(1) below shall not apply unless he is convicted before the Crown Court of one or more of the related offences.

(5) Where section 5(1) below does not apply, the Crown Court may deal with the offender in respect of the offence in any way in which the magistrates' court could deal with him if it had just convicted him of the offence.

(6) Where the court commits a person under subsection (2) above, section 6 below (which enables a magistrates' court, where it commits a person under this section in respect of an offence, also to commit him to the Crown Court to be dealt with in respect of certain other offences) shall apply accordingly.

(7) For the purposes of this section one offence is related to another if, were they both to be prosecuted on indictment, the charges for them could be joined in the same indictment.

5 Power of Crown Court on committal for sentence under sections 3 and 4

(1) Where an offender is committed by a magistrates' court for sentence under section 3 or 4 above, the Crown Court shall inquire into the circumstances of the case and may deal with the offender in any way in which it could deal with him if he had just been convicted of the offence on indictment before the court.

(2) In relation to committals under section 4 above, subsection (1) above has effect subject to section 4(4) and (5) above.

6 Committal for sentence in certain cases where offender committed in respect of another offence

(1) This section applies where a magistrates' court ('the committing court') commits a person in custody or on bail to the Crown Court under any enactment mentioned in subsection (4) below to be sentenced or otherwise dealt with in respect of an offence ('the relevant offence').

(2) Where this section applies and the relevant offence is an indictable offence, the committing court may also commit the offender, in custody or on bail as the case may require, to the Crown Court to be dealt with in respect of any other offence whatsoever in respect of which the committing court has power to deal with him (being an offence of which he has been convicted by that or any other court).

(3) Where this section applies and the relevant offence is a summary offence, the committing court may commit the offender, in custody or on bail as the case may require, to the Crown Court to be dealt with in respect of–

    (a) any other offence of which the committing court has convicted him, being either—

        (i) an offence punishable with imprisonment; or

        (ii) an offence in respect of which the committing court has a power or duty to order him to be disqualified under section 34, 35 or 36 of the Road Traffic Offenders Act 1988 (disqualification for certain motoring offences); or

    (b) any suspended sentence in respect of which the committing court has under paragraph 11(1) of Schedule 12 to the Criminal Justice Act 2003 power to deal with him.

(4) The enactments referred to in subsection (1) above are—

    (a) the Vagrancy Act 1824 (incorrigible rogues);

    (b) sections 3 to 4A above (committal for sentence for offences triable either way);

    (c) section 13(5) below (conditionally discharged person convicted of further offence);

(e) paragraph 11(2) of Schedule 12 to the Criminal Justice Act 2003 (committal to Crown Court where offender convicted during operational period of suspended sentence).

 See *Blackstone's Criminal Practice 2012* **D6**

D9 **Committal for Sentence: Dangerous Young Offender**

D9.1 **Age requirements**

Offender aged under 18 years. See also **D21**.

D9.2 **Criteria**

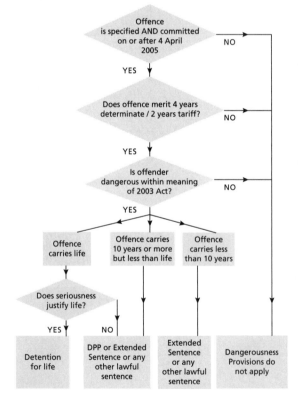

Section 3C of the PCCS(A) 2000 provides:

Powers of Criminal Courts (Sentencing) Act 2000, s 3C

(1) This section applies where on the summary trial of a specified offence [see **D9.3** below] a person aged under 18 is convicted of the offence.

(2) If, in relation to the offence, it appears to the court that the criteria for the imposition of a sentence under section 226(3) or 228(2) of the Criminal Justice Act 2003 would be met [ie the assessment of dangerousness], the court must commit the offender in custody or on bail to the Crown Court for sentence in accordance with section 5A (1) below.

(3) Where the court commits a person under subsection (2) above, section 6 below (which enables a magistrates' court, where it commits a person under this section in respect of an offence, also to commit him to the Crown Court to be dealt with in respect of certain other offences) shall apply accordingly.

(4) Nothing in this section shall prevent the court from committing a specified offence to the Crown Court for sentence under section 3B above if the provisions of that section are satisfied.

(5) In this section, references to a specified offence are to a specified offence within the meaning of section 224 of the Criminal Justice Act 2003.

Given the changes made by the Criminal Justice and Immigration Act 2008, a court will have a much wider discretion when considering imposing extended sentences and sentences of detention for public protection. It is likely, therefore, that advocates will be able to persuade a youth court to retain jurisdiction in a great many more cases.

The Sentencing Guidelines Council has issued this general guidance:

> The court should be particularly rigorous before concluding that a youth is a dangerous offender. When assessing likely future conduct and whether it may give rise to a significant risk of serious harm, the court should consider the offender's level of maturity and that he or she may change and develop in a shorter period of time than an adult.
>
> When assessing the risk of the offender committing further specified offences, a young person is less likely than an adult to have an extensive criminal record. Accordingly, when preparing a pre-sentence report, the Youth Offending Team looks not only at the offender's previous convictions but also at any evidence of violence or sexual aggression at home, at school or amongst the offender's peer group that may not have resulted in a conviction.
>
> The Youth Justice Board anticipates that normally the court would find a youth to be a dangerous offender only if he or she was assessed in a pre-sentence report to pose a very high risk of serious harm or, in a small number of cases and due to specific circumstances, a high risk of serious harm. However, the court is not bound by the assessment of risk in the pre-sentence report; it does not follow automatically that, because an offender has been assessed as posing a high risk or very high risk of serious harm, he or she is a dangerous offender.

D9.3 **Specified offences**

Specified offences are those listed in Schedule 15 to the Criminal Justice Act 2003:

Criminal Justice Act 2003, Sch 15, Part 1

Part 1: Specified violent offences

1. Manslaughter.
2. Kidnapping.
3. False imprisonment.
4. An offence under section 4 of the Offences against the Person Act 1861 (c 100) (soliciting murder).
5. An offence under section 16 of that Act (threats to kill).
6. An offence under section 18 of that Act (wounding with intent to cause grievous bodily harm).
7. An offence under section 20 of that Act (malicious wounding).
8. An offence under section 21 of that Act (attempting to choke, suffocate, or strangle in order to commit or assist in committing an indictable offence).
9. An offence under section 22 of that Act (using chloroform etc to commit or assist in the committing of any indictable offence).
10. An offence under section 23 of that Act (maliciously administering poison etc so as to endanger life or inflict grievous bodily harm).
11. An offence under section 27 of that Act (abandoning children).
12. An offence under section 28 of that Act (causing bodily injury by explosives).
13. An offence under section 29 of that Act (using explosives etc with intent to do grievous bodily harm).
14. An offence under section 30 of that Act (placing explosives with intent to do bodily injury).
15. An offence under section 31 of that Act (setting spring guns etc with intent to do grievous bodily harm).
16. An offence under section 32 of that Act (endangering the safety of railway passengers).
17. An offence under section 35 of that Act (injuring persons by furious driving).
18. An offence under section 37 of that Act (assaulting officer preserving wreck).
19. An offence under section 38 of that Act (assault with intent to resist arrest).
20. An offence under section 47 of that Act (assault occasioning actual bodily harm).
21. An offence under section 2 of the Explosive Substances Act 1883 (c 3) (causing explosion likely to endanger life or property).
22. An offence under section 3 of that Act (attempt to cause explosion, or making or keeping explosive with intent to endanger life or property).
23. An offence under section 1 of the Infant Life (Preservation) Act 1929 (c 34) (child destruction).
24. An offence under section 1 of the Children and Young Persons Act 1933 (c 12) (cruelty to children).

---

25. An offence under section 1 of the Infanticide Act 1938 (c 36) (infanticide).
26. An offence under section 16 of the Firearms Act 1968 (c 27) (possession of firearm with intent to endanger life).
27. An offence under section 16A of that Act (possession of firearm with intent to cause fear of violence).
28. An offence under section 17(1) of that Act (use of firearm to resist arrest).
29. An offence under section 17(2) of that Act (possession of firearm at time of committing or being arrested for offence specified in Schedule 1 to that Act).
30. An offence under section 18 of that Act (carrying a firearm with criminal intent).
31. An offence under section 8 of the Theft Act 1968 (c 60) (robbery or assault with intent to rob).
32. An offence under section 9 of that Act of burglary with intent to— inflict grievous bodily harm on a person, or do unlawful damage to a building or anything in it.
33. An offence under section 10 of that Act (aggravated burglary).
34. An offence under section 12A of that Act (aggravated vehicle-taking) involving an accident which caused the death of any person.
35. An offence of arson under section 1 of the Criminal Damage Act 1971 (c 48).
36. An offence under section 1(2) of that Act (destroying or damaging property) other than an offence of arson.
37. An offence under section 1 of the Taking of Hostages Act 1982 (c 28) (hostage-taking).
38. An offence under section 1 of the Aviation Security Act 1982 (c 36) (hijacking).
39. An offence under section 2 of that Act (destroying, damaging or endangering safety of aircraft).
40. An offence under section 3 of that Act (other acts endangering or likely to endanger safety of aircraft).
41. An offence under section 4 of that Act (offences in relation to certain dangerous articles).
42. An offence under section 127 of the Mental Health Act 1983 (c 20) (ill-treatment of patients).
43. An offence under section 1 of the Prohibition of Female Circumcision Act 1985 (c 38) (prohibition of female circumcision).
44. An offence under section 1 of the Public Order Act 1986 (c 64) (riot).
45. An offence under section 2 of that Act (violent disorder).
46. An offence under section 3 of that Act (affray).
47. An offence under section 134 of the Criminal Justice Act 1988 (c 33) (torture).
48. An offence under section 1 of the Road Traffic Act 1988 (c 52) (causing death by dangerous driving).
49. An offence under section 3A of that Act (causing death by careless driving when under influence of drink or drugs).
50. An offence under section 1 of the Aviation and Maritime Security Act 1990 (c 31) (endangering safety at aerodromes).
51. An offence under section 9 of that Act (hijacking of ships).

52. An offence under section 10 of that Act (seizing or exercising control of fixed platforms).
53. An offence under section 11 of that Act (destroying fixed platforms or endangering their safety).
54. An offence under section 12 of that Act (other acts endangering or likely to endanger safe navigation).
55. An offence under section 13 of that Act (offences involving threats).
56. An offence under Part II of the Channel Tunnel (Security) Order 1994 (SI 1994/570) (offences relating to Channel Tunnel trains and the tunnel system).
57. An offence under section 4 of the Protection from Harassment Act 1997 (c 40) (putting people in fear of violence).
58. An offence under section 29 of the Crime and Disorder Act 1998 (c 37) (racially or religiously aggravated assaults).
59. An offence falling within section 31(1) (a) or (b) of that Act (racially or religiously aggravated offences under section 4 or 4A of the Public Order Act 1986 (c 64)).
60. An offence under section 51 or 52 of the International Criminal Court Act 2001 (c 17) (genocide, crimes against humanity, war crimes and related offences), other than one involving murder.
61. An offence under section 1 of the Female Genital Mutilation Act 2003 (c 31) (female genital mutilation).
62. An offence under section 2 of that Act (assisting a girl to mutilate her own genitalia).
63. An offence under section 3 of that Act (assisting a non-UK person to mutilate overseas a girl's genitalia).
64. An offence of—
    (a) aiding, abetting, counselling, procuring or inciting the commission of an offence specified in this Part of this Schedule,
    (b) conspiring to commit an offence so specified, or
    (c) attempting to commit an offence so specified.
65. An attempt to commit murder or a conspiracy to commit murder.

Part 2: Specified sexual offences

66. An offence under section 1 of the Sexual Offences Act 1956 (c 69) (rape).
67. An offence under section 2 of that Act (procurement of woman by threats).
68. An offence under section 3 of that Act (procurement of woman by false pretences).
69. An offence under section 4 of that Act (administering drugs to obtain or facilitate intercourse).
70. An offence under section 5 of that Act (intercourse with girl under 13).
71. An offence under section 6 of that Act (intercourse with girl under 16).
72. An offence under section 7 of that Act (intercourse with a defective).
73. An offence under section 9 of that Act (procurement of a defective).
74. An offence under section 10 of that Act (incest by a man).
75. An offence under section 11 of that Act (incest by a woman).
76. An offence under section 14 of that Act (indecent assault on a woman).
77. An offence under section 15 of that Act (indecent assault on a man).

78. An offence under section 16 of that Act (assault with intent to commit buggery).
79. An offence under section 17 of that Act (abduction of woman by force or for the sake of her property).
80. An offence under section 19 of that Act (abduction of unmarried girl under 18 from parent or guardian).
81. An offence under section 20 of that Act (abduction of unmarried girl under 16 from parent or guardian).
82. An offence under section 21 of that Act (abduction of defective from parent or guardian).
83. An offence under section 22 of that Act (causing prostitution of women).
84. An offence under section 23 of that Act (procuration of girl under 21).
85. An offence under section 24 of that Act (detention of woman in brothel).
86. An offence under section 25 of that Act (permitting girl under 13 to use premises for intercourse).
87. An offence under section 26 of that Act (permitting girl under 16 to use premises for intercourse).
88. An offence under section 27 of that Act (permitting defective to use premises for intercourse).
89. An offence under section 28 of that Act (causing or encouraging the prostitution of, intercourse with or indecent assault on girl under 16).
90. An offence under section 29 of that Act (causing or encouraging prostitution of defective).
91. An offence under section 32 of that Act (soliciting by men).
92. An offence under section 33 of that Act (keeping a brothel).
93. An offence under section 128 of the Mental Health Act 1959 (c 72) (sexual intercourse with patients).
94. An offence under section 1 of the Indecency with Children Act 1960 (c 33) (indecent conduct towards young child).
95. An offence under section 4 of the Sexual Offences Act 1967 (c 60) (procuring others to commit homosexual acts).
96. An offence under section 5 of that Act (living on earnings of male prostitution).
97. An offence under section 9 of the Theft Act 1968 (c 60) of burglary with intent to commit rape.
98. An offence under section 54 of the Criminal Law Act 1977 (c 45) (inciting girl under 16 to have incestuous sexual intercourse).
99. An offence under section 1 of the Protection of Children Act 1978 (c 37) (indecent photographs of children).
100. An offence under section 170 of the Customs and Excise Management Act 1979 (c 2) (penalty for fraudulent evasion of duty etc) in relation to goods prohibited to be imported under section 42 of the Customs Consolidation Act 1876 (c 36) (indecent or obscene articles).
101. An offence under section 160 of the Criminal Justice Act 1988 (c 33) (possession of indecent photograph of a child).
102. An offence under section 1 of the Sexual Offences Act 2003 (c 42) (rape).
103. An offence under section 2 of that Act (assault by penetration).
104. An offence under section 3 of that Act (sexual assault).

105. An offence under section 4 of that Act (causing a person to engage in sexual activity without consent).
106. An offence under section 5 of that Act (rape of a child under 13).
107. An offence under section 6 of that Act (assault of a child under 13 by penetration).
108. An offence under section 7 of that Act (sexual assault of a child under 13).
109. An offence under section 8 of that Act (causing or inciting a child under 13 to engage in sexual activity).
110. An offence under section 9 of that Act (sexual activity with a child).
111. An offence under section 10 of that Act (causing or inciting a child to engage in sexual activity).
112. An offence under section 11 of that Act (engaging in sexual activity in the presence of a child).
113. An offence under section 12 of that Act (causing a child to watch a sexual act).
114. An offence under section 13 of that Act (child sex offences committed by children or young persons).
115. An offence under section 14 of that Act (arranging or facilitating commission of a child sex offence).
116. An offence under section 15 of that Act (meeting a child following sexual grooming etc).
117. An offence under section 16 of that Act (abuse of position of trust: sexual activity with a child).
118. An offence under section 17 of that Act (abuse of position of trust: causing or inciting a child to engage in sexual activity).
119. An offence under section 18 of that Act (abuse of position of trust: sexual activity in the presence of a child).
120. An offence under section 19 of that Act (abuse of position of trust: causing a child to watch a sexual act).
121. An offence under section 25 of that Act (sexual activity with a child family member).
122. An offence under section 26 of that Act (inciting a child family member to engage in sexual activity).
123. An offence under section 30 of that Act (sexual activity with a person with a mental disorder impeding choice).
124. An offence under section 31 of that Act (causing or inciting a person with a mental disorder impeding choice to engage in sexual activity).
125. An offence under section 32 of that Act (engaging in sexual activity in the presence of a person with a mental disorder impeding choice).
126. An offence under section 33 of that Act (causing a person with a mental disorder impeding choice to watch a sexual act).
127. An offence under section 34 of that Act (inducement, threat or deception to procure sexual activity with a person with a mental disorder).
128. An offence under section 35 of that Act (causing a person with a mental disorder to engage in or agree to engage in sexual activity by inducement, threat or deception).
129. An offence under section 36 of that Act (engaging in sexual activity in the presence, procured by inducement, threat or deception, of a person with a mental disorder).

130. An offence under section 37 of that Act (causing a person with a mental disorder to watch a sexual act by inducement, threat or deception).
131. An offence under section 38 of that Act (care workers: sexual activity with a person with a mental disorder).
132. An offence under section 39 of that Act (care workers: causing or inciting sexual activity).
133. An offence under section 40 of that Act (care workers: sexual activity in the presence of a person with a mental disorder).
134. An offence under section 41 of that Act (care workers: causing a person with a mental disorder to watch a sexual act).
135. An offence under section 47 of that Act (paying for sexual services of a child).
136. An offence under section 48 of that Act (causing or inciting child prostitution or pornography).
137. An offence under section 49 of that Act (controlling a child prostitute or a child involved in pornography).
138. An offence under section 50 of that Act (arranging or facilitating child prostitution or pornography).
139. An offence under section 52 of that Act (causing or inciting prostitution for gain).
140. An offence under section 53 of that Act (controlling prostitution for gain).
141. An offence under section 57 of that Act (trafficking into the UK for sexual exploitation).
142. An offence under section 58 of that Act (trafficking within the UK for sexual exploitation).
143. An offence under section 59 of that Act (trafficking out of the UK for sexual exploitation).
144. An offence under section 61 of that Act (administering a substance with intent).
145. An offence under section 62 of that Act (committing an offence with intent to commit a sexual offence).
146. An offence under section 63 of that Act (trespass with intent to commit a sexual offence).
147. An offence under section 64 of that Act (sex with an adult relative: penetration).
148. An offence under section 65 of that Act (sex with an adult relative: consenting to penetration).
149. An offence under section 66 of that Act (exposure).
150. An offence under section 67 of that Act (voyeurism).
151. An offence under section 69 of that Act (intercourse with an animal).
152. An offence under section 70 of that Act (sexual penetration of a corpse).
153. An offence of—
    (a) aiding, abetting, counselling, procuring or inciting the commission of an offence specified in this Part of this Schedule,
    (b) conspiring to commit an offence so specified, or
    (c) attempting to commit an offence so specified.

See *Blackstone's Criminal Practice 2012* D24.30

D10 Community Orders and Sentences: General

D10.1 Age requirements

The availability of community orders and sentences for young offenders depends upon the age of the offender:

Age when convicted	10–15 years	16–17 years	18–20 years
Action plan	Yes*	Yes*	No
Attendance centre	Yes*	Yes*	If committed before 4 April 2005
Community orders—CJA 2003	No	No	If committed on or after 4 April 2005
Community punishment	No	Yes*	If committed before 4 April 2005
Community rehabilitation	No	Yes*	If committed before 4 April 2005
Community punishment and rehabilitation	No	Yes*	If committed before 4 April 2005
Curfew	Yes* (maximum 3 months)	Yes* (maximum 3 months)	If committed before 4 April 2005
Drug treatment and testing	No	Yes*	If committed before 4 April 2005
Exclusion order	Yes* (maximum 3 months)	Yes* (maximum 3 months)	If committed before 4 April 2005
Referral order	Yes	Yes	No
Reparation	Yes	Yes	No
Supervision	Yes*	Yes*	No
Youth Rehabiitation Order	Yes	Yes	No

* indicates for an offence prior to 30 November 2009

D10.2 **Criteria**

Section 148 of the Criminal Justice Act 2003 (as amended by the Criminal Justice and Immigration Act 2008) provides:

Criminal Justice Act 2003, s 148

(1) A court must not pass a community sentence on an offender unless it is of the opinion that the offence, or the combination of the offence and one or more offences associated with it, was serious enough to warrant such a sentence.

(2) Where a court passes a community sentence which consists of or includes a community order—

    (a) the particular requirement or requirements forming part of the community order must be such as, in the opinion of the court, is, or taken together are, the most suitable for the offender, and

    (b) the restrictions on liberty imposed by the order must be such as in the opinion of the court are commensurate with the seriousness of the offence, or the combination of the offence and one or more offences associated with it.

(2A) Subsection (2) is subject to paragraph 3(4) of Schedule 1 to the Criminal Justice and Immigration Act 2008 (youth rehabilitation order with intensive supervision and surveillance).

(3) Where a court passes a community sentence which consists of or includes one or more youth community orders—

    (a) the particular order or orders forming part of the sentence must be such as, in the opinion of the court, is, or taken together are, the most suitable for the offender, and

    (b) the restrictions on liberty imposed by the order or orders must be such as in the opinion of the court are commensurate with the seriousness of the offence, or the combination of the offence and one or more offences associated with it.

(4) Subsections (1) and (2)(b) have effect subject to section 151(2).

(5) The fact that by virtue of any provision of this section—

    (a) a community sentence may be passed in relation to an offence; or

    (b) particular restrictions on liberty may be imposed by a community order or youth rehabilitation order,

does not require a court to pass such a sentence or to impose those restrictions.

Section 10 of the Criminal Justice and Immigration Act 2008 clarifies the courts' sentencing powers to make it clear that a court is not required to impose a community sentence in cases where the offence is serious enough to justify such a sentence. The practical effect of this is to give courts wider discretion to impose financial penalties. Section 11 of the Criminal Justice and Immigration Act 2008 inserted a new section 150A into the Criminal Justice Act 2003. The effect of this provision is to restrict community orders for those aged 18 or above to offences that are punishable with imprisonment:

Criminal Justice Act 2003, s 150A

(1) The power to make a community order is only exercisable in respect of an offence if—
   (a) the offence is punishable with imprisonment; or
   (b) in any other case, section 151(2) confers power to make such an order.
(2) For the purposes of this section and section 151 an offence triable either way that was tried summarily is to be regarded as punishable with imprisonment only if it is so punishable by the sentencing court (and for this purpose section 148(1) is to be disregarded).

D10.3 Reports

The court must obtain a report unless the court is of the view that one is unnecessary. In a case where the offender is aged under 18, the court must not determine a report unnecessary unless:

• there exists a previous pre-sentence report obtained in respect of the offender; and
• the court has had regard to the information contained in that report, or, if there is more than one such report, the most recent report (Criminal Justice Act 2003, s 156(5)).

For a person aged under 18 years the report must be in writing.

It should be noted, however, that no custodial sentence or community sentence is invalidated by the failure of a court to obtain and consider a pre-sentence report (s 156(6)).

D10.4 Sentencing guidelines: general

The Council's guideline provides that the seriousness of the offence should be the initial factor in determining which requirements to include in a community order. It establishes three sentencing ranges within the community order band based on offence seriousness (low, medium, and high), and identifies non-exhaustive examples of requirements that might be appropriate in each. These are set out below. The examples focus on punishment in the community; other requirements of a rehabilitative nature may be more appropriate in some cases.

The particular requirements imposed within the range must be suitable for the individual offender and will be influenced by a wide range of factors, including the stated purpose(s) of the sentence, the risk of reoffending, the ability of the offender to comply, and the availability of the requirements in the local area. Sentencers must ensure that the sentence strikes the right balance between proportionality and suitability. The resulting restriction on liberty must be a proportionate response to the offence that was committed.

Low	Medium	High
Offences only just cross community order threshold, where the seriousness of the offence or the nature of the offender's record means that a discharge or fine is inappropriate.	Offences that obviously fall within the community order band.	Offences only just fall below the custody threshold or the custody threshold is crossed but a community order is more appropriate in the circumstances.
In general, only one requirement will be appropriate and the length may be curtailed if additional requirements are necessary.		More intensive sentences which combine two or more requirements may be appropriate.
Suitable requirements might include: • 40–80 hours unpaid work • curfew requirement within the lowest range (eg up to 12 hours per day for a few weeks) • exclusion requirement, without electronic monitoring, for a few months • prohibited activity requirement • attendance centre requirement (where available).	Suitable requirements might include: • greater number of hours of unpaid work (eg 80–150 hours) • curfew requirement within the middle range (eg up to 12 hours per day for 2–3 months) • exclusion requirement lasting in the region of 6 months • prohibited activity requirement.	Suitable requirements might include: • 150–300 hours unpaid work • activity requirement up to the maximum of 60 days • curfew requirement up to 12 hours per day for 4–6 months • exclusion order lasting in the region of 12 months.

D10.5 Community order made after long remand in custody

It is not uncommon in a magistrates' court for the offender to have served time on remand equivalent to the maximum custodial sentence available. Some courts, instead of imposing a custodial sentence that allows for immediate release, go on to sentence the offender to a community penalty, effectively visiting upon the offender a greater punishment than is deserved for the crime. In *R v Hemmings* [2008] 1 Cr App R (S) 106 the court held:

A sentence of a community order, and all the more so one coupled with requirements which have a real impact on the offender's liberty, is a form of punishment. It does not seem to us to be right that the appellant should receive a substantial further punishment in circumstances where he has already received what was in practice the maximum punishment by way of imprisonment which the law could have imposed. That reasoning seems to

us to be in line with the reasoning in [earlier cases where] . . . the court took
the course of imposing a conditional discharge.

The court went on to impose a conditional discharge that expired
immediately upon sentence to ensure that the appellant could not
fall foul of the consequences of any breach of the order. In *R v Rakib*
[2011] EWCA Crim 870 the court, considering *Hemmings*, held that
time spent in custody was not a determinative factor and the rehabilitative aims of sentencing (s 142(1) of the Criminal Justice Act 2003)
may in some cases justify a community penalty even if the offender
had served on remand the equivalent of the maximum custodial
sentence. See **D45.2** for the position in relation to costs.

D10.6 Requirements

When imposing requirements on the offender as part of the community order, a court should balance the requirements, or combination of requirements, with the offender's personal circumstances, and
avoid conflict with work, schooling, or religious beliefs.

D10.7 Breach

Schedule 8 to the Criminal Justice Act 2003 details the consequences
that flow from breach. Note that the 2003 Act only applies to community orders made for offences committed on or after 4 April 2005.
The court has only three options:

1. make the offender subject to more onerous community requirements; or
2. resentence the offender if the order was made by a magistrates'
   court. The court can deal with him in any manner in which it
   could deal with him if he had just been convicted by the court of
   the offence. Wilful and persistent breach by an offender aged at
   least 18 years may result in imprisonment for a period not exceeding six months even if the offence does not otherwise carry imprisonment, or the general requirements for the passing of a custodial
   sentence are not met (Sch 8 para 9(c)); or
3. if the order was made in the Crown Court, commit the offender to
   that court.

When dealing with the offender, a court must consider and take into
account the level of compliance with the original order (if any).

If a person breaches an order that does not already include an unpaid
work requirement, and the court is minded to impose such a requirement, the minimum hours to be worked shall be 20 (Criminal Justice
and Immigration Act 2008, s 38).

  See *Blackstone's Criminal Practice 2012* **E8**

D11 Community Punishment and Rehabilitation Orders

D11.1 Age requirements

Aged at least 16 years. For offenders aged 18 or over, the offence must have been committed before 4 April 2005. For offenders aged 16 or 17 years the offence must have been committed before 30 November 2009.

D11.2 Criteria

A community punishment order and rehabilitation order can be made for any offence that carries imprisonment, provided that the general requirements for the making of a community order are satisfied (see **D10.2**). In addition, the order must be in the interests of securing the rehabilitation of the defendant or protecting the public from harm or further offences. Consent is not necessary for offences committed on or after 1 October 1997.

The court must impose not less than 40 and not more than 100 hours of unpaid work. The supervision period must be between one and three years.

D11.3 Breach

See **D12.3**.

 See *Blackstone's Criminal Practice 2012* **E8**

D12 **Community Punishment Order**

D12.1 **Age requirements**

Aged at least 16 years. For offenders aged 18 or over, the offence must have been committed before 4 April 2005. For offenders aged 16 or 17 years the offence must have been committed before 30 November 2009.

D12.2 **Criteria**

A community punishment order can be made for any offence that carries imprisonment, provided that the general requirements for the making of a community order are satisfied (see **D10.2**). Consent is not necessary for offences committed on or after 1 October 1997. For offenders aged 18–20 years, the court must impose not less than 40 and not more than 240 hours of unpaid work.

D12.3 **Breach**

Breach is dealt with under Schedule 3 to the PCC(S)A 2000. The court has the following options:

1. Impose a fine not exceeding £1,000.
2. Impose a community punishment order (max 60 hours, and any aggregate order not to exceed 240 hours).
3. If the offender is under 21, impose an attendance centre order.
4. Revoke and resentence (but note that committal for sentence would not be an option).

 See *Blackstone's Criminal Practice 2012* **E8**

D13 **Community Rehabilitation Order**

D13.1 **Age requirements**

Aged at least 16 years. For offenders 18 or over, the offence must have been committed before 4 April 2005. For offenders aged 16 or 17 years the offence must have been committed before 30 November 2009.

D13.2 **Criteria**

A community rehabilitation order can be made for any offence that carries imprisonment, provided that the general requirements for the making of a community order are satisfied (see **D10.2**). In addition, the order must be in the interests of securing the rehabilitation of the defendant or protecting the public from harm or further offences. Consent is not necessary for offences committed on or after 1 October 1997.

The supervision period must be between six months and three years. In addition, the court may impose one or more of the following requirements:

Requirement	Notes
Residence	Court must specify period of residence.
Specified activities	Maximum of 60 days attendance (save in the case of defendants convicted of certain sexual offences).
Refraining from specified activities	–
Attendance at a probation centre	Maximum of 60 days attendance (save in the case of defendants convicted of certain sexual offences).
Mental health treatment	The court must receive evidence from an approved doctor that the condition is susceptible to treatment and a hospital order is not required. Defendant must consent.
Drug or alcohol treatment	Defendant must consent.
Drug abstinence	Defendant must be over 18 years on conviction and be dependent on, or have a propensity to misuse Class A drugs (and that has contributed to the offence before the court). Orders in force in pilot areas only: in the case of trigger offences, such a requirement must be imposed with a rehabilitation order.
Curfew	During first six months of the order only, and for between 2–12 hours per day.
Exclusion	Maximum two years' duration.

D13.3 **Breach**

See D12.3.

📖 See *Blackstone's Criminal Practice 2012* **E8**

D14 **Compensation Order**

D14.1 **Age requirements**

Any offender subject to means.

D14.2 **Criteria**

> **Powers of Criminal Courts (Sentencing) Act 2000, s 130(1)–(10)**
>
> (1) A court by or before which a person is convicted of an offence, instead of or in addition to dealing with him in any other way, may, on application or otherwise, make an order (in this Act referred to as a 'compensation order') requiring him—
>
>   (a) to pay compensation for any personal injury, loss or damage resulting from that offence or any other offence which is taken into consideration by the court in determining sentence; or
>
>   (b) to make payments for funeral expenses or bereavement in respect of a death resulting from any such offence, other than a death due to an accident arising out of the presence of a motor vehicle on a road; but this is subject to the following provisions of this section and to section 131 below.
>
> (2) Where the person is convicted of an offence the sentence for which is fixed by law or falls to be imposed under 110(2) or 111(2) above, section 51A(2) of the Firearms Act 1968, section 225, 226, 227 or 228 of the Criminal Justice Act 2003 or section 29(4) or (6) of the Violent Crime Reduction Act 2006, subsection (1) above shall have effect as if the words 'instead of or' were omitted.
>
> (3) A court shall give reasons, on passing sentence, if it does not make a compensation order in a case where this section empowers it to do so.
>
> (4) Compensation under subsection (1) above shall be of such amount as the court considers appropriate, having regard to any evidence and to any representations that are made by or on behalf of the accused or the prosecutor.
>
> (5) In the case of an offence under the Theft Act 1968 or Fraud Act 2006, where the property in question is recovered, any damage to the property occurring while it was out of the owner's possession shall be treated for the purposes of subsection (1) above as having resulted from the offence, however and by whomever the damage was caused.
>
> (6) A compensation order may only be made in respect of injury, loss or damage (other than loss suffered by a person's dependants in consequence of his death) which was due to an accident arising out of the presence of a motor vehicle on a road, if—
>
>   (a) it is in respect of damage which is treated by subsection (5) above as resulting from an offence under the Theft Act 1968 or Fraud Act 2006; or

(b) it is in respect of injury, loss or damage as respects which—

    (i) the offender is uninsured in relation to the use of the vehicle; and

    (ii) compensation is not payable under any arrangements to which the Secretary of State is a party.

(7) Where a compensation order is made in respect of injury, loss or damage due to an accident arising out of the presence of a motor vehicle on a road, the amount to be paid may include an amount representing the whole or part of any loss of or reduction in preferential rates of insurance attributable to the accident.

(8) A vehicle the use of which is exempted from insurance by section 144 of the Road Traffic Act 1988 is not uninsured for the purposes of subsection (6) above.

(9) A compensation order in respect of funeral expenses may be made for the benefit of any one who incurred the expenses.

(10) A compensation order in respect of bereavement may be made only for the benefit of a person for whose benefit a claim for damages for bereavement could be made under section 1A of the Fatal Accidents Act 1976; and the amount of compensation in respect of bereavement shall not exceed the amount for the time being specified in section 1A (3) of that Act.

D14.3 **Principles**

A magistrates' court can order compensation up to a maximum of £5,000 for each offence, and may also award compensation in relation to offences taken into consideration (but may not exceed the total arrived at by multiplying offences × £5,000).

In relation to motor vehicle damage the maximum payable will generally be the excess not paid by the Motor Insurer's Bureau (currently £300), save where it is in respect to a vehicle stolen or taken without consent and there is damage to that vehicle, or the claim is not covered by the MIB.

If the amount of compensation is not agreed, the prosecution must be in a position to call evidence. In cases where the loss is unclear or subject to complex argument, the best course of action is to leave the matter to the civil courts to resolve (*R v Horsham Justices, ex p Richards* [1985] 2 All ER 1114); the court of appeal did, however, uphold a compensation order made in respect of injuries occasioned as a result of health and safety related failures, in the sum of £90,000 (*R (Health and Safety Executive) v Pola*, unreported, 7 April 2009). In *R v Bewick* [2007] EWCA Crim 3297 the court observed that it would generally not be appropriate to resolve compensation applications where it was necessary to hear from a third party in evidence. A court can, however, make a common sense determination (eg £50 for a small broken window). Where a person receives state benefit over a period of time as a result of a false declaration it is not wrong to make a confiscation order in the sum of the full amount paid to the fraudulent claimant (*Revenue and Customs Prosecutions Office v Duffy* [2008] EWHC 848 (Admin)).

D14.4 Assessment of means

In determining whether to make a compensation order against any person, and in determining the amount to be paid by any person under such an order, the court shall have regard to his means so far as they appear or are known to the court. An order made in the absence of a means enquiry is at risk of being ruled unlawful (*R v Gray* [2011] EWCA 225).

Where the court considers:

- that it would be appropriate both to impose a fine and to make a compensation order; but
- that the offender has insufficient means to pay both an appropriate fine and appropriate compensation, the court shall give preference to compensation (though it may impose a fine as well).

Save where a sentence of custody impacts on the offender's ability to pay, there is nothing wrong in principle with imposing compensation in addition to a custodial penalty.

D14.5 Suggested levels of compensation

The Magistrates' Court Sentencing Guidelines set out the following scales for the award of compensation:

Physical injury		
Type of injury	**Description**	**Starting point**
Graze	Depending on size	Up to £75
Bruise	Depending on size	Up to £100
Cut: no permanent scar	Depending on size and whether stitched	£100–500
Black eye		£125
Eye	Blurred or double vision lasting up to 6 weeks	Up to £1,000
	Blurred or double vision lasting for 6–13 weeks	£1,000
	Blurred or double vision lasting for more than 13 weeks (recovery expected)	£1,750
Brain	Concussion lasting one week	£1,500
Nose	Undisplaced fracture of nasal bone	£1,000

D14 Compensation Order

	Displaced fracture requiring manipulation	£2,000
	Deviated nasal septum requiring septoplasty	£2,000

Physical injury		
Type of injury	Description	Starting point
Loss of non-front tooth	Depending on cosmetic effect	£1,250
Loss of front tooth		£1,750
Facial scar	Minor disfigurement (permanent)	£1,500
Arm	Fractured humerus, radius, ulna (substantial recovery)	£3,300
Shoulder	Dislocated (substantial recovery)	£1,750
Wrist	Dislocated/fractured—including scaphoid fracture (substantial recovery)	£3,300
	Fractured—colles type (substantial recovery)	£4,400
Sprained wrist, ankle	Disabling for up to 6 weeks	Up to £1,000
	Disabling for 6–13 weeks	£1,000
	Disabling for more than 13 weeks	£2,500
Finger	Fractured finger other than index finger (substantial recovery)	£1,000
	Fractured index finger (substantial recovery)	£1,750
	Fractured thumb (substantial recovery)	£2,000
Leg	Fractured fibula (substantial recovery)	£2,500
	Fractured femur, tibia (substantial recovery)	£3,800
Abdomen	Injury requiring laprotomy	£3,800

Mental injury	
Description	Starting point
Temporary mental anxiety (including terror, shock, distress), not medically verified	Up to £1,000
Disabling mental anxiety, lasting more than 6 weeks, medically verified	£1,000
Disability mental illness, lasting up to 28 weeks, confirmed by psychiatric diagnosis	£2,500

Physical and sexual abuse		
Type of abuse	**Description**	**Starting point**
Physical abuse of adult	Intermittent physical assaults resulting in accumulation of healed wounds, burns or scalds, but with no appreciable disfigurement	£2,000
Physical abuse of child	Isolated or intermittent assault(s) resulting in weals, hair pulled from scalp etc	£1,000
	Intermittent physical assaults resulting in accumulation of healed wounds, burns, or scalds, but with no appreciable disfigurement	£2,000
Sexual abuse of adult	Non-penetrative indecent physical acts over clothing	£1,000
	Non-penetrative indecent act(s) under clothing	£2,000
Sexual abuse of child (under 18)	Non-penetrative indecent physical act(s) over clothing	£1,000
	Non-penetrative frequent assaults over clothing or non-penetrative indecent act under clothing	£2,000
	Repetitive indecent acts under clothing	£3,300

 See *Blackstone's Criminal Practice 2012* **E16**

D15 **Conditional and Absolute Discharge**

D15.1 **Age requirements**

Any offender.

D15.2 **Criteria**

An order can be imposed where it is inexpedient to inflict any punishment. A conditional discharge can be for up to three years. Only the orders mentioned in section 12(7) of the PCC(S)A 2000 can be made alongside a discharge and therefore a magistrates' court should not commit an offender to the Crown Court for the purposes of activating the confiscation regime under the Proceeds of Crime Act 2002 where a discharge is considered the proper sentence (see *R v Clarke* [2009] EWCA Crim 1074).

> ### **Powers of Criminal Courts (Sentencing) Act 2000, s 12(7)**
>
> (7) Nothing in this section shall be construed as preventing a court, on discharging an offender absolutely or conditionally in respect of any offence, from making an order for costs against the offender or imposing any disqualification on him or from making in respect of the offence an order under section 130, 143 or 148 below (compensation orders, deprivation orders and restitution orders).

Where a person who has received a warning under section 65 of the Crime and Disorder Act 1998 is convicted of an offence committed within two years of the warning, the court by or before which he is so convicted:

(a) shall not impose a conditional discharge in respect of the offence unless it is of the opinion that there are exceptional circumstances relating to the offence or the offender which justify its doing so; and

(b) where it does so, shall state in open court that it is of that opinion and why it is.

If a person commits an offence during the life of a conditional discharge he may be resentenced for that original offence, even if the period of discharge has expired at the date of sentence. The offender will be sentenced with reference to his age at the date of sentence, not the date of the previous offence, and can be sentenced in any way as if he had just been convicted of the offence. If the conditional discharge was imposed by the Crown Court the offender can be committed to that court for resentence.

There is no requirement to resentence and a court could sentence for a new offence and leave the conditional discharge in place if it saw fit to do so.

 See *Blackstone's Criminal Practice 2012* E12

D16 **Confiscation, Proceeds of Crime Act 2002**

D16.1 **Criteria**

A magistrates' court has no power to make a confiscation order. However, in some cases it will be appropriate to retain jurisdiction for an offence, but find that the prosecution or court later considers that confiscation proceedings are appropriate (a common example is in relation to counterfeit goods). A magistrates' court should not commit an offender to the Crown Court for the purposes of activating the confiscation regime under the Proceeds of Crime Act 2002 where a discharge is considered the proper sentence (see *R v Clarke* [2009] EWCA Crim 1074 and **D15** above).

In the event that the prosecution wish to proceed with confiscation proceedings the court *must* commit the offender to the Crown Court for sentence.

Proceeds of Crime Act 2002, s 70

(1) This section applies if—
  (a) a defendant is convicted of an offence by a magistrates' court, and
  (b) the prosecutor asks the court to commit the defendant to the Crown Court with a view to a confiscation order being considered under section 6.
(2) In such a case the magistrates' court—
  (a) must commit the defendant to the Crown Court in respect of the offence, and
  (b) may commit him to the Crown Court in respect of any other offence falling within subsection (3).
(3) An offence falls within this subsection if—
  (a) the defendant has been convicted of it by the magistrates' court or any other court, and
  (b) the magistrates' court has power to deal with him in respect of it.
(4) If a committal is made under this section in respect of an offence or offences—
  (a) section 6 applies accordingly, and
  (b) the committal operates as a committal of the defendant to be dealt with by the Crown Court in accordance with section 71.
(5) If a committal is made under this section in respect of an offence for which (apart from this section) the magistrates' court could have committed the defendant for sentence under section 3(2) of the Sentencing Act (offences triable either way) the court must state whether it would have done so.
(6) A committal under this section may be in custody or on bail.

Particular note should be made of section 70(5), with the court being invited to confirm that it would not otherwise have committed for sentence. Later clarification can be relied upon and it is therefore essential that a full contemporaneous note is taken (*R v Blakeburn* [2007] EWCA Crim 1803).

 See *Blackstone's Criminal Practice 2012* E19

D17 **Custodial Sentences**

D17.1 Age requirements

See below.

D17.2 Criteria

The court must not pass a custodial sentence unless it is of the opinion that the offence, or the combination of the offence and one or more offences associated with it, was so serious that neither a fine alone nor a community sentence can be justified for the offence.

Nothing prevents the court from passing a custodial sentence on the offender if:

- he fails to express his willingness to comply with a requirement which is proposed by the court to be included in a community order and which requires an expression of such willingness; or
- he fails to comply with an order under section 161(2) (pre-sentence drug testing).

The custodial sentence must be for the shortest term (not exceeding the permitted maximum) that in the opinion of the court is commensurate with the seriousness of the offence, or the combination of the offence and one or more offences associated with it.

Type of sentence	Age requirement	Notes
Detention and training order	10–12 years (not in force) 12–14 years—only if a persistent offender 15–17 years	See **D22**. Maximum 24 months, subject to any statutory maximum.
Detention in young offender institution	18–20 years	Minimum sentence of 21 days. Maximum 6 months for any one offence. Maximum 12 months for two or more either way offences. Subject always to the statutory maximum for the offences in question. See **D24**.
Imprisonment	21 years+	Minimum 5 days save for imprisonment imposed under Magistrates' Courts Act 1980, ss 135 and 136. Maximum 6 months for any one offence. Maximum 12 months for two or more either way offences. Subject always to the statutory maximum for the offences in question.

 See *Blackstone's Criminal Practice 2012* **E2**

D18 Dangerous Offenders

D18.1 Criteria

Generally speaking, the dangerous offender provisions are only of concern to the magistrates' court when determining venue, and can raise particular difficulties in relation to young offenders in the youth court (for which see **D9**).

The Administrative Court in *Crown Prosecution Service v South East Surrey Youth Court* [2006] 2 Cr App R (S) 26 held that the following provisions should apply:

(i) the policy of the legislature is that those who are under 18 should, wherever possible, be tried in a Youth Court, which is best designed for their specific needs;

(ii) the guidance given by the Court of Appeal, in particular in paragraph 17 of the judgment in *Lang & Ors* [2006] 2 Cr App R (S) 3, particularly in (iv) in relation to non-serious specified offences;

(iii) the need, in relation to those under 18, to be particularly rigorous before concluding that there is a significant risk of serious harm by the commission of further offences: such a conclusion is unlikely to be appropriate in the absence of a pre-sentence report following assessment by a young offender team;

(iv) in most cases where a non-serious specified offence is charged, an assessment of dangerousness will not be appropriate until after conviction, when, if the dangerousness criteria are met, the defendant can be committed to the Crown Court for sentence;

(v) when a youth under 18 is jointly charged with an adult, an exercise of judgement will be called for by the Youth Court when assessing the competing presumptions in favour of (a) joint trial of those jointly charged and (b) the trial of youths in the Youth Court. Factors relevant to that judgement will include the age and maturity of the youth, the comparative culpability in relation to the offence and the previous convictions of the two, and whether the trial can be severed without either injustice or undue inconvenience to witnesses.

Section 17 of the Criminal Justice and Immigration Act 2008 removed the presumption of dangerousness in relation to defendants facing a specified offence who had previously been convicted of a specified offence (the so-called 'two-strikes' rule).

In relation to adults the issues are usually so cut and dried that recourse to case law is almost unheard of. The general framework for the dangerous offender provisions in relation to adults can be found at <http://http://www.sentencingcouncil.org.uk>.

 See *Blackstone's Criminal Practice 2012* **E4**

D19 **Deferment of Sentence**

D19.1 **Age requirements**

None.

D19.2 **Criteria**

The magistrates' court can defer sentence, on one occasion, for a maximum period of six months to enable the court to assess the offender's capacity to change or carry out reparation to the victim. Such cases are simply adjourned (not on bail), and a warrant can be issued (PCC(S) A 2000, s 1(7)(b)) if the offender fails to attend for sentence (the court also has the option of issuing a summons and the court should always be invited to try this option first). If the offender reoffends before the period of deferment has expired he may be dealt with for the deferred matter.

The power to defer shall be exercisable only if:

(a) the offender consents;
(b) the offender undertakes to comply with any requirements as to his conduct during the period of the deferment that the court considers it appropriate to impose; and
(c) the court is satisfied, having regard to the nature of the offence and the character and circumstances of the offender, that it would be in the interests of justice to exercise the power.

See **D19.4** for legislative framework.

D19.3 **Sentencing Council Guideline on use of deferred sentences**

Use of deferred sentences:

> Under the new framework, there is a wider range of sentencing options open to the courts, including the increased availability of suspended sentences, and deferred sentences are likely to be used in very limited circumstances. A deferred sentence enables the court to review the conduct of the defendant before passing sentence, having first prescribed certain requirements. It also provides several opportunities for an offender to have some influence as to the sentence passed—
> a) it tests the commitment of the offender not to re-offend;
> b) it gives the offender an opportunity to do something where progress can be shown within a short period;
> c) it provides the offender with an opportunity to behave or refrain from behaving in a particular way that will be relevant to sentence.

Given the new power to require undertakings and the ability to enforce those undertakings before the end of the period of deferral, the decision to defer sentence should be predominantly for a small group of cases at either the custody threshold or the community sentence threshold where the sentencer feels that there would be particular value in giving the offender the opportunities listed because, if the offender complies with the requirements, a different sentence will be justified at the end of the deferment period.

This could be a community sentence instead of a custodial sentence or a fine or discharge instead of a community sentence. It may, rarely, enable a custodial sentence to be suspended rather than imposed immediately.

> The use of deferred sentences should be predominantly for a small group of cases close to a significant threshold where, should the defendant be prepared to adapt his behaviour in a way clearly specified by the sentencer, the court may be prepared to impose a lesser sentence.

A court may impose any conditions during the period of deferment that it considers appropriate. These could be specific requirements as set out in the provisions for community sentences, or requirements that are drawn more widely. These should be specific, measurable conditions so that the offender knows exactly what is required and the court can assess compliance; the restriction on liberty should be limited to ensure that the offender has a reasonable expectation of being able to comply whilst maintaining his or her social responsibilities.

Given the need for clarity in the mind of the offender and the possibility of sentence by another court, the court should give a clear indication (and make a written record) of the type of sentence it would be minded to impose if it had not decided to defer and ensure that the offender understands the consequences of failure to comply with the court's wishes during the deferral period.

> When deferring sentence, the sentencer must make clear the consequence of not complying with any requirements and should indicate the type of sentence it would be minded to impose. Sentencers should impose specific, measurable conditions that do not involve a serious restriction on liberty.

D19.4 Legislation

Sections 1-1D of the Powers of Criminal Courts (Sentencing) Act 2000 provide:

Powers of Criminal Courts (Sentencing) Act 2000, ss 1, 1A(1)–(2), 1B, 1C, and 1D

1 Deferment of sentence

(1) The Crown Court or a magistrates' court may defer passing sentence on an offender for the purpose of enabling the court, or any other court to which it falls to deal with him, to have regard in dealing with him to—

    (a) his conduct after conviction (including, where appropriate, the making by him of reparation for his offence); or

    (b) any change in his circumstances;

but this is subject to subsections (3) and (4) below.

(2) Without prejudice to the generality of subsection (1) above, the matters to which the court to which it falls to deal with the offender may have regard by virtue of paragraph (a) of that subsection include the extent to which the offender has complied with any requirements imposed under subsection (3)(b) below.

(3) The power conferred by subsection (1) above shall be exercisable only if—

    (a) the offender consents;

    (b) the offender undertakes to comply with any requirements as to his conduct during the period of the deferment that the court considers it appropriate to impose; and

    (c) the court is satisfied, having regard to the nature of the offence and the character and circumstances of the offender, that it would be in the interests of justice to exercise the power.

(4) Any deferment under this section shall be until such date as may be specified by the court, not being more than six months after the date on which the deferment is announced by the court; and, subject to section 1D(3) below, where the passing of sentence has been deferred under this section it shall not be further so deferred.

(5) Where a court has under this section deferred passing sentence on an offender, it shall forthwith give a copy of the order deferring the passing of sentence and setting out any requirements imposed under subsection (3)(b) above—

    (a) to the offender,

    (b) . . .

(6) Notwithstanding any enactment, a court which under this section defers passing sentence on an offender shall not on the same occasion remand him.

(7) Where—

    (a) a court which under this section has deferred passing sentence on an offender proposes to deal with him on the date originally specified by the court, or

---

   (b) the offender does not appear on the day so specified, the court may issue a summons requiring him to appear before the court at a time and place specified in the summons, or may issue a warrant to arrest him and bring him before the court at a time and place specified in the warrant.

(8) Nothing in this section or sections 1A to 1D below shall affect—

   (a) the power of the Crown Court to bind over an offender to come up for judgment when called upon; or

   (b) the power of any court to defer passing sentence for any purpose for which it may lawfully do so apart from this section.

1A Further provision about undertakings

(1) Without prejudice to the generality of paragraph (b) of section 1(3) above, the requirements that may be imposed by virtue of that paragraph include requirements as to the residence of the offender during the whole or any part of the period of deferment.

(2) Where an offender has undertaken to comply with any requirements imposed under section 1(3)(b) above the court may appoint—

   (a) an officer of a local probation board or an officer of a provider of probation services, or

   (b) any other person whom the court thinks appropriate, to act as a supervisor in relation to him.

1B Breach of undertakings

(1) A court which under section 1 above has deferred passing sentence on an offender may deal with him before the end of the period of deferment if—

   (a) he appears or is brought before the court under subsection (3) below; and

   (b) the court is satisfied that he has failed to comply with one or more requirements imposed under section 1(3)(b) above in connection with the deferment.

(2) Subsection (3) below applies where—

   (a) a court has under section 1 above deferred passing sentence on an offender;

   (b) the offender undertook to comply with one or more requirements imposed under section 1(3)(b) above in connection with the deferment; and

   (c) a person appointed under section 1A(2) above to act as a supervisor in relation to the offender has reported to the court that the offender has failed to comply with one or more of those requirements.

(3) Where this subsection applies, the court may issue—

   (a) a summons requiring the offender to appear before the court at a time and place specified in the summons; or

   (b) a warrant to arrest him and bring him before the court at a time and place specified in the warrant.

1C Conviction of offence during period of deferment

(1) A court which under section 1 above has deferred passing sentence on an offender may deal with him before the end of the period of deferment if during that period he is convicted in Great Britain of any offence.

(2) Subsection (3) below applies where a court has under section 1 above deferred passing sentence on an offender in respect of one or more offences and during the period of deferment the offender is convicted in England and Wales of any offence ('the later offence').

(3) Where this subsection applies, then (without prejudice to subsection (1) above and whether or not the offender is sentenced for the later offence during the period of deferment), the court which passes sentence on him for the later offence may also, if this has not already been done, deal with him for the offence or offences for which passing of sentence has been deferred, except that—

    (a) the power conferred by this subsection shall not be exercised by a magistrates' court if the court which deferred passing sentence was the Crown Court; and

    (b) the Crown Court, in exercising that power in a case in which the court which deferred passing sentence was a magistrates' court, shall not pass any sentence which could not have been passed by a magistrates' court in exercising that power.

(4) Where a court which under section 1 above has deferred passing sentence on an offender proposes to deal with him by virtue of subsection (1) above before the end of the period of deferment, the court may issue—

    (a) a summons requiring him to appear before the court at a time and place specified in the summons; or

    (b) a warrant to arrest him and bring him before the court at a time and place specified in the warrant.

1D Deferment of sentence: supplementary

(1) In deferring the passing of sentence under section 1 above a magistrates' court shall be regarded as exercising the power of adjourning the trial conferred by section 10(1) of the Magistrates' Courts Act 1980, and accordingly sections 11(1) and 13(1) to (3A) and (5) of that Act (non-appearance of the accused) apply (without prejudice to section 1(7) above) if the offender does not appear on the date specified under section 1(4) above.

(2) Where the passing of sentence on an offender has been deferred by a court ('the original court') under section 1 above, the power of that court under that section to deal with the offender at the end of the period of deferment and any power of that court under section 1B(1) or 1C(1) above, or of any court under section 1C(3) above, to deal with the offender—

    (a) is power to deal with him, in respect of the offence for which passing of sentence has been deferred, in any way in which the original court could have dealt with him if it had not deferred passing sentence; and

    (b) without prejudice to the generality of paragraph (a) above, in the case of a magistrates' court, includes the power conferred by section 3 below to commit him to the Crown Court for sentence.

(3) Where—

    (a) the passing of sentence on an offender in respect of one or more offences has been deferred under section 1 above, and

    (b) a magistrates' court deals with him in respect of the offence or any of the offences by committing him to the Crown Court under section 3 below, the power of the Crown Court to deal with him includes the same power to defer passing sentence on him as if he had just been convicted of the offence or offences on indictment before the court.

(4) Subsection (5) below applies where—

    (a) the passing of sentence on an offender in respect of one or more offences has been deferred under section 1 above;

    (b) it falls to a magistrates' court to determine a relevant matter; and

    (c) a justice of the peace is satisfied—

        (i) that a person appointed under section 1A(2)(b) above to act as a supervisor in relation to the offender is likely to be able to give evidence that may assist the court in determining that matter; and

        (ii) that that person will not voluntarily attend as a witness.

(5) The justice may issue a summons directed to that person requiring him to attend before the court at the time and place appointed in the summons to give evidence.

(6) For the purposes of subsection (4) above a court determines a relevant matter if it—

    (a) deals with the offender in respect of the offence, or any of the offences, for which the passing of sentence has been deferred; or

    (b) determines, for the purposes of section 1B(1)(b) above, whether the offender has failed to comply with any requirements imposed under section 1(3)(b) above.

 See *Blackstone's Criminal Practice 2012* **D20.101–D20.107**

D20 **Deportation, Automatic**

D20.1 **Age requirements**

Applies only to those aged 18 years or over at date of conviction.

D20.2 **Criteria**

Section 32 of the UK Borders Act 2007 provides for the automatic deportation of some offenders sentenced to imprisonment for a period of at least 12 months. The 12 months must be for a single offence, and the Act only applies to those aged 18 or over. Accordingly, this power is not available to a magistrates' court until such time as sentencing powers are increased (a provision in the Criminal Justice Act 2003 that is not yet in force).

 See *Blackstone's Criminal Practice 2012* **E20**

D21 **Deprivation Order**

D21.1 **Age requirements**

None.

D21.2 **Criteria**

Orders of this kind (commonly referred to as 'forfeiture and destruction orders') should not be made without warning the defendant in advance and inviting representations, otherwise they are liable to be quashed on appeal (*R v Ball* [2002] EWCA Crim 2777). The court should not proceed without first ascertaining the value of the property, and should also ensure that an order made against just one offender does not result in an overly disproportionate sentence (*Ball*). The power can be used to forfeit property intended to be used for any offence, not just the particular offence before the court (*R v O'Farrell* [1988] Crim LR 387). Deprivation orders are intended only for straightforward cases involving unencumbered property (*R v Troth* [1980] Crim LR 249).

Powers of Criminal Courts (Sentencing) Act 2000, s 143

(1) Where a person is convicted of an offence and the court by or before which he is convicted is satisfied that any property which has been lawfully seized from him, or which was in his possession or under his control at the time when he was apprehended for the offence or when a summons in respect of it was issued—

    (a) has been used for the purpose of committing, or facilitating the commission of, any offence, or

    (b) was intended by him to be used for that purpose, the court may (subject to subsection (5) below) make an order under this section in respect of that property.

(2) Where a person is convicted of an offence and the offence, or an offence which the court has taken into consideration in determining his sentence, consists of unlawful possession of property which—

    (a) has been lawfully seized from him, or

    (b) was in his possession or under his control at the time when he was apprehended for the offence of which he has been convicted or when a summons in respect of that offence was issued,

the court may (subject to subsection (5) below) make an order under this section in respect of that property.

(3) An order under this section shall operate to deprive the offender of his rights, if any, in the property to which it relates, and the property shall (if not already in their possession) be taken into the possession of the police.

(4) Any power conferred on a court by subsection (1) or (2) above may be

---

exercised—

    (a) whether or not the court also deals with the offender in any other way in respect of the offence of which he has been convicted; and

    (b) without regard to any restrictions on forfeiture in any enactment contained in an Act passed before 29th July 1988.

(5) In considering whether to make an order under this section in respect of any property, a court shall have regard—

    (a) to the value of the property; and

    (b) to the likely financial and other effects on the offender of the making of the order (taken together with any other order that the court contemplates making).

(6) Where a person commits an offence to which this subsection applies by—

    (a) driving, attempting to drive, or being in charge of a vehicle, or

    (b) failing to comply with a requirement made under section 7 or 7A of the Road Traffic Act 1988 (failure to provide specimen for analysis or laboratory test or to give permission for such a test) in the course of an investigation into whether the offender had committed an offence while driving, attempting to drive or being in charge of a vehicle, or

    (c) failing, as the driver of a vehicle, to comply with subsection (2) or (3) of section 170 of the Road Traffic Act 1988 (duty to stop and give information or report accident),

the vehicle shall be regarded for the purposes of subsection (1) above (and section 144(1)(b) below) as used for the purpose of committing the offence (and for the purpose of committing any offence of aiding, abetting, counselling or procuring the commission of the offence).

(7) Subsection (6) above applies to—

    (a) an offence under the Road Traffic Act 1988 which is punishable with imprisonment;

    (b) an offence of manslaughter; and

    (c) an offence under section 35 of the Offences Against the Person Act 1861 (wanton and furious driving).

(8) Facilitating the commission of an offence shall be taken for the purposes of subsection (1) above to include the taking of any steps after it has been committed for the purpose of disposing of any property to which it relates or of avoiding apprehension or detection.

 See *Blackstone's Criminal Practice 2012* **E18**

D22 **Detention and Training Order**

D22.1 **Age requirements**

10–11 years—not in force.

12–14 years—if offender is a persistent offender (see below).

15–17 years.

The relevant age is age at time of commission of the offence, and therefore an offender who turns 18 during the proceedings can receive this order (*Aldis v Director of Public Prosecutions* [2002] 2 Cr App R (S) 88).

D22.2 **Criteria**

A youth court can impose a detention and training order, provided it does not exceed the maximum sentence for the offence, of up to two years duration.

The general conditions justifying a custodial sentence must be met (see **D17.2**), and the sentence must only be expressed in one of the following durations:

4, 6, 8, 10, 12, 18, or 24 months

A court can pass consecutive orders for multiple offences, and make an order consecutive to an existing order. Aggregate orders can be for a term not allowed in respect to a single order (*Norris* (2000) 164 JP 689). For example, a court could sentence an offender to four months for one offence, and ten months consecutive for another, making 14 months in total (but would not be able to sentence to 14 months for a single offence as that is not a permissible single sentence). It follows that a detention and training order cannot be imposed for an offence that carries less than four months' detention.

D22.3 **Persistent offenders**

Previous case law which set out to define who qualified as a persistent offender has been superseded by the youth sentencing guideline at paras 6.3–6.6:

> 6.3 'Persistent offender' is not defined in legislation but has been considered by the Court of Appeal on a number of occasions. However, following the implementation of the 2008 Act, the sentencing framework is different from that when the definition was judicially developed, particularly the greater emphasis on the requirement to use a custodial sentence as 'a measure of last resort'.

6.4 A dictionary definition of 'persistent offender' is 'persisting or having a tendency to persist'; 'persist' is defined as 'to continue firmly or obstinately in a course of action in spite of difficulty or opposition'.

6.5 In determining whether an offender is a persistent offender for these purposes, a court should consider the simple test of whether the young person is one who persists in offending:

i) in most circumstances, the normal expectation is that the offender will have had some contact with authority in which the offending conduct was challenged before being classed as 'persistent'; a finding of persistence in offending may be derived from information about previous convictions but may also arise from orders which require an admission or finding of guilt – these include reprimands, final warnings, restorative justice disposals and conditional cautions; since they do not require such an admission, penalty notices for disorder are unlikely to be sufficiently reliable;

ii) a young offender is certainly likely to be found to be persistent (and, in relation to a custodial sentence, the test of being a measure of last resort is most likely to be satisfied) where the offender has been convicted of, or made subject to a pre-court disposal that involves an admission or finding of guilt in relation to, imprisonable offences on at least 3 occasions in the past 12 months.

6.6 Even where a young person is found to be a persistent offender, a court is not obliged to impose the custodial sentence or youth rehabilitation order with intensive supervision and surveillance or fostering that becomes available as a result of that finding. The other tests continue to apply and it is clear that Parliament expects custodial sentences to be imposed only rarely on those aged 14 or less.

It will not ordinarily be proper to decline jurisdiction on grave crime grounds simply in order to allow for the Crown Court to impose detention under section 91 of the PCC(S)A 2000, when an offender is not a persistent offender and could, therefore, not receive a detention and training order (see **D24**).

D22.4 Time on remand

A court must give credit for any time spent on remand, but need not apply a precise discount for time served (*R v Fieldhouse* [2000] Crim LR 1020).

D22.5 Breach of supervision requirement

Where a person has breached the supervision element of the order and is being returned to custody, the words 'remainder of the term of the detention and training order' under section 104(3) of the PCC(S)A 2000, meant the period between the date of the breach being proved and the expiry of the order (*H v Doncaster Youth Court* [2009] EWHC 3463 (Admin)).

Powers of Criminal Courts (Sentencing) Act 2000, s 104

(1) Where a detention and training order is in force in respect of an offender and it appears on information to a justice of the peace that the offender has failed to comply with requirements under section 103(6)(b) above, the justice—

    (a) may issue a summons requiring the offender to appear at the place and time specified in the summons; or

    (b) if the information is in writing and on oath, may issue a warrant for the offender's arrest.

(2) Any summons or warrant issued under this section shall direct the offender to appear or be brought—

    (a) before a youth court acting in the local justice area in which the offender resides; or

    (b) if it is not known where the offender resides, before a youth court acting in the same local justice area as the justice who issued the summons or warrant.

(3) If it is proved to the satisfaction of the youth court before which an offender appears or is brought under this section that he has failed to comply with requirements under section 103(6)(b) above, that court may—

    (a) order the offender to be detained, in such youth detention accommodation as the Secretary of State may determine, for such period, not exceeding the shorter of three months or the remainder of the term of the detention and training order, as the court may specify; or

    (b) impose on the offender a fine not exceeding level 3 on the standard scale.

(4) An offender detained in pursuance of an order under subsection (3)(a) above shall be deemed to be in legal custody.

(5) A fine imposed under subsection (3)(b) above shall be deemed, for the purposes of any enactment, to be a sum adjudged to be paid by a conviction.

(6) An offender may appeal to the Crown Court against any order made under subsection (3)(a) or (b) above.

D22.6 Breach due to further offending

Powers of Criminal Courts (Sentencing) Act 2000, s 105(1)–(4)

(1) This section applies to a person subject to a detention and training order if—

    (a) after his release and before the date on which the term of the order ends, he commits an offence punishable with imprisonment in the case of a person aged 21 or over ('the new offence'); and

    (b) whether before or after that date, he is convicted of the new offence.

(2) Subject to section 8(6) above (duty of adult magistrates' court to remit young offenders to youth court for sentence), the court by or before which

a person to whom this section applies is convicted of the new offence may, whether or not it passes any other sentence on him, order him to be detained in such youth detention accommodation as the Secretary of State may determine for the whole or any part of the period which—

    (a) begins with the date of the court's order; and

    (b) is equal in length to the period between the date on which the new offence was committed and the date mentioned in subsection (1) above.

(3) The period for which a person to whom this section applies is ordered under subsection (2) above to be detained in youth detention accommodation—

    (a) shall, as the court may direct, either be served before and be followed by, or be served concurrently with, any sentence imposed for the new offence; and

    (b) in either case, shall be disregarded in determining the appropriate length of that sentence.

(4) Where the new offence is found to have been committed over a period of two or more days, or at some time during a period of two or more days, it shall be taken for the purposes of this section to have been committed on the last of those days.

📖 See *Blackstone's Criminal Practice 2012* E7.10–E7.16

D23 Detention in Young Offender Institution

D23.1 Age requirements

Aged 18 to 20 years.

D23.2 Criteria

The general requirements for the imposition of a custodial sentence (see **D17.2**) must be met. A minimum sentence of 21 days must be imposed.

A suspended sentence order (see **D60**) may be imposed.

 See *Blackstone's Criminal Practice 2012* E7.3

D24 **Detention under section 91 PCC(S)A 2000**

D24.1 **Age requirements**

| 10–17 years | In respect to an offence punishable, in the case of an adult, with 14 years or more imprisonment (excluding an offence for which the sentence is fixed by law). In respect to an offence under sections 3, 13, 25, 26 of the Sexual Offences Act 2003 (or equivalent under predecessor legislation). |
| 16 and 17 years | Certain firearms offences and section 28 of the Violent Crime Reduction Act 2006. |

D24.2 **Criteria**

A youth court has no power to impose imprisonment for 'grave crimes' and will decline jurisdiction (see **B2.4**). A Crown Court may sentence the offender up to the maximum penalty permitted in respect to an adult offender.

Powers of Criminal Courts (Sentencing) Act 2000, s 91

(1) Subsection (3) below applies where a person aged under 18 is convicted on indictment of—

    (a) an offence punishable in the case of a person aged 21 or over with imprisonment for 14 years or more, not being an offence the sentence for which is fixed by law; or

    (b) an offence under section 3 of the Sexual Offences Act 2003 (in this section, 'the 2003 Act') (sexual assault); or

    (c) an offence under section 13 of the 2003 Act (child sex offences committed by children or young persons); or

    (d) an offence under section 25 of the 2003 Act (sexual activity with a child family member); or

    (e) an offence under section 26 of the 2003 Act (inciting a child family member to engage in sexual activity).

(1A) Subsection (3) below also applies where—

    (a) a person aged under 18 is convicted on indictment of an offence—

        (i) under subsection (1)(a), (ab), (aba), (ac), (ad), (ae), (af) or (c) of section 5 of the Firearms Act 1968 (prohibited weapons), or

        (ii) under subsection (1A)(a) of that section,

    (b) the offence was committed after the commencement of section 51A of that Act and for the purposes of subsection (3) of that section at a time when he was aged 16 or over, and

    (c) the court is of the opinion mentioned in section 51A(2) of that Act (exceptional circumstances which justify its not imposing required custodial sentence).

(1B) Subsection (3) below also applies where—

(a) a person aged under 18 is convicted on indictment of an offence under the Firearms Act 1968 that is listed in section 51A(1A)(b), (e) or (f) of that Act and was committed in respect of a firearm or ammunition specified in section 5(1)(a), (ab), (aba), (ac), (ad), (ae), (af) or (c) or section 5(1A)(a) of that Act;

(b) the offence was committed after the commencement of section 30 of the Violent Crime Reduction Act 2006 and for the purposes of section 51A(3) of the Firearms Act 1968 at a time when he was aged 16 or over; and

(c) the court is of the opinion mentioned in section 51A(2) of the Firearms Act 1968.

(1C) Subsection (3) below also applies where—

(a) a person aged under 18 is convicted of an offence under section 28 of the Violent Crime Reduction Act 2006 (using someone to mind a weapon);

(b) section 29(3) of that Act applies (minimum sentences in certain cases); and

(c) the court is of the opinion mentioned in section 29(6) of that Act (exceptional circumstances which justify not imposing the minimum sentence).

(3) If the court is of the opinion that neither a community sentence nor a detention and training order is suitable, the court may sentence the offender to be detained for such period, not exceeding the maximum term of imprisonment with which the offence is punishable in the case of a person aged 21 or over, as may be specified in the sentence.

(4) Subsection (3) above is subject to (in particular) section 152 and 153 of the Criminal Justice Act 2003.

(5) Where—

(a) subsection (2) of section 51A of the Firearms Act 1968, or

(b) subsection (6) of section 29 of the Violent Crime Reduction Act 2006,

requires the imposition of a sentence of detention under this section for a term of at least the term provided for in that section, the court shall sentence the offender to be detained for such period, of at least the term so provided for but not exceeding the maximum term of imprisonment with which the offence is punishable in the case of a person aged 18 or over, as may be specified in the sentence.

 See *Blackstone's Criminal Practice 2012* **E7.7–E7.9**

D25 Discounts for Early Plea

D25.1 Age requirements

None.

D25.2 Criteria

Generally speaking, a court must discount a sentence in return for a guilty plea. In rare cases the discount may be withheld, and a magistrates' court could impose a maximum sentence as an alternative to committing the case for sentence to the Crown Court. The full reduction also need not be given if the prosecution case is overwhelming. The amount of discount will depend upon the timing of the plea, the *Magistrates' Sentencing Guidelines* state:

> The reduction has no impact on sentencing decisions in relation to ancillary orders, including disqualification. The level of the reduction should reflect the stage at which the offender indicated a willingness to admit guilt and will be gauged on a sliding scale, ranging from a recommended one third (where the guilty plea was entered at the first reasonable opportunity), reducing to a recommended one quarter (where a trial date has been set) and to a recommended one tenth (for a guilty plea entered at the 'door of the court' or after the trial has begun). There is a presumption that the recommended reduction will be given unless there are good reasons for a lower amount. The application of the reduction may affect the type, as well as the severity, of the sentence. It may also take the sentence below the range in some cases. The court must state that it has reduced a sentence to reflect a guilty plea. It should usually indicate what the sentence would have been if there had been no reduction as a result of the plea.

In each category, there is a presumption that the recommended reduction will be given unless there are good reasons for a lower amount		
First reasonable opportunity	After a trial date is set	Door of the court/after trial has begun
recommended 1/3	**recommended 1/4**	**recommended 1/10**

It is commonly believed that there is no benefit to entering a guilty plea at plea before venue stage as most judges will give full credit for a plea at plea and case management hearings. This is an erroneous approach and all advocates should be aware of *R v Cundell* [2008] EWCA Crim 1420:

> As is well known, the maximum discount of one-third is usually available in circumstances where a defendant in criminal proceedings accepts his guilt at the earliest opportunity. That may be at the first hearing before the Magistrates' Court, but it is well recognised that the earliest reasonable

opportunity may come rather sooner. In our judgement, this is one of those cases. When the appellant was arrested he was confronted with the account of what had happened and the DNA evidence. He persisted in his denials, causing an identification process to be gone through, and then he failed to take the opportunity of accepting his guilt when he appeared before the Magistrates' Court. As we have indicated, he first accepted responsibility in December 2007, when speaking to the police about other matters, and then of course he confirmed it at his first appearance at the Crown Court, at which time a trial date would have been set. Taking account of all those factors, in our judgement a discount of about 25 per cent would have been reasonable. That is consonant with the recommendations of the Sentencing Guidelines Council. He was not entitled to full credit.

D26 **Disqualification from Driving**

D26.1 **Age requirements**

None.

D26.2 **Criteria**

Disqualification (or in the fifth example, more accurately a revocation) may arise in one of five ways:

1. Offence carrying obligatory disqualification (see **D26.4**).
2. Offence carrying discretionary disqualification (see **D26.6**).
3. As a result of accumulating 12 or more penalty points (see **D26.7**).
4. As a result of conviction for any offence, or an offence where a vehicle was used for crime (PCC(S)A 2000, ss 146, 147) (see **D26.9**).
5. As a result of a 'new driver' accumulating six penalty points (see **D26.10**).

D26.3 **Interim disqualification**

An interim disqualification can be imposed when the court commits an offender for sentence to the Crown Court, remits the case to another court, or defers or adjourns sentence. More than one interim disqualification can be imposed but the total term must not exceed six months.

D26.4 **Obligatory disqualification**

Where a person is convicted of an offence involving obligatory disqualification, the court must order him to be disqualified for such period not less than 12 months as the court thinks fit unless the court for special reasons (see **D26.5**) thinks fit to order him to be disqualified for a shorter period or not to order him to be disqualified.

A person disqualified for dangerous driving must also be ordered to undertake an extended driving test.

A mandatory disqualification does not have the effect of removing any penalty points existing on the licence.

There are certain exceptions to the minimum 12-month period that are applicable to those sentenced in the magistrates' court:

D26.4.1 *A minimum three-year disqualification follows:*

Where a person convicted of an offence under any of the following provisions of the Road Traffic Act 1988, that is:

(aa) section 3A (causing death by careless driving when under the influence of drink or drugs),

(a) section 4(1) (driving or attempting to drive while unfit),

(b) section 5(1)(a) (driving or attempting to drive with excess alcohol),

(c) section 7(6) (failing to provide a specimen) where that is an offence involving obligatory disqualification,

(d) section 7A(6) (failing to allow a specimen to be subjected to laboratory test) where that is an offence involving obligatory disqualification;

has within the ten years immediately preceding the commission of the offence been convicted of any such offence.

D26.4.2 *A minimum two-year disqualification follows:*

In relation to a person on whom more than one disqualification for a fixed period of 56 days or more has been imposed within the three years immediately preceding the commission of the offence.

D26.4.3 *A minimum six months disqualification follows:*

Where a person convicted of an offence under section 40A of the Road Traffic Act 1988 (using vehicle in dangerous condition etc) has within the three years immediately preceding the commission of the offence been convicted of any such offence.

D26.5 Special reasons

There is no statutory definition of special reasons, but it must not amount to a defence in law, must be directly connected with the offence in question (not the offender), and must be a mitigating or extenuating circumstance. The burden (civil standard) falls on the defendant. Good character, personal service to the community (for example being a doctor), financial hardship as a result of a disqualification, and the fact the offence was not particularly serious have all been held not to amount to special reasons.

An ignorance of the terms of motor insurance cannot generally amount to special reasons (*Rennison v Knowler* [1947] 1 All ER 302) unless the person was misled or there is a particularly good reason for the ignorance (eg illness, confusion brought about by others).

If special reasons are found the court has a discretion not to endorse points, and to reduce or not impose a mandatory period of disqualification. Note, however, that for an offence involving mandatory disqualification, where special reasons are found and the court does not disqualify, it must impose points.

Common special reasons are:

- spiked drinks or mistake as to item drunk;
- shortness of distance driven;
- medical or other emergencies.

In *R v Mander*, unreported, 13 May 2008, CA, the court found special reasons where a taxi driver, upon three of five passengers alighting without paying, drove dangerously for approximately nine-tenths of a mile. The court declined, however, to exercise its discretion to reduce the period of disqualification on the grounds that the defendant had overreacted to the circumstances.

In *Warring-Davies v Director of Public Prosecutions* [2009] EWHC 1172 (Admin) the court emphasized the need to find a causal link between any alleged medical condition and the driving in question.

In *Director of Public Prosecutions v Harrison* [2007] EWHC 556 (Admin) the court held it wrong to find special reasons where a drunken person drove 446 yards in order to find youths who had harassed him earlier.

In *Director of Public Prosecutions v Oram* [2005] EWHC 964 (Admin) the court held that special reasons would not be arguable to a drunk driver who relied upon shortness of distance driven alone.

Taylor v Rajan [1974] RTR 304 deals with the principles involved in 'emergency' cases:

> This is not the first case in which the court has had to consider whether driving in an emergency could justify a conclusion that there are special reasons for not disqualifying the driver. If a man, in the well-founded belief that he will not drive again, puts his car in the garage, goes into his house and has a certain amount to drink in the belief that he is not going to drive again, and if thereafter is an emergency which requires him in order to deal with it to take his car out despite his intention to leave it in the garage, then that is a situation which can in law amount to a special reason for not disqualifying a driver. On the other hand, Justices who are primarily concerned with dealing with this legislation should approach the exercise of the resulting discretion with great care. The mere fact that the facts disclose a special reason does not mean that the driver is to escape disqualification as a matter of course. There is a very serious burden upon the Justices, even when a special reason has been disclosed, to decide whether in their discretion they should decline to disqualify a particular case. The Justices should have very much in mind that if a man deliberately drives when he knows he has consumed a considerable quantity of drink, he presents a potential source of danger to the public which

no private crisis can likely excuse. One of the most important matters which Justices have to consider in the exercise of this discretion is whether the emergency (and I call it such for want of a more convenient word) was sufficiently acute to justify the driver taking his car out. The Justices should only exercise a discretion in favour of the driver in clear and compelling circumstances . . . The Justices therefore must consider the whole of the circumstances. They must consider the nature and degree of the crisis or emergency which has caused the defendant to take the car out. They must consider with particular care whether there were alternative means of transport or methods of dealing with the crisis other than and alternative to the use by the defendant of his own car. They should have regard to the manner in which the defendant drove . . . and they should generally have regard to whether the defendant acted responsibly or otherwise . . . The matter must be considered objectively and the quality and gravity of the crisis must be assessed in that way. Last, but by no means least, if the alcohol content in the defendant's blood and body is very high, that is a powerful reason for saying that the discretion should not be exercised in his favour. Indeed, if the alcohol content exceeds 100 milligrammes per hundred millilitres of blood, the Justices should rarely, if ever, exercise this discretion in favour of the defendant driver . . .

Chatters v Burke [1986] 3 All ER 168 details the seven factors relevant to a shortness of distance driven argument:

- distance;
- manner of driving;
- state of the vehicle;
- whether there was an intention to drive further;
- road and traffic conditions;
- possibility of danger to road users and pedestrians;
- reason for the driving.

In order to establish a spiked drinks defence it will be necessary to prove that the drink was laced, the defendant did not know it was laced, and that but for the lacing of the drink his alcohol level would not have exceeded the legal limit. It will normally be necessary to call expert evidence in relation to the last point. The higher the reading, the less likely it is that a defendant will be able to prove he had no knowledge. If a court is of the view that the defendant ought to have realized his drink was spiked it will not find special reasons (*Pridige v Grant* [1985] RTR 196).

D26.6 Discretionary disqualification

Where an offence carries discretionary disqualification, the court must consider disqualification before it considers the imposition of penalty points. This is the case even if the offender would be liable to disqualification under the 'totting up' provisions.

Practitioners must think of the tactical considerations of inviting a court to impose a discretionary disqualification as opposed to points that could trigger a totting-up disqualification. The benefit of a discretionary disqualification is that it can be for as short a period as the court directs; the negative side is that any previous points remain on the licence. If a totting-up disqualification were imposed, all the points would be removed, but the defendant would face a minimum six-month period of disqualification. You do, however, have to be sure that the court is minded to impose a shorter period, as a defendant may prefer to tot-up and clear his licence after a six-month disqualification, rather than have, say, four months disqualified and still have the existing points hanging over him. It is clear that the approach and sympathy of the court to this dilemma tends to vary across the country.

If a court disqualifies, then no additional penalty points are imposed. The period of disqualification can be for any period the court thinks proper.

D26.7 As a result of accumulating 12 or more penalty points 'totting-up'

In calculating the points on the licence, the court will have regard to:

- the points to be imposed for the new offence, and
- any points on the licence for offences committed no longer than three years from the date of commission of the new offence (therefore, points run from date of old offence to date of new offence).

If there has been in the three-year period a disqualification under the totting-up provisions, then points imposed prior to that disqualification would be disregarded.

The minimum period of disqualification is:

- six months if no previous disqualification;
- 12 months if one previous disqualification (for 56 days or more);
- two years if two or more previous disqualifications (for 56 days or more).

The previous disqualifications must have been imposed within three years of the date of the new offence to count.

D26.8 Exceptional hardship

Exceptional hardship (more properly titled 'mitigating circumstances') can be argued in order to escape disqualification as a result of totting-up (see **D26.7**).

Section 35 of the Road Traffic Offenders Act 1988 provides:

Road Traffic Offenders Act 1988, s 35

(1) Where—

    (a) a person is convicted of an offence to which this subsection applies, and

    (b) the penalty points to be taken into account on that occasion number twelve or more,

the court must order him to be disqualified for not less than the minimum period unless the court is satisfied, having regard to all the circumstances, that there are grounds for mitigating the normal consequences of the conviction and thinks fit to order him to be disqualified for a shorter period or not to order him to be disqualified.

(1A) Subsection (1) above applies to—

    (a) an offence involving discretionary disqualification and obligatory endorsement, and

    (b) an offence involving obligatory disqualification in respect of which no order is made under section 34 of this Act.

(2) The minimum period referred to in subsection (1) above is—

    (a) six months if no previous disqualification imposed on the offender is to be taken into account, and

    (b) one year if one, and two years if more than one, such disqualification is to be taken into account;

and a previous disqualification imposed on an offender is to be taken into account if it was for a fixed period of 56 days or more and was imposed within the three years immediately preceding the commission of the latest offence in respect of which penalty points are taken into account under section 29 of this Act.

(3) Where an offender is convicted on the same occasion of more than one offence to which subsection (1) above applies—

    (a) not more than one disqualification shall be imposed on him under subsection (1) above,

    (b) in determining the period of the disqualification the court must take into account all the offences, and

    (c) for the purposes of any appeal any disqualification imposed under subsection (1) above shall be treated as an order made on the conviction of each of the offences.

(4) No account is to be taken under subsection (1) above of any of the following circumstances—

    (a) any circumstances that are alleged to make the offence or any of the offences not a serious one,

    (b) hardship, other than exceptional hardship, or

    (c) any circumstances which, within the three years immediately preceding the conviction, have been taken into account under that subsection in ordering the offender to be disqualified for a shorter period or not ordering him to be disqualified.

(5) References in this section to disqualification do not include a disqualification imposed under section 26 of this Act or section 147 of the Powers of Criminal Courts (Sentencing) Act 2000 or section 223A or 436A of

> the Criminal Procedure (Scotland) Act 1975 (offences committed by using
> vehicles) or a disqualification imposed in respect of an offence of stealing a
> motor vehicle, an offence under section 12 or 25 of the Theft Act 1968, an
> offence under section 178 of the Road Traffic Act 1988, or an attempt to
> commit such an offence.
>
> (5A) The preceding provisions of this section shall apply in relation to a convic-
> tion of an offence committed by aiding, abetting, counselling, procuring, or
> inciting to the commission of, an offence involving obligatory disqualification
> as if the offence were an offence involving discretionary disqualification.

It should be noted that the burden of establishing mitigating circumstances is on the defendant and will generally need to be proved by way
of evidence as opposed to submission.

D26.9 As a result of conviction for any offence, or an offence where a vehicle was used for crime

Section 146 of the PCC(S)A 2000 gives a court the power to disqualify
an offender from holding a driving licence following a conviction for
any offence. There need be no nexus between driving and the offence
in question, and nothing additional should be written into the statute
over and above what is already present; this allows a court to use the
provision whenever it feels it to be appropriate in all of the circumstances (*R v Sofekun* [2008] EWCA Crim 2035). This penalty can only
be imposed by courts if they have been notified of its availability by the
Secretary of State.

Section 147 of the PCC(S)A 2000 gives courts a narrower power to
disqualify where a motor vehicle was involved in the commission of
the offence. In the magistrates' court the power is limited solely to the
offences of assault:

> **Powers of Criminal Courts (Sentencing) Act 2000,
> s 147(2)–(4)**
>
> (2) This section [. . .] applies where a person is convicted by or before any court
> of common assault or of any other offence involving an assault (including
> an offence of aiding, abetting, counselling or procuring, or inciting to the
> commission of, an offence).
>
> (3) [. . .]
>
> (4) If, in a case to which this section applies by virtue of subsection (2) above,
> the court is satisfied that the assault was committed by driving a motor
> vehicle, the court may order the person convicted to be disqualified, for such
> period as the court thinks fit, for holding or obtaining a driving licence.

D26.10 Road Traffic (New Drivers) Act 1995

Newly qualified drivers are subject to a two-year probationary period. If at any time during that period the points to be endorsed on a driving licence amounts to six or more, the licence will be automatically revoked. The relevant date is the date of offence not conviction, so revocation cannot be avoided by delaying court proceedings.

In appropriate cases, advocates should invite courts to disqualify instead of endorse points in order to try to avoid the draconian consequences of accumulating six or more penalty points. Wiser magistrates and their advisers will, however, be alive to this, so do not count on it working.

D26.11 Return of driving licence

D26.11.1 *Overview*

Section 42 of the Road Traffic Offenders Act 1988 provides for a disqualified driver to apply to the court for the return of his driving licence, prior to the expiry of the disqualification period. These proceedings are funded at the magistrates' court by way of a means tested representation order.

Period of disqualification	Minimum period of disqualification that must have elapsed before court can consider an application
Less than 4 years	2 years
4 years, but less than 10 years	One half of the disqualification period
10 years or more	5 years

It should be noted that the Coroners and Justice Act 2009 makes amendments to the periods above in relation to disqualifications that are ordered to begin upon expiry of any prison term. Those provisions were not at the time of writing in force.

If a disqualification is imposed by virtue of section 36(1) of the Act (disqualification until test is passed), there is no power to return a licence under section 43.

D26.11.2 *Criteria to be applied*

On any such application the court may, as it thinks proper having regard to—

(a) the character of the person disqualified and his conduct subsequent to the order,

(b) the nature of the offence, and

(c) any other circumstances of the case,

either by order remove the disqualification as from such date as may be specified in the order or refuse the application.

D26.11.3 *Further application following refusal*

Where an application is refused, a further application shall not be entertained if made within three months after the date of the refusal.

 See *Blackstone's Criminal Practice 2012* E21.9–E21.10

D27 **Disqualification of Company Directors**

D27.1 **Age requirements**

None.

D27.2 **Criteria**

Section 2 of the Company Directors Disqualification Act 1986 provides:

> **Company Directors Disqualification Act 1986, s 2(1)**
>
> The court may make a disqualification order against a person where he is convicted of an indictable offence (whether on indictment or summarily) in connection with the promotion, formation, management, liquidation or striking off of a company with the receivership of a company's property or with his being an administrative receiver of a company.

Section 5 provides:

> **Company Directors Disqualification Act 1986, s 5**
>
> (1) An offence counting for the purposes of this section is one of which a person is convicted (either on indictment or summarily) in consequence of a contravention of, or failure to comply with, any provision of the companies legislation requiring a return, account or other document to be filed with, delivered or sent, or notice of any matter to be given, to the registrar of companies (whether the contravention or failure is on the person's own part or on the part of any company).
> (2) Where a person is convicted of a summary offence counting for those purposes, the court by which he is convicted (or, in England and Wales, any other magistrates' court acting in the same local justice area) may make a disqualification order against him if the circumstances specified in the next subsection are present.
> (3) Those circumstances are that, during the 5 years ending with the date of the conviction, the person has had made against him, or has been convicted of, in total not less than 3 default orders and offences counting for the purposes of this section; and those offences may include that of which he is convicted as mentioned in subsection (2) and any other offence of which he is convicted on the same occasion.
> (4) For the purposes of this section—
>   (a) the definition of 'summary offence' in Schedule 1 to the Interpretation Act 1978 applies for Scotland as for England and Wales, and
>   (b) 'default order' means the same as in section 3(3)(b).
> (5) The maximum period of disqualification under this section is 5 years.

D27 Disqualification of Company Directors

The effect of the order (s 1) is that the offender:

- will not be a director of a company, act as receiver of a company's property, or in any way, whether directly or indirectly, be concerned or take part in the promotion, formation, or management of a company unless (in each case) he has the leave of a court; and
- will not act as an insolvency practitioner.

The management of the company relates to both internal and external activities, so a director who obtains goods from another during the course of his business can properly be made subject to an order for disqualification (*R v Corbin* (1984) 6 Cr App R (S) 17).

A magistrates' court can make such an order for a maximum period of five years. An order cannot run consecutively to an existing order. It is wrong to also impose compensation if the defendant has, by virtue of being disqualified as a director, been deprived of his means to earn money in order to pay compensation (*R v Holmes* (1992) 13 Cr App R (S) 29).

 See *Blackstone's Criminal Practice 2012* **E21.8**

D28 **Drinking Banning Order**

D28.1 **Age requirements**

16 years or over.

D28.2 **Criteria**

As of 1 November 2010 the orders can be made in the following Local Justice Areas: Birmingham; Bristol; Burnley, Pendle and Rossendale; Cardiff Central and South West Staffordshire; City of London; City of Salford; City of Westminster; Corby; Coventry District; Denbighshire; Doncaster; East Berkshire; East Dorset; East Kent; Fenland; Fylde Coast; Grimsby and Cleethorpes; Gwent; Hackney and Tower Hamlets; Halton; Hull and Holderness; Hammersmith and Fulham, and Kensington and Chelsea; Hartlepool; Lambeth and Southwark; Leicester; Lincoln District; Manchester City; Mansfield; Merthyr Tydfil; Newcastle Upon Tyne District; North East Derbyshire and Dales; North East Suffolk; North Kent; North Staffordshire; North Tyneside District; Northampton; Nottingham; Plymouth District; Reading; Sedgemoor; South Devon; South East Hampshire; Southampton; Southern Derbyshire; Sussex (Central); Teesside; Wakefield; West Cornwall; West Hertfordshire .

Following conviction for any offence, the court must determine whether the offence was committed while under the influence of alcohol, and if so, whether a banning order is necessary for the purpose of protecting others from further criminal or disorderly conduct by the offender while he is under the influence of alcohol.

An order may last between two months and two years and may impose any prohibition on the offender which is necessary to prevent criminal or disorderly conduct while under the influence of alcohol, and must include prohibitions as the court considers necessary on the offender's entering licensed premises. Breach of an order carries a maximum penalty of a fine (level 4).

> **Violent Crime Reduction Act 2006, s 6**
>
> (1) This section applies where—
>   (a) an individual aged 16 or over is convicted of an offence (the 'offender'); and
>   (b) at the time he committed the offence, he was under the influence of alcohol.
> (2) The court must consider whether the conditions in section 3(2) are satisfied in relation to the offender.

(3) If the court decides that the conditions are satisfied in relation to the offender, it may make a drinking banning order against him.

(4) If the court—
   (a) decides that the conditions are satisfied in relation to the offender, but
   (b) does not make a drinking banning order,
   it must give its reasons for not doing so in open court.

(5) If the court decides that the conditions are not satisfied in relation to the offender, it must state that fact in open court and give its reasons.

The conditions in section 3(2) are:

Violent Crime Reduction Act 2006, s 3(2)

(2) The conditions are—
   (a) that the individual has, after the commencement of this section, engaged in criminal or disorderly conduct while under the influence of alcohol; and
   (b) that such an order is necessary to protect other persons from further conduct by him of that kind while he is under the influence of alcohol.

The section 7 Supplementary provision about orders on conviction:

Violent Crime Reduction Act 2006, s 7

(1) For the purpose of deciding whether to make a drinking banning order under section 6 the court may consider evidence led by the prosecution and evidence led by the defence.

(2) It is immaterial whether the evidence would have been admissible in the proceedings in which the offender was convicted.

(3) A drinking banning order under section 6 must not be made except—
   (a) in addition to a sentence imposed in respect of the offence; or
   (b) in addition to an order discharging the offender conditionally.

(4) The court may adjourn any proceedings in relation to a drinking banning order under section 6 even after sentencing the offender.

(5) If the offender does not appear for any adjourned proceedings, the court may further adjourn the proceedings or may issue a warrant for his arrest.

(6) But the court may not issue a warrant for the offender's arrest unless it is satisfied that he has had adequate notice of the time and place of the adjourned proceedings.

(7) A drinking banning order under section 6 takes effect on—
   (a) the day on which it is made; or
   (b) if on that day the offender is detained in legal custody, the day on which he is released from that custody.

(8) Subsection (9) applies in relation to proceedings in which a drinking banning order is made under section 6 against a young person.

(9) In so far as the proceedings relate to the making of the order—
- (a) section 49 of the Children and Young Persons Act 1933 (c 12) (restrictions on reports of proceedings in which children and young persons are concerned) does not apply in respect of the young person against whom the order is made; and
- (b) section 39 of that Act (power to prohibit publication of certain matters) does so apply.

(10) In section 3(2)(fa) of the Prosecution of Offences Act 1985 (c 23) (functions of the Director), after the first occurrence of 'conviction of certain offences)' insert ', section 6 of the Violent Crime Reduction Act 2006 (orders on conviction in criminal proceedings)'.

(11) In this section and section 6 'the court' in relation to an offender means—
- (a) the court by or before which he is convicted of the offence; or
- (b) if he is committed to the Crown Court to be dealt with for the offence, the Crown Court.

 See *Blackstone's Criminal Practice 2012* **E21.2**

D29 Exclusion from Licensed Premises

D29.1 Age requirements

None.

D29.2 Criteria

The term of the order must be between three months and two years.

Section 1 of the Licensed Premises (Exclusion of Certain Persons) Act 1980 provides:

Licensed Premises (Exclusion of Certain Persons) Act 1980, s 1(1)–(2)

(1) Where a court by or before which a person is convicted of an offence committed on licensed premises is satisfied that in committing that offence he resorted to violence or offered or threatened to resort to violence, the court may, subject to subsection (2) below, make an order (in this Act referred to as an 'exclusion order') prohibiting him from entering those premises or any other specified premises, without the express consent of the licensee of the premises or his servant or agent.

(2) An exclusion order may be made either—
   (a) in addition to any sentence which is imposed in respect of the offence of which the person is convicted; or
   (b) where the offence was committed in England and Wales, notwithstanding the provisions of sections 12 and 14 of the Powers of Criminal Courts (Sentencing) Act 2000 (cases in which absolute and conditional discharges may be made, and their effect), in addition to an order discharging him absolutely or conditionally.

 See *Blackstone's Criminal Practice 2012* E21.1

D30 **Exclusion Order**

D30.1 **Age requirements**

None. But note that the order can only be made for an offender aged 18 years or over if the offence was committed prior to 4 April 2005.

D30.2 **Criteria**

The general requirements for a community order must be met (see **D10.2**). An exclusion order can last for a maximum of three months in respect to an offender under 16 years, or two years in respect to any other offender.

 See *Blackstone's Criminal Practice 2012* **E21.1**

D31 **Financial Circumstances Order**

D31.1 **Age requirements**

None.

D31.2 **Criteria**

Section 162 of the Criminal Justice Act 2003 provides:

Criminal Justice Act 2003, s 162

(1) Where an individual has been convicted of an offence, the court may, before sentencing him, make a financial circumstances order with respect to him.

(2) Where a magistrates' court has been notified in accordance with section 12(4) of the Magistrates' Courts Act 1980 (c 43) that an individual desires to plead guilty without appearing before the court, the court may make a financial circumstances order with respect to him.

(3) In this section 'a financial circumstances order' means, in relation to any individual, an order requiring him to give to the court, within such period as may be specified in the order, such a statement of his financial circumstances as the court may require.

(4) An individual who without reasonable excuse fails to comply with a financial circumstances order is liable on summary conviction to a fine not exceeding level 3 on the standard scale.

(5) If an individual, in furnishing any statement in pursuance of a financial circumstances order—
   (a) makes a statement which he knows to be false in a material particular,
   (b) recklessly furnishes a statement which is false in a material particular, or
   (c) knowingly fails to disclose any material fact, he is liable on summary conviction to a fine not exceeding level 4 on the standard scale.

(6) Proceedings in respect of an offence under subsection (5) may, notwithstanding anything in section 127(1) of the Magistrates' Courts Act 1980 (c 43) (limitation of time), be commenced at any time within two years from the date of the commission of the offence or within six months from its first discovery by the prosecutor, whichever period expires the earlier.

 See *Blackstone's Criminal Practice 2012* **E15.9**

D32 **Financial Reporting Order**

D32.1 **Age requirements**

None.

D32.2 **Criteria**

Section 76 of the Serious Organised Crime and Police Act 2005 provides:

Serious Organised Crime and Police Act 2005, s 76

(1) A court sentencing or otherwise dealing with a person convicted of an offence mentioned in subsection (3) may also make a financial reporting order in respect of him.

(2) But it may do so only if it is satisfied that the risk of the person's committing another offence mentioned in subsection (3) is sufficiently high to justify the making of a financial reporting order.

(3) The offences are—

  (aa) an offence under either of the following provisions of the Fraud Act 2006—

   (i) section 1 (fraud),

   (ii) section 11 (obtaining services dishonestly),

  (ab) a common law offence of conspiracy to defraud,

  (ac) an offence under section 17 of the Theft Act 1968 (c 60) (false accounting),

  (c) any offence specified in Schedule 2 to the Proceeds of Crime Act 2002 (c 29) ('lifestyle offences').

  (d) a common law offence of bribery,

  (e) an offence under section 1 of the Public Bodies Corrupt Practices Act 1889 (c 69) (corruption in office),

  (f) the first two offences under section 1 of the Prevention of Corruption Act 1906 (c 34) (bribes obtained by or given to agents),

  (g) an offence under any of the following provisions of the Criminal Justice Act 1988 (c 33)—

   — section 93A (assisting another to retain the benefit of criminal conduct),

   — section 93B (acquisition, possession or use of proceeds of criminal conduct),

   — section 93C (concealing or transferring proceeds of criminal conduct),

  (h) an offence under any of the following provisions of the Drug Trafficking Act 1994 (c 37)—

   — section 49 (concealing or transferring proceeds of drug trafficking),

   — section 50 (assisting another person to retain the benefit of drug trafficking),

   — section 51 (acquisition, possession or use of proceeds of drug trafficking),

---

    (i) an offence under any of the following provisions of the Terrorism Act 2000 (c 11)—
-    section 15 (fund-raising for purposes of terrorism),
-    section 16 (use and possession of money etc. for purposes of terrorism),
-    section 17 (funding arrangements for purposes of terrorism),
-    section 18 (money laundering in connection with terrorism),

    (j) an offence under section 329 of the Proceeds of Crime Act 2002 (c 29) (acquisition, use and possession of criminal property),

    (k) a common law offence of cheating in relation to the public revenue,

    (l) an offence under section 170 of the Customs and Excise Management Act 1979 (c 2) (fraudulent evasion of duty),

    (m) an offence under section 72 of the Value Added Tax Act 1994 (c 23) (offences relating to VAT),

    (n) an offence under section 144 of the Finance Act 2000 (c 17) (fraudulent evasion of income tax),

    (o) an offence under section 35 of the Tax Credits Act 2002 (c 21) (tax credit fraud),

    (p) an offence of attempting, conspiring in or inciting the commission of an offence mentioned in paragraphs (aa), (ac) or (d) to (o),

    (q) an offence of aiding, abetting, counselling or procuring the commission of an offence mentioned in paragraphs (aa), (ac) or (d) to (o).

(4) The Secretary of State may by order amend subsection (3) so as to remove an offence from it or add an offence to it.

(5) A financial reporting order—
    (a) comes into force when it is made, and
    (b) has effect for the period specified in the order, beginning with the date on which it is made.

(6) If the order is made by a magistrates' court, the period referred to in subsection (5)(b) must not exceed 5 years.

Section 79 sets out the effect of a financial reporting order:

Serious Organised Crime and Police Act 2005, s 79

(1) A person in relation to whom a financial reporting order has effect must do the following.

(2) He must make a report, in respect of—
    (a) the period of a specified length beginning with the date on which the order comes into force, and
    (b) subsequent periods of specified lengths, each period beginning immediately after the end of the previous one.

(3) He must set out in each report, in the specified manner, such particulars of his financial affairs relating to the period in question as may be specified.

(4) He must include any specified documents with each report.

(5) He must make each report within the specified number of days after the end of the period in question.

(6) He must make each report to the specified person.

(7) Rules of court may provide for the maximum length of the periods which may be specified under subsection (2).

(8) In this section, 'specified' means specified by the court in the order.

(9) . . .

(10) A person who without reasonable excuse includes false or misleading information in a report, or otherwise fails to comply with any requirement of this section, is guilty of an offence and is liable on summary conviction to—

    (a) imprisonment for a term not exceeding—

        (i) in England and Wales, 6 months,

        (ii) . . .,

        (iii) . . ., or

    (ab) a fine not exceeding level 5 on the standard scale, or to both.

In *R v Adams* [2008] EWCA Crim 914 the court held financial reporting orders to be preventative in nature, and that any retrospective effect did not infringe Article 7 of the European Convention.

 See *Blackstone's Criminal Practice 2012* **E21.16**

D33 **Fines**

D33.1 **Age requirements**

None.

D33.2 **Criteria**

The *Magistrates' Court Sentencing Guidelines* sets out the following approach to fines.

D33.3 **Fine band starting points and ranges**

In these guidelines, where the starting point or range for an offence is or includes a fine, it is expressed as one of three fine bands (A, B, or C). Each fine band has both a starting point and a range.

On some offence guidelines, both the starting point and the range are expressed as a single fine band; see, for example, careless driving, where the starting point and range for the first level of offence activity are 'fine band A'. This means that the starting point will be the starting point for fine band A (50 per cent of the offender's relevant weekly income) and the range will be the range for fine band A (25–75 per cent of relevant weekly income). On other guidelines, the range encompasses more than one fine band; see, for example, drunk and disorderly in a public place on page 55 of the Sentencing Guidelines, where the starting point for the second level of offence activity is 'fine band B' and the range is 'fine band A to fine band C'. This means that the starting point will be the starting point for fine band B (100 per cent of relevant weekly income) and the range will be the lowest point of the range for fine band A to the highest point of the range for fine band C (125–175 per cent of relevant weekly income).

1. The amount of a fine must reflect the seriousness of the offence.

2. The court must also take into account the financial circumstances of the offender; this applies whether it has the effect of increasing or reducing the fine. Normally a fine should be of an amount that is capable of being paid within 12 months.

3. The aim is for the fine to have an equal impact on offenders with different financial circumstances; it should be a hardship but should not force the offender below a reasonable 'subsistence' level.

4. The guidance below aims to establish a clear, consistent, and principled approach to the assessment of fines that will apply fairly in the majority of cases. However, it is impossible to anticipate every

situation that may be encountered and in each case the court will need to exercise its judgement to ensure that the fine properly reflects the seriousness of the offence and takes into account the financial circumstances of the offender.

5. For the purpose of the offence guidelines, a fine is based on one of three bands (A, B, or C). The selection of the relevant fine band, and the position of the individual offence within that band, is determined by the seriousness of the offence.

	Starting point	**Range**
Fine band A	50% of relevant weekly income	25–75% of relevant weekly income
Fine band B	100% of relevant weekly income	75–125% of relevant weekly income
Fine band C	150% of relevant weekly income	125–175% of relevant weekly income

D33.4 Definition of relevant weekly income

6. The seriousness of an offence determines the choice of fine band and the position of the offence within the range for that band. The offender's financial circumstances are taken into account by expressing that position as a proportion of the offender's relevant weekly income.

7. Where an offender is in receipt of income from employment or is self-employed and that income is more than £100 per week after deduction of tax and national insurance (or equivalent where the offender is self-employed), the actual income is the relevant weekly income.

8. Where an offender's only source of income is state benefit (including where there is relatively low additional income as permitted by the benefit regulations) or the offender is in receipt of income from employment or is self-employed but the amount of income after deduction of tax and national insurance is £100 or less, the relevant weekly income is deemed to be £100.

9. In calculating relevant weekly income, no account should be taken of tax credits, housing benefit, child benefit, or similar.

D33.5 No reliable information

10. Where an offender has failed to provide information, or the court is not satisfied that it has been given sufficient reliable information, it is entitled to make such determination as it thinks fit regarding the financial circumstances of the offender. Any determination should be clearly stated on the court records for use in any subsequent variation or enforcement proceedings. In such cases, a record should also be

made of the applicable fine band and the court's assessment of the position of the offence within that band based on the seriousness of the offence.

11. Where there is no information on which a determination can be made, the court should proceed on the basis of an assumed relevant weekly income of £350. This is derived from national median pre-tax earnings; a gross figure is used as, in the absence of financial information from the offender, it is not possible to calculate appropriate deductions.

12. Where there is some information that tends to suggest a significantly lower or higher income than the recommended £350 default sum, the court should make a determination based on that information.

13. A court is empowered to remit a fine in whole or part if the offender subsequently provides information as to means. The assessment of offence seriousness and, therefore, the appropriate fine band and the position of the offence within that band is not affected by the provision of this information.

D33.6 Assessment of financial circumstances

14. While the initial consideration for the assessment of a fine is the offender's relevant weekly income, the court is required to take account of the offender's financial circumstances more broadly. Guidance on important parts of this assessment is set out below.

15. An offender's financial circumstances may have the effect of increasing or reducing the amount of the fine; however, they are not relevant to the assessment of offence seriousness. They should be considered separately from the selection of the appropriate fine band and the court's assessment of the position of the offence within the range for that band.

D33.7 Out-of-the-ordinary expenses

16. In deciding the proportions of relevant weekly income that are the starting points and ranges for each fine band, account has been taken of reasonable living expenses. Accordingly, no further allowance should normally be made for these. In addition, no allowance should normally be made where the offender has dependants.

17. Outgoings will be relevant to the amount of the fine only where the expenditure is out of the ordinary and substantially reduces the ability to pay a financial penalty so that the requirement to pay a fine based on the standard approach would lead to undue hardship.

D33.8 Unusually low outgoings

18. Where the offender's living expenses are substantially lower than would normally be expected, it may be appropriate to adjust the amount of the fine to reflect this. This may apply, for example, where an offender does not make any financial contribution towards his or her living costs.

D33.9 Savings

19. Where an offender has savings these will not normally be relevant to the assessment of the amount of a fine although they may influence the decision on time to pay.

20. However, where an offender has little or no income but has substantial savings, the court may consider it appropriate to adjust the amount of the fine to reflect this.

D33.10 Household has more than one source of income

21. Where the household of which the offender is a part has more than one source of income, the fine should normally be based on the income of the offender alone.

22. However, where the offender's part of the income is very small (or the offender is wholly dependent on the income of another), the court may have regard to the extent of the household's income and assets which will be available to meet any fine imposed on the offender.

D33.11 Potential earning capacity

23. Where there is reason to believe that an offender's potential earning capacity is greater than his or her current income, the court may wish to adjust the amount of the fine to reflect this. This may apply, for example, where an unemployed offender states an expectation to gain paid employment within a short time. The basis for the calculation of fine should be recorded in order to ensure that there is a clear record for use in variation or enforcement proceedings.

D33.12 High income offenders

24. Where the offender is in receipt of very high income, a fine based on a proportion of relevant weekly income may be disproportionately high when compared with the seriousness of the offence. In such cases, the court should adjust the fine to an appropriate level; as a general

indication, in most cases the fine for a first time offender pleading not guilty should not exceed 75 per cent of the maximum fine.

D33.13 Offence committed for 'commercial' purposes

25. Some offences are committed with the intention of gaining a significant commercial benefit. These often occur where, in order to carry out an activity lawfully, a person has to comply with certain processes which may be expensive. They include, for example, 'taxi-touting' (where unauthorized persons seek to operate as taxi drivers) and 'fly-tipping' (where the cost of lawful disposal is considerable).

26. In some of these cases, a fine based on the standard approach set out above may not reflect the level of financial gain achieved or sought through the offending.

Accordingly:

(a) where the offender has generated income or avoided expenditure to a level that can be calculated or estimated, the court may wish to consider that amount when determining the financial penalty;

(b) where it is not possible to calculate or estimate that amount, the court may wish to draw on information from the enforcing authorities about the general costs of operating within the law.

D33.14 Reduction for a guilty plea

27. Where a guilty plea has been entered, the amount of the fine should be reduced by the appropriate proportion.

D33.15 Maximum fines

28. A fine must not exceed the statutory limit. Where this is expressed in terms of a 'level', the maxima are:

Level 1	£200
Level 2	£500
Level 3	£1,000
Level 4	£2,500
Level 5	£5,000

D33.16 Victims' surcharge

29. Whenever a court imposes a fine in respect of an offence committed after 1 April 2007, it must order the offender to pay a surcharge of £15.

30. Where the offender is of adequate means, the court must not reduce the fine to allow for imposition of the surcharge. Where the offender does not have sufficient means to pay the total financial penalty considered appropriate by the court, the order of priority is: compensation, surcharge, fine, costs.

31. Further guidance is set out in *Guidance on Victims Surcharge* issued by the Justices' Clerks' Society and Magistrates' Association (30 March 2007).

D33.17 Costs

32. Where the offender does not have sufficient means to pay the total financial penalty considered appropriate by the court, the order of priority is: compensation, surcharge, fine, costs.

D33.18 Multiple offences

33. Where an offender is to be fined for two or more offences that arose out of the same incident, it will often be appropriate to impose on the most serious offence a fine which reflects the totality of the offending where this can be achieved within the maximum penalty for that offence. 'No separate penalty' should be imposed for the other offences.

34. Where compensation is being ordered, that will need to be attributed to the relevant offence as will any necessary ancillary orders.

D33.19 Fine bands D and E

35. Two further fine bands are provided to assist a court in calculating a fine where the offence and general circumstances would otherwise warrant a community order (band D) or a custodial sentence (band E) but the court has decided that it need not impose such a sentence and that a financial penalty is appropriate. See pages 160 and 163 of the *Magistrates' Court Sentencing Guidelines* for further guidance.

36. The following starting points and ranges apply:

	Starting point	Range
Band D	250% of relevant weekly income	200–300% of relevant weekly income
Band E	400% of relevant weekly income	300–500% of relevant weekly income

D33.20 Imposition of fines with custodial sentences

37. A fine and a custodial sentence may be imposed for the same offence, although there will be few circumstances in which this is appropriate, particularly where the custodial sentence is to be served immediately. One example might be where an offender has profited financially from an offence but there is no obvious victim to whom compensation can be awarded. Combining these sentences is most likely to be appropriate only where the custodial sentence is short and/ or the offender clearly has, or will have, the means to pay.

38. Care must be taken to ensure that the overall sentence is proportionate to the seriousness of the offence and that better-off offenders are not able to 'buy themselves out of custody'.

D33.21 Payment

39. A fine is payable in full on the day on which it is imposed. The offender should always be asked for immediate payment when present in court and some payment on the day should be required wherever possible.

40. Where that is not possible, the court may, in certain circumstances, require the offender to be detained. More commonly, a court will allow payments to be made over a period set by the court:

(a) if periodic payments are allowed, the fine should normally be payable within a maximum of 12 months. However, it may be unrealistic to expect those on very low incomes to maintain payments for as long as a year;

(b) compensation should normally be payable within 12 months. However, in exceptional circumstances it may be appropriate to allow it to be paid over a period of up to three years.

41. Where fine bands D and E apply (see paras 35–36 above), it may be appropriate for the fine to be of an amount that is larger than can be repaid within 12 months. In such cases, the fine should normally be payable within a maximum of 18 months (band D) or two years (band E).

42. It is generally recognized that the maximum weekly payment by a person in receipt of state benefit should rarely exceed £5.

43. When allowing payment by instalments by an offender in receipt of earned income, the following approach may be useful. If the offender has dependants or larger than usual commitments, the weekly payment is likely to be decreased.

Net weekly income	Starting point for weekly payment
£60	£5
£120	£10
£200	£25
£250	£30
£300	£50
£400	£80

D33.22 Youth default order

Section 39 of and Schedule 7 to the Criminal Justice and Immigration Act 2008 (not in force at time of writing) introduce youth default orders which will enable a court to impose an unpaid work requirement, curfew requirement, or attendance centre requirement on a young offender in lieu of an unpaid fine.

 See *Blackstone's Criminal Practice 2012* E15

D34 **Forfeiture Order**

D34.1 **Age requirements**

None.

D34.2 **Criteria**

Section 27 of the Misuse of Drugs Act 1971 provides:

> **Misuse of Drugs Act 1971, s 27**
>
> (1) Subject to subsection (2) below, the court by or before which a person is convicted of an offence under this Act or an offence falling within subsection (3) below or an offence to which section 1 of the Criminal Justice (Scotland) Act 1987 relates may order anything shown to the satisfaction of the court to relate to the offence, to be forfeited and either destroyed or dealt with in such other manner as the court may order.
> (2) The court shall not order anything to be forfeited under this section, where a person claiming to be the owner of or otherwise interested in it applies to be heard by the court, unless an opportunity has been given to him to show cause why the order should not be made.
> (3) An offence falls within this subsection if it is an offence which is specified in—
>   (a) paragraph 1 of Schedule 2 to the Proceeds of Crime Act 2002 (drug trafficking offences), or
>   (b) so far as it relates to that paragraph, paragraph 10 of that Schedule.

 See *Blackstone's Criminal Practice 2012* **E18**

D35 **Guardianship and Hospital Orders**

D35.1 **Age requirements**

None.

D35.2 **Criteria**

Section 37 of the Mental Health Act 1983 provides:

> **Mental Health Act 1983, s 37**
>
> (1) Where a person is convicted . . . by a magistrates' court of an offence punishable on summary conviction with imprisonment, and the conditions mentioned in subsection (2) below are satisfied, the court may by order authorise his admission to and detention in such hospital as may be specified in the order or, as the case may be, place him under the guardianship of a local social services authority or of such other person approved by a local social services authority as may be so specified.
>
> (1A) . . .
>
> (1B) . . .
>
> (2) The conditions referred to in subsection (1) above are that—
>
>   (a) the court is satisfied, on the written or oral evidence of two registered medical practitioners, that the offender is suffering from mental illness, psychopathic disorder, severe mental impairment or mental impairment and that either—
>
>   (i) the mental disorder from which the offender is suffering is of a nature or degree which makes it appropriate for him to be detained in a hospital for medical treatment and, in the case of psychopathic disorder or mental impairment, that such treatment is likely to alleviate or prevent a deterioration of his condition; or
>
>   (ii) in the case of an offender who has attained the age of 16 years, the mental disorder is of a nature or degree which warrants his reception into guardianship under this Act; and
>
>   (b) the court is of the opinion, having regard to all the circumstances including the nature of the offence and the character and antecedents of the offender, and to the other available methods of dealing with him, that the most suitable method of disposing of the case is by means of an order under this section.
>
> (3) Where a person is charged before a magistrates' court with any act or omission as an offence and the court would have power, on convicting him of that offence, to make an order under subsection (1) above in his case as being a person suffering from mental illness or severe mental impairment, then, if the court is satisfied that the accused did the act or made the omission charged, the court may, if it thinks fit, make such an order without convicting him.

(4) An order for the admission of an offender to a hospital (in this Act referred to as 'a hospital order') shall not be made under this section unless the court is satisfied on the written or oral evidence of the registered medical practitioner who would be in charge of his treatment or of some other person representing the managers of the hospital that arrangements have been made for his admission to that hospital, and for his admission to it within the period of 28 days beginning with the date of the making of such an order; and the court may, pending his admission within that period, give such directions as it thinks fit for his conveyance to and detention in a place of safety.

(8) Where an order is made under this section, the court shall not—

(a) pass sentence of imprisonment or impose a fine or make a community order (within the meaning of Part 12 of the Criminal Justice Act 2003) in respect of the offence,

(b) if the order under this section is a hospital order, make a referral order (within the meaning of the Powers of Criminal Courts (Sentencing) Act 2000) in respect of the offence, or

(c) make in respect of the offender an order under section 150 of that Act (binding over of parent or guardian),

but the court may make any other order which it has power to make apart from this section; and for the purposes of this subsection 'sentence of imprisonment' includes any sentence or order for detention.

 See *Blackstone's Criminal Practice 2012* **E22**

D36 **Newton Hearings**

D36.1 **Age requirements**

None.

D36.2 **Criteria**

Updated guidance in relation to the holding of Newton hearings were set down in *R v Underwood* [2004] EWCA Crim 2256:

(1) The starting point has to be the defendant's instructions. His advocate will appreciate whether any significant facts about the prosecution evidence are disputed and the factual basis on which the defendant intends to plead guilty. Responsibility for taking initiative and alerting the prosecutor to the disputed areas rests with the defence.

(2) Where the Crown accepts the defendant's account of the disputed facts, the agreement should be written down and signed by both advocates. It should then be made available to the judge. If pleas have already been accepted and approved then it should be available before the sentencing hearing begins. If the agreed basis of plea is not signed by both advocates, the judge is entitled to ignore it. The Crown might reject the defendant's version. If so, the areas of dispute should be identified in writing, focusing the court's attention on the precise facts in dispute.

(3) The prosecution's position might be that they have no evidence to contradict the defence's assertions. In those circumstances, particularly if the facts relied on by the defendant arise from his personal knowledge and depend on his own account of the facts, the Crown should not normally agree the defendant's account unless supported by other material. The court should be notified at the outset in writing of the points in issue and the Crown's responses.

(4) After submissions, the judge will decide how to proceed. If not already decided, he would address the question of whether he should approve the Crown's acceptance of pleas. Then he would address the proposed basis of plea. It should be emphasized that whether or not the basis of plea is agreed, the judge is not bound by any such agreement and is entitled of his own motion to insist that any evidence relevant to the facts in dispute should be called before him, paying appropriate regard to any agreement reached by the advocates and any reasons which the Crown, in particular, might advance to justify him proceeding immediately to sentence. The judge is responsible for the sentencing decision and may order a Newton hearing to ascertain the truth about disputed facts.

(5) Relevant evidence should be called by prosecution and defence, particularly where the issue arises from facts which are within the exclusive knowledge of the defendant. If the defendant is willing to give evidence he should be called and, if not, subject to any explanation offered, the judge may draw such inference as he sees fit. The judge can reject the evidence called by the prosecution or by the defendant or his witnesses

even if the Crown has not called contradictory evidence. The judge's conclusions should be explained in the judgment.

(6) There are occasions when a Newton hearing would be inappropriate. Some issues require a jury's verdict; if a defendant denies that a specific criminal offence has been committed, the tribunal for deciding whether the offence has been proved is the jury. At the end of a Newton hearing the judge cannot make findings of fact and sentence on a basis which is inconsistent with the pleas to counts which have already been accepted and approved by the court. Particular care is needed in relation to a multi-count indictment involving one defendant or, an indictment involving a number of defendants. Where there are a number of defendants to a joint enterprise, the judge, while reflecting on the individual basis of pleas, should bear in mind the relative seriousness of the joint enterprise on which the defendants were involved.

(7) Normally, matters of mitigation are not dealt with by way of a Newton hearing but it is always open to the court to allow a defendant to give evidence on matters of mitigation which are within his own knowledge. The judge is entitled to decline to hear evidence about disputed facts if the case advanced is, for good reason, to be regarded as absurd or obviously untenable.

(8) If the issues at the Newton hearing are wholly resolved in the defendant's favour, mitigation for guilty pleas should not be reduced. If the defendant is disbelieved or obliges the prosecution to call evidence from the victim, who is then subjected to cross-examination which, because it is entirely unfounded, causes unnecessary and inappropriate distress, or if the defendant conveys that he has no insight into the consequences of his offence, and no genuine remorse, the judge might reduce the discount for the guilty pleas. There may be a few exceptional cases in which the normal entitlement to credit for a plea of guilty is wholly dissipated by the Newton hearing, and, in such cases, the judge should explain his reasons.

See *Blackstone's Criminal Practice 2012* D20.8–D20.29

D37 Offences Taken into Consideration

D37.1 Age requirements

None.

D37.2 Criteria

In *R v Miles* [2006] EWCA Crim 256 the court made the following observations:

. . . the sentence is intended to reflect a defendant's overall criminality. Offences cannot be taken into consideration without the express agreement of the offender. That is an essential prerequisite. The offender is pleading guilty to the offences. If they are to be taken into account (and the court is not obliged to take them into account) they have relevance to the overall criminality. When assessing the significance of TICs, as they are often called, of course the court is likely to attach weight to the demonstrable fact that the offender has assisted the police, particularly if they are enabled to clear up offences which might not otherwise be brought to justice. It is also true that cooperative behaviour of that kind will often provide its own very early indication of guilt, and usually means that no further proceedings at all need be started. They may also serve to demonstrate a genuine determination by the offender (and we deliberately use the colloquialism) to wipe the slate clean, so that when he emerges from whatever sentence is imposed on him, he can put his past completely behind him, without having worry or concern that offences may be revealed and that he is then returned to court. As in so many aspects of sentencing, of course, the way in which the court deals with offences to be taken into consideration depends on context. In some cases the offences taken into consideration will end up by adding nothing or nothing very much to the sentence which the court would otherwise impose. On the other hand, offences taken into consideration may aggravate the sentence and lead to a substantial increase in it. For example, the offences may show a pattern of criminal activity which suggests careful planning or deliberate rather than casual involvement in a crime. They may show an offence or offences committed on bail, after an earlier arrest. They may show a return to crime immediately after the offender has been before the court and given a chance that, by committing the crime, he has immediately rejected. There are many situations where similar issues may arise. One advantage to the defendant, of course, is that if once an offence is taken into consideration, there is no likely risk of any further prosecution for it. If, on the other hand, it is not, that risk remains. In short, offences taken into consideration are indeed taken into consideration. They are not ignored or expunged or disregarded.

 See *Blackstone's Criminal Practice 2012* **D20**

D38 **Parenting Order**

D38.1 **Age requirements**

None.

D38.2 **Criteria**

An order may be made against a parent or guardian (being a person in charge or control of the child), and must be made where a referral order is not made in respect to a child under 16 years unless it is not desirable to prevent further offending. Note that the order will generally be made following conviction of the child, but section 8(1) sets out numerous other instances when an order can be made.

The Crime and Security Act 2010 makes changes to section 8(1)(c) of the Act, and inserts a new section 8A. Those changes are inserted below (in brackets) but at the time of writing were not in force.

The order must not exceed 12 months, and a requirement to attend guidance sessions (which must be imposed) must not exceed three months.

Consent is not required.

Sections 8 and 8A of the Crime and Disorder Act 1998 provide:

Crime and Disorder Act 1998, ss 8(1)–(7A), [8A]

(1) This section applies where, in any court proceedings—
  (a) a child safety order is made in respect of a child or the court determines on an application under section 12(6) below that a child has failed to comply with any requirement included in such an order;
  (aa) a parental compensation order is made in relation to a child's behaviour;
  (b) an anti-social behaviour order or sex offender order is made in respect of a child or young person;
  (c) a child or young person is convicted of an offence [, except in a case where section 8A below applies (parenting order on breach of anti-social behaviour order)]; or
  (d) a person is convicted of an offence under section 443 (failure to comply with school attendance order) or section 444 (failure to secure regular attendance at school of registered pupil) of the Education Act 1996.
(2) Subject to subsection (3) and section 9(1) below, if in the proceedings the court is satisfied that the relevant condition is fulfilled, it may make a parenting order in respect of a person who is a parent or guardian of the child or young person or, as the case may be, the person convicted of the offence under section 443 or 444 ('the parent').

---

(3) A court shall not make a parenting order unless it has been notified by the Secretary of State that arrangements for implementing such orders are available in the area in which it appears to the court that the parent resides or will reside and the notice has not been withdrawn.

(4) A parenting order is an order which requires the parent—

    (a) to comply, for a period not exceeding twelve months, with such requirements as are specified in the order, and

    (b) subject to subsection (5) below, to attend, for a concurrent period not exceeding three months, such counselling or guidance programme as may be specified in directions given by the responsible officer.

(5) A parenting order may, but need not, include such a requirement as is mentioned in subsection (4)(b) above in any case where a parenting order under this section or any other enactment has been made in respect of the parent on a previous occasion.

(6) The relevant condition is that the parenting order would be desirable in the interests of preventing—

    (a) in a case falling within paragraph (a), (aa) or (b) of subsection (1) above, any repetition of the kind of behaviour which led to the child safety order, parental compensation order, anti-social behaviour order or sex offender order being made;

    (b) in a case falling within paragraph (c) of that subsection, the commission of any further offence by the child or young person;

    (c) in a case falling within paragraph (d) of that subsection, the commission of any further offence under section 443 or 444 of the Education Act 1996.

(7) The requirements that may be specified under subsection (4)(a) above are those which the court considers desirable in the interests of preventing any such repetition or, as the case may be, the commission of any such further offence.

(7A) A counselling or guidance programme which a parent is required to attend by virtue of subsection (4)(b) above may be or include a residential course but only if the court is satisfied—

    (a) that the attendance of the parent at a residential course is likely to be more effective than his attendance at a non-residential course in preventing any such repetition or, as the case may be, the commission of any such further offence, and

    (b) that any interference with family life which is likely to result from the attendance of the parent at a residential course is proportionate in all the circumstances.

8A Parenting order on breach of anti-social behaviour order

(1) This section applies where a person under the age of 16 is convicted of an offence under section 1(10) above in respect of an anti-social behaviour order.

(2) The court by or before which the person is so convicted must make a parenting order in respect of a person who is a parent or guardian of the person convicted, unless it is of the opinion that there are exceptional circumstances that would make a parenting order inappropriate.

(3) The parenting order must specify such requirements as the court considers would be desirable in the interests of preventing—
  (a) any repetition of the kind of behaviour which led to the anti-social behaviour order being made; or
  (b) the commission of any further offence by the person convicted.
(4) If the court does not make a parenting order because it is of the opinion that there are exceptional circumstances that would make it inappropriate, it must state in open court that it is of that opinion and what those circumstances are.
(5) The following subsections of section 8 above apply to parenting orders made under this section—
  (a) subsection (3) (court not to make parenting order unless arrangements available in local area);
  (b) subsection (4) (definition of parenting order);
  (c) subsection (5) (counselling or guidance programme not necessary if previous parenting order);
  (d) subsection (7A) (residential courses).

 See *Blackstone's Criminal Practice 2012* E14

D39 **Parents and Guardians, Liability and Responsibility**

D39.1 **Age requirements**

None.

D39.2 **Criteria**

Fines, costs, or compensation awarded against a person under 16 years must be ordered to be paid by a parent or guardian, unless such an order is unreasonable.

In respect to a child aged 16–17 years the court may make the orders above against a parent or guardian.

An order should not be made against a local authority unless that local authority has failed in its duty towards the child, and that failure is causative of the criminal behaviour.

In relation to a child under 16 years the court must bind over the parent or guardian to take proper care and control of the child. It has a discretion to do so in relation to a child aged 16–17 years. The bind over cannot exceed a period of three years, or until the child attains 18 years (whichever is the earlier); the recognizance must not exceed £1,000. If a parent refuses to be bound over, a fine not exceeding £1,000 can be imposed.

 See *Blackstone's Criminal Practice 2012* E14

D40 Penalty Points for Driving Offences

D40.1 Criteria

Penalty points must be imposed for all offences that are subject to obligatory endorsement, unless the court finds special reasons for not imposing points (see **D26.5**).

A person who acts as a secondary party to an offence carrying obligatory disqualification is liable to 10 penalty points.

If a person is found guilty of more than one offence on the same occasion, the range of penalty points is taken as being whichever is the highest available for any one offence (eg a person convicted of speeding (3–6 points) and no insurance (6–8 points) is liable to receive up to 8 points). A court does, however, have discretion to ignore any of the offences (Road Traffic Act 1988, s 28).

Where a court orders obligatory disqualification and there are further offences to be sentenced (eg driving with excess alcohol and no insurance), it should not order points for the further offences (Road Traffic Act 1988, s 44(1)).

 See *Blackstone's Criminal Practice 2012* **C7.12–C7.16**

D41 **Prescribed Minimum Sentences**

D41.1 **Criteria**

Burglary	• Latest offence committed on or after 1 December 1999. • Offender aged 18 or over at date of offence. • Convicted of two previous domestic burglaries, both of which occurred after 1 December 1999, and had been convicted of the first burglary before he committed the second. Must have been sentenced to a penalty greater than a discharge. • Minimum three year sentence (discount of 20% permissible for guilty plea).
Drug Trafficking	• Latest offence committed on or after 1 October 1997. • Offender aged 18 or over at date of offence. • Convicted of two previous drug trafficking offences (date of conviction is not relevant). Must have been sentenced to a penalty greater than a discharge. • Minimum seven year sentence (discount of 20% permissible for guilty plea).

Firearms	Minimum five years, or three years (depending on whether offender aged under or over 18 years at time of commission of offence):
	Section 51A of the Firearms Act 1968
	(1) This section applies where—
	    (a) an individual is convicted of—
	        (i) an offence under section 5(1)(a), (ab), (aba), (ac), (ad), (ae), (af) or (c) of this Act,
	        (ii) an offence under section 5(1A)(a) of this Act, or
	        (iii) an offence under any of the provisions of this Act listed in subsection (1A) in respect of a firearm or ammunition specified in section 5(1)(a), (ab), (aba), (ac), (ad), (ae), (af) or (c) or section 5(1A)(a) of this Act, and
	    (b) the offence was committed after the commencement of this section and at a time when he was aged 16 or over.
	(1A) The provisions are—
	    (a) section 16 (possession of firearm with intent to injure);
	    (b) section 16A (possession of firearm with intent to cause fear of violence);
	    (c) section 17 (use of firearm to resist arrest);
	    (d) section 18 (carrying firearm with criminal intent);
	    (e) section 19 (carrying a firearm in a public place);
	    (f) section 20(1) (trespassing in a building with firearm).
	(2) The court shall impose an appropriate custodial sentence (or order for detention) for a term of at least the required minimum term (with or without a fine) unless the court is of the opinion that there are exceptional circumstances relating to the offence or to the offender which justify its not doing so.
	The relevant date for the section 51(1A) offences is 6 April 2007. For all other offences, it is 22 January 2004.

D42 **Pre-Sentence Drug Testing**

D42.1 **Age requirements**

14 years or over.

D42.2 **Criteria**

Note: not in force at time of writing.

Section 161 of the Criminal Justice Act 2003 provides:

Criminal Justice Act 2003, s 161(1)–(4)

(1) Where a person aged 14 or over is convicted of an offence and the court is considering passing a community sentence or a suspended sentence, it may make an order under subsection (2) for the purpose of ascertaining whether the offender has any specified Class A drug in his body.

(2) The order requires the offender to provide, in accordance with the order, samples of any description specified in the order.

(3) Where the offender has not attained the age of 17, the order must provide for the samples to be provided in the presence of an appropriate adult.

(4) If it is proved to the satisfaction of the court that the offender has, without reasonable excuse, failed to comply with the order it may impose on him a fine of an amount not exceeding level 4.

D43 **Pre-Sentence Reports**

D43.1 **Age requirements**

None.

D43.2 **Criteria**

Section 156 of the Criminal Justice Act 2003 provides:

Criminal Justice Act 2003, s 156

(1) In forming any such opinion as is mentioned in section 148(1) or (2)(b), section 152(2) or section 153(2), or in section 1(4)(b) or (c) of the Criminal Justice and Immigration Act 2008 (youth rehabilitation orders with intensive supervision and surveillance or fostering), a court must take into account all such information as is available to it about the circumstances of the offence or (as the case may be) of the offence and the offence or offences associated with it, including any aggravating or mitigating factors.

(2) In forming any such opinion as is mentioned in section 148(2)(a), the court may take into account any information about the offender which is before it.

(3) Subject to subsection (4), a court must obtain and consider a pre-sentence report before—

    (a) in the case of a custodial sentence, forming any such opinion as is mentioned in section 152(2), section 153(2), section 225(1)(b), section 226(1)(b), section 227(1)(b) or section 228(1)(b)(i), or

    (b) in the case of a community sentence, forming any such opinion as is mentioned in section 148(1) or (2)(b), or in section 1(4)(b) or (c) of the Criminal Justice and Immigration Act 2008, or any opinion as to the suitability for the offender of the particular requirement or requirements to be imposed by the community order or youth rehabilitation order.

(4) Subsection (3) does not apply if, in the circumstances of the case, the court is of the opinion that it is unnecessary to obtain a pre-sentence report.

(5) In a case where the offender is aged under 18, the court must not form the opinion mentioned in subsection (4) unless—

    (a) there exists a previous pre-sentence report obtained in respect of the offender, and

    (b) the court has had regard to the information contained in that report, or, if there is more than one such report, the most recent report.

(6) No custodial sentence or community sentence is invalidated by the failure of a court to obtain and consider a pre-sentence report before forming an opinion referred to in subsection (3), but any court on an appeal against such a sentence—

    (a) must, subject to subsection (7), obtain a pre-sentence report if none was obtained by the court below, and

---

    (b) must consider any such report obtained by it or by that court.

(7) Subsection (6)(a) does not apply if the court is of the opinion—

    (a) that the court below was justified in forming an opinion that it was unnecessary to obtain a pre-sentence report, or

    (b) that, although the court below was not justified in forming that opinion, in the circumstances of the case at the time it is before the court, it is unnecessary to obtain a pre-sentence report.

(8) In a case where the offender is aged under 18, the court must not form the opinion mentioned in subsection (7) unless—

    (a) there exists a previous pre-sentence report obtained in respect of the offender, and

    (b) the court has had regard to the information contained in that report, or, if there is more than one such report, the most recent report.

 See *Blackstone's Criminal Practice 2012* **E1.18**

D44 **Previous Convictions**

D44.1 **Age requirements**

None.

D44.2 **Criteria**

Section 143 of the Criminal Justice Act 2003 provides:

Criminal Justice Act 2003, s 143

(1) In considering the seriousness of any offence, the court must consider the offender's culpability in committing the offence and any harm which the offence caused, was intended to cause or might foreseeably have caused.

(2) In considering the seriousness of an offence ('the current offence') committed by an offender who has one or more previous convictions, the court must treat each previous conviction as an aggravating factor if (in the case of that conviction) the court considers that it can reasonably be so treated having regard, in particular, to—
    (a) the nature of the offence to which the conviction relates and its relevance to the current offence, and
    (b) the time that has elapsed since the conviction.

(3) In considering the seriousness of any offence committed while the offender was on bail, the court must treat the fact that it was committed in those circumstances as an aggravating factor.

(4) Any reference in subsection (2) to a previous conviction is to be read as a reference to—
    (a) a previous conviction by a court in the United Kingdom, or
    (b) a previous finding of guilt in service disciplinary proceedings.

(5) Subsections (2) and (4) do not prevent the court from treating—
    (a) a previous conviction by a court outside both the United Kingdom and any other member State, or
    (b) a previous conviction by a court in any member State (other than the United Kingdom) of an offence which is not a relevant offence,
as an aggravating factor in any case where the court considers it appropriate to do so.

(6) For the purposes of this section—
    (a) an offence is 'relevant' if the offence would constitute an offence under the law of any part of the United Kingdom if it were done in that part at the time of the conviction of the defendant for the current offence,

---

(b) 'member State service offence' means an offence which—
  (i) was the subject of proceedings under the service law of a member State other than the United Kingdom, and
  (ii) would constitute an offence under the law of any part of the United Kingdom, or a service offence (within the meaning of the Armed Forces Act 2006), if it were done in any part of the United Kingdom, by a member of Her Majesty's forces, at the time of the conviction of the defendant for the current offence,

 See *Blackstone's Criminal Practice 2012* **D20.45** and **D20.51**

D45 **Prosecution Costs**

D45.1 **Age requirements**

None.

D45.2 **Criteria**

The following principles can be derived from the *Criminal Practice Direction* and *R v Northallerton Magistrates' Court, ex p Dove* [2000] 1 Cr App R (S) 136:

(1) An order to pay costs to the prosecutor should never exceed the sum which, having regard to the defendant's means and any other financial order imposed upon him, the defendant was able to pay and which it was reasonable to order the defendant to pay.

(2) Such an order should never exceed the sum that the prosecutor had actually and reasonably incurred (or was liable to a third-party to pay, for example, when that third-party commissions a report on behalf of the prosecution).

(3) The purpose of such an order was to compensate the prosecutor and not punish the defendant. Where the defendant had by his conduct put the prosecutor to avoidable expense he might, subject to his means, be ordered to pay some or all of that sum to the prosecutor. However, he was not to be punished for exercising his constitutional right to defend himself.

(4) Whilst there was no requirement that any sum ordered by justices to be paid to a prosecutor by way of costs should stand in any arithmetical relationship to any fine imposed, the costs ordered to be paid should not in any ordinary way be grossly disproportionate to the fine. Justices should ordinarily begin by deciding on the appropriate fine to reflect the criminality of the defendant's offence, always bearing in mind his means and ability to pay, and then consider what, if any, costs he should be ordered to pay to the prosecutor. If, when the costs sought by the prosecutor were added to the proposed fine, the total exceeded the sum which in the light of the defendant's means and all other relevant circumstances the defendant could reasonably be ordered to pay, it was preferable to achieve an acceptable total by reducing the sum of costs which the defendant was ordered to pay rather than by reducing the fine.

(5) If the offender fails to disclose properly his means to the court, reasonable inferences can be drawn as to his means from evidence they had heard and all the circumstances of the case.

In determining the amount of costs to be paid by an offender, consideration should be given to any time that the offender has spent in custody on remand, if the court is to go on to impose any further punishment (for example, a community order) (*R v Rakib* [2011] EWCA Crim 870).

D45.3 **Costs scale**

The CPS has issued the policy in relation to costs in **Appendix 1**.

 See *Blackstone's Criminal Practice 2012* **D31**

D46 Racially and Religiously Aggravated Crimes

D46.1 Age requirements

None.

D46.2 Criteria

Section 145 of the Criminal Justice Act 2003 provides:

Criminal Justice Act 2003, s 145

(1) This section applies where a court is considering the seriousness of an offence other than one under sections 29 to 32 of the Crime and Disorder Act 1998 (c 37) (racially or religiously aggravated assaults, criminal damage, public order offences and harassment etc).

(2) If the offence was racially or religiously aggravated, the court—
   (a) must treat that fact as an aggravating factor, and
   (b) must state in open court that the offence was so aggravated.

(3) Section 28 of the Crime and Disorder Act 1998 (meaning of 'racially or religiously aggravated') applies for the purposes of this section as it applies for the purposes of sections 29 to 32 of that Act. An offence is racially or religiously aggravated if—
   (a) at the time of committing the offence, or immediately before or after doing so, the offender demonstrates towards the victim of the offence hostility based on the victim's membership (or presumed membership) of a racial or religious group; or
   (b) the offence is motivated (wholly or partly) by hostility towards members of a racial or religious group based on their membership of that group.

Following the guidance given by the court in *R v Kelly and Donnelly* [2001] 2 Cr App R (S) 73 (p 341), the court should follow a two-stage process, identifying first the sentence it would have passed if the offence had not been racially aggravated and then adding an appropriate uplift to reflect the racial element so that the sentencing process is transparent and the public could see to what extent the racial element had been reflected. There is no fixed uplift, but in *Kelly and Donnelly*, an uplift of 50 per cent was applied.

 See *Blackstone's Criminal Practice 2012* **B11.131–B11.134**

D47 **Referral Orders**

D47.1 **Age requirements**

Under 18 years.

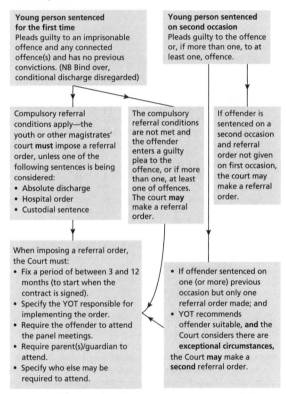

Young person sentenced for the first time
Pleads guilty to an imprisonable offence and any connected offence(s) and has no previous convictions. (NB Bind over, conditional discharge disregarded)

Young person sentenced on second occasion
Pleads guilty to the offence or, if more than one, to at least one, offence.

Compulsory referral conditions apply—the youth or other magistrates' court **must** impose a referral order, unless one of the following sentences is being considered:
• Absolute discharge
• Hospital order
• Custodial sentence

The compulsory referral conditions are not met and the offender enters a guilty plea to the offence, or if more than one, at least one of offences. The court **may** make a referral order.

If offender is sentenced on a second occasion and referral order not given on first occasion, the court may make a referral order.

When imposing a referral order, the Court must:
• Fix a period of between 3 and 12 months (to start when the contract is signed).
• Specify the YOT responsible for implementing the order.
• Require the offender to attend the panel meetings.
• Require parent(s)/guardian to attend.
• Specify who else may be required to attend.

• If offender sentenced on one (or more) previous occasion but only one referral order made; and
• YOT recommends offender suitable, **and** the Court considers there are **exceptional circumstances**, the Court **may** make a **second** referral order.

D47.2 **Requirements**

The court must make an order (PCC(S)A 2000, s 17(1)) where:

• the offence is punishable with imprisonment;
• the offender has pleaded guilty to the offence(s);
• the court is not imposing an absolute discharge, hospital order, or a custodial sentence;

- the offender has never previously been convicted (in the United Kingdom) of an offence or bound over.

The court may make an order where:

- the offender has never previously been convicted (in the United Kingdom) of an offence other than the offence and any connected offence; or
- the offender has been dealt with by a UK court for any offence other than the offence and any connected offence on only one previous occasion, but was not referred to a youth offender panel on that occasion; or
- the offender has been dealt with by a UK court for any offence other than the offence and any connected offence on only one previous occasion, and was referred to a youth offender panel on that occasion, and an appropriate officer recommends that the offender is suitable for a further referral order, and the court considers that there are exceptional circumstances justifying the offender to be so referred.

The Ministry of Justice has given examples of when a further referral order might be appropriate:

The court must specify a compliance period of between three and 12 months.

Example one:

1. The first referral order has been completed; and
2. A substantive period of time (a minimum of at least a year) had passed without any further offences being committed; and
3. The YOT recommends a second referral order on the basis that it is the most effective way of reducing further offending.

Example two:

1. The first referral order has been completed—the offence had no clear victim; and
2. A substantive period of time (a minimum of at least a year) had passed without any further offences being committed; and
3. The YOT recommends a second referral order on the basis that the second offence involved a clear victim and there is a clear opportunity to engage the restorative justice approach of referral to prevent reoffending.

D47.3 Breach

- Failure to comply with the order can result in resentence for the offence(s).
- Commission of a new offence during the life of the referral order can result in revocation of the order, or, if there are exceptional circumstances, an extension to the order (but note that the order may not extend beyond 12 months).
- Conviction for an offence committed prior to the order can result in a custodial sentence, hospital order, absolute discharge, or an extension to the compliance period of the order.

If an offender is sentenced to a custodial sentence or hospital order, any referral order must be revoked and the offender resentenced for the original offence.

Schedule 1, Part II, paras 10–12 to the PCCS(A) 2000 detail the powers when a further offence is sentenced during the period of the order:

Powers of Criminal Courts (Sentencing) Act 2000, Sch 1, Pt II, paras 10–12

10 Extension of referral for further offences

(1) Paragraphs 11 and 12 below apply where, at a time when an offender aged under 18 is subject to referral, a youth court or other magistrates' court ('the relevant court') is dealing with him for an offence in relation to which paragraphs (a) to (c) of section 16(1) of this Act are applicable.

(2) But paragraphs 11 and 12 do not apply unless the offender's compliance period is less than twelve months.

11 Extension where further offences committed pre-referral

If—
(a) the occasion on which the offender was referred to the panel is the only other occasion on which it has fallen to a court in the United Kingdom to deal with the offender for any offence or offences, and
(b) the offender committed the offence mentioned in paragraph 10 above, and any connected offence, before he was referred to the panel,
the relevant court may sentence the offender for the offence by making an order extending his compliance period.

12 Extension where further offence committed after referral

(1) If—
(a) paragraph 11(a) above applies, but
(b) the offender committed the offence mentioned in paragraph 10 above, or any connected offence, after he was referred to the panel,
the relevant court may sentence the offender for the offence by making an order extending his compliance period, but only if the requirements of sub-paragraph (2) below are complied with.

---

(2) Those requirements are that the court must—
   (a) be satisfied, on the basis of a report made to it by the relevant body, that there are exceptional circumstances which indicate that, even though the offender has re-offended since being referred to the panel, extending his compliance period is likely to help prevent further re-offending by him; and
   (b) state in open court that it is so satisfied and why it is.

(3) In sub-paragraph (2) above 'the relevant body' means the panel to which the offender has been referred or, if no contract has yet taken effect between the offender and the panel under section 23 of this Act, the specified team.

See *Blackstone's Criminal Practice 2012* **E10**

D48 **Remand to Hospital for Reports**

D48.1 **Age requirements**

None.

D48.2 **Criteria**

Section 35 of the Mental Health Act 1983 provides:

Mental Health Act 1983, s 35

(1) Subject to the provisions of this section, the Crown Court or a magistrates' court may remand an accused person to a hospital specified by the court for a report on his mental condition.

(2) For the purposes of this section an accused person is—

   (a) . . .

   (b) in relation to a magistrates' court, any person who has been convicted by the court of an offence punishable on summary conviction with imprisonment and any person charged with such an offence if the court is satisfied that he did the act or made the omission charged or he has consented to the exercise by the court of the powers conferred by this section.

(3) Subject to subsection (4) below, the powers conferred by this section may be exercised if—

   (a) the court is satisfied, on the written or oral evidence of a registered medical practitioner, that there is reason to suspect that the accused person is suffering from mental illness, psychopathic disorder, severe mental impairment or mental impairment; and

   (b) the court is of the opinion that it would be impracticable for a report on his mental condition to be made if he were remanded on bail; but those powers shall not be exercised by the Crown Court in respect of a person who has been convicted before the court if the sentence for the offence of which he has been convicted is fixed by law.

(4) The court shall not remand an accused person to a hospital under this section unless satisfied, on the written or oral evidence of the registered medical practitioner who would be responsible for making the report or of some other person representing the managers of the hospital, that arrangements have been made for his admission to that hospital and for his admission to it within the period of seven days beginning with the date of the remand; and if the court is so satisfied it may, pending his admission, give directions for his conveyance to and detention in a place of safety.

(5) Where a court has remanded an accused person under this section it may further remand him if it appears to the court, on the written or oral evidence of the registered medical practitioner responsible for making the report, that a further remand is necessary for completing the assessment of the accused person's mental condition.

---

(6) The power of further remanding an accused person under this section may be exercised by the court without his being brought before the court if he is represented by an authorised person who is given an opportunity of being heard.

(7) An accused person shall not be remanded or further remanded under this section for more than 28 days at a time or for more than 12 weeks in all; and the court may at any time terminate the remand if it appears to the court that it is appropriate to do so.

(8) An accused person remanded to hospital under this section shall be entitled to obtain at his own expense an independent report on his mental condition from a registered medical practitioner or approved clinician chosen by him and to apply to the court on the basis of it for his remand to be terminated under subsection (7) above.

(9) Where an accused person is remanded under this section—
   (a) a constable or any other person directed to do so by the court shall convey the accused person to the hospital specified by the court within the period mentioned in subsection (4) above; and
   (b) the managers of the hospital shall admit him within that period and thereafter detain him in accordance with the provisions of this section.

(10) If an accused person absconds from a hospital to which he has been remanded under this section, or while being conveyed to or from that hospital, he may be arrested without warrant by any constable and shall, after being arrested, be brought as soon as practicable before the court that remanded him; and the court may thereupon terminate the remand and deal with him in any way in which it could have dealt with him if he had not been remanded under this section.

 See *Blackstone's Criminal Practice 2012* D20.74

D49 **Remitting a Juvenile**

D49.1 **Age requirements**

None.

D49.2 **Criteria**

If a youth is convicted before a magistrates' court, that court must remit the case to a youth court for sentence unless it proposes to deal with him by way of discharge, fine, or parental bind over. An offender who was a youth at the start of the proceedings and falls to be sentenced when an adult should be remitted to the youth court in the same manner (PCC(S)A 2000, s 8). Where a case is remitted under section 8, the offender has no right of appeal against the order of remission, but shall have the same right of appeal against any order of the court to which the case is remitted as if he had been convicted by that court.

 See *Blackstone's Criminal Practice 2012* **D24**

D50 **Reparation Order**

D50.1 **Age requirements**

Offender aged under 18 years.

D50.2 **Criteria**

Section 73 of the PCC(S)A 2000 provides:

> **Powers of Criminal Courts (Sentencing) Act 2000, s 73(1)–(3)**
>
> (1) Where a child or young person (that is to say, any person aged under 18) is convicted of an offence other than one for which the sentence is fixed by law, the court by or before which he is convicted may make an order requiring him to make reparation specified in the order—
>   (a) to a person or persons so specified; or
>   (b) to the community at large;
>   and any person so specified must be a person identified by the court as a victim of the offence or a person otherwise affected by it.
> (2) . . .
> (3) In this section and section 74 below 'make reparation', in relation to an offender, means make reparation for the offence otherwise than by the payment of compensation; and the requirements that may be specified in a reparation order are subject to section 74(1) to (3).

The court shall not make a reparation order in respect of the offender if it proposes to pass on him a custodial sentence; or to make in respect of him a community order under section 177 of the Criminal Justice Act 2003, a supervision order which includes requirements authorized by Schedule 6 to this Act, an action plan order, or a referral order.

 See *Blackstone's Criminal Practice 2012* E11

493

D51 Restitution Order

D51.1 Age requirements

None.

D51.2 Criteria

A court passing sentence in handling cases should always have in mind the power to make restitution orders (*R v Webbe and others* [2002] 1 Cr App R (S) 22).

Section 148 of the PCC(S)A 2000 provides:

Powers of Criminal Courts (Sentencing) Act 2000, s 148(1)–(5)

(1) This section applies where goods have been stolen, and either—
   (a) a person is convicted of any offence with reference to the theft (whether or not the stealing is the gist of his offence); or
   (b) a person is convicted of any other offence, but such an offence as is mentioned in paragraph (a) above is taken into consideration in determining his sentence.
(2) Where this section applies, the court by or before which the offender is convicted may on the conviction (whether or not the passing of sentence is in other respects deferred) exercise any of the following powers—
   (a) the court may order anyone having possession or control of the stolen goods to restore them to any person entitled to recover them from him; or
   (b) on the application of a person entitled to recover from the person convicted any other goods directly or indirectly representing the stolen goods (as being the proceeds of any disposal or realisation of the whole or part of them or of goods so representing them), the court may order those other goods to be delivered or transferred to the applicant; or
   (c) the court may order that a sum not exceeding the value of the stolen goods shall be paid, out of any money of the person convicted which was taken out of his possession on his apprehension, to any person who, if those goods were in the possession of the person convicted, would be entitled to recover them from him;
   and in this subsection 'the stolen goods' means the goods referred to in subsection (1) above.
(3) Where the court has power on a person's conviction to make an order against him both under paragraph (b) and under paragraph (c) of subsection (2) above with reference to the stealing of the same goods, the court may make orders under both paragraphs provided that the person in whose favour the orders are made does not thereby recover more than the value of those goods.

(4) Where the court on a person's conviction makes an order under subsection (2)(a) above for the restoration of any goods, and it appears to the court that the person convicted—

(a) has sold the goods to a person acting in good faith, or

(b) has borrowed money on the security of them from a person so acting, the court may order that there shall be paid to the purchaser or lender, out of any money of the person convicted which was taken out of his possession on his apprehension, a sum not exceeding the amount paid for the purchase by the purchaser or, as the case may be, the amount owed to the lender in respect of the loan.

(5) The court shall not exercise the powers conferred by this section unless in the opinion of the court the relevant facts sufficiently appear from evidence given at the trial or the available documents, together with admissions made by or on behalf of any person in connection with any proposed exercise of the powers.

 See *Blackstone's Criminal Practice 2012* E17

D52 **Restraining Order**

D52.1 **Age requirements**

None.

D52.2 **Criteria**

A court may impose a restraining order following conviction or acquittal (acquittal includes where the prosecution offer no evidence on a charge). Sections 5 and 5A provide:

> **Protection from Harassment Act 1997, s 5**
>
> (1) . . .
> (2) The order may, for the purpose of protecting the victim or victims of the offence, or any other person mentioned in the order, from further conduct which—
>   (a) amounts to harassment, or
>   (b) will cause a fear of violence,
>   prohibit the defendant from doing anything described in the order.
> (3) The order may have effect for a specified period or until further order.
> (4) The prosecutor, the defendant or any other person mentioned in the order may apply to the court which made the order for it to be varied or discharged by a further order.
> (5) If without reasonable excuse the defendant does anything which he is prohibited from doing by an order under this section, he is guilty of an offence.
> (6) A person guilty of an offence under this section is liable—
>   (a) on conviction on indictment, to imprisonment for a term not exceeding five years, or a fine, or both, or
>   (b) on summary conviction, to imprisonment for a term not exceeding six months, or a fine not exceeding the statutory maximum, or both.

The terms of the order must be proportionate and not violate the offender's human rights. However, a person can harass someone by publishing truthful things (eg that someone is gay), and an order can be made preventing publication of information that is the truth, and such an order will not violate a person's right of freedom of expression under the European Convention (*R v Debnath* [2006] 2 Cr App R (S) 25).

An order must name the person that it is seeking to protect (*R v Mann* The Times, 11 April 2000), but there is no reason in principle why an order cannot be made to protect a group of individuals or a company (*R v Buxton*, unreported, 1 December 2010).

In relation to restraining orders after acquittal, a new legal aid order should be sought from the court, and the matter billed separately (as a cds7 non-standard claim).

The following points emerge from *R v Major*, unreported, 1 December 2010:

It was not Parliament's intention that orders be made only when the facts are uncontested, nor that orders should only rarely be made.

The civil standard of proof applies.

There is no contradiction in making an order post-acquittal as the standard of proof required for a conviction is higher than that for making a restraining order:

- The evidence did not have to establish on the balance of probabilities that there had been harassment; it was enough if the evidence established conduct which fell short of harassment but which might well, if repeated in the future, amount to harassment and so make an order necessary.
- The court should set out the factual basis for making an order.

Section 5A of the Protection from Harassment Act 1997 provides:

Protection from Harassment Act 1997, s 5A

(1) A court before which a person ('the defendant') is acquitted of an offence may, if it considers it necessary to do so to protect a person from harassment by the defendant, make an order prohibiting the defendant from doing anything described in the order.

(2) Subsections (3) to (7) of section 5 apply to an order under this section as they apply to an order under that one.

(3) . . .

(4) . . .

(5) A person made subject to an order under this section has the same right of appeal against the order as if—

    (a) he had been convicted of the offence in question before the court which made the order, and

    (b) the order had been made under section 5.

 See *Blackstone's Criminal Practice 2012* **E21.14**

D53 **Return to Custody**

D53.1 **Age requirements**

None.

D53.2 **Criteria**

This power applies to those released on determinate sentences under the Criminal Justice Act 1991 (ie for offences committed prior to 4 April 2005—irrespective of when they are sentenced), and to those released from a sentence of less than 12 months imposed under the Criminal Justice Act 2003 for offences on or after 4 April 2005.

A court has the power (but is not obliged) to return a prisoner for the unexpired part of his sentence if at any time during that unexpired part he commits an imprisonable offence. It does not matter that the sentence for the original offence might have expired at the time of sentence for the new matter. An offender will be returned to prison for the whole or part of the period beginning with the date of new offence, and ending with the sentence expiry date, remembering to credit any period during which the offender has been recalled by the parole board. It is important that the offender is sentenced to serve the ordered return period before any additional sentence of imprisonment. If the unexpired part is more than six months the magistrates' court can commit the matter to the Crown Court for sentence.

D54 Sentencing Guidelines Issued by the Sentencing Council

D54.1 Age requirements

None.

D54.2 Criteria

On 5 April 2010 the Sentencing Council took over the role previously carried out by the Sentencing Guidelines Council and Sentencing Advisory Panel. A court must follow sentencing guidelines issued by the Sentencing Council unless it is contrary to the interests of justice to do so (Coroners and Justice Act 2009, s 125).

Section 174(2) of the Criminal Justice Act 2003 provides:

> **Criminal Justice Act 2003, s 174(2)**
>
> . . . the court must—
> (a) identify any definitive sentencing guidelines relevant to the offender's case and explain how the court discharged any duty imposed on it by section 125 of the Coroners and Justice Act 2009,
> (aa) where the court did not follow any such guidelines because it was of the opinion that it would be contrary to the interests of justice to do so, state why it was of that opinion,

Relevant guidelines are reproduced in the offences section of this book.

 See *Blackstone's Criminal Practice 2012* E1

D55 Sexual Offences Notification Requirements

D55.1 Age requirements

None.

D55.2 Criteria

It is not a requirement that a court 'orders' a notification requirement, as it will follow automatically as a result of a qualifying conviction (ie those offences specified in Schedule 3 to the Sexual Offences Act 2003).

An offender will be given a notice to sign and be provided with his own copy that sets down the requirements to be satisfied. In *R v D*, unreported, 3 November 2008 D was ordered to complete 220 hours of unpaid work within a 12-month period. An issue arose as to whether the defendant was, therefore, subject to notification requirements (Sexual Offences Act 2003). D submitted that a community order which contains solely an unpaid work requirement to be completed within 12 months is not a community sentence of at least 12 months duration as it is open to the offender to complete the work within the 12-month period and on completion of the work the community order ceases. He relied on *Odam* [2008] EWCA Crim 1087. The court held:

> We have had the benefit of helpful written and oral argument on behalf of both the applicant and the respondent which were not available to the court in *Odam*. These have led us to the conclusion that the length of a community order must be capable of being determined on the date it is made. In our judgement the period specified under section 177(5) of the Criminal Justice Act 2003 by a court when imposing a community order is the relevant period for the purpose of determining the duration of the order under paragraph 18(b)(ii)(c) of Schedule 3 to the Sexual Offences Act 2003 however long it in fact takes the offender to carry out the requirements under the order. It follows that in our judgement the opinion expressed in *Odam* was wrong.

Penalty	Notification period for an adult	Notification period for an offender aged under 18 years
Conditional discharge	Period of discharge	Period of discharge
Imprisonment for a term of 6 months or less	7 years	3½ years
Imprisonment for a minimum term of 6 months but less than 30 months	10 years	5 years
Detention element of a detention and training order not exceeding 12 months	3½ years (an adult can receive a detention and training order in certain circumstances)	3½ years
Detention element of a detention and training order exceeding 12 months	5 years	5 years

D55.3 Transfer of responsibility to those with parental responsibility

In respect to offenders under 18 years, however, the court has a discretion to impose the notification obligations onto a person with parental responsibility for the young offender. Given that non-compliance is a criminal offence, advocates should always try to persuade a court to do this in order to remove the obligation from the child (Sexual Offences Act 2003, s 89).

See *Blackstone's Criminal Practice 2012* **E23**

D56 **Sexual Offences Prevention Order**

D56.1 Age requirements

None.

D56.2 Criteria

Following conviction for an offence specified in Schedule 3 (other than paragraph 60) or 5 to the Sexual Offences Act 2003, the court may go on to consider whether or not to make a sexual offences prevention order (Sexual Offences Act 2003, s 104). It is important to be aware that Schedule 5 contains a wide range of non-sexual offences.

A court may make such an order if satisfied that it is necessary to make such an order, for the purpose of protecting the public or any particular members of the public from serious sexual harm from the defendant. The offence in question may predate 1 May 2004. It is important to note that there is nothing in section 104 to indicate that a court must believe a defendant to be 'dangerous' (within the meaning of the public protection sentencing regime) before it can make such an order (*R v Richards* [2006] EWCA Crim 2519).

A sexual offences prevention order:

- prohibits the defendant from doing anything described in the order; and
- has effect for a fixed period (not less than five years) specified in the order or until further order.

The only prohibitions that may be included in the order are those necessary for the purpose of protecting the public or any particular members of the public from serious sexual harm from the defendant.

An order must be made for a period not less than five years, and may be indefinite.

 See *Blackstone's Criminal Practice 2012* **E21.13**

D57 Sexual Orientation or Disability

Section 146 of the Criminal Justice Act 2003 provides:

Criminal Justice Act 2003, s 146

(1) This section applies where the court is considering the seriousness of an offence committed in any of the circumstances mentioned in subsection (2).

(2) Those circumstances are—

    (a) that, at the time of committing the offence, or immediately before or after doing so, the offender demonstrated towards the victim of the offence hostility based on—

        (i) the sexual orientation (or presumed sexual orientation) of the victim, or

        (ii) a disability (or presumed disability) of the victim, or

    (b) that the offence is motivated (wholly or partly)—

        (i) by hostility towards persons who are of a particular sexual orientation, or

        (ii) by hostility towards persons who have a disability or a particular disability.

(3) The court—

    (a) must treat the fact that the offence was committed in any of those circumstances as an aggravating factor, and

    (b) must state in open court that the offence was committed in such circumstances.

(4) It is immaterial for the purposes of paragraph (a) or (b) of subsection (2) whether or not the offender's hostility is also based, to any extent, on any other factor not mentioned in that paragraph.

(5) In this section 'disability' means any physical or mental impairment.

 See *Blackstone's Criminal Practice 2012* E1.10

D58 **Supervision Order**

D58.1 **Age requirements**

Offender aged under 18 years. For offenders aged 16 or 17 years the offence must have been committed before 30 November 2009.

D58.2 **Criteria**

The general requirements for the making of a community order must be satisfied (see **D10.2**).

A supervision order may impose one or more of the following requirements:

- residence requirement;
- reparation requirement;
- specified activities;
- refraining from specific activities;
- school attendance;
- psychiatric treatment.

 See *Blackstone's Criminal Practice 2012* **E9**

D59 **Surcharge Order**

D59.1 **Age requirements**

None.

D59.2 **Criteria**

In any case relating to an offence committed on or after 1 April 2007, the court must impose a surcharge order if a fine is imposed (Criminal Justice Act 2003, s 161A). The surcharge, currently £15, may be reduced if the offender were not able to pay both the surcharge and compensation. If the offender were not able to pay both a surcharge and fine, the surcharge takes precedence and the fine should be reduced.

 See *Blackstone's Criminal Practice 2012* E15.15

D60 Suspended Sentences

D60.1 Age requirements

None.

D60.2 Offences committed on or after 4 April 2005: suspended sentence orders

A magistrates' court may suspend a sentence of not less than 14 days, and not more than six months (Criminal Justice Act 2003, s 189). The minimum and maximum periods can be made up from single or consecutive sentences. Where a person has served such time on remand that a custodial sentence would result in immediate release, it is not appropriate to impose a suspended sentence order (*R v Waters and Young*, unreported, 8 October 2008).

The court must order:

(a) An operational period of between six months and two years (which may extend beyond the operational period).

(b) A supervision period of between six months and two years (which must not extend beyond the operational period).

(c) Community requirement(s) to be completed as part of the order. (Note: the court must impose at least one community requirement: *R v Lees-Wolfenden* [2007] 1 Cr App R (S) 119, CA.)

D60.3 Breach of suspended sentence order

An order will be breached if the offender does not comply with a community requirement during the supervision period, or commits a further offence during the operational period. Following conviction for a new offence a magistrates' court has no jurisdiction to deal with breach of a suspended sentence order imposed by the Crown Court; it must either commit the offender for sentence upon conviction for the new offence, or notify the Crown Court of the breach so that that court can take action if it so wishes. A Crown Court order will specify whether or not any breach of its requirments should result in a return to the Crown Court, or be left to the magistrates' court (it is the norm for a Crown Court to order any breach be reserved to itself).

Upon a breach being proved the court has the following options open:

(a) order the sentence to take effect (ie send the offender to prison), or
(b) order the sentence to take effect but with a reduced term of imprisonment; or
(c) impose more onerous community requirements.

Note: the court must order (a) or (b) unless it would be unjust to do so in all the circumstances. A court must give reasons for so ordering.

 See *Blackstone's Criminal Practice 2012* **E6**

D61 **Time on Remand**

D61.1 **Age requirements**

None.

D61.2 **Criteria**

Section 240 of the Criminal Justice Act 2003 provides that time spent on remand in custody should be taken into account when sentencing an offender. A court declining to allow credit for time on remand must state its reasons for so ruling. A person sentenced to a community order which is subsequently breached, resulting in imprisonment, is entitled to credit for any time on remand served prior to the community order being imposed (and indeed if on remand subsequently). Section 240 does not apply in relation to detention and training orders, but credit should be given in the same way (see **D22.4**).

Section 240A of the Criminal Justice Act 2003 enables the sentencing court to direct that time spent on bail under an electronically monitored curfew should be credited against a custodial sentence in a similar way to the manner in which remands in custody are credited. A person will receive credit at the rate of a half a day for every day spent subject to a qualifying electronically monitored curfew (that is a curfew of nine hours a day or more).

 See *Blackstone's Criminal Practice 2012* **E2.8**

D62 Youth Rehabilitation Order: Criminal Justice and Immigration Act 2008

D62.1 Overview

As of 30 November 2009 the only community order available for a youth is a youth rehabilitation order (YRO)—comprising one or more requirements tailored to meeting the statutory sentencing purposes. To assist the court in tailoring the order to the offender's needs a 'tailored approach' to intervention will be adopted. In addition regard should be had to principles of youth sentencing issued by the Sentencing Council. There are no restrictions on the number of times an offender can be sentenced to a YRO. Courts would be expected to use the YRO on multiple occasions, adapting the menu as appropriate to deal with the offending behaviour.

For the court to sentence a young person to a YRO, the court must consider the offence serious enough to warrant a YRO, and the restriction of liberty involved must be proportionate to seriousness of offence (Criminal Justice Act 2003, ss 147–148).

The court will specify the date or dates by which particular requirements must be completed; the maximum period of a YRO is three years. If the young person is already subject to a YRO or reparation order, the court cannot sentence to a YRO, unless the existing orders have been revoked. The court will also have the power to order a sentence review in particular YRO cases.

The Act sets the threshold for a YRO with Intensive Supervision and Surveillance Requirement (ISSR) or Intensive Fostering provisions that the offence(s) must be imprisonable and so serious that if a YRO with ISSR and/or Intensive Fostering was not available then a sentence of custody would be appropriate; and in addition for under 15-year-olds the young person must be a persistent offender. A YRO with ISSR or Intensive Fostering requirement must be for a minimum six months; the ISSR must be a minimum of 90 days and a maximum of 180 days.

The new youth sentence structure following the Criminal Justice and Immigration Act 2008 is:

Custody

Detention & Training Order

s 91—serious offence

s 228—extended sentence/ public protection

s 226—indeterminate/ public protection

s 90—mandatory life/ Murder

Intensive Supervision and Surveillance Requirement

Intensive Fostering Requirement

Youth Rehabilitation Order

Exclusion Requirement

Education Requirement

Prohibited Activity Requirement

Electronic Monitoring Requirement

Drug Testing Requirement

Drug Treatment Requirement

LA Residence Requirement

Unpaid Work Requirement (16/17 yr olds only)

Intoxicating substance treatment requirement

Activity Requirement

Supervision Requirement

Curfew Requirement

Programme Requirement

Residence Requirement (16/17 yr olds only)

Mental Health Treatment Requirement

Attendance Centre Requirement

- YRO can be used by courts on multiple occasions
- YRO cannot exceed 3 years
- Parenting Orders available

Pre-Court

Police Reprimand

Final Warning

Youth Conditional Caution

First Tier

Absolute Discharge

Conditional Discharge

Compensation Order

Fine

Referral Order

Reparation Order

Sentence Deferred

Sentencing will follow a two-stage process: identifying the intervention level, and then tailoring a sentence to meet that need.

D62.1.1 *Intervention level*

Child/young person profile	Intervention level
Low likelihood of reoffending (as indicated by *Asset* score [dynamic and static factors] between 0 and 14 inclusive) AND **Low risk of serious harm** (as indicated by no risk of serious harm assessment being required, or low risk of serious harm assessment)	**STANDARD**
Medium likelihood of reoffending (as indicated by *Asset* score [dynamic and static factors] between 15 and 32 inclusive) OR **Medium risk of serious harm** (as indicated by risk of serious harm assessment)	**ENHANCED**
High likelihood of reoffending (as indicated by *Asset* score [dynamic and static factors] between 33 and 64 inclusive) OR **High or very high risk of serious harm** (as indicated by risk of serious harm assessment)	**INTENSIVE**

Source: Youth Justice Board: 'Youth Justice—The Scaled Approach 2009'

D62.1.2 *Tailored sentencing*

Intervention level	Function	Typical case management approach	Possible sentence requirement/component (not exclusive)
STANDARD	Enabling compliance and repairing harm	• Organizing interventions to meet basic requirements of order • Engaging parents in interventions and/or to support young person • Monitoring compliance • Enforcement	• Reparation • Stand-alone unpaid work • Supervision • Stand-alone attendance centre
ENHANCED	Enabling compliance and repairing harm AND Enabling help/change	• Brokering access to external interventions • Coordinating interventions with specialists in YOT • Providing supervision • Engaging parents in interventions and/or supporting young person • Providing motivation to encourage compliance • Proactively addressing reasons for non-compliance • Enforcement	• Supervision • Reparation • Requirement/component to help young person or change behaviour, eg drug treatment, offending behaviour programme, education programme • Combination of the above
INTENSIVE	Enabling compliance and repairing harm AND Enabling help/change AND Ensuring control	• Extensive • Help/change function plus additional controls, restrictions and monitoring	• Supervision • Reparation PLUS • Requirement/component to monitor or restrict movement, eg prohibited activity, curfew, exclusion, or electronic monitoring • Combination of the above

D62.2 Requirements

An order must be made up of one or more of the following requirements (along with the options of electronic monitoring, intensive supervision and surveillance or fostering):

(a) an activity requirement (maximum 90 days, or 180 if ISSR imposed);
(b) a supervision requirement;
(c) in a case where the offender is aged 16 or 17 at the time of the conviction, an unpaid work requirement (40–240 hours);
(d) a programme requirement;
(e) an attendance centre requirement (Age 14: maximum 12 hours; 14–15: 12–24 hours; 16–17: 12–36 hours);
(f) a prohibited activity requirement;
(g) a curfew requirement (2–12 hours daily for maximum of 6 months);
(h) an exclusion requirement (maximum three months);
(i) a residence requirement;
(j) a local authority residence requirement (maximum six months or until offender aged 18 years if sooner);
(k) a mental health treatment requirement;
(l) a drug treatment requirement;
(m) a drug testing requirement;
(n) an intoxicating substance treatment requirement;
(o) an education requirement.

Intensive supervision and surveillance is only for those aged 15 years and over, unless a persistent offender.

Fostering is for a maximum period of 12 months or until offender aged 18 years if sooner.

D62.3 Legislation

Section 1 provides:

Criminal Justice and Immigration Act 2008, s 1

(1) Where a person aged under 18 is convicted of an offence, the court by or before which the person is convicted may in accordance with Schedule 1 make an order (in this Part referred to as a 'youth rehabilitation order') imposing on the person any one or more of the following requirements—
    (a) an activity requirement (see paragraphs 6 to 8 of Schedule 1),
    (b) a supervision requirement (see paragraph 9 of that Schedule),
    (c) in a case where the offender is aged 16 or 17 at the time of the conviction, an unpaid work requirement (see paragraph 10 of that Schedule),

     (d) a programme requirement (see paragraph 11 of that Schedule),

     (e) an attendance centre requirement (see paragraph 12 of that Schedule),

     (f) a prohibited activity requirement (see paragraph 13 of that Schedule),

     (g) a curfew requirement (see paragraph 14 of that Schedule),

     (h) an exclusion requirement (see paragraph 15 of that Schedule),

     (i) a residence requirement (see paragraph 16 of that Schedule),

     (j) a local authority residence requirement (see paragraph 17 of that Schedule),

     (k) a mental health treatment requirement (see paragraph 20 of that Schedule),

     (l) a drug treatment requirement (see paragraph 22 of that Schedule),

     (m) a drug testing requirement (see paragraph 23 of that Schedule),

     (n) an intoxicating substance treatment requirement (see paragraph 24 of that Schedule), and

     (o) an education requirement (see paragraph 25 of that Schedule).

(2) A youth rehabilitation order—

     (a) may also impose an electronic monitoring requirement (see paragraph 26 of Schedule 1), and

     (b) must do so if paragraph 2 of that Schedule so requires.

(3) A youth rehabilitation order may be—

     (a) a youth rehabilitation order with intensive supervision and surveillance (see paragraph 3 of Schedule 1), or

     (b) a youth rehabilitation order with fostering (see paragraph 4 of that Schedule).

(4) But a court may only make an order mentioned in subsection (3)(a) or (b) if—

     (a) the court is dealing with the offender for an offence which is punishable with imprisonment,

     (b) the court is of the opinion that the offence, or the combination of the offence and one or more offences associated with it, was so serious that, but for paragraph 3 or 4 of Schedule 1, a custodial sentence would be appropriate (or, if the offender was aged under 12 at the time of conviction, would be appropriate if the offender had been aged 12), and

     (c) if the offender was aged under 15 at the time of conviction, the court is of the opinion that the offender is a persistent offender.

(5) Schedule 1 makes further provision about youth rehabilitation orders.

(6) This section is subject to—

     (a) sections 148 and 150 of the Criminal Justice Act 2003 (c 44) (restrictions on community sentences etc), and

     (b) the provisions of Parts 1 and 3 of Schedule 1.

D62.4 Breach of youth rehabilitation order

In a YRO case a warning is required if the supervising officer finds there is a failure to comply without reasonable excuse. If following a further second warning, within the 12-month 'warned period', there is then a third failure to comply without reasonable excuse, the officer must refer the case to court for breach proceedings, although YOTs will have additional discretion in exceptional circumstances following a third failure to comply. The officer also has the discretion to refer the case to court at an earlier warning stage.

When dealing with the breach of a YRO, the court has the following options:

- no action;
- fine;
- amend the YRO, but not with ISSR or Intensive Fostering unless that already applies;
- revoke the YRO and resentence.

Custody is an option for breach of a YRO only if the original offence is imprisonable or in the case of a non-imprisonable offence if, following 'wilful and persistent' non-compliance, a YRO with an ISSR or Intensive Fostering provision is made and that further YRO is then also subject to non-compliance. The court, if passing a custodial sentence, must state that a YRO with an ISSR or Intensive Fostering provision is not appropriate and the reasons why. This is in addition to meeting the existing criteria, ie the court forming the opinion that the offence(s) is so serious that a community sentence cannot be justified.

Breach of a youth community order will be dealt with under Schedule 2 to the Act.

Paragraph 6 provides:

Criminal Justice and Immigration Act 2008, Sch 2, para 6

(1) This paragraph applies where—
   (a) an offender appears or is brought before a youth court or other magistrates' court under paragraph 5, and
   (b) it is proved to the satisfaction of the court that the offender has failed without reasonable excuse to comply with the youth rehabilitation order.
(2) The court may deal with the offender in respect of that failure in any one of the following ways—
   (a) by ordering the offender to pay a fine of an amount not exceeding—
      (i) £250, if the offender is aged under 14, or
      (ii) £1,000, in any other case;
   (b) by amending the terms of the youth rehabilitation order so as to impose any requirement which could have been included in the order when it was made—
      (i) in addition to, or
      (ii) in substitution for,
      any requirement or requirements already imposed by the order;

  (c) by dealing with the offender, for the offence in respect of which the order was made, in any way in which the court could have dealt with the offender for that offence (had the offender been before that court to be dealt with for it).

(3) Sub-paragraph (2)(b) is subject to sub-paragraphs (6) to (9).

(4) In dealing with the offender under sub-paragraph (2), the court must take into account the extent to which the offender has complied with the youth rehabilitation order.

(5) A fine imposed under sub-paragraph (2)(a) is to be treated, for the purposes of any enactment, as being a sum adjudged to be paid by a conviction.

(6) Any requirement imposed under sub-paragraph (2)(b) must be capable of being complied with before the date specified under paragraph 32(1) of Schedule 1.

(7) Where—

  (a) the court is dealing with the offender under sub-paragraph (2)(b), and

  (b) the youth rehabilitation order does not contain an unpaid work requirement,

paragraph 10(2) of Schedule 1 applies in relation to the inclusion of such a requirement as if for '40' there were substituted '20'.

(8) The court may not under sub-paragraph (2)(b) impose—

  (a) an extended activity requirement, or

  (b) a fostering requirement,

if the order does not already impose such a requirement.

(9) Where—

  (a) the order imposes a fostering requirement (the 'original requirement'), and

  (b) under sub-paragraph (2)(b) the court proposes to substitute a new fostering requirement ('the substitute requirement') for the original requirement,

paragraph 18(2) of Schedule 1 applies in relation to the substitute requirement as if the reference to the period of 12 months beginning with the date on which the original requirement first had effect were a reference to the period of 18 months beginning with that date.

(10) Where—

  (a) the court deals with the offender under sub-paragraph (2)(b), and

  (b) it would not otherwise have the power to amend the youth rehabilitation order under paragraph 13 (amendment by reason of change of residence),

that paragraph has effect as if references in it to the appropriate court were references to the court which is dealing with the offender.

(11) Where the court deals with the offender under sub-paragraph (2)(c), it must revoke the youth rehabilitation order if it is still in force.

(12) Sub-paragraphs (13) to (15) apply where—

  (a) the court is dealing with the offender under sub-paragraph (2)(c), and

  (b) the offender has wilfully and persistently failed to comply with a youth rehabilitation order.

(13) The court may impose a youth rehabilitation order with intensive supervision and surveillance notwithstanding anything in section 1(4)(a) or (b).

(14) If—
   (a) the order is a youth rehabilitation order with intensive supervision and surveillance, and
   (b) the offence mentioned in sub-paragraph (2)(c) was punishable with imprisonment,

the court may impose a custodial sentence notwithstanding anything in section 152(2) of the Criminal Justice Act 2003 (c 44) (general restrictions on imposing discretionary custodial sentences).

(15) If—
   (a) the order is a youth rehabilitation order with intensive supervision and surveillance which was imposed by virtue of sub-paragraph (13) or paragraph 8(12), and
   (b) the offence mentioned in sub-paragraph (2)(c) was not punishable with imprisonment,

for the purposes of dealing with the offender under sub-paragraph (2)(c), the court is to be taken to have had power to deal with the offender for that offence by making a detention and training order for a term not exceeding 4 months.

(16) An offender may appeal to the Crown Court against a sentence imposed under sub-paragraph (2)(c).

📖 See *Blackstone's Criminal Practice 2012* **E9.2–E9.22**

Application for costs against convicted defendants

Scales of Cost

1. The policy of CPS is to apply for costs against convicted defendants unless the particular circumstances of a case mean that such an application would lack merit or an order for costs would be impractical.

2. The following scales provide guidance on the level of costs incurred by the CPS in various types of proceedings. The scales represent the average costs incurred in a wide range of cases and provide a benchmark to estimate the costs in individual cases (excluding very high-cost cases). The scales are indicative of single-defendant cases only and the figure should be increased by 20 per cent for each additional defendant.

3. More complex cases should attract the higher range of costs and relatively straightforward cases the lower range. The figures include all staff preparation costs, including advocacy in magistrates' courts and time spent in the Crown Court by paralegal officers/assistants. Add to these figures witness expenses, counsel fees or Crown Advocate's advocacy costs (for Crown Court cases), and other specific costs, where appropriate.

4. When seeking a costs order, prosecutors should inform the court of all costs incurred and invite the court to consider what should be paid. Discretion should be exercised in putting forward a reasonable estimate of the costs incurred in the individual case.

5. The average hourly rates appropriate to CPS staff are:

Lawyers	£69 per hour
Paralegals	£51 per hour
Support staff	£44 per hour

Appendix 1

6. Types of Proceedings

Magistrates' Court	Lower	Average	Higher
Proof in Absence		£85 (set amount)	
Early Guilty Plea (EFH)		£85	£100
Summary Guilty Plea	£105	£135	£160
Summary Trial	£620	£775	£930
Either way Guilty Plea	£145	£185	£220
Either way Trial	£770	£965	£1,150
Crown Court	Lower	Average	Higher
Committal for Sentence	£340	£425	£510
Appeal against Sentence	£260	£330	£395
Appeal against Conviction	£415	£520	£620
Section 51 Early Guilty Plea	£535	£670	£800
* Committal for Trial (Plea)	£1,200	£1,500	£1,800
* Committal for Trial (Trial)	£2,800	£3,500	£4,200

* These scales include the costs of committal/transfer/sending proceedings

1 September 2009

Bar Council Guidance: Court Appointed Legal Representatives

Commentary

1. The Criminal Bar Association has been asked by the General Management Committee of the Bar Council to draft brief guidance to assist with the issues which arise when the court appoints legal representatives to act on behalf of defendants and to consider whether a list of suitable counsel and solicitors should be drawn up from which the courts can make such appointments.

There have been previous reports written on this subject[1] and, although in practice, the appointment of counsel by the court is not likely to occur often, as a matter of common sense, when it does occur, it is likely to involve a defendant who is either not cooperating or who is 'playing the system' and such guidance will have to be interpreted liberally if the interests of the defendant are to be preserved and justice is seen to be done.

We have set out in full the background and statutory basis for these issues in order to explain why we have drafted the guidance in the terms we have. The draft guidance itself is annexed to the report.

2. The Background

2.1 The legislation which has provided for this procedure was passed as a result of two widely publicised cases in which a defendant acting in person cross-examined the complainant on an allegation of rape.[2] The Lord Chief Justice gave guidance (in the then absence of statutory reform) in the case of R v Brown (Milton) [1998] 2.Cr.App.R.364 to assist trial judges confronted with such a problem:

'It will often be desirable, before any question is asked by the defendant in cross-examination, for the trial judge to discuss the course of the proceedings with the defendant in the absence of the jury. The judge can then elicit the general nature of the defence and identify the specific points in the complainant's evidence with which the defendant takes issue and any points he wishes to put to her. If the defendant proposes to call witnesses in his own defence, the substance of their

---

[1] Peter Rook QC 27th January, 2001 and Nicholas Price QC March 2002
[2] R v Brown (Milton) [1998] 2Cr.App.R.364 and R v Ralston Edwards

evidence can be elicited so that the complainant's observations on it may, so far as it is relevant, be invited.'

There was further guidance set out as to the steps to be taken to restrict repetition or the intimidation or humiliation of the witness by way of the defendant's dress, bearing, manner or questions.

2.2 Statutory restrictions on cross-examination of the complainant by a defendant in person charged with a sexual offence[3] were imposed by Section 34 of the Youth Justice and Criminal Evidence Act, 1999 (the Act) and this provision is now in force in respect of proceedings commencing on or after 4th September, 2000. This prohibition covers any other offence (of whatever nature) with which that person is charged in the proceedings.[4]

2.3 Section 34A of the Criminal Justice Act, 1988 prohibited cross-examination in person of child witnesses in certain cases and Section 35 of the Act extended this to include the alleged victims of kidnapping, false imprisonment and abduction. This prohibition also extends to cross-examination in respect of other offences with which a defendant is charged in the proceedings.[5]

2.4 There is a further power under Sections 36 and 37 of the Act to prohibit a defendant in person from cross-examining witnesses not covered by Sections 34 & 35 if the court is satisfied, first, that the quality of the witness's evidence is likely to be diminished if the defendant is allowed to proceed and improved if he is prohibited from doing so and secondly, that it would not be contrary to the interests of justice to give such a direction. These provisions came into force on the 24th July, 2002.

2.5 Section 38 of the Act makes provision for the appointment of a qualified legal representative for the purposes of cross-examination of a witness where an accused in person has been prevented from so doing by virtue of Section 34, 35 or 36.

3. Section 38

3.1 Section 38 allows the accused to have the opportunity of appointing his own legal representative to conduct the cross-examination on his behalf. If he does not, Section 38(4) of the Act specifies that where the court has decided that it is necessary in the interests of justice for the witness to be cross-examined by a court appointed legal representative, the court must appoint a qualified legal representative[6] (chosen by the court) to cross-examine the witness in the interests

---

[3] Defined in S.62 YJ&CEA, 1999
[4] S.34(b) YJ&CEA, 1999
[5] S.35(b) YJ&CEA, 1999
[6] Defined in S.38(8)(b) as a legal representative who has a right of audience (within the meaning of the Courts and Legal Services Act 1990) in relation to the proceedings before the court

of the accused. A person so appointed shall not be responsible to the accused.[7] Any reference to cross-examination includes (in a case where a direction under Section 36 has been given after the accused has begun cross-examining the witness) a reference to further cross-examination.[8] Even after the appointment by the court under Section 38(4) of such a legal representative, the accused may arrange for that legal representative to be appointed to act for him and it is then as though he had done so at the outset under Section 38(2)(a) of the Act.[9]

The legal representative is then no longer the representative of the Court.

3.2 We have set out the statutory framework in some detail because the provisions themselves make it clear that there are the two under-lying principles behind the appointment of such a legal representa-tive, namely, that such an appointment is in the interests of justice and that the legal representative is appointed to represent the inter-ests of the accused although not responsible to him. They may sound obvious principles but the tensions which are likely to flow from such a situation make any court appointed legal representative liable to face a number of extremely difficult decisions and it will be a testing task for the judge to ensure that the balance between the interests of justice and the interests of the accused is maintained. One of the obvious problems which we try to deal with in the guidance is the effect of dis-closure material. This may well contain material which could properly be used in cross-examination where it was relevant but in the absence of specific issues identified by the defendant to the Court, it will be extremely difficult for its relevance to be assessed.

4. Code of Conduct

Paragraph 401(a) of the Code of Conduct has been amended to allow for a barrister in independent practice to be appointed by the court but it seems to us very likely that there will have to be other amend-ments made since the role of court appointed counsel who is expressly not responsible to the defendant is quite different from the role of counsel appointed to represent the defendant. An example is under Paragraph 708(a) which deals with conduct in court and which requires that a barrister is personally responsible for the conduct and presentation of his case and must exercise personal judgement upon the substance and purpose of statements made and questions asked. This is likely to be very difficult since the questions asked are likely to be constrained

---

by the judge who will ultimately be responsible for parameters of appropriate cross-examination.

It will also be very important that any court-appointed counsel is as clear as possible as to the purpose and the parameters of any questions to be asked since it is not difficult to foresee a situation where questions asked without instructions may receive answers which either make matters worse for the defendant or open up previously unexplored areas which the Crown may use to their advantage. This may be unavoidable but if both the judge and counsel are fully aware of the nature of the questions to be asked, the danger will be lessened and, if it occurs, counsel will not be at fault. A simple instruction from the court to 'test the evidence' will not be sufficient and the judge will have to be as specific as possible and counsel equally careful as to the questions asked to avoid unnecessarily exposing themselves to complaint from the defendant of unfairness.

5. List of Suitably Qualified Legal Representatives

5.1 As previously set out, 'qualified legal representative' is defined in Section 38(8)(b) as a 'legal representative who has a right of audience (within the meaning of the Courts and Legal Services Act, 1990) in relation to the proceedings before the Court'.

It is, in our view, essential that only legal representatives with the appropriate number of years experience (we suggest seven) in predominantly criminal law with previous experience of cross-examining complainants in sexual cases and children be considered for what is going to be a difficult task. Whilst these cases may not be restricted to allegations of sexual abuse, they are more likely to be generated by them. The Code of Conduct provisions would in any event apply to the Bar which would prevent counsel from accepting any instructions if to do so would cause him to be professionally embarrassed which includes having insufficient experience or competence to handle the matter.[10]

5.2 The task of appointing counsel is likely to be done on a practical level by the associate in consultation with the judge and perhaps the List Office. Who is appointed will depend on the stage at which the appointment is made. If it is early in the proceedings, there should be ample time to appoint an appropriate representative. In the absence of a list, this is likely to be from counsel who regularly appear in that court or who are well known. It seems to us there should at least be the opportunity for counsel to have their name on the list. It may be the appropriate course would be for all Chambers to be asked to provide a list of counsel with the appropriate experience who would like to

---

[10] Paragraph 603(a)

be included on the list. Remuneration would have to be appropriate[11] because it will be necessary for counsel to familiarise themselves with all the material including unused which in these unusual circumstances should also be made available to the judge.

5.3 Although an appointment of a legal representative will normally terminate at the conclusion of the cross-examination,[12] there is provision for the court to determine otherwise and we consider that it may well be necessary for counsel to remain for the duration of the trial if case evidence is given by the defendant or another witness which needs to be put to the complainant who will then have to be recalled and re-cross-examined. This situation may arise where the defence is not known and the issues have not been fully identified because the defendant is being uncooperative and may have given a no comment interview. The cross-examination will have been based on the papers and, whilst obvious issues will have been covered, it may well be that the questions asked do not, in fact, cover the defendant's case as given from the witness box. To avoid the whole scenario becoming a sham, the defendant's case will have to be put to the complainant. It follows from this that counsel appointed by the court will have to be available for the whole trial as opposed to simply cross-examination. There is also the possibility that the judge may intervene during the trial to make a direction under Section 36 preventing the defendant from cross-examining other witnesses.

5.4 Such a list will need maintaining as well as setting up. Although there are a number of sources which could probably provide the relevant information, for example, the individual Bar Messes, the CBA, the circuit, none of these include solicitor advocates and although there may not presently be many with the necessary experience, the Law Society will need to be involved in this process to maintain equal opportunity for all those with suitable qualifications.

5.5 Once such a list is set up, it will be for the court to select the appropriate advocate and the cab-rank principle should apply to all approached, subject to an advocate feeling they are insufficiently experienced.

6. Duties of Court Appointed Legal Representative

6.1 It is expressly set out that the legal representative is not responsible to the defendant[13]. It follows that there will not be any meetings with the defendant nor any instructions taken directly from him unless he chooses to 'adopt' the court appointed representative as his own (see para 3.1).

---

[11] S.40 YJ&CEA,2002 makes provision for payment out of central funds
[12] Crown Court Rules 1982 r24C-(2)
[13] S.38(5) YJ&CEA, 1999

6.2 Rules of court may make provision in particular for securing that the legal representative will be provided with 'evidence or other material relating to the proceedings'[14] and this can include disclosure of material in connection with criminal proceedings under Part 1 of the Criminal Procedure and Investigations Act, 1996.[15] It will be the duty of the legal representative to read all such material and watch any videos of disclosure interviews.

6.3 If the appointment is made at a relatively early stage in the proceedings, presence at preparatory hearings may seem sensible if there is to be a ruling on the admissibility of evidence or any similar ruling prior to the swearing of the jury and it may well be useful to attend simply to clarify the issues. It should be borne in mind, however, that the role of the legal representative is clearly intended to be limited to cross-examining witnesses whom the defendant is prohibited from cross-examining and although it may be thought that such a representative could be useful to the court in other areas, that does not seem to be intended by the legislation. Ultimately, it will be matter for the judge to decide and, no doubt if there is a point which can be properly taken on admissibility of a witness's evidence which is not dependent on the defendant's instructions, the legal representative will make the appropriate submissions, either of his own volition or at the invitation of the judge and these are areas which may well be identifiable at an early stage in the proceedings.

6.4 If it is possible, the legal representative should be present during the opening of the case to the jury and it is after this that there should be a hearing in the absence of the jury but in the presence of the defendant and both prosecuting counsel and the legal representative at which the judge will have to take steps to establish the issues in the case. Concern has been expressed that the defendant may refuse to tell the judge anything in the presence of prosecuting counsel and there is always the possibility that the defendant may inadvertently say something to the judge which could provide material in cross-examination. The problem is that prosecuting counsel has an ongoing duty of disclosure and they have to know what the defence is in order to comply with their duty. If the defendant makes it clear that he will not say anything if prosecuting counsel remains present, the Judge must decide what to do and this may well include explaining to the defendant the duty of the Crown and how limited the judge's powers are on disclosure without input from the Crown. Subject to that, if the Judge feels that the interests of justice are best served by a hearing in the absence of the Crown, then, no doubt, that is what he will do.

---

[14] S.38(6)(b) YJ&CEA, 1999
[15] S.38(7)(a) YJ&CEA, 1999

There are a number of possible scenarios:

(i) The defendant has given a full interview to the police setting out his defence. In this case, the defendant can simply be asked whether he will confirm the defence set out in the interview. If he does so, then it seems to us that the legal representative is justified in putting a positive case to the witness although no doubt in a moderate way. This will assist the jury to assess the credibility of the witness. If the defendant will not confirm that this is his defence, the witness should nonetheless be cross-examined on that basis but not as a positive case and any other relevant points need to be identified before cross-examination.

(ii) There is a defence statement setting out a defence. The same question can be asked but as the defendant will have presumably sacked whoever was responsible for that statement, care will need to be taken in putting that forward even if the defendant confirms that is his defence. There are often significant differences between an interview and a defence statement and all that will be required will be to give the witness the opportunity of dealing with any points made in either. It is important, however, that the cross-examination is not conducted in a way which invites scepticism because of how it is put as opposed to the actual content of the questions being put because the legal representative has been appointed to represent the interests of the defendant.

(iii) There is a no comment interview and no defence statement. Although the defendant can be asked by the judge if he will outline the points on which he takes issue in the case, it is not hard to foresee the scenario where a defendant is being completely uncooperative, no doubt wishing to make a point to the jury (which some may think has some force) that he has not been able to defend himself properly because he has been unable to cross-examine the main witness against him. In those circumstances, the legal representative is likely to be constrained by the issues which the judge directs are relevant as far as can be ascertained from the papers although no doubt the submissions of the legal representative will be sought. Once those issues have been identified, they should be explained to the defendant and he should again be asked whether he is now willing to indicate his defence. It should be noted that it is for the court to decide in the first place whether it is necessary in the interests of justice for the witness to be cross-examined by a legal representative appointed to represent the interests of the defendant and it is only if the court does so decide that a legal representative has to be appointed. Strictly speaking, if there is no sensible basis upon which a witness can be cross-examined, it may not be in the interests of justice for this to be done and it is open to the judge to refuse to appoint a legal representative to do so. This would be a brave decision to take and one which would seem likely to strike the average juror as unfair. The more likely scenario and the more sensible one would be for the legal representative to be invited to test the evidence as if a certain line of defence was being put forward but not putting any positive case to the witness.

(iv) Where the defendant refuses to be represented because of a psychiatric condition such as mental illness or a personality disorder. It is obvious in these very unfortunate cases that every effort should be made to persuade the defendant to be represented but that if they will not, then all proper and available lines of defence should be put to the witness and all proper legal arguments mounted.

6.5 Once the relevant areas of cross-examination have been identified, the legal representative must consider any proper legal arguments relevant to the cross-examination. This would include questions relating to the sexual history of the witness for which leave must be given or whether a particular line of cross-examination may lead to an application to adduce the defendant's previous convictions in the event of him giving evidence. We do not consider it is the duty of the legal representative to raise other legal arguments which are not relevant to cross-examination. It may be that such representatives would wish to ensure that either the court or the prosecution was made aware of such points to avoid a miscarriage of justice but it would not appear to be within the limited confines of their duty which is to cross-examine. There will no doubt be a strong temptation for the legal representative to be treated as amicus in the trial generally. We do not consider that to be appropriate unless the judge specifically requests that that role be adopted as it will be extremely difficult for the legal representative then to be confident that he or she is fully aware of the parameters of their role in the case. It would also be confusing for the jury who may well think that the defendant has actually got full representation even though he didn't want it.

6.6 There will be circumstances where the legal representative considers that it is in the interests of the defendant that they remain until the end of the evidence. If so, application should be made to the judge for leave to remain.

6.7 It may also be sensible for the defendant to be reminded at the end of the cross-examination that they can 'adopt' the legal representative. If that is done, there will need to be the opportunity for the defendant to give instructions and, if necessary, further cross-examination but care will have to be taken to prevent a defendant manipulating or appearing to manipulate the court process and also to prevent a witness being cross-examined more than is necessary.

7. It is our view that many of these decisions can only be taken on an individual case basis and will depend upon the sensible handling of the defendant by the judge. The legal representative will need to

be alive to the limitations of their role and not to be beguiled into acting as the defendant's representative generally. There is a requirement in Section 40 of the Act that the judge gives such warning to the jury as he considers necessary to prevent prejudicial inferences being drawn either from the fact that the defendant is not cross-examining or (where this occurs) the fact that a court appointed representative has cross-examined on his behalf. It remains to be seen whether the difficult balance between maintaining the interests of justice whilst making sure that justice is being seen to be done can be achieved in practice.

Guidance for Court Appointed Legal Representatives

1. A court appointed legal representative will not meet privately with the defendant nor take instructions directly from the defendant.

2. All matters relevant to the cross-examination to be conducted by the legal representative will ordinarily be dealt with in open court in the presence of the prosecution and the defendant but in the absence of the jury.

3. The legal representative will be provided with the evidence in the case comprising all prosecution statements and exhibits and have access to unused material. It will be the duty of the legal representative to familiarise him/herself with the evidence and be in a position to assist the judge as to the likely material issues as disclosed on the papers.

4. Before the start of the trial, the judge will identify as far as possible the likely issues in the case. This will involve the prosecution and the legal representative and where possible, the defendant.

5. Where the defendant has given a full account in interview and has confirmed to the judge that this account is to be maintained at trial identifying, if appropriate, any material differences etc, the legal representative should prepare cross-examination on the basis of that defence. It is a matter for the legal representative's judgement in each case as to whether that is put forward as a positive defence in cross-examination or simply used as a basis for testing the evidence.

6. Where there is only a defence statement which the defendant has not confirmed as his defence, the legal representative should not put this forward as a positive defence. It should only be used as a basis from which to test the evidence of the witness.

7. Where there is only a defence statement but the judge has elicited from the defendant that this accurately represents his defence, the legal representative should prepare cross-examination on the basis of that defence but should not generally put it as a positive defence unless there is good reason so to do, for example, if the defendant indicates that the defence to a rape allegation is to be one of consent.

8. Where the defendant has made no comment in interview and there is no defence statement but the judge has elicited from the defendant

what his defence is to be, the legal representative should prepare cross-examination on the basis of that defence but should not generally put it as a positive defence unless there is good reason so to do, for example, if the defendant indicates that the defence to a rape allegation is to be one of consent.

9. Where the defendant has made no comment in interview and there is no defence statement and declines to indicate what his defence is to be, the legal representative should prepare cross-examination in accordance with the directions of the judge after discussion with both prosecution and the legal representative as to the material issues in the case. This should not be put forward as a positive case. The only proper basis is to test the evidence of the witness on the specific areas identified by the judge.

10. Where the defendant has given an account in interview and/or his defence statement but has indicated that his defence is different and will not indicate in what way it differs, the same approach as in para 9 above should be followed.

11. Although the appointment by the court of a legal representative implies that the court considers that cross-examination of the relevant witness will be in the interests of the defendant, it is a matter for the legal representative to judge whether, in the event, it is in the interests of the defendant for there to be cross-examination as, for example, where the witness has not come up to proof on a material point.

12. It will be the duty of the legal representative to raise any points of law relevant to the conduct of the cross-examination prior to the cross-examination such as whether there are relevant and admissible questions on the witness's sexual history or whether a particular line of cross-examination is likely to result in the defendant's 'shield' being lost in the event of him giving evidence.

13. Whilst in the normal course of events, the appointment of the legal representative terminates at the conclusion of the cross-examination of the particular witness, the legal representative should consider whether there is a need for the appointment to remain until a later stage in the trial if, for example, it may be necessary for the witness to be recalled for further cross-examination and if there is, to make the appropriate application to the judge.

November 2003

Penalty Notices for Disorder

Upper Tier Penalty—£80 for 16-year-olds and over (£40 for 10–15-year-olds)

Offence	Notice
Causing wasteful use of police time/ wasting police time, Giving false report	Criminal Law Act 1967, s 5
Send false message/persistently use a public electronic communications network in order to cause annoyance, inconvenience, or needless anxiety	Communications Act 2003, s 127(2)
Knowingly give a false alarm to a person acting on behalf of a fire and rescue authority	Fire and Rescue Services Act 2004, s 49
Use words/conduct likely to cause fear of harassment, alarm, or distress	Public Order Act 1986, s 5
Fire/throw firework(s)	Explosives Act 1875, s 80
Drunk & disorderly in a public place	Criminal Justice Act 1967, s 91
Destroying or damaging property (under £300)	Criminal Damage Act 1971, s 1(1)
Theft from a shop (retail under £100)	Theft Act 1968, s 1
Breach of fireworks curfew (11 pm–7 am)	Fireworks Regulations 2004 under Fireworks Act 2003, s 11
Possession of a category 4 firework	Fireworks Regulations 2004 under Fireworks Act 2003, s 11
Possession by a person under 18 of an adult firework	Fireworks Regulations 2004 under Fireworks Act 2003, s 11
Sells or attempts to sell alcohol to a person who is drunk	Licensing Act 2003, s 141

Offence	Notice
Supply of alcohol by or on behalf of a club to a person aged under 18	Licensing Act 2003, s 146(3)
Sale of alcohol anywhere to a person under 18	Licensing Act 2003, s 146(1)
Buys or attempts to buy alcohol on behalf of person under 18	Licensing Act 2003, s 149(3)
Buys or attempts to buy alcohol for consumption on relevant premises by person under 18	Licensing Act 2003, s 149(4)
Delivery of alcohol to person under 18 or allowing such delivery	Licensing Act 2003, s 151
Possess a controlled drug of Class B—cannabis/cannabis resin	Misuse of Drugs Act 1971, s 5(2) and Sch 4

Lower Tier Penalty—£50 for 16-year-olds and over (£30 for 10–15-year-olds)

Offence	Notice
Trespass on a railway	British Transport Commission Act 1949, s 55
Throwing stones/matter/thing at a train	British Transport Commission Act 1949, s 56
Drunk in highway	Licensing Act 1872, s 12
Consume alcohol in designated public place, contrary to requirement by constable not to do so	Criminal Justice and Police Act 2001, s 12
Depositing and leave litter	Environmental Protection Act 1990, s 87(1) and (5)
Consumption of alcohol by a person under 18 on relevant premises	Licensing Act 2003, s 150(1)
Allowing consumption of alcohol by a person under 18 on relevant premises	Licensing Act 2003, s 150(2)
Buying or attempting to buy alcohol by a person under 18	Licensing Act 2003, s 149(1)

Criminal Procedure Rules 2010

The following rules are reproduced in this appendix:

- Rule 1 (the overriding objective)
- Rule 3 (case management)

Part 1 The Overriding Objective

The overriding objective

1.1.—(1) The overriding objective of this new code is that criminal cases be dealt with justly.

(2) Dealing with a criminal case justly includes—

    (a) acquitting the innocent and convicting the guilty;

    (b) dealing with the prosecution and the defence fairly;

    (c) recognising the rights of a defendant, particularly those under Article 6 of the European Convention on Human Rights;

    (d) respecting the interests of witnesses, victims and jurors and keeping them informed of the progress of the case;

    (e) dealing with the case efficiently and expeditiously;

    (f) ensuring that appropriate information is available to the court when bail and sentence are considered; and

    (g) dealing with the case in ways that take into account—

        (i) the gravity of the offence alleged,

        (ii) the complexity of what is in issue,

        (iii) the severity of the consequences for the defendant and others affected, and

        (iv) the needs of other cases.

The duty of the participants in a criminal case

1.2.—(1) Each participant, in the conduct of each case, must—

    (a) prepare and conduct the case in accordance with the overriding objective;

    (b) comply with these Rules, practice directions and directions made by the court; and

    (c) at once inform the court and all parties of any significant failure (whether or not that participant is responsible for that failure) to take any procedural step required by these Rules, any practice direction or any direction of the court. A failure is significant if it might hinder the court in furthering the overriding objective.

(2) Anyone involved in any way with a criminal case is a participant in its conduct for the purposes of this rule.

The application by the court of the overriding objective

1.3. The court must further the overriding objective in particular when—
- (a) exercising any power given to it by legislation (including these Rules);
- (b) applying any practice direction; or
- (c) interpreting any rule or practice direction.

Part 3 Case Management

The scope of this Part

3.1. This Part applies to the management of each case in a magistrates' court and in the Crown Court (including an appeal to the Crown Court) until the conclusion of that case.

[Note. Rules that apply to procedure in the Court of Appeal are in Parts 65 to 73 of these Rules.]

The duty of the court

3.2.—(1) The court must further the overriding objective by actively managing the case.

(2) (2) Active case management includes—
- (a) the early identification of the real issues;
- (b) the early identification of the needs of witnesses;
- (c) achieving certainty as to what must be done, by whom, and when, in particular by the early setting of a timetable for the progress of the case;
- (d) monitoring the progress of the case and compliance with directions;
- (e) ensuring that evidence, whether disputed or not, is presented in the shortest and clearest way;
- (f) discouraging delay, dealing with as many aspects of the case as possible on the same occasion, and avoiding unnecessary hearings;
- (g) encouraging the participants to co-operate in the progression of the case; and
- (h) making use of technology.

(3) The court must actively manage the case by giving any direction appropriate to the needs of that case as early as possible.

The duty of the parties

3.3. Each party must—
   (a) actively assist the court in fulfilling its duty under rule 3.2, without or if necessary with a direction; and
   (b) apply for a direction if needed to further the overriding objective.

Case progression officers and their duties

3.4.—(1) At the beginning of the case each party must, unless the court otherwise directs—
   (a) nominate an individual responsible for progressing that case; and
   (b) tell other parties and the court who he is and how to contact him.
(2) In fulfilling its duty under rule 3.2, the court must where appropriate—
   (a) nominate a court officer responsible for progressing the case; and
   (b) make sure the parties know who he is and how to contact him.
(3) In this Part a person nominated under this rule is called a case progression officer.
(4) A case progression officer must—
   (a) monitor compliance with directions;
   (b) make sure that the court is kept informed of events that may affect the progress of that case;
   (c) make sure that he can be contacted promptly about the case during ordinary business hours;
   (d) act promptly and reasonably in response to communications about the case; and
   (e) if he will be unavailable, appoint a substitute to fulfil his duties and inform the other case progression officers.

The court's case management powers

3.5.—(1) In fulfilling its duty under rule 3.2 the court may give any direction and take any step actively to manage a case unless that direction or step would be inconsistent with legislation, including these Rules.
(2) In particular, the court may—
   (a) nominate a judge, magistrate or justices' legal adviser to manage the case;

(b) give a direction on its own initiative or on application by a party;

(c) ask or allow a party to propose a direction;

(d) for the purpose of giving directions, receive applications and representations by letter, by telephone or by any other means of electronic communication, and conduct a hearing by such means;

(e) give a direction without a hearing;

(f) fix, postpone, bring forward, extend or cancel a hearing;

(g) shorten or extend (even after it has expired) a time limit fixed by a direction;

(h) require that issues in the case should be determined separately, and decide in what order they will be determined; and

(i) specify the consequences of failing to comply with a direction.

(3) A magistrates' court may give a direction that will apply in the Crown Court if the case is to continue there.

(4) The Crown Court may give a direction that will apply in a magistrates' court if the case is to continue there.

(5) Any power to give a direction under this Part includes a power to vary or revoke that direction.

(6) If a party fails to comply with a rule or a direction, the court may—

(a) fix, postpone, bring forward, extend, cancel or adjourn a hearing;

(b) exercise its powers to make a costs order; and

(c) impose such other sanction as may be appropriate.

[*Note. Depending upon the nature of a case and the stage that it has reached, its progress may be affected by other Criminal Procedure Rules and by other legislation. The note at the end of this Part lists other rules and legislation that may apply.*

See also rule 3.10.

The court may make a costs order under—

(a) section 19 of the Prosecution of Offences Act 1985[(1)], where the court decides that one party to criminal proceedings has incurred costs as a

---

[1] 1985 c. 23; section 19 was amended by section 166 of the Criminal Justice Act 1988 (c. 33), section 45 of, and Schedule 6 to, the Legal Aid Act 1988 (c. 34), section 7 of, and paragraph 8 of Schedule 3 to, the Criminal Procedure (Insanity and Unfitness to Plead) Act 1991 (c. 25), section 24 of, and paragraphs 27 and 28 of Schedule 4 to, the Access to Justice Act 1999 (c. 22), sections 40 and 67 of, and paragraph 4 of Schedule 7 to, the Youth Justice and Criminal Evidence Act 1999 (c. 23), section 165 of, and paragraph 99 of Schedule 9 to, the Powers of Criminal Courts (Sentencing) Act 2000 (c. 6) and section 378 of, and paragraph 107 of Schedule 16 to, the Armed Forces Act 2006 (c. 52). It is further amended by sections 6 and 148 of, and paragraph 32 of Schedule 4 and paragraphs 1 and 5 of Schedule 27 to, the Criminal Justice and Immigration Act 2008 (c. 4), with effect from a date to be appointed.

result of an unnecessary or improper act or omission by, or on behalf of, another party;

(b) section 19A of that Act[2], where the court decides that a party has incurred costs as a result of an improper, unreasonable or negligent act or omission on the part of a legal representative;

(c) section 19B of that Act[3], where the court decides that there has been serious misconduct by a person who is not a party.

Under some other legislation, including Parts 33, 34 and 35 of these Rules, if a party fails to comply with a rule or a direction then in some circumstances—

(a) the court may refuse to allow that party to introduce evidence;

(b) evidence that that party wants to introduce may not be admissible;

(c) the court may draw adverse inferences from the late introduction of an issue or evidence.

See also—

(a) section 81(1) of the Police and Criminal Evidence Act 1984[4] and section 20(3) of the Criminal Procedure and Investigations Act 1996[5] (advance disclosure of expert evidence);

(b) section 11(5) of the Criminal Procedure and Investigations Act 1996[6] (faults in disclosure by accused);

(c) section 132(5) of the Criminal Justice Act 2003[7] (failure to give notice of hearsay evidence).]

Application to vary a direction

3.6.—(1) A party may apply to vary a direction if—

    (a) the court gave it without a hearing;

    (b) the court gave it at a hearing in his absence; or

    (c) circumstances have changed.

(2) A party who applies to vary a direction must—

    (a) apply as soon as practicable after he becomes aware of the grounds for doing so; and

    (b) give as much notice to the other parties as the nature and urgency of his application permits.

---

[2] 1985 c. 23; section 19A was inserted by section 111 of the Courts and Legal Services Act 1990 (c. 41).

[3] 1985 c. 23; section 19B was inserted by section 93 of the Courts Act 2003 (c. 39).

[4] 1984 c. 60; section 81(1) was amended by section 109(1) of, and paragraph 286 of Schedule 8 to, the Courts Act 2003 (c.39).

[5] 1996 c. 25; section 20(3) was amended by section 109(1) of, and paragraph 378 of Schedule 8 to, the Courts Act 2003 (c.39).

[6] 1996 c. 25; section 11 was substituted by section 39 of the Criminal Justice Act 2003 (c. 44) and amended by section 60 of the Criminal Justice and Immigration Act 2008 (c. 4).

[7] 2003 c. 44.

Appendix 4

Agreement to vary a time limit fixed by a direction

3.7.—(1) The parties may agree to vary a time limit fixed by a direction, but only if—

    (a) the variation will not—

        (i) affect the date of any hearing that has been fixed, or

        (ii) significantly affect the progress of the case in any other way;

    (b) the court has not prohibited variation by agreement; and

    (c) the court's case progression officer is promptly informed.

(2) The court's case progression officer must refer the agreement to the court if he doubts the condition in paragraph (1)(a) is satisfied.

Case preparation and progression

3.8.—(1) At every hearing, if a case cannot be concluded there and then the court must give directions so that it can be concluded at the next hearing or as soon as possible after that.

(2) At every hearing the court must, where relevant—

    (a) if the defendant is absent, decide whether to proceed nonetheless;

    (b) take the defendant's plea (unless already done) or if no plea can be taken then find out whether the defendant is likely to plead guilty or not guilty;

    (c) set, follow or revise a timetable for the progress of the case, which may include a timetable for any hearing including the trial or (in the Crown Court) the appeal;

    (d) in giving directions, ensure continuity in relation to the court and to the parties' representatives where that is appropriate and practicable; and

    (e) where a direction has not been complied with, find out why, identify who was responsible, and take appropriate action.

(3) In order to prepare for a trial in the Crown Court, the court must conduct a plea and case management hearing unless the circumstances make that unnecessary.

(4) In order to prepare for the trial, the court must take every reasonable step to encourage and to facilitate the attendance of witnesses when they are needed.

Readiness for trial or appeal

3.9.—(1) This rule applies to a party's preparation for trial or appeal, and in this rule and rule 3.10 trial includes any hearing at which evidence will be introduced.

(2) In fulfilling his duty under rule 3.3, each party must—

    (a) comply with directions given by the court;

    (b) take every reasonable step to make sure his witnesses will attend when they are needed;

    (c) make appropriate arrangements to present any written or other material; and

    (d) promptly inform the court and the other parties of anything that may—

        (i) affect the date or duration of the trial or appeal, or

        (ii) significantly affect the progress of the case in any other way.

  (3) The court may require a party to give a certificate of readiness.

Conduct of a trial or an appeal

3.10. In order to manage a trial or an appeal—

(a) the court must establish, with the active assistance of the parties, what disputed issues they intend to explore; and

(b) the court may require a party to identify—

    (i) which witnesses that party wants to give oral evidence,

    (ii) the order in which that party wants those witnesses to give their evidence,

    (iii) whether that party requires an order compelling the attendance of a witness,

    (iv) what arrangements are desirable to facilitate the giving of evidence by a witness,

    (v) what arrangements are desirable to facilitate the participation of any other person, including the defendant,

    (vi) what written evidence that party intends to introduce,

    (vii) what other material, if any, that person intends to make available to the court in the presentation of the case,

    (viii) whether that party intends to raise any point of law that could affect the conduct of the trial or appeal, and

    (ix) what timetable that party proposes and expects to follow.

[*Note.* See also rule 3.5.]

Case management forms and records

3.11.—(1) The case management forms set out in the Practice Direction must be used, and where there is no form then no specific formality is required.

  (2) The court must make available to the parties a record of directions given.

Appendix 5

Relevant Offences for the purposes of special measures direction

Schedule 14 Coroners and Justice Act 2009

RELEVANT OFFENCES FOR THE
PURPOSES OF SECTION 17

Murder and manslaughter

1 Murder in a case where it is alleged that a firearm or knife was used to cause the death in question.

2 Manslaughter in a case where it is alleged that a firearm or knife was used to cause the death in question.

3 Murder or manslaughter in a case (other than a case falling within paragraph 1 or 2) where it is alleged that—
    (a) the accused was carrying a firearm or knife at any time during the commission of the offence, and
    (b) a person other than the accused knew or believed at any time during the commission of the offence that the accused was carrying a firearm or knife.

Offences against the Person Act 1861 (c. 100)

4 An offence under section 18 of the Offences against the Person Act 1861 (wounding with intent to cause grievous bodily harm etc) in a case where it is alleged that a firearm or knife was used to cause the wound or harm in question.

5 An offence under section 20 of that Act (malicious wounding) in a case where it is alleged that a firearm or knife was used to cause the wound or inflict the harm in question.

6 An offence under section 38 of that Act (assault with intent to resist arrest) in a case where it is alleged that a firearm or knife was used to carry out the assault in question.

7 An offence under section 47 of the Offences against the Person Act 1861 (assault occasioning actual bodily harm) in a case where it is alleged that a firearm or knife was used to inflict the harm in question.

8 An offence under sections 18, 20, 38 or 47 of the Offences against the Person Act 1861 in a case (other than a case falling within any of paragraphs 4 to 7) where it is alleged that—

(a) the accused was carrying a firearm or knife at any time during the commission of the offence, and

(b) a person other than the accused knew or believed at any time during the commission of the offence that the accused was carrying a firearm or knife.

Prevention of Crime Act 1953 (c. 14)

9 An offence under section 1 of the Prevention of Crime Act 1953 (having an offensive weapon in a public place).

Firearms Act 1968 (c. 27)

10 An offence under section 1 of the Firearms Act 1968 (requirement of firearm certificate).

11 An offence under section 2(1) of that Act (possession etc of a shot gun without a certificate).

12 An offence under section 3 of that Act (business and other transactions with firearms and ammunition).

13 An offence under section 4 of that Act (conversion of weapons).

14 An offence under section 5(1) of that Act (weapons subject to general prohibition).

15 An offence under section 5(1A) of that Act (ammunition subject to general prohibition).

16 An offence under section 16 of that Act (possession with intent to injure).

17 An offence under section 16A of that Act (possession with intent to cause fear of violence).

18 An offence under section 17 of that Act (use of firearm to resist arrest).

19 An offence under section 18 of that Act (carrying firearm with criminal intent).

20 An offence under section 19 of that Act (carrying firearm in a public place).

21 An offence under section 20 of that Act (trespassing with firearm).

22 An offence under section 21 of that Act (possession of firearms by person previously convicted of crime).

23 An offence under section 21A of that Act (firing an air weapon beyond premises).

24 An offence under section 24A of that Act (supplying imitation firearms to minors).

Criminal Justice Act 1988 (c. 33)

25 An offence under section 139 of the Criminal Justice Act 1988 (having article with blade or point in public place).

26 An offence under section 139A of that Act (having article with blade or point (or offensive weapon) on school premises).

Appendix 5

Violent Crime Reduction Act 2006 (c. 38)

27 An offence under section 28 of the Violent Crime Reduction Act 2006 (using someone to mind a weapon).

28 An offence under section 32 of that Act (sales of air weapons by way of trade or business to be face to face).

29 An offence under section 36 of that Act (manufacture, import and sale of realistic imitation firearms).

General

30 A reference in any of paragraphs 1 to 8 to an offence ('offence A') includes—

   (a) a reference to an attempt to commit offence A in a case where it is alleged that it was attempted to commit offence A in the manner or circumstances described in that paragraph,

   (b) a reference to a conspiracy to commit offence A in a case where it is alleged that the conspiracy was to commit offence A in the manner or circumstances described in that paragraph,

   (c) a reference to an offence under Part 2 of the Serious Crime Act 2007 in relation to which offence A is the offence (or one of the offences) which the person intended or believed would be committed in a case where it is alleged that the person intended or believed offence A would be committed in the manner or circumstances described in that paragraph, and

   (d) a reference to aiding, abetting, counselling or procuring the commission of offence A in a case where it is alleged that offence A was committed, or the act or omission charged in respect of offence A was done or made, in the manner or circumstances described in that paragraph.

31 A reference in any of paragraphs 9 to 29 to an offence ('offence A') includes—

   (a) a reference to an attempt to commit offence A,

   (b) a reference to a conspiracy to commit offence A,

   (c) a reference to an offence under Part 2 of the Serious Crime Act 2007 in relation to which offence A is the offence (or one of the offences) which the person intended or believed would be committed, and

   (d) a reference to aiding, abetting, counselling or procuring the commission of offence A.

Interpretation

32 In this Schedule—

'firearm' has the meaning given by section 57 of the Firearms Act 1968;

'knife' has the meaning given by section 10 of the Knives Act 1997.

Appendix 6

Fraud Guideline

Fraud—banking and insurance fraud, and obtaining credit through fraud, benefit fraud, and revenue fraud—factors to take into consideration

This guideline and accompanying notes are taken from the Sentencing Guidelines Council's definitive guideline *Sentencing for Fraud—Statutory offences*, published 26 October 2009.

The starting points and ranges for fraud against HM Revenue and Customs, for benefit fraud and for banking and insurance and obtaining credit through fraud are the same since the seriousness of all offences of organisational fraud derives from the extent of the fraudulent activity (culpability) and the financial loss caused or likely to be caused (harm).

Key factors common to these types of fraud

(a) As the determinants of seriousness include the 'value of property or consequential loss involved', the table provides both a fixed amount (on which the starting point is based) and a band (on which the sentencing range is based). Where the value is larger or smaller than the amount on which the starting point is based, this should lead to upward or downward movement from the starting point as appropriate. Where the amount the offender intended to obtain cannot be established, the appropriate measure will be the amount that was likely to be achieved in all the circumstances. Where the offender was entitled to part or all of the amount obtained, the starting point should be based on the amount to which they were not entitled.

(b) A further determinant of seriousness is whether the fraud was a single fraudulent transaction or a multiple fraud. Where one false declaration or a failure to disclose a change in circumstances results in multiple payments, this should be regarded as multiple fraud.

(c) In general terms, the greater the loss, the more serious will be the offence. However, the financial value of the loss may not reflect the full extent of the harm caused. The court should also take into account; the impact of the offence on the victim (particularly where the loss may be significantly greater than the monetary value); harm to persons other than the direct victim (including the aggravation and stress of unscrambling the consequences of an offence); erosion of public confidence; and the difference between the loss intended and that which results (which may involve adjusting the assessment of seriousness to reflect the degree of loss caused).

(d) When the offending involves a number of people acting co-operatively, this will aggravate an offence as it indicates planning or professional activity, and may also increase the degree of loss caused or intended. The role of each offender is important in determining the appropriate level of seriousness and movement above or below the starting point within the applicable level.

(e) Use of another person's identity is an aggravating factor; the extent to which it aggravates an offence will be based on the degree of planning and the impact that the offence has had on the living victim or relatives of the deceased – whether the identity belongs to a living or deceased person is neutral for this purpose.

(f) Matters of offender mitigation which may be particularly relevant to these types of fraud include:

— *Voluntary cessation of offending* – a claim, supported by objective evidence, that an offender stopped offending before being apprehended should be treated as mitigation, particularly where accompanied by a genuine expression of remorse. The lapse of time since commission of the last offence is relevant to whether the claim is genuine, and reasons for the cessation will assist the court in determining whether it amounts to mitigation and if so, to what degree.

— *Complete and unprompted disclosure of the extent of the fraud* – An admission that a greater sum has been obtained than that known to the authorities ensures that an offender is sentenced for the complete extent of the fraud. This is ready co-operation with the authorities and should be treated as mitigation. Provision of information about others involved in the fraud should also be treated as mitigation. Generally, the earlier the disclosure is given and the higher the degree of assistance, the greater the allowance for mitigation.

— *Voluntary restitution* – the timing of the voluntary restitution will indicate the degree to which it reflects genuine remorse. Generally, the earlier the property or money is returned the greater the degree of mitigation the offender should receive. If circumstances beyond the control of the offender prevent return of defrauded items, the degree of mitigation will depend on the point in time at which, and the determination with which the offender tried to return the items.

— *Financial pressure* – financial pressure neither increases nor diminishes an offender's culpability. However, where such pressure is **exceptional** and not of the offender's own making, it may in very rare circumstances constitute mitigation.

(g) A court should be aware that a confiscation order is an important sanction. Such an order may only be made in the Crown Court. The court must commit the offender to the Crown Court where this is requested by the prosecution with a view to an order being considered.

(h) Ancillary orders should be considered in all cases, principally compensation, deprivation and disqualification from driving, as well as other powers particular to the type of offending behaviour.

Additional notes:

Banking and insurance fraud and obtaining credit through fraud

(i) A payment card or bank account fraud is unlikely to be committed in circumstances where the offender's intention was not fraudulent from the outset.

(ii) Use of another person's identity is a feature of nearly all payment card and bank account frauds since in most cases the offender claims to be the account holder or a person authorised to deal with the account. Courts should therefore increase the starting point to reflect the presence of this aggravating factor.

Benefit fraud

(i) This guideline is based on an understanding that the prosecutor will generally seek summary trial for appropriate benefit fraud cases involving sums up to £35,000.

(ii) The fact that defrauded sums may have been recovered is not relevant to the choice of the type of sentence to be imposed.

(iii) The court should have regard to personal and family circumstances of offenders which will vary greatly and may be particularly significant to sentencing this type of fraud.

Revenue fraud

(i) The proposals for the sentencing of revenue fraud take as a starting point an offender who acts intentionally. Where the offender has acted recklessly (relevant only to offences under the Value Added Tax Act 1994), courts should adjust the assessment of seriousness to take account of this lower level of culpability.

(ii) Payments <u>to</u> HMRC may be evaded in order to increase the profitability of a legitimate business or the level of an individual's legitimate remuneration; payments may be fraudulently obtained <u>from</u> HMRC without any underlying legitimate activity at all as in a Carousel Fraud. Although the type of harm is the same since both result in a loss to HMRC, where payment is sought from HMRC in such circumstances, culpability is likely to be higher. Accordingly, such offences are likely to be regarded as more serious.

All offences: Triable either way:

Maximum when tried summarily: Level 5 fine and/or 6 months

Maximum when tried on indictment: Fraud 10 years, other offences, 7 years

Offences under s. 112, Social Security Administration Act 1992 are not covered by this guideline.

This guideline does not apply to offences under s. 50 or s. 170, Customs and Excise Management Act 1979 which involve prohibited weapons and have a maximum penalty of 10 years.

Offence seriousness (culpability and harm) A. Identify the appropriate starting point Starting points based on first time offender pleading not guilty		
Examples of nature of activity	**Starting point**	**Range**
Single fraudulent transaction, not fraudulent from the outset	Value £2,500*—Band B fine Value £12,500*—Medium level community order Value £60,000*—12 weeks custody	Value less than £5,000—Band A fine to low level community order Value £5,000 to less than £20,000—Band B fine to 6 weeks custody Value £20,000 to less than £100,000—Medium level community order to Crown Court
Single fraudulent transaction, fraudulent from the outset	Value £2,500*—Low level community order Value £12,500*—High level community order Value £60,000*—26 weeks custody	Value less than £5,000—Band A fine to medium level community order Value £5,000 to less than £20,000—Band C fine to 18 weeks custody Value £20,000 to less than £100,000—6 weeks custody to Crown Court
Not fraudulent from the outset, **and either** • fraud carried out over a significant period of time **or** • multiple frauds	Value £2,500*—Medium level community order Value £12,500*—6 weeks custody Value £60,000*—Crown Court	Value less than £5,000—Band B fine to high level community order Value £5,000 to less than £20,000—Medium level community order to 26 weeks custody Value £20,000 to less than £100,000—12 weeks custody to Crown Court
Where value exceeds £100,000	Crown Court	Crown Court

Appendix 6

	Offence seriousness (culpability and harm)	
	A. Identify the appropriate starting point	
	Starting points based on first time offender pleading not guilty	
Examples of nature of activity	**Starting point**	**Range**
Fraudulent from the outset, **and either** • fraud carried out over a significant period of time **or** • multiple frauds	Value £2,500*—High level community order	Value less than £5,000—Low level community order to 6 weeks custody
	Value £12,500*—12 weeks custody Value £60,000*—Crown Court Crown Court	Value £5,000 to less than £20,000—High level community order to Crown Court Value £20,000 to less than £100,000—18 weeks custody to Crown Court Crown Court
Where value £100,000 or more or fraud was professionally planned		

* Where the actual amount is greater or smaller than the value on which the starting point is based, that is likely to be one of the factors which will move the sentence within range (see (a) on page 62b)

Offence seriousness (culpability and harm)
B. Consider the effect of aggravating and mitigating factors
(other than those within examples above)
Common aggravating and mitigating factors are identified in the pullout card— the following may be particularly relevant but **these lists are not exhaustive**

Factors indicating higher culpability	**Factors indicating lower culpability**
1. Number involved in the offence and role of the offender 2. Making repeated importations, particularly in the face of warnings from the authorities 3. Dealing in goods with an additional health risk **Factors indicating greater degree of harm** 1. Use of another person's identity 2. Disposing of goods to under-aged purchasers	1. Peripheral involvement 2. Misleading or incomplete advice

Form a preliminary view of the appropriate sentence, **then consider offender mitigation** Common factors are identified in the pullout card

Consider a reduction for a guilty plea

> **Consider ancillary orders**
> Refer to pages 168–174 for guidance on available ancillary orders

> **Decide sentence**
> **Give reasons**

Fraud—confidence—factors to take into consideration

This guideline and accompanying notes are taken from the Sentencing Guidelines Council's definitive guideline *Sentencing for Fraud—Statutory offences*, published October 2009

Key factors

(a) This type of offending involves a victim transferring money and/or property as a result of being deceived or misled by the offender. An example of a simple confidence fraud is a person claiming to be collecting money for charity when, in fact, he or she intends to keep the money. Other examples of common confidence frauds are *Advance fee frauds* (such as lottery/prize draw scams and foreign money-making frauds) and *Fraudulent sales of goods and services* (where goods or services are never received/performed or are worth less than represented.

(b) As the determinants of seriousness include the 'value of property or consequential loss involved', the table provides both a fixed amount (on which the starting point is based) and a band (on which the sentencing range is based). Where the value is larger or smaller than the amount on which the starting point is based, this should lead to upward or downward movement as appropriate. Where the amount the offender intended to obtain cannot be established, the appropriate measure will be the amount that was likely to be achieved in all the circumstances.

(c) A further determinant of seriousness is whether the fraud was a single fraudulent transaction or a multiple fraud. Most confidence frauds will by their nature involve many actual or potential victims and multiple transactions and should be regarded as multiple fraud.

(d) Targeting a vulnerable victim is also a determinant of seriousness. A victim might be vulnerable as a result of old age, youth or disability. In addition, some victims of advance fee frauds may have personalities which make them 'vulnerable in a way and to a degree not typical of the general population' because they fall for scams many times and may be targeted using 'sucker lists' of people who have previously fallen victim to scams. Care should be taken to ensure that where targeting a vulnerable victim is used to determine the appropriate level of seriousness and starting point, that it is not used again as an aggravating factor to move within the sentencing range.

(e) In general terms, the greater the loss, the more serious will be the offence. However, the financial value of the loss may not reflect the full extent of the harm caused. The court should also take into account; the impact of the offence on the victim (particularly where the loss may be significantly greater than the monetary value); harm to persons other than the direct victim (including the aggravation and stress of unscrambling the consequences of an offence); erosion of public confidence; and the difference between the loss intended and that which results (which may involve adjusting the assessment of seriousness to reflect the degree of loss caused).

(f) When the offending involves a number of people acting co-operatively, this will aggravate an offence as it indicates planning or professional activity, and may also increase the degree of loss caused or intended. The role of each offender is important in determining the appropriate level of seriousness and movement above or below the starting point within the applicable level.

(g) Use of another person's identity is an aggravating factor; the extent to which it aggravates an offence will be based on the degree of planning and the impact that the offence has had on the living victim or relatives of the deceased – whether the identity belongs to a living or deceased person is neutral for this purpose.

(h) Matters of offender mitigation which may be particularly relevant to this type of fraud include:

— *Voluntary cessation of offending* – a claim, supported by objective evidence, that an offender stopped offending before being apprehended should be treated as mitigation, particularly where accompanied by a genuine expression of remorse. The lapse of time since commission of the last offence is relevant to whether the claim is genuine, and reasons for the cessation will assist the court in determining whether it amounts to mitigation and if so, to what degree.

— *Complete and unprompted disclosure of the extent of the fraud* – an admission that a greater sum has been obtained than that known to the authorities ensures that an offender is sentenced for the complete extent of the fraud. This amounts to ready co-operation with the authorities and should be treated as mitigation. Provision of information about others involved in the fraud should also be treated as mitigation. Generally, the earlier the disclosure is given and the higher the degree of assistance, the greater the allowance for mitigation.

— *Voluntary restitution* – the timing of the voluntary restitution will indicate the degree to which it reflects genuine remorse. Generally, the earlier the property or money is returned the greater the degree of mitigation the offender should receive. If circumstances beyond the control of the offender prevent return of defrauded items, the degree of mitigation will depend on the point in time at which, and the determination with which the offender tried to return the items.

— *Financial pressure* – financial pressure neither increases nor diminishes an offender's culpability. However, where such pressure is **exceptional** and not of the offender's own making, it may in very rare circumstances constitute mitigation.

(i) A court should be aware that a confiscation order is an important sanction. Such an order may only be made in the Crown Court. The court must commit the offender to the Crown Court where this is requested by the prosecution with a view to an order being considered.

(j) Ancillary orders should be considered in all cases, principally compensation and deprivation.

All offences: Triable either way:

Maximum when tried summarily: Level 5 fine and/or 6 months

Maximum when tried on indictment: Fraud 10 years, other offences, 7 years

Offence seriousness (culpability and harm)		
A. Identify the appropriate starting point		
Starting points based on first time offender pleading not guilty		
Examples of nature of activity	**Starting point**	**Range**
Single fraudulent transaction confidence fraud not targeting a vulnerable victim, and involving no or limited planning	Value £10,000*—Medium level community order Value £60,000*—12 weeks custody	Value less than £20,000—Band B fine to 6 weeks custody Value £20,000 to less than £100,000—Medium level community order to Crown Court
Single fraudulent transaction confidence fraud involving targeting of a vulnerable victim	Value £10,000*—6 weeks custody Value £60,000*—26 weeks custody	Value less than £20,000—Medium level community order to 26 weeks custody Value £20,000 to less than £100,000—High level community order to Crown Court

Appendix 6

Offence seriousness (culpability and harm)		
A. Identify the appropriate starting point		
Starting points based on first time offender pleading not guilty		
Examples of nature of activity	**Starting point**	**Range**
Lower scale advance fee fraud **or** other confidence fraud characterised by a degree of planning and/or multiple transactions	Value £10,000*— Crown Court Value £60,000*— Crown Court	Value less than £20,000—26 weeks custody to Crown Court Value £20,000 to less than £100,000—Crown Court
Large scale advance fee fraud or other confidence fraud involving the deliberate targeting of a large number of vulnerable victims	Value £10,000*— Crown Court Value £60,000*— Crown Court	Value less than £20,000— Crown Court Value £20,000 to less than £100,000—Crown Court

* Where the actual amount is greater or smaller than the value on which the starting point is based, that is likely to be one of the factors which will move the sentence within range (see (b) on page 62f)

Offence seriousness (culpability and harm)	
B. Consider the effect of aggravating and mitigating factors	
(other than those within examples above)	
Common aggravating and mitigating factors are identified in the pullout card— the following may be particularly relevant but **these lists are not exhaustive**	
Factors indicating higher culpability	**Factors indicating lower culpability**
1. Number involved in the offence and role of the offender 2. Offending carried out over a significant period of time **Factors indicating greater degree of harm** 1. Use of another person's identity 2. Offence has lasting effect on the victim	1. Peripheral involvement 2. Behaviour not fraudulent from the outset 3. Misleading or inaccurate advice

Form a preliminary view of the appropriate sentence, then consider offender mitigation
Common factors are identified in the pullout card

Consider a reduction for a guilty plea

Consider ancillary orders
Refer to pages 168–174 for guidance on available ancillary orders

Decide sentence
Give reasons

Fraud—possessing, making or supplying articles for use in fraud—factors to take into consideration

This guideline and accompanying notes are taken from the Sentencing Guidelines Council's definitive guideline *Sentencing for Fraud—Statutory offences*, published 26 October 2009.

Key factors

(a) There are many ways in which offenders may commit this group of offences. 'Articles' will include any electronic programs or data stored electronically, false fronts for cash machines, computer programs for generating credit card numbers, lists of credit card or bank account details, 'sucker lists' and draft letters or emails for use in advance fee frauds.

(b) Offenders who possess, make or supply articles for use in fraud intend their actions to lead to a fraud, and therefore have the highest level of culpability. The three offences in this group all involve an element of planning (whether by the offender or by another person) which indicates a higher level of culpability; this has been incorporated into the proposed starting points.

(c) In relation to harm, the value of the fraud (either that intended by the offender where that can be ascertained, or that which was likely to be achieved) is not a determinant of seriousness for these offences but is a factor that should be taken into account in determining the appropriate sentence within the sentencing range.

(d) Whilst in many cases no financial harm will have been caused, in some cases, particularly where the 'article' is a list of credit card or bank account details, the victim(s) may have been inconvenienced despite not suffering any financial loss. In all cases, the harm must be judged in light of the offender's culpability.

(e) When the offending involves a number of people acting co-operatively, this will aggravate an offence as it indicates planning or professional activity, and may also increase the degree of loss caused or intended. The role of each offender is important in determining the appropriate level of seriousness and movement above or below the starting point within the applicable level.

(f) Matters of offender mitigation which may be particularly relevant to this type of fraud include:

— *Voluntary cessation of offending* – a claim, supported by objective evidence, that an offender stopped offending before being apprehended should be treated as mitigation, particularly where accompanied by a genuine expression of remorse. The lapse of time since commission of the last offence is relevant to whether the claim is genuine, and reasons for the cessation will assist the court in determining whether it amounts to mitigation and if so, to what degree.

— *Complete and unprompted disclosure of the extent of the fraud* – An admission that a greater sum has been obtained than that known to the authorities ensures that an offender is sentenced for the complete extent of the fraud. This amounts to ready co-operation with the authorities and should be treated as mitigation. Provision of information about others involved in the fraud should also be treated as mitigation. Generally, the earlier the disclosure is given and the higher the degree of assistance, the greater the allowance for mitigation.

— *Voluntary restitution* – the timing of the voluntary restitution will indicate the degree to which it reflects genuine remorse. Generally, the earlier the property or money is returned the greater the degree of mitigation the offender should receive. If circumstances beyond the control of the offender prevent return of defrauded items, the degree of mitigation will depend on the point in time at which, and the determination with which the offender tried to return the items.

— *Financial pressure* – financial pressure neither increases nor diminishes an offender's culpability. However, where such pressure is **exceptional** and not of the offender's own making, it may in very rare circumstances constitute mitigation.

(g) A court should be aware that a confiscation order is an important sanction. Such an order may only be made in the Crown Court. The court must commit the offender to the Crown Court where this is requested by the prosecution with a view to an order being considered.

(h) Ancillary orders should be considered in all cases, principally compensation and deprivation.

Possession of articles: Triable either way
Maximum when tried summarily: Level 5 fine and/or 6 months
Maximum when tried on indictment: 5 years

Making or supplying articles, and Fraud (s.1): Triable either way
Maximum when tried summarily: Level 5 fine and/or 6 months
Maximum when tried on indictment: 10 years

Offence seriousness (culpability and harm)		
A. Identify the appropriate starting point		
Starting points based on first time offender pleading not guilty		
Examples of nature of activity	**Starting point**	**Range**
Possessing articles intended for use in a less extensive and less skillfully planned fraud	Medium level community order	Low level community order to 26 weeks custody
Possessing articles for use in an extensive and skillfully planned fraud	Crown Court	6 weeks custody to Crown Court
Making or adapting, supplying or offering to supply articles intended for use in a less extensive and less skillfully planned fraud	26 weeks custody	High level community order to Crown Court
Making or adapting, supplying or offering to supply articles for use in an extensive and skillfully planned fraud	Crown Court	Crown Court

Offence seriousness (culpability and harm)	
B. Consider the effect of aggravating and mitigating factors	
(other than those within examples above)	
Common aggravating and mitigating factors are identified in the pullout card— the following may be particularly relevant but **these lists are not exhaustive**	
Factors indicating higher culpability	**Factor indicating lower**
1. Number involved in the offence and role of the offender	**culpability**
2. Offending carried out over a significant period of time	1. Peripheral involvement
Factors indicating greater degree of harm	
1. Use of another person's identity	
2. Offence has lasting effect on the victim	

Form a preliminary view of the appropriate sentence,
then consider offender mitigation
Common factors are identified in the pullout card

Consider a reduction for a guilty plea

Consider ancillary orders
Refer to pages 168–174 for guidance on available ancillary orders

Decide sentence
Give reasons

Appendix 7

Assault Guidelines

The guidelines set out below were published by the Sentencing Guidelines Council and have effect in respect of all sentences passed after 13 June 2011 on offenders aged 18 or older. They replace the guidelines which previously applied and which continue to have effect until that date.

Inflicting grievous bodily harm/Unlawful wounding

Offences against the Person Act 1861 (section 20)

Racially/religiously aggravated GBH/Unlawful wounding

Crime and Disorder Act 1998 (section 29)

These are specified offences for the purposes of section 224 of the Criminal Justice Act 2003

Triable either way

Section 20

Maximum when tried summarily: Level 5 fine and/or 26 weeks' custody
Maximum when tried on indictment: 5 years' custody

Section 29

Maximum when tried summarily: Level 5 fine and/or 26 weeks' custody
Maximum when tried on indictment: 7 years' custody

Offence range: Community order – 4 years' custody

This guideline applies to all offenders aged 18 and older, who are sentenced on or after 13 June 2011. The definitions at page 145 of 'starting point' and 'first time offender' do not apply for this guideline. Starting point and category ranges apply to all offenders in all cases, irrespective of plea or previous convictions.

STEP ONE
Determining the offence category
The court should determine the offence category using the table below:

Category 1	Greater harm (serious injury must normally be present) **and** higher culpability
Category 2	Greater harm (serious injury must normally be present) **and** lower culpability; **or** lesser harm and higher culpability
Category 3	Lesser harm and lower culpability

The court should determine the offender's culpability and the harm caused, or intended, by reference **only** to the factors below (as demonstrated by the presence of one or more). These factors comprise the principal factual elements of the offence and should determine the category.

Factors indicating greater harm
Injury (which includes disease transmission and/or psychological harm) which is serious in the context of the offence (must normally be present)
Victim is particularly vulnerable because of personal circumstances
Sustained or repeated assault on the same victim
Factors indicating higher culpability
Statutory aggravating factors:
Offence motivated by, or demonstrating, hostility to the victim based on his or her sexual orientation (or presumed sexual orientation)
Offence motivated by, or demonstrating, hostility to the victim based on the victim's disability (or presumed disability)
Other aggravating factors:
A significant degree of premeditation
Use of weapon or weapon equivalent (for example, shod foot, headbutting, use of acid, use of animal)
Intention to commit more serious harm than actually resulted from the offence
Deliberately causes more harm than is necessary for commission of offence
Deliberate targeting of vulnerable victim
Leading role in group or gang
Offence motivated by, or demonstrating, hostility based on the victim's age, sex, gender identity (or presumed gender identity)

Factor indicating lesser harm
Injury which is less serious in the context of the offence
Factors indicating lower culpability
Subordinate role in a group or gang
A greater degree of provocation than normally expected
Lack of premeditation
Mental disorder or learning disability, where linked to commission of the offence
Excessive self defence

Appendix 7

STEP TWO

Starting point and category range

Having determined the category, the court should use the corresponding starting points to reach a sentence within the category range below. The starting point applies to all offenders irrespective of plea or previous convictions. A case of particular gravity, reflected by multiple features of culpability in step one, could merit upward adjustment from the starting point before further adjustment for aggravating or mitigating features, set out below.

Offence Category	Starting Point (Applicable to all offenders)	Category Range (Applicable to all offenders)
Category 1	Crown Court	Crown Court
Category 2	Crown Court	Crown Court
Category 3	High level community order	Low level community order – Crown Court (51 weeks' custody)

The table below contains a **non-exhaustive** list of additional factual elements providing the context of the offence and factors relating to the offender. Identify whether any combination of these, or other relevant factors, should result in an upward or downward adjustment from the starting point. In some cases, having considered these factors, it may be appropriate to move outside the identified category range.

When sentencing **category 3** offences, the court should also consider the custody threshold as follows:

- has the custody threshold been passed?
- if so, is it unavoidable that a custodial sentence be imposed?
- if so, can that sentence be suspended?

Factors increasing seriousness	Factors reducing seriousness or reflecting personal mitigation
Statutory aggravating factors:	No previous convictions or no relevant/recent convictions
Previous convictions, having regard to a) the nature of the offence to which the conviction relates and its relevance to the current offence; and b) the time that has elapsed since the conviction	Single blow
	Remorse
	Good character and/or exemplary conduct
Offence committed whilst on bail	Determination and/or demonstration of steps taken to address addiction or offending behaviour
Other aggravating factors include:	Serious medical conditions requiring urgent, intensive or long-term treatment
Location of the offence	Isolated incident
Timing of the offence	
Ongoing effect upon the victim	

Offence committed against those working in the public sector or providing a service to the public	Age and/or lack of maturity where it affects the responsibility of the offender
Presence of others including relatives, especially children or partner of the victim	Lapse of time since the offence where this is not the fault of the offender
Gratuitous degradation of victim	Mental disorder or learning disability, where not linked to the commission of the offence
In domestic violence cases, victim forced to leave their home	Sole or primary carer for dependent relatives
Failure to comply with current court orders	
Offence committed whilst on licence	
An attempt to conceal or dispose of evidence	
Failure to respond to warnings or concerns expressed by others about the offender's behaviour	
Commission of offence whilst under the influence of alcohol or drugs	
Abuse of power and/or position of trust	
Exploiting contact arrangements with a child to commit an offence	
Established evidence of community impact	
Any steps taken to prevent the victim reporting an incident, obtaining assistance and/or from assisting or supporting the prosecution	
Offences taken into consideration (TICs)	

Section 29 offences only: The court should determine the appropriate sentence for the offence without taking account of the element of aggravation and then make an addition to the sentence, considering the level of aggravation involved. It may be appropriate to move outside the identified category range, taking into account the increased statutory maximum.

STEP THREE
Consider any other factors which indicate a reduction, such as assistance to the prosecution
The court should take into account any rule of law by virtue of which an offender may receive a discounted sentence in consequence of assistance given (or offered) to the prosecutor or investigator.

STEP FOUR
Reduction for guilty plea
The court should take account of any potential reduction for a guilty plea in accordance with section 144 of the Criminal Justice Act 2003 and the Guilty Plea guideline.

STEP FIVE
Dangerousness

Inflicting grievous bodily harm/Unlawful wounding and racially/religiously aggravated GBH/Unlawful wounding are specified offences within the meaning of Chapter 5 of the Criminal Justice Act 2003 and at this stage the court should consider whether having regard to the criteria contained in that Chapter it would be appropriate to award an extended sentence.

STEP SIX
Totality principle

If sentencing an offender for more than one offence, or where the offender is already serving a sentence, consider whether the total sentence is just and proportionate to the offending behaviour.

STEP SEVEN
Compensation and ancillary orders

In all cases, the court should consider whether to make compensation and/or other ancillary orders.

STEP EIGHT
Reasons

Section 174 of the Criminal Justice Act 2003 imposes a duty to give reasons for, and explain the effect of, the sentence.

STEP NINE
Consideration for remand time

Sentencers should take into consideration any remand time served in relation to the final sentence. The court should consider whether to give credit for time spent on remand in custody or on bail in accordance with sections 240 and 240A of the Criminal Justice Act 2003.

Assault occasioning actual bodily harm

Offences against the Person Act 1861 (section 47)

Racially/religiously aggravated ABH

Crime and Disorder Act 1998 (section 29)

These are specified offences for the purposes of section 224 of the Criminal Justice Act 2003

Triable either way

Section 47

Maximum when tried summarily: Level 5 fine and/or 26 weeks' custody

Maximum when tried on indictment: 5 years' custody

Section 29

Maximum when tried summarily: Level 5 fine and/or 26 weeks' custody

Maximum when tried on indictment: 7 years' custody

Offence range: Fine – 3 years' custody

This guideline applies to all offenders aged 18 and older, who are sentenced on or after 13 June 2011. The definitions at page 145 of 'starting point' and 'first time offender' do not apply for this guideline. Starting point and category ranges apply to all offenders in all cases, irrespective of plea or previous convictions.

STEP ONE

Determining the offence category

The court should determine the offence category using the table below.

Category 1	Greater harm (serious injury must normally be present) **and** higher culpability
Category 2	Greater harm (serious injury must normally be present) **and** lower culpability; **or** lesser harm and higher culpability
Category 3	Lesser harm and lower culpability

The court should determine the offender's culpability and the harm caused, or intended, by reference only to the factors identified in the table below (as demonstrated by the presence of one or more). These factors comprise the principal factual elements of the offence and should determine the category.

Factors indicating greater harm	**Factors indicating lesser harm**
Injury (which includes disease transmission and/or psychological harm) which is serious in the context of the offence (must normally be present)	Injury which is less serious in the context of the offence
Victim is particularly vulnerable because of personal circumstances	**Factors indicating lower culpability**
Sustained or repeated assault on the same victim	Subordinate role in group or gang
	A greater degree of provocation than normally expected
	Lack of premeditation

Factors indicating higher culpability	Mental disorder or learning disability, where linked to commission of the offence
Statutory aggravating factors: Offence motivated by, or demonstrating, hostility to the victim based on his or her sexual orientation (or presumed sexual orientation) Offence motivated by, or demonstrating, hostility to the victim based on the victim's disability (or presumed disability) *Other aggravating factors:* A significant degree of premeditation Use of weapon or weapon equivalent (for example, shod foot, headbutting, use of acid, use of animal) Intention to commit more serious harm than actually resulted from the offence Deliberately causes more harm than is necessary for commission of offence Deliberate targeting of vulnerable victim Leading role in group or gang Offence motivated by, or demonstrating, hostility based on the victim's age, sex, gender identity (or presumed gender identity)	Excessive self defence

STEP TWO

Starting point and category range

Having determined the category, the court should use the corresponding starting points to reach a sentence within the category range below. The starting point applies to all offenders irrespective of plea or previous convictions. A case of particular gravity, reflected by multiple features of culpability in step one, could merit upward adjustment from the starting point before further adjustment for aggravating or mitigating features, set out below.

Offence Category	Starting Point (Applicable to all offenders)	Category Range (Applicable to all offenders)
Category 1	Crown Court	Crown Court
Category 2	26 weeks' custody	Low level community order – Crown Court (51 weeks' custody)
Category 3	Medium level community order	Band A fine – High level community order

The table below contains a **non-exhaustive** list of additional factual elements providing the context of the offence and factors relating to the offender. Identify whether any combination of these, or other relevant factors, should result in an upward or downward adjustment from the starting point. In some cases, having considered these factors, it may be appropriate to move outside the identified category range.

When sentencing **category 2** offences, the court should also consider the custody threshold as follows:

- has the custody threshold been passed?

- if so, is it unavoidable that a custodial sentence be imposed?

- if so, can that sentence be suspended?

When sentencing **category 3** offences, the court should also consider the community order threshold as follows:

- has the community order threshold been passed?

Factors increasing seriousness	Factors reducing seriousness or reflecting personal mitigation
Statutory aggravating factors:	No previous convictions **or** no relevant/recent convictions
Previous convictions, having regard to a) the nature of the offence to which the conviction relates and its relevance to the current offence; and b) the time that has elapsed since the conviction	Single blow
	Remorse
	Good character and/or exemplary conduct
Offence committed whilst on bail	Determination and/or demonstration of steps taken to address addiction or offending behaviour
Other aggravating factors include:	
Location of the offence	Serious medical conditions requiring urgent, intensive or long-term treatment
Timing of the offence	Isolated incident
Ongoing effect upon the victim	Age and/or lack of maturity where it affects the responsibility of the offender
Offence committed against those working in the public sector or providing a service to the public	Lapse of time since the offence where this is not the fault of the offender
Presence of others including relatives, especially children or partner of the victim	Mental disorder or learning disability, where **not** linked to the commission of the offence
Gratuitous degradation of victim	Sole or primary carer for dependent relatives
In domestic violence cases, victim forced to leave their home	
Failure to comply with current court orders	
Offence committed whilst on licence	
An attempt to conceal or dispose of evidence	
Failure to respond to warnings or concerns expressed by others about the offender's behaviour	
Commission of offence whilst under the influence of alcohol or drugs	
Abuse of power and/or position of trust	
Exploiting contact arrangements with a child to commit an offence	
Established evidence of community impact	
Any steps taken to prevent the victim reporting an incident, obtaining assistance and/or from assisting or supporting the prosecution	
Offences taken into consideration (TICs)	

Appendix 7

Section 29 offences only: The court should determine the appropriate sentence for the offence without taking account of the element of aggravation and then make an addition to the sentence, considering the level of aggravation involved. It may be appropriate to move outside the identified category range, taking into account the increased statutory maximum.

Assault with intent to resist arrest

Offences against the Person Act 1861 (section 38)

This is a specified offence for the purposes of section 224 of the Criminal Justice Act 2003

Triable either way

Maximum when tried summarily: Level 5 fine and/or 26 weeks' custody
Maximum when tried on indictment: 2 years' custody

Offence range: Fine - 51 weeks' custody

This guideline applies to all offenders aged 18 and older, who are sentenced on or after 13 June 2011. The definitions at page 145 of 'starting point' and 'first time offender' do not apply for this guideline. Starting point and category ranges apply to all offenders in all cases, irrespective of plea or previous convictions.

STEP ONE
Determining the offence category
The court should determine the offence category using the table below.

Category 1	Greater harm **and** higher culpability
Category 2	Greater harm **and** lower culpability; **or** lesser harm **and** higher culpability
Category 3	Lesser harm **and** lower culpability

The court should determine the offender's culpability and the harm caused, or intended, by reference only to the factors identified in the table below (as demonstrated by the presence of one or more). These factors comprise the principal factual elements of the offence and should determine the category.

Factors indicating greater harm	Factor indicating lesser harm
Sustained or repeated assault on the same victim	Injury which is less serious in the context of the offence
Factors indicating higher culpability	**Factors indicating lower culpability**
Statutory aggravating factors:	Subordinate role in group or gang
Offence racially or religiously aggravated	Lack of premeditation
Offence motivated by, or demonstrating, hostility to the victim based on his or her sexual orientation (or presumed sexual orientation)	Mental disorder or learning disability, where linked to commission of the offence
Offence motivated by, or demonstrating, hostility to the victim based on the victim's disability (or presumed disability)	
Other aggravating factors:	
A significant degree of premeditation	
Use of weapon or weapon equivalent (for example, shod foot, headbutting, use of acid, use of animal)	
Intention to commit more serious harm than actually resulted from the offence	
Deliberately causes more harm than is necessary for commission of offence	
Leading role in group or gang	
Offence motivated by, or demonstrating, hostility based on the victim's age, sex, gender identity (or presumed gender identity)	

STEP TWO

Starting point and category range

Having determined the category, the court should use the corresponding starting points to reach a sentence within the category range below. The starting point applies to all offenders irrespective of plea or previous convictions. A case of particular gravity, reflected by multiple features of culpability in step one, could merit upward adjustment from the starting point before further adjustment for aggravating or mitigating features, set out below.

Offence Category	Starting Point (Applicable to all offenders)	Category Range (Applicable to all offenders)
Category 1	26 weeks' custody	12 weeks' custody – Crown Court (51 weeks' custody)
Category 2	Medium level community order	Low level community order – High level community order
Category 3	Band B fine	Band A fine – Band C fine

The table below contains a non-exhaustive list of additional factual elements providing the context of the offence and factors relating to the offender. Identify whether any combination of these, or other relevant factors, should result in an upward or downward adjustment from the starting point. In some cases, having considered these factors, it may be appropriate to move outside the identified category range.

When sentencing **category 1** offences, the court should consider whether the sentence can be suspended.

Factors increasing seriousness	Factors reducing seriousness or reflecting personal mitigation
Statutory aggravating factors:	No previous convictions **or** no relevant/recent convictions
Previous convictions, having regard to a) the nature of the offence to which the conviction relates and its relevance to the current offence; and b) the time that has elapsed since the conviction	Single blow
	Remorse
	Good character and/or exemplary conduct
Offence committed whilst on bail	Determination and/or demonstration of steps taken to address addiction or offending behaviour
Other aggravating factors include:	
Location of the offence	
Timing of the offence	Serious medical conditions requiring urgent, intensive or long-term treatment
Ongoing effect upon the victim	Isolated incident
Gratuitous degradation of victim	Age and/or lack of maturity where it affects the responsibility of the defendant
Failure to comply with current court orders	
Offence committed whilst on licence	Mental disorder or learning disability, where **not** linked to the commission of the offence
An attempt to conceal or dispose of evidence	Sole or primary carer for dependent relatives
Failure to respond to warnings or concerns expressed by others about the offender's behaviour	
Commission of offence whilst under the influence of alcohol or drugs	
Established evidence of community impact	
Any steps taken to prevent the victim reporting an incident, obtaining assistance and/or from assisting or supporting the prosecution	
Offences taken into consideration (TICs)	

Assault on a police constable in execution of his duty

Police Act 1996 (section 89)

Triable only summarily

Maximum: Level 5 fine and/or 26 weeks' custody

Offence range: Fine – 26 weeks' custody

This guideline applies to all offenders aged 18 and older, who are sentenced on or after 13 June 2011. The definitions at page 145 of 'starting point' and 'first time offender' do not apply for this guideline. Starting point and category ranges apply to all offenders in all cases, irrespective of plea or previous convictions.

STEP ONE

Determining the offence category

The court should determine the offence category using the table below.

Category 1	Greater harm and higher culpability
Category 2	Greater harm and lower culpability; or lesser harm and higher culpability
Category 3	Lesser harm and lower culpability

The court should determine the offender's culpability and the harm caused, or intended, by reference **only** to the factors below (as demonstrated by the presence of one or more). These factors comprise the principal factual elements of the offence and should determine the category.

Factor indicating greater harm	**Factor indicating lesser harm**
Sustained or repeated assault on the same victim	Injury which is less serious in the context of the offence
Factors indicating higher culpability	**Factors indicating lower culpability**
Statutory aggravating factors:	Subordinate role in group or gang
Offence racially or religiously aggravated	Lack of premeditation
Offence motivated by, or demonstrating, hostility to the victim based on his or her sexual orientation (or presumed sexual orientation)	Mental disorder or learning disability, where linked to commission of the offence
Offence motivated by, or demonstrating, hostility to the victim based on the victim's disability (or presumed disability)	
Other aggravating factors:	
A significant degree of premeditation	
Use of weapon or weapon equivalent (for example, shod foot, headbutting, use of acid, use of animal)	
Intention to commit more serious harm than actually resulted from the offence	
Deliberately causes more harm than is necessary for commission of offence	
Leading role in group or gang	
Offence motivated by, or demonstrating, hostility based on the victim's age, sex, gender identity (or presumed gender identity)	

STEP TWO

Starting point and category range

Having determined the category, the court should use the corresponding starting points to reach a sentence within the category range below. The starting point applies to all offenders irrespective of plea or previous convictions. A case of particular gravity, reflected by multiple features of culpability in step one, could merit upward adjustment from the starting point before further adjustment for aggravating or mitigating features, set out below.

Offence Category	Starting Point (Applicable to all offenders)	Category Range (Applicable to all offenders)
Category 1	12 weeks' custody	Low level community order – 26 weeks' custody
Category 2	Medium level community order	Low level community order – High level community order
Category 3	Band B fine	Band A fine – Band C fine

The table below contains a **non-exhaustive** list of additional factual elements providing the context of the offence and factors relating to the offender. Identify whether any combination of these, or other relevant factors, should result in an upward or downward adjustment from the starting point. In some cases, having considered these factors, it may be appropriate to move outside the identified category range.

When sentencing **category 1** offences, the court should also consider the custody threshold as follows:

- has the custody threshold been passed?
- if so, is it unavoidable that a custodial sentence be imposed?
- if so, can that sentence be suspended?

Factors increasing seriousness	Factors reducing seriousness or reflecting personal mitigation
Statutory aggravating factors:	No previous convictions **or** no relevant/recent convictions
Previous convictions, having regard to a) the nature of the offence to which the conviction relates and its relevance to the current offence; and b) the time that has elapsed since the conviction	Single blow
Offence committed whilst on bail	Remorse
Other aggravating factors include:	Good character and/or exemplary conduct
Location of the offence	Determination and/or demonstration of steps taken to address addiction or offending behaviour
Timing of the offence	Serious medical conditions requiring urgent, intensive or long-term treatment
Ongoing effect upon the victim	Isolated incident
Gratuitous degradation of victim	Age and/or lack of maturity where it affects the responsibility of the offender
Failure to comply with current court orders	Lapse of time since the offence where this is not the fault of the offender
Offence committed whilst on licence	Mental disorder or learning disability, where **not** linked to the commission of the offence
An attempt to conceal or dispose of evidence	Sole or primary carer for dependent relatives
Failure to respond to warnings or concerns expressed by others about the offender's behaviour	
Commission of offence whilst under the influence of alcohol or drugs	

Established evidence of community impact	
Any steps taken to prevent the victim report-ing an incident, obtaining assistance and/or from assisting or supporting the prosecution	
Offences taken into consideration (TICs)	

STEP THREE
Consider any other factors which indicate a reduction, such as assistance to the prosecution
The court should take into account any rule of law by virtue of which an offender may receive a discounted sentence in consequence of assistance given (or offered) to the prosecutor or investigator.

STEP FOUR
Reduction for guilty plea
The court should take account of any potential reduction for a guilty plea in accordance with section 144 of the Criminal Justice Act 2003 and the Guilty Plea guideline.

STEP FIVE
Totality principle
If sentencing an offender for more than one offence, or where the offender is already serving a sentence, consider whether the total sentence is just and proportionate to the offending behaviour.

STEP SIX
Compensation and ancillary orders
In all cases, courts should consider whether to make compensation and/or other ancillary orders.

STEP SEVEN
Reasons
Section 174 of the Criminal Justice Act 2003 imposes a duty to give reasons for, and explain the effect of, the sentence.

STEP EIGHT
Consideration for remand time
Sentencers should take into consideration any remand time served in relation to the final sentence. The court should consider whether to give credit for time spent on remand in custody or on bail in accordance with sections 240 and 240A of the Criminal Justice Act 2003.

Appendix 7

Common Assault

Criminal Justice Act 1988 (section 39)

Racially/religiously aggravated common assault

Crime and Disorder Act 1998 (section 29)

Racially/religiously aggravated assault is a specified offence for the purposes of section 224 of the Criminal Justice Act 2003

Section 39

Triable only summarily

Maximum when tried summarily: Level 5 fine and/or 26 weeks' custody

Section 29

Triable either way

Maximum when tried summarily: Level 5 fine and/or 26 weeks' custody
Maximum when tried on indictment: 2 years' custody

Offence range: Discharge – 26 weeks' custody

This guideline applies to all offenders aged 18 and older, who are sentenced on or after 13 June 2011. The definitions at page 145 of 'starting point' and 'first time offender' do not apply for this guideline. Starting point and category ranges apply to all offenders in all cases, irrespective of plea or previous convictions.

STEP ONE
Determining the offence category
The court should determine the offence category using the table below.

Category 1	Greater harm (injury or fear of injury must normally be present) **and** higher culpability
Category 2	Greater harm (injury or fear of injury must normally be present) **and** lower culpability; **or** lesser harm and higher culpability
Category 3	Lesser harm **and** lower culpability

The court should determine the offender's culpability and the harm caused, or intended, by reference only to the factors below (as demonstrated by the presence of one or more). These factors comprise the principal factual elements of the offence and should determine the category.

Factors indicating greater harm	Factor indicating lesser harm
Injury or fear of injury which is serious in the context of the offence (must normally be present)	Injury which is less serious in the context of the offence
Victim is particularly vulnerable because of personal circumstances	**Factors indicating lower culpability**
Sustained or repeated assault on the same victim	Subordinate role in group or gang
Factors indicating higher culpability	A greater degree of provocation than normally expected
Statutory aggravating factors:	Lack of premeditation
Offence motivated by, or demonstrating, hostility to the victim based on his or her sexual orientation (or presumed sexual orientation)	Mental disorder or learning disability, where linked to commission of the offence
Offence motivated by, or demonstrating, hostility to the victim based on the victim's disability (or presumed disability)	Excessive self defence
Other aggravating factors:	
A significant degree of premeditation	
Threatened or actual use of weapon or weapon equivalent	
(for example, shod foot, headbutting, use of acid, use of animal)	
Intention to commit more serious harm than actually resulted from the offence	
Deliberately causes more harm than is necessary for commission of offence	
Deliberate targeting of vulnerable victim	
Leading role in group or gang	
Offence motivated by, or demonstrating, hostility based on the victim's age, sex, gender identity (or presumed gender identity)	

STEP TWO

Starting point and category range

Having determined the category, the court should use the corresponding starting points to reach a sentence within the category range below. The starting point applies to all offenders irrespective of plea or previous convictions. A case of particular gravity, reflected by multiple features of culpability in step one, could merit upward adjustment from the starting point before further adjustment for aggravating or mitigating features, set out below.

Offence Category	Starting Point (Applicable to all offenders)	Category Range (Applicable to all offenders)
Category 1	High level community order	Low level community order – 26 weeks' custody
Category 2	Medium level community order	Band A fine – High level community order
Category 3	Band A fine	Discharge – Band C fine

The table below contains a **non-exhaustive** list of additional factual elements providing the context of the offence and factors relating to the offender. Identify whether any combination of these, or other relevant factors, should result in an upward or downward adjustment from the starting point. In some cases, having considered these factors, it may be appropriate to move outside the identified category range.

When sentencing **category 1** offences, the court should also consider the custody threshold as follows:

- has the custody threshold been passed?
- if so, is it unavoidable that a custodial sentence be imposed?
- if so, can that sentence be suspended?

When sentencing **category 2** offences, the court should also consider the community order threshold as follows:

- has the community order threshold been passed?

Factors increasing seriousness	Factors reducing seriousness or reflecting personal mitigation
Statutory aggravating factors: Previous convictions, having regard to a) the nature of the offence to which the conviction relates and its relevance to the current offence; and b) the time that has elapsed since the conviction Offence committed whilst on bail *Other aggravating factors include:* Location of the offence Timing of the offence Ongoing effect upon the victim Offence committed against those working in the public sector or providing a service to the public	No previous convictions or no relevant/recent convictions Single blow Remorse Good character and/or exemplary conduct Determination and/or demonstration of steps taken to address addiction or offending behaviour Serious medical conditions requiring urgent, intensive or long-term treatment Isolated incident Age and/or lack of maturity where it affects the responsibility of the offender

Presence of others including relatives, especially children or partner of the victim	Lapse of time since the offence where this is not the fault of the offender
Gratuitous degradation of victim	Mental disorder or learning disability, where not linked to the commission of the offence
In domestic violence cases, victim forced to leave their home	Sole or primary carer for dependent relatives
Failure to comply with current court orders	
Offence committed whilst on licence	
An attempt to conceal or dispose of evidence	
Failure to respond to warnings or concerns expressed by others about the offender's behaviour	
Commission of offence whilst under the influence of alcohol or drugs	
Abuse of power and/or position of trust	
Exploiting contact arrangements with a child to commit an offence	
Established evidence of community impact	
Any steps taken to prevent the victim reporting an incident, obtaining assistance and/or from assisting or supporting the prosecution	
Offences taken into consideration (TICs)	

Section 29 offences only: The court should determine the appropriate sentence for the offence without taking account of the element of aggravation and then make an addition to the sentence, considering the level of aggravation involved. It may be appropriate to move outside the identified category range, taking into account the increased statutory maximum.

Index

Index

Index

Index

Index

Index

Index

Index

Index

Index

Index

Index

Index

Index

2011

January

M		3	10	17	24	31
T		4	11	18	25
W		5	12	19	26
T		6	13	20	27
F		7	14	21	28
S	1	8	15	22	29
S	2	9	16	23	30

February

M		7	14	21	28
T	1	8	15	22
W	2	9	16	23
T	3	10	17	24
F	4	11	18	25
S	5	12	19	26
S	6	13	20	27

March

M		7	14	21	28
T	1	8	15	22	29
W	2	9	16	23	30
T	3	10	17	24	31
F	4	11	18	25
S	5	12	19	26
S	6	13	20	27

April

M		4	11	18	25
T		5	12	19	26
W		6	13	20	27
T		7	14	21	28
F	1	8	15	22	29
S	2	9	16	23	30
S	3	10	17	24

May

M	2	9	16	23	30
T	3	10	17	24	31
W	4	11	18	25
T	5	12	19	26
F	6	13	20	27
S	7	14	21	28
S	1	8	15	22	29

June

M		6	13	20	27
T		7	14	21	28
W	1	8	15	22	29
T	2	9	16	23	30
F	3	10	17	24
S	4	11	18	25
S	5	12	19	26

July

M		4	11	18	25
T		5	12	19	26
W		6	13	20	27
T		7	14	21	28
F	1	8	15	22	29
S	2	9	16	23	30
S	3	10	17	24	31

August

M	1	8	15	22	29
T	2	9	16	23	30
W	3	10	17	24	31
T	4	11	18	25
F	5	12	19	26
S	6	13	20	27
S	7	14	21	28

September

M		5	12	19	26
T		6	13	20	27
W		7	14	21	28
T	1	8	15	22	29
F	2	9	16	23	30
S	3	10	17	24
S	4	11	18	25

October

M		3	10	17	24	31
T		4	11	18	25
W		5	12	19	26
T		6	13	20	27
F		7	14	21	28
S	1	8	15	22	29
S	2	9	16	23	30

November

M		7	14	21	28
T	1	8	15	22	29
W	2	9	16	23	30
T	3	10	17	24
F	4	11	18	25
S	5	12	19	26
S	6	13	20	27

December

M		5	12	19	26
T		6	13	20	27
W		7	14	21	28
T	1	8	15	22	29
F	2	9	16	23	30
S	3	10	17	24	31
S	4	11	18	25